# THE CAMBRIDGE COMPANION TO ROMANTICISM AND RACE

Amidst the popularization of race science and rapid colonial expansion that characterized the Romantic era, newly urgent discussions about the morality and legality of slavery emerged that would pave the way for formal abolition. The thirteen essays collected here make clear that these developments thoroughly informed Romantic-era literature: the very terms that have long defined Romanticism – revolution and radicalism, poetry and "powerful feeling," the solitary self and the social world – were shaped by a changing global order in which race figured centrally. Combining academic rigor with accessibility, this diverse group of scholars presents specialists and nonspecialists alike with a rich picture of this key moment in the literary and cultural history of race. Engaging with the distinctly Romantic meanings of race, chapters invite readers to consider how eighteenth- and nineteenth-century ideas about difference continue to shape the modern world.

MANU SAMRITI CHANDER is Associate Professor of English at Georgetown University. He is the author of *Brown Romantics: Poetry and Nationalism in the Global Nineteenth Century* (2017) and coeditor, with Tricia A. Matthew, of the series Race in Nineteenth-Century Literature and Culture.

*A complete list of books in the series is at the back of the book.*

# THE CAMBRIDGE COMPANION TO ROMANTICISM AND RACE

EDITED BY

MANU SAMRITI CHANDER

*Georgetown University*

Shaftesbury Road, Cambridge CB2 8EA, United Kingdom

One Liberty Plaza, 20th Floor, New York, NY 10006, USA

477 Williamstown Road, Port Melbourne, VIC 3207, Australia

314–321, 3rd Floor, Plot 3, Splendor Forum, Jasola District Centre,
New Delhi – 110025, India

103 Penang Road, #05–06/07, Visioncrest Commercial, Singapore 238467

Cambridge University Press is part of Cambridge University Press & Assessment,
a department of the University of Cambridge.

We share the University's mission to contribute to society through the pursuit of
education, learning and research at the highest international levels of excellence.

www.cambridge.org
Information on this title: www.cambridge.org/9781009180160
DOI: 10.1017/9781009180177

© Cambridge University Press & Assessment 2024

This publication is in copyright. Subject to statutory exception and to the provisions
of relevant collective licensing agreements, no reproduction of any part may take
place without the written permission of Cambridge University Press & Assessment.

When citing this work, please include a reference to the DOI 10.1017/9781009180177

First published 2024

*A catalogue record for this publication is available from the British Library*

*Library of Congress Cataloging-in-Publication Data*
NAMES: Chander, Manu Samriti, editor.
TITLE: The Cambridge companion to Romanticism and race / edited by Manu Samriti
Chander, Georgetown University.
OTHER TITLES: Companion to Romanticism and race
DESCRIPTION: Cambridge ; New York : Cambridge University Press, 2024. |
Series: Cambridge companions to literature | Includes bibliographical references and index.
IDENTIFIERS: LCCN 2024019592 | ISBN 9781009180160 (hardback) | ISBN 9781009180153
(paperback) | ISBN 9781009180177 (ebook)
SUBJECTS: LCSH: English literature – 19th century – History and criticism – Handbooks,
manuals, etc. | English literature – 18th century – History and criticism – Handbooks,
manuals, etc. | Race in literature. | Literature and society – Great Britain – History – Handbooks,
manuals, etc. | Romanticism – Great Britain – Handbooks, manuals, etc.
CLASSIFICATION: LCC PR457 .C335 2024 | DDC 820.9/145–dc23/eng/20240515
LC record available at https://lccn.loc.gov/2024019592

ISBN 978-1-009-18016-0 Hardback
ISBN 978-1-009-18015-3 Paperback

Cambridge University Press & Assessment has no responsibility for the persistence
or accuracy of URLs for external or third-party internet websites referred to in this
publication and does not guarantee that any content on such websites is, or will remain,
accurate or appropriate.

## Contents

| | | |
|---|---|---|
| List of Figures | | *page* vii |
| List of Contributors | | viii |
| Acknowledgments | | xi |
| | Introduction<br>*Manu Samriti Chander* | 1 |
| 1 | Burke and Kant on Color and Inheritance<br>*Yoon Sun Lee* | 7 |
| 2 | Breathing Freedom in the Era of the Haitian Revolution<br>*Catherine R. Peters* | 22 |
| 3 | Afropessimism, Queer Negativity, and the Limits of Romanticism<br>*Deanna P. Koretsky* | 37 |
| 4 | Samuel Taylor Coleridge's Racial Imaginary<br>*Mathelinda Nabugodi* | 56 |
| 5 | (Not)freedom<br>*DJ Lee and Aaron Ngozi Oforlea* | 78 |
| 6 | Disability and Race<br>*Essaka Joshua* | 98 |
| 7 | The Crip Foundations of Romantic Medicine<br>*Travis Chi Wing Lau* | 116 |
| 8 | The Voice of Complaint<br>*Joseph Albernaz* | 130 |
| 9 | Romantic Manscapes<br>*Devin M. Garofalo* | 150 |

| | | |
|---|---|---|
| 10 | Romantic Poetry and Constructions of Indigeneity<br>*Nikki Hessell* | 168 |
| 11 | Romanticism and the Novel(ty) of Race<br>*Atesede Makonnen* | 186 |
| 12 | Reading Race Along the "Bounding Line"<br>*Lauren Dembowitz* | 204 |
| 13 | The Racecraft of Romantic Stagecraft<br>*Yasser Shams Khan* | 227 |

*Further Reading* 246
*Index* 264

# *Figures*

| | | |
|---|---|---|
| 1.1 | Princess Sophia, dressed as an American Indian, 1644. Painted by her sister, Louise Hollandine of the Palatinate. Oil on canvas. Museum Wasserburg Anholt | *page* 19 |
| 12.1 | Reverse of William Blake, "Flagellation of a Female Samboe Slave" | 207 |
| 12.2 | William Grainger after Thomas Stothard, *Voyage of the Sable Venus* | 208 |
| 12.3 | Isaac Cruikshank, *Abolition of the Slave Trade* | 210 |
| 12.4 | William Blake, *Visions of the Daughters of Albion*, Copy I, 1793, frontispiece. Courtesy of the Yale Center for British Art, Paul Mellon Collection / Public Domain. | 217 |
| 13.1 | Schematic representation of the rethinking of the relations between racial identity and racism | 233 |
| 13.2 | The Harrison Watercolor/Orme engraving depicting the scene in Jack's cave (1801) | 241 |

## Contributors

JOSEPH ALBERNAZ is an assistant professor of English and comparative literature at Columbia University. His first book, on conceptions of community and the common in Romanticism and its legacies, is forthcoming from Stanford University Press. Recent and forthcoming publications include essays on the history of the word "communism," the origins of the general strike in the Black Atlantic, and Mary Shelley's pandemic novel *The Last Man*.

MANU SAMRITI CHANDER is Associate Professor of English at Georgetown University. He is the author of *Brown Romantics: Poetry and Nationalism in the Global Nineteenth Century* (Bucknell, 2017).

LAUREN DEMBOWITZ is an independent scholar in Boulder, Colorado. Her current book project is titled *The Black Venus and the (Un)Making of Whiteness in the Atlantic World*. It layers together representations of the Black Venus figure in eighteenth-century British and contemporary African American poetry, performance, and visual culture to explore entanglements of race, gender, commerce, and intimacy.

DEVIN M. GAROFALO is an assistant professor of English at the University of California, San Diego. She is currently working on a monograph about the nineteenth-century concomitance of the normative lyric subject and colonial anthropogenic enterprise. Portions of this project have appeared in *European Romantic Review*, *Victorian Literature and Culture*, and *Diacritics*.

NIKKI HESSELL is a settler-scholar and Professor of English Literatures at Te Herenga Waka–Victoria University of Wellington in Aotearoa. She is the author of *Romantic Literature and the Colonised World: Lessons from Indigenous Translations* (Palgrave, 2018) and *Sensitive Negotiations: Indigenous Diplomacy and British Romantic Poetry* (SUNY Press, 2021). Her new project is *The Poetics of Treaties: Settler Treaty-Making and Eighteenth-Century Poetry*.

*List of Contributors*

ESSAKA JOSHUA is Professor of English Literature at the University of Notre Dame, and specializes in nineteenth-century British literature and disability studies. Her latest book is *Physical Disability in British Romantic Literature* (Cambridge University Press, 2020).

YASSER SHAMS KHAN is Assistant Professor of Literature in the Department of English Literature and Linguistics at Qatar University. His work on the theatricality and performance of race and empire in the long eighteenth and early nineteenth century has appeared in *Studies in Romanticism* and *The Eighteenth Century: Theory and Interpretation*. He is currently working on a monograph on the representation and performance of blackness in Georgian-period drama, methodologically exploring the convergence of critical theory, performance, and race studies in his analysis of the formal transformations of pathetic tragedy, sentimental comedy, farce, and melodrama.

DEANNA P. KORETSKY is Associate Professor of English at Spelman. Her first book, *Death Rights: Romantic Suicide, Race, and the Bounds of Liberalism* (2021), shows how cultural representations of suicide inherited from the nineteenth century continue to reinforce anti-Blackness in the modern world.

TRAVIS CHI WING LAU is Assistant Professor of English at Kenyon College. His research and teaching focus on eighteenth- and nineteenth-century British literature and culture, health humanities, and disability studies. Alongside his scholarship, Lau frequently writes for venues of public scholarship like *Synapsis: A Journal of Health Humanities*, *Public Books*, *Lapham's Quarterly*, and *The Los Angeles Review of Books*.

DJ LEE is a scholar, writer, editor, artist, Regents Professor of English at Washington State University, and a scholar-fellow at the Black Earth Institute. She has published more than 100 articles, essays, and prose poems, the memoir *Remote: Finding Home in the Bitterroots* (Oregon State University Press, 2020), and eight scholarly books, including *The Land Speaks* (Oxford University Press, 2017), and *Slavery and the Romantic Imagination* (University of Pennsylvania Press, 2004). Artist residencies include the Arctic Circle Artist Residency in the International Territory of Svalbard, the Women's Studio Workshop, and the Wilderness Art Collective. Her forthcoming book is a collection of lyric essays called *The Edge Is What We Have: Awe and Wonder in a Dimming World*.

*List of Contributors*

YOON SUN LEE is Anne Pierce Rogers Professor in American Literature and Professor of English at Wellesley College. She is the author of *Nationalism and Irony* (Oxford University Press, 2004), *Modern Minority: Asian American Literature and Everyday Life* (Oxford University Press, 2013), and *The Natural Laws of Plot: How Things Happen in Realist Novels* (University of Pennsylvania Press, 2023).

ATESEDE MAKONNEN is Assistant Professor of English at Carnegie Mellon University. Her current book project focuses on the visualization of blackness in nineteenth-century British culture. Her previous work has been published in *Studies in Romanticism*, the *European Romantic Review*, the *Keats–Shelley Journal*, *Victorian Studies*, *Symbiosis: A Journal of Transatlantic Literary and Cultural Relations*, and *The Visual Life of Romantic Theatre, 1770–1830*.

MATHELINDA NABUGODI is Lecturer in Comparative Literature at University College London. She is the author of *Shelley with Benjamin: A Critical Mosaic* (UCL Press, 2023) and one of the editors on the Longman edition of *The Poems of Shelley* (2024). Her current book project explores the connections between British Romanticism and the Black Atlantic through a series of objects found in the archives of the Romantic poets.

AARON NGOZI OFORLEA is Associate Professor of English at Washington State University, specializing in African American literature, rhetoric, and folklore. He has published *James Baldwin, Toni Morrison, and The Rhetorics of Black Male Subjectivity* (Ohio State University Press, 2017), several essays, and articles; co-edited the "African American Folklore and Critical Race Theory" issue of *The Western Journal of Black Studies*; and has constructed three digital archive projects.

CATHERINE R. PETERS is Lecturer in Race, Colonialism, and Diaspora Studies at Tufts University. Her manuscript-in-progress centers on the ecologies and sociopolitical genres through which people of Asian and African descent forged communities in the nineteenth-century Caribbean.

## *Acknowledgments*

I am grateful to the truly exceptional scholars who contributed to this volume – their dedication, rigor, and creativity has made editing this book a genuine pleasure. I wish to also thank Bethany Thomas and George Laver at Cambridge University Press for their commitment to this project. Bethany Qualls, who assisted with formatting and copyediting, and Kavita Mudan Finn, who prepared the index, have been invaluable in the production of the manuscript. The founding members of the Bigger 6 Collective – Nikki Hessell, Tina Iemma, Deanna Koretsky, Tricia Matthew, Matt Sandler, Rebecca Schneider, and Eugenia Zuroski – model the forms of engaged and committed scholarship to which I aspire. I am indebted to many, many scholars beyond the research collective, including David Ben-Merre, Thora Brylowe, Elaine Freedgood, and Alex Milsom, as well as my colleagues at Rutgers-Newark and Georgetown. Thanks as always to my sprawling brown kinship network: my parents, Madhu and Mahesh Chander; my sisters, Nivedita and Geetanjali Chander; and all the aunties, uncles, and cousins who make up the community of care that sustains me. This book, like everything in my life, is for Patricia, P. J., and Yogi.

# Introduction

## Manu Samriti Chander

The need for a *Companion to Romanticism and Race* stems from the slipperiness of "romanticism" and "race," two terms that are notoriously difficult to define. Arthur O. Lovejoy's oft-cited argument that we need to speak of romanticisms in the plural attests to the fact that, at least since the early twentieth century, the effort to pin down exactly what "romanticism" is has troubled literary scholars, even as we continue to publish books and articles and host conferences and symposia with the word in the title.[1] A period in history that spans variously from 1776 or 1789 (or earlier) to 1832 or 1837 (or later); an aesthetic movement that emphasized subjective, emotional experience over objective knowledge and rationality; a political commitment centered on revolution and the rights of men – all of these understandings of Romanticism illuminate but fail to exhaust its possible meanings.

No less tricky a term to pin down, "race" refers variously to physical characteristics, national origin, religious identity, and ethnicity, among others. In the nineteenth century, "race" still held its longtime association with family line, but it was increasingly informed by scientific usages, where it referred to phenotypically and geographically differentiated peoples. This relatively new conception of race did not displace but intertwined with the "older" sense of race as family line, such that to speak of lineage was also to speak of phenotypic characteristics that implied positive or negative behaviors.[2] Further complicating the issue, as it became more common to talk about the universal rights of man in the Age of Revolutions, race was used to refer not only to social difference but also to common humanity – the "human race," according to the ideals of *liberté*, *égalité*, and *fraternité*, was bound together by rights and responsibilities that knew no borders. Often, even within such liberal discourse, race was used contradictorily to refer to similarity and difference at once, pointing to both shared attributes and irreconcilable distinctions.

The essays collected in this volume work through various understandings of "romanticism" and "race," addressing how these terms acquire meaning via other concepts taking shape in the eighteenth and nineteenth centuries, such as "blackness," "whiteness," "sovereignty," "property," and "freedom." They look for these meanings in literary works by those commonly associated with Romanticism – Wordsworth, Coleridge, Blake, Byron – and by those who appear less frequently on course syllabi – Jane Johnston Schoolcraft, John Fawcett, Juan Francisco Manzano, Uriah Derick D'Arcy. They look to the philosophical writings of Kant and Burke, the political works of Edward Rushton and Thomas Clarkson, and the scientific inquiries of Cornelius de Pauw and Robert Knox.

The collection opens with Yoon Sun Lee's discussion of how Enlightenment understandings of race shaped ideas about inheritance, such that property ownership came to be understood in racialized terms and race came to be understood in economic terms. Burke's and Kant's writings about heritability thus shed light on the doctrine of *partus sequitur ventrem*, whereby, as Lee puts it, "The children of enslaved women of African counted as property that could be inherited by others, on the basis of a color that had to be ascribed as the material sign of a legal condition."

The question of race and kinship that Lee introduces is taken up in the chapter that follows, where Catherine R. Peters discusses how writers such as the Cuban poet Juan Francisco Manzano reworked the Romantic trope of the revolutionary "common wind" to forge kinship networks among forcibly displaced peoples. In formulating this argument, Peters shifts the conventional focus on the French Revolution as the hub of radical Romantic thought to the Haitian Revolution, where "fraternité" refers not to an abstract ideal but a very real desire to reconstitute those family relations disrupted by the institution of slavery.

Kinship in the Atlantic world is central as well to Deanna P. Koretsky's analysis of the pseudonymous Uriah Derick D'Arcy's *The Black Vampyre*, set in Sainte-Domingue, Haiti. While the Romantic vampire has often been read as disrupting heteropatriarchal norms, D'Arcy's novel, Koretsky argues via Afropessimism and theories of queer futurity, exposes how the supposedly liberatory figure of the vampire upholds the antiblackness at the heart of the Gothic tradition. Koretsky sharply and counterintuitively argues that there is in fact nothing more representative of the human than the figure of the vampire, and that D'Arcy's Black vampire thus threatens the modern sociopolitical order built on expelling blackness from the category of the human.

Mathelinda Nabugodi traces the shifts in Coleridge's thoughts on race from his early abolitionist writings to his later reflections on beauty and aesthetics. Focusing on his comments about Africans, Nabugodi demonstrates a crucial tension between the Romantic poet's youthful commitment to abolition and the embrace of scientific racism in his later writings. This tension also informs the revisions that Coleridge made to *The Rime of the Ancient Mariner* (1798) when he prepared it for republication in *Sibylline Leaves* (1817). Nabugodi's careful comparative reading of the 1798 and the 1817 versions highlights the way a representative poet's work embodies the contradictions of a Romanticism in which freedom could be imagined as universal even as European superiority was taken for granted.

DJ Lee and Aaron Ngozi Oforlea's chapter approaches Coleridge from a different angle, counterposing his vision of freedom with that of the Black Loyalists who supported the English during the American Revolution. Lee and Oforlea's titular phrase "(not)Freedom" refers to "the fragmentation, resistance, and transgression with which Black Loyalists lived," which is exemplified in the Loyalists' linguistic practices. Whether by mimicking the language of white Europeans or by developing a distinctive lingo that infused poetry into the language of transactions, the Loyalists demonstrated a model of freedom – (not)freedom – that was local and transitory, contextually dependent and always precarious.

Just as the Romantic era witnessed dramatic changes in the understanding of race, so too did it see new ideas about intellectual and physical ability and disability. Essaka Joshua discusses the relationship between disability and race, both where they intersect in literary and nonliterary discourses and, importantly, where they are deliberately opposed. For example, in the writing of the blind writer and staunch abolitionist Edward Rushton, the critique of racism hinges on the idea that racial prejudice derives from sightedness. Rushton thus serves as an important counterpoint to the more widely taught Edmund Burke, whose ableist assumptions about blindness in *A Philosophical Enquiry into the Origin of Our Ideas of the Sublime and Beautiful* undergirds a belief in Blackness and Black subjects as inherently terrifying.

In a related discussion, Travis Chi Wing Lau addresses the place of race within Romantic-era medical discourse, calling attention to the disabling forms of experimentation on Black bodies that enabled anatomical research. There is, Lau points out, a key irony in these experiments, as the study of those who were understood to be fundamentally *pathological* led to universalizing conclusions about the nature of the normative, white man. If this sounds like a moment of merely historical interest, Lau assures us it is not. Rather, the legacy of the racialized discourse of medicine can be witnessed in ongoing health disparities among differently racialized groups.

Romanticism has been all but synonymous with poetry – the art "more capable than any other art of completely unfolding the totality of an event," per Hegel – and the poet qua "legislator of the world" (Percy Shelley) who "brings the whole soul of man into activity" (Coleridge) occupies a privileged place in Romanticism. Joseph Albernaz and Devin M. Garofalo examine in their respective chapters how, as Albernaz puts it, "the modern category of lyric voice is entangled with processes of racialization." Albernaz focuses on the complaint poem, a subgenre that was especially important to Romantic-era abolitionists, who often ventriloquized enslaved Africans. And yet, Albernaz contends, Romantic poetry, particularly as it is taken up by Black writers, is also capable of refusing the racial logics it has traditionally upheld. In such instances, complaint negates the world as it is and reveals, however briefly, "the collective undersong of *No*, the depthless well of non-sense from which all sense springs."

Riffing on the narcissism of male grooming, Devin M. Garofalo discusses the Romantic impulse to "manscape" – that is, to "read ... a culturally specific conception of the human into the landscape such that it is invisibilized as the world's structuring principle." This culturally specific conception of the human, she clarifies, building on the pathbreaking work of Sylvia Wynter, is that of man as a bourgeois colonialist, a tamer, and a conqueror. He is Hannibal and Napoleon and the Wordsworthian poet all in one. The Romantic nature poem that is the hallmark of early nineteenth century poetry, then, recruits the ecological imagination as it consolidates and eradicates all threats to whiteness.

Nikki Hessell's "Romantic Poetry and Constructions of Indigeneity" understands the Romantic racialization of Indigenous peoples as means of denying these groups sovereignty. The trope of the Indian in representative European texts is, by this reading, complicit with the "desire to own, define, and administer *everything*." By reading Romantic poetry for its recurring tropes, however, we can also locate the Romantic tradition in the work of those generally excluded from conversations about Romanticism. Thus, Hessell reads Romanticism in the works of Indigenous poets Jane Johnston Schoolcraft (Ojibwe) and John Rollin Ridge (Cherokee). This is not merely a matter of expanding the Romantic canon; rather, by centering those whose presence in Romantic literature has generally been restricted to object of interest, Hessell shows that those who have been used as tropes are wielders of Romantic tropes in their own right.

The final three chapters look beyond the poetic tradition that has long been emphasized in Romanticist criticism. Atesede Makonnen's "Romanticism and the Novel(ty) of Race" argues that not only did the Romantic novel take up questions about race, but the novel form was itself racialized during the Romantic era. Makonnen studies in particular Clara Reeve and Anna Letitia Barbauld, who attempted to taxonomize various "species" of prose in a mirror of the categorization central to that of eighteenth and nineteenth-century racial philosophy and science. For both Reeve and Barbauld, the evolution of the modern novel is a move away from other forms – tales and fables, for instance – linked to the primitive and the non-European. Thus, both writers link literary development as a mark of cultural, national, and, implicitly, racial progress.

Lauren Dembowitz's chapter focuses on race and visual culture, drawing on Blake's notion of the "bounding line" with its "infinite inflexions and movements" that recast the visual image without relying on the inhumanity and philistinism of mass production. These "inflexions and movements" allow us to imagine new possibilities for familiar images, such as that of the "Hottentot Venus," Sarah Baartman. Rather than write off these images as racist stereotypes, we can, with Dembowitz's Blakean method, attend closely to how the material history of the visual text is imbricated with the history of race, which is subtly transformed with each new iteration. As Dembowitz powerfully concludes, the image compels us to "contend with the ways we are 'intimately connected' with, 'bound up in,' and 'dependent upon' that figure and the real women she overwrites for understanding how racial capitalism lives on in our present."

In the chapter that concludes this volume, Yasser Shams Khan reminds us that race, simply put, is made. It is the consequence of painstaking and deliberate work, whether in the meticulous anthropological taxonomies offered by Kant and Blumenbach, or in the line of poetry, or, as Khan argues, in the representation of racial differences on the Romantic-era stage. Drawing on the notion of "racecraft," which "foregrounds racism as a reality that produces 'race' to rationalize the dispossession of wealth, power, and rights," Khan shows how stagecraft in John Fawcett's *Obi; or Three-Finger'd Jack* (1800) establishes the terms by which racialized subjects come to be understood as fundamentally exploitable.

The chapters are as varied in their conclusions as they are in their scope: while none is forgiving of Romanticism's sometimes tacit, sometimes explicit endorsement of racist ideologies, each suggests a different solution for combatting these ideologies, whether by reading more widely, or reading more deeply, or even refusing to read Romantic literatures altogether. What binds these pieces together, despite their diversity, is a shared commitment to understanding how Romanticism positions us as critics invested in emancipatory politics, and how we position ourselves in turn.

## Notes

1. Arthur O. Lovejoy, "On the Discrimination of Romanticisms," *PMLA* 39/2 (June 1924): 229–53.
2. Indeed, as recent work in the field of premodern critical race studies has shown us, race in its pre-Enlightenment usage (i.e. race *qua* family) was bound up with notions of phenotype, ethnicity, geography, and behavior well before the advent of scientific racism. See, for example, Geraldine Heng, *The Invention of Race in the European Middle Ages* (Cambridge: Cambridge University Press, 2018); M. Lindsay Kaplan, *Figuring Racism in Medieval Christianity* (New York: Oxford University Press, 2019); and Urvashi Chakravarty, *Fictions of Consent: Slavery, Servitude, and Free Service in Early Modern England* (Philadelphia: University of Pennsylvania Press, 2022).

CHAPTER 1

# Burke and Kant on Color and Inheritance

## Yoon Sun Lee

Historians agree that race began to be imagined and perceived differently in the second half of the European eighteenth century. Skin color, in particular, started to receive much more attention, even though its significance was far from settled.[1] An example can be found in a 1741 essay contest sponsored by the Royal Academy of Bordeaux on the topic of the "'degeneration' of black skin and hair." Henry Louis Gates, Jr. and Andrew Curran explain why there was this degree of interest. The wealth not only of the port city of Bordeaux but of the expanding empire of Britain was increasingly dependent on a particular color of skin: "the color of sub-Saharan bodies had become synonymous with human bondage ... the color black was a metonym for Africans, [and] Black Africans themselves were undoubtedly a metonym for slavery and the trans-Atlantic slave trade."[2]

Skin color had not always been at the center of racial thinking or colonizing activities. Earlier in the century, British colonization had relied on categories such as "Christian and savage."[3] Instead of color, other features, such as the presence of clothing or the state of agricultural development, were invoked. Still, by the final two decades of the century, skin color had become an inescapable consideration, as for the formerly enslaved author of *The Interesting Narrative of the Life of Olaudah Equiano or Gustavus Vassa, the African* (1789), even if its meaning remained unclear.

This chapter undertakes to examine the strange and shifting role that color plays in the writings of two major figures of the late eighteenth century. The philosopher Immanuel Kant is better known for his critical or transcendental philosophy than for his views on racial difference. But Kant taught anthropology and geography throughout his career, and he considered these disciplines essential to all other forms of knowledge.[4] In a 1777 essay, "Of the Different Human Races," he asserts that humans can be classified by their four skin colors: "First race/Noble blond (northern Europe) ... Second race/Copper red (America) ... Third race/Black

(Senegambia) ... Fourth race/Olive-yellow (Asian-Indian)."[5] Edmund Burke, politician and philosopher, first made his name by writing about the beautiful and the sublime – sensations that arose from color, size, sound, and touch, among other factors. In his most famous work, *Reflections on the Revolution in France* (1790), Burke makes his central theme the idea of inheritance. This same concept – inheritance – lies at the heart of the way that Kant comes to define race philosophically. Kant and Burke are usually associated on the ground of aesthetic theory. By bringing together their discussions of human difference and similarity, however, we can see how race in this historical moment occupied a supremely ambiguous, slippery position in thought and discourse, even as it supplied a foundation for the development of capitalism and empire. Color and inheritance do not bear any necessary relation to each other, but they were brought together in and through the very concept of necessity. What we find at their complex intersection is an uneasy, perhaps even wishful exploration of the limits of human freedom.

The concept of race had already undergone many changes. Before the early modern period, race had referred to "the flow of traits or of kinship across generations," something more like a line of descent, while the concept of "species" had relied on "the inspectable surface of a thing ... the kind to which a thing belongs in virtue of its current, apparent conformation, rather than in virtue of its origins, of where it flows from."[6] But in the seventeenth century, the natural philosopher François Bernier, in "A New Division of the Earth" (1684), used the term "race" as if it referred to "species." In a way now familiar, Bernier posited four or five "Species or Races of men," characterized by morphological difference and geographical distribution; the two went hand in hand.[7] As a result, the concept of race "ceases to denote a potentially morphologically variable chain of descent, and comes to denote a fixed and bounded population of morphologically homogeneous individuals" (148).[8] Bernier did not offer a definitive explanation of how these different features came about in various parts of the world.[9] But this way of thinking about race would endure. It allowed morphological or phenotypical differences to be assumed rather than observed to be uniform across certain groups.

Kant would take up the task of explaining these differences, arguing that skin color was functional; it allowed humans to adapt to different climates all over the globe. Ultimately, the definition of race that he constructs has to do less with the function of skin color than with its transmission. Race is defined by the inheritance of skin color, passed on from parent to child. Kant insists that color inheritance is necessary; it happens in every case without exception. But color ceases to be a sensation or experience one might have. Rather, it is used as an abstract concept to sustain a philosophical definition of race.

Burke develops his thinking about color in the *Philosophical Enquiry into the Origin of our Ideas of the Sublime and the Beautiful* (1757). In that aesthetic treatise, color matters for the physiological effect that it produces on an observer. When Burke takes up the idea of inheritance later in his 1790 *Reflections*, he does not bring it together with skin color in the way that Kant does. And yet, Burke is even more deeply invested in inheritance: biological, legal, English culture as inheritance. Inheritance becomes a metonym for the very order of nature. This is where Kant's argument offers a link back to race. Both thinkers seem to value inheritance because it precludes individual choice. In Burke's somewhat paradoxical version, it becomes an active renunciation of choice, a decision not to decide. Inheritance becomes a structure that can explain and legitimate all other structures. It lends significance to something as superficial as skin color. It also grounds an institution that stands behind their arguments: racial slavery across the Atlantic world.

Edmund Burke's influence was as far-reaching as his views were complex. Echoes of his thought and language can be found in nearly all genres of writing in the Romantic period. Historians today seem divided on whether Burke was a critic of British Empire or its greatest defender. From 1774 to 1780, Burke served as Member of Parliament for the city of Bristol, the second largest port in Britain, whose wealth relied on sugar from West Indian plantations. Judging from his "Sketch of a Negro Code," apparently drafted in 1780, Burke, like many others of his time, looked at the institution of slavery in an economic light, or as an economic problem. However, his views on race or racial difference are not easy to determine.

Burke's *Philosophical Enquiry* can be read in the context of a relatively new preoccupation with skin color, what it means, and how it can be used to produce value. In this work, slavery emerges as a subtext, a set of concerns barely beneath the surface. It ties together Burke's often heterogeneous observations. When Kant later reworks Burke's ideas in the *Critique of Judgment* (1790), the sublime comes to point toward a higher destiny for humans as rational beings able to give themselves a law. In Burke, though, this tranche of aesthetic experience is defined in relation to the involuntary experience of fear, pain, labor, and, implicitly, bondage. "The passions which belong to self-preservation, turn on pain and danger," and these are the causes of the sublime. The other class of passions points us toward "society," toward other people, and those are linked to the beautiful.[10] It was Burke's most important claim that both the sublime and the beautiful originate in the structures of the body rather than of the mind. As we will see, the experiences that define the sublime revolve around darkness. The experience of beauty has at its core the sensation of sweetness. A link between them can be found in sugar, a final cause of the slavery that can be glimpsed through the discussion of the sublime. As Gates and Curran remind us, the color black was already by 1741 becoming a metonymic representation of slavery.

Burke offers this concise account of the sublime: "the idea of bodily pain, in all the modes and degrees of labour, pain, anguish, torment, is productive of the sublime" (*Enquiry*, 86). Burke insists that fear, pain, and labor are physiologically identical because they rely on the same "tension, contraction, or violent emotion of the nerves" (*Enquiry*, 132). (In keeping with eighteenth-century usage, Burke does not distinguish between nerves and muscles.)

> A man who suffers under violent bodily pain (I suppose the most violent, because the effect may be the more obvious) ... has his teeth set, his eyebrows are violently contracted, his forehead is wrinkled, his eyes are dragged inwards, and rolled ... his hair stands on end ... the whole fabric totters. Fear or terror ... exhibits exactly the same effects. (*Enquiry*, 131)

While Burke's description suggests a separation between the person experiencing pain and the one observing it, that separation actually does not hold. The distinction between labor and pain likewise collapses. "As common labour, which is a mode of pain, is the exercise of the grosser, a mode of terror is the exercise of the finer parts of the system" (*Enquiry*, 136). He notes that "pain is always inflicted by a power in some way superior, because we never submit to pain willingly" (*Enquiry*, 65). The experience of the sublime, then, which results from the labor of "these finer and more delicate organs," is also presumably forced, not voluntary. It collapses the distinction between involuntary and voluntary sensation.

The question of color arises through a series of associations that is worth tracing. Burke first argues that the perceptual causes of the sublime must be large and unified objects. But the sublime can also be produced, he notes, by the repetition of one element, which he calls "the artificial infinite." He offers repeating sounds as an instance, then imagines a "colonnade of uniform pillars planted in a right line" (*Enquiry*, 141). Then this section ends abruptly at a blank wall. Burke is unsure about how the "view of a bare wall, if it be of a great height and length" affects us. He concludes that it is not productive of the sublime. But the example, over which he lingers, places the reader imaginatively in a situation of captivity.

The discussion of the bare wall leads Burke directly to "Locke's opinion concerning darkness, considered" (*Enquiry*, 143). The subsequent sections cannot let go of the idea of darkness. They are titled, "Darkness terrible in its own nature," "Why Darkness is terrible," "The effects of Blackness," "The effects of Blackness moderated" (*Enquiry*, 144–48). The first of these sections cites the story of a boy who received his vision through surgery at age thirteen or fourteen, and who felt "great uneasiness" when he first saw a black object. This is the only time that the *Enquiry* mentions "a negro woman," whose sight strikes this boy with terror (*Enquiry*, 144–45). The story is meant to prove that such fear was not contingent on association with other ideas, since the boy had never seen anything at all before. It results from a "natural operation" of the structure of the human eye. The "radial fibres of the iris," Burke writes, "may by great darkness come to be so contracted, as to strain the nerves that compose it beyond their natural tone; and by this means to produce a painful sensation" (*Enquiry*, 145). The eye has to labor, and labor causes pain. Yet paradoxes quickly accumulate. It turns out that the reason the eye labors is because blackness is not actually seen. In a passage that says perhaps more than it intends, Burke writes, "Black bodies, reflecting none, or but a few rays, with regard to sight, are but as so many vacant spaces dispersed among the objects we view. When the eye lights on one of these vacuities . . . it suddenly falls into a relaxation; out of which it as suddenly recovers by a convulsive spring" (*Enquiry*, 147). After citing awkward physical analogies to explain this "convulsive spring," Burke ends with an admission of defeat: "To enter into every particular, or to answer every objection, would be an endless labour" (*Enquiry*, 148–49).

Unwilling to shoulder the burden of endless labor to which so many bodies were condemned, Burke turns to "The physical cause of Love," the passion behind the beautiful. He finds it in the quality of smoothness, which produces ease, comfort. But smoothness emerges as a haptic sweetness, a sweetness perceived through other organs of touch. Burke proceeds immediately from "Why smoothness is beautiful" to sugar itself. In "Sweetness, its nature," he observes, "In all sweet bodies, sugar . . . is constantly found." Sugar "has its own distinct, regular, invariable form . . . a perfect globe." The round shape on "that nice organ the tongue . . . will induce that sense called sweetness" (*Enquiry*, 152–53). In his theory, sweetness serves as a hinge. It is a structure that links the senses of taste, touch, and sight, both in ordinary linguistic usage and in its physiological operation.

Though Burke does not explicitly connect sugar, labor, and color, all the elements that link them are present in his treatise: terror, obscurity, power, and privation, the very first elements of the sublime Burke had discussed. These go into the making of material sweetness. Burke does evoke black and white as an analogy to the sublime and beautiful in order to argue that these categories are and must remain distinct, even when blended: "If the qualities of the sublime and the beautiful are sometimes found united, does this prove, that they are the same ... that they are not opposite and contradictory? Black and white may soften, they may blend, but they are not therefore the same" (*Enquiry*, 124–25). Even though the opposite conclusion could be drawn, Burke insists that the fact that two colors can blend into each other proves that they are eternally different. This logic, applied to humans of different colors, grounds Kant's argument that racial categories exist in nature and are not merely the result of human judgment.

Kant's lectures on physical geography and anthropology were a mainstay of his career as a teacher, philosopher, and public intellectual. He began lecturing on the former subject in the 1750s and continued to teach both throughout his tenure at the University of Königsberg, including the period of his critical turn. Though they strike us now as full of outdated prejudices, Kant saw fit to publish his collected anthropology lectures in 1798. Two earlier essays focused on the definition of race form part of this same project. "Determination of the Concept of a Human Race" appeared in 1785, the same year that he published the *Groundwork for the Metaphysics of Morals*. Kant also developed many of the same ideas in his 1775 essay "Of the Different Human Races."

Both essays elaborate the claim that "all humans everywhere on the earth belong to one and the same natural species" ("Different," 46). Kant cites the criterion popularized by the natural historian Buffon: "animals that produce fertile young with one another belong to one and the same *physical* species (no matter how different in form they may be)" ("Different," 45). The unity of the species, however, matters far less to him than differences of skin color. The four races that Kant enumerates in the 1775 essay are defined by little more than color. This was not a universally accepted standard. Johann Friedrich Blumenbach, often regarded as the father of modern race theory, insists in his 1775 essay, "On the Natural Variety of Mankind," that lines cannot be drawn between skin colors: "there is an almost insensible and indefinable transition from the pure white skin of the German lady through the yellow, the red, and the dark nations, to the Ethiopian of the very deepest black ... [and even] in the space of a few degrees of latitude."[11] Skin color, Blumenbach asserts, is "an adventitious and easily changeable thing, and can never constitute a diversity of species."[12] Taking into account the effects of social class, gender, and climate, he even cites examples of people who have changed color: "An Englishman who had spent only three years with the Virginians, became exactly like them in colour."[13] Blumenbach thus turns to what he considers more quantifiable features, such as skull shape and size, with significant consequences for the future development of Western scientific racism.

Two of Kant's claims about skin color can be noted. The first is that skin color is adaptive. It has changed in different parts of the world to allow humans to survive in different climates. Kant draws on the chemistry of his time when he notes, for instance, that "human blood becomes black simply by being overloaded with phlogiston," which was believed to be the element in things that made them combustible.[14] In Africa, where there is supposedly a high amount of phlogiston in the atmosphere, "nature must have organized the skin in them in such a way" that their skin can somehow remove the excess of this element ("Determination," 139). Likewise, he conjectures that the "reddish rust color" of native Americans is the result of having been exposed to "acidic air" (carbon dioxide) from "the ice of the Arctic Ocean": "nature might in the organization of the skin have cared in advance for the removal of the fixed air" ("Determination," 140).

Kant also asserts that skin color results from nature's wise advance planning. There must have been "germs" or seeds that were "preformed" in original humans, that allowed them to adapt to different climates and soils: "Something that is meant to reproduce itself must instead have already, in advance, been situated in the generative power ... for an occasional development appropriate to the circumstances into which the creature can land and in which it should continuously preserve itself," since "Human beings were destined for living in every climate and any condition of the land" ("Different," 50). Kant even describes, in a kind of fast-forward sequence, the process whereby one of these original "germs" developed in the northern Arctic in order to produce the "Kalmuckish" race, which he also refers to as the "Hunnish" or "Mongolish" race. The human body gets smaller, the legs get shorter, "juices" dry up so that less hair emerges, the face gets flat to protect itself from the cold, and the eyes permanently half-close to protect against the "light of the snow":

> Thus, little by little, the beardless chin, the snarled nose, thin lips, squinting eyes, the flat face, and the red-brown skin color with black hair, or, in one word, the Kalmuckish facial formation arises. This formation takes root after a long succession of generations in the same climate up to the point of becoming an enduring race and preserves itself when such a people immediately thereafter acquires a new place to live in a more temperate climate. ("Different," 51)

While many things could be said about this narrative, it certainly shows Kant's commitment to teleological thinking. This type of thinking, described in the *Critique of Judgment*, looks for the final cause or purpose served by the parts of a whole that is supposed to exist. Kant thus arrives at a concept of a single human species "whose internal possibility presupposes throughout the idea of a whole on which depend the constitution and mode of action of the parts, as we must represent to ourselves an organized body."[15] But Kant emphasizes the miraculous adaptability of the human species in order to locate it in the past, "up to the point of becoming an enduring race." This move does not make sense even in its immediate context. Why must there be a cut-off point beyond which humans cannot continue to adapt to their surroundings?

The answer can be found in the second major point Kant makes about race, which is that it is simply another word for inheritance: "Among the deviations, that is, the heritable differences of animals that belong to a single line of descent, are those called *races*. Races are deviations preserved invariably over many generations, both in all transplantations ... and in interbreeding with other deviations ... that always produce half-breed offspring" ("Different," 46). The 1785 essay is more streamlined and more adamant: "Only that in an animal species which passes on can justify a class distinction in that species" ("Determination," 129). The concept of human race is grounded exclusively in skin color, which is "invariably" inherited by offspring. Kant remarks that many different traits are inherited across generations. He thus finds it "a noteworthy phenomenon that no single one of them within a class of beings characterized by means of simple skin color passes on necessarily, but this last character, skin color – even though it might seem insignificant – passes on universally and invariably both within the class as well as in the interbreeding of one class with the remaining three" ("Determination," 133). At this point, Kant seems unconcerned with the adaptive significance of skin color and concedes that "it might seem insignificant" were it not for the fact that it "passes on... invariably." Most strange is his insistence that

> The character of the class is passed on invariably in heterogeneous interbreeding, and there exist absolutely no exceptions to this... This transmission is, then, every time two-sided and never simply one-sided in one and the same child. The white father imprints the child with the character of his class, and the black mother that of hers. Consequently, an intermediate breed... must arise every time in unions such as these. ("Determination," 132)

Kant's way of reasoning and calculating with skin color appears even more odd when compared with Blumenbach's. In the case of "hybrid offspring," Blumenbach notes that "It is plain therefore that the traces of blackness are propagated... but they do not keep completely the degrees which we have just noticed, for twins sometimes are born of different colours."[16]

Kant does not, however, entirely forget the adaptive argument about color, and restates the importance of the skin's function as an organ. He concludes that "purposive suitability in an organized system is surely the general reason" for these color differences (139):

> different classes of human beings must have emerged that necessarily also had to bring their determined character in the succession into the generation with every other class. This is because the character appertained to the possibility of their existence... it also appertained to the possibility of the reproduction of the kind... We are, therefore, compelled to conclude from such invariably transmitting properties... that their derivation is from a unified lineal stem stock, because without this it would not be possible to understand the *necessity* of the transmission. ("Determination," 135–36)

Kant balances precariously between observation and logical deduction. Skin color is observable and therefore justifies this division of the single species into races. It also helped ensure survival, "the possibility of their existence." Yet when Kant finds it necessary for skin color to become an "invariably transmitting property," it opens the possibility for the division of humans by skin color to become "an organized system" that is an end in itself.

We can note, however, that this belief rests on a contradiction. In the 1775 essay, Kant had explained how Buffon's definition of a species was superior to the Linnaean system based on morphology: "A scholastic division is based upon classes and divides things up according to *similarities*, but a natural division is based upon identifying lines of descent that classify the animals according to reproductive *relationships*... The first has only the intent of bringing the creatures under headings, but the second, of bringing them under laws" ("Different," 45–46, original emphasis). In other words, classification based on morphological similarities and differences, on features that strike the eye, is merely contingent, a lesser form of knowledge. Buffon's more scientific or "natural" taxonomy studies "reproductive relationships," or heredity. But an idea of *visible* color appears to be the basis of Kant's taxonomy. Unless it were possible to group people together on the basis of not just similar but *identical* color, Kant's definition of race could not stand. In the process, color is taken up into the idea of inheritance. Moreover, the idea of inheritance becomes conflated with that of natural lawfulness.

In Burke, we can observe the same movement. We recall that François Bernier's "A New Division of the Earth" managed "to effectively decouple the concept of race from considerations of lineage, and instead to conceptualize it in biogeographical terms in which the precise origins or causes of the original differences of human physical appearance from region to region remain underdetermined."[17] What we see in Burke is the next turn in the emergence of this concept. If race had begun to refer to a geographically fixed set of "morphologically homogeneous individuals," or, in Kant's version, a set of individuals of identical skin color, Burke reimmerses the concept of race even more fully in the flow of time, and more particularly in "kinship across generations."[18] Without referring to color, he transforms inheritance from what might be thought of as a natural mechanism into a supreme act of cultural wisdom and a uniquely English intentionality. Englishness becomes not a matter of external morphological traits or even of hereditary national character, but of a constitutional morphology, which in turn determines what one holds in one's mind or as property.

Burke's most extensive criticism of the French Revolution and its supporters in England is actually aimed at a particular interpretation of the English revolution of 1688 and the establishment of the Hanoverian monarchy (George I and his successors). According to the Dissenting clergyman Richard Price, "the people of England have acquired three fundamental rights ... 1. 'To choose our own governors.' 2. 'To cashier them for misconduct.' 3. 'To frame a government for ourselves.'"[19] Burke quotes these lines and asserts that "The body of the people of England ... utterly disclaim it" (*Reflections*, 27). The last right is what Burke will most energetically dispute. On the abdication of James II in 1688, Burke argues, Parliament did not choose a monarch or "frame a government," but chose instead to reaffirm emphatically the hereditary status of the British monarchy. When neither King William nor Queen Anne had surviving children, Parliament decided again to emphasize the hereditary principle, only "indicating with more precision the persons who were to inherit in the Protestant line" (*Reflections*, 28). "Instead of a right to choose our own governors, they declared that the succession in that line (the Protestant line drawn from James the First) was absolutely necessary" (*Reflections*, 29). They chose not to choose, reaffirming instead an original "stock" (*Reflections*, 34).

But Burke does more than correct certain details of political history. He shapes inheritance into the racial identity of the English people. This is not inheritance as an empirical fact; Burke is not saying that English people share the same genetic inheritance, much less the same color. Rather, inheritance as an idea or "analogy" serves as the basis of English self-consciousness. Burke argues that those acts of Parliament only gave formal expression to an immanent knowledge and practice. Experience taught the English, he says, that inheritance is the strongest claim of all, that it secures the future better than any mere choice or decision:

> We wished at the period of the [1688] Revolution, and do now wish, to derive all we possess as an inheritance from our forefathers ... they preferred this positive, recorded, hereditary title to all which can be dear to the man and the citizen, to that vague speculative right, which exposed their sure inheritance to be scrambled for and torn to pieces by every wild litigious spirit ... claiming their franchises not on abstract principles "as the rights of men," but as the rights of Englishmen, and as a patrimony derived from their forefathers. (*Reflections*, 43–44)

Burke is referring to the Declaration of the Rights of Man and of Citizens, one of the first acts to emerge when the French Estates General transformed itself in 1789 into a National Assembly. Burke describes this latter body with horror as "the organic moleculae of a disbanded people." In 1688,

> when England found itself without a king ... they regenerated the deficient part of the old constitution through the parts which were not impaired. They kept these old parts exactly as they were, that the part recovered might be suited to them. They acted by the ancient organized states in the shape of their old organization, and not by the organic moleculae of a disbanded people. (*Reflections*, 33)

Burke is describing England's revolution in the terms of natural regeneration, how a creature can regrow a missing part. It also resembles how human races, in Kant's account, perpetuate their color differences, making sure that the new parts exactly resemble the existing members of the group.

The phenomenon of regeneration is key to Kant's account of teleological judgment in the third Critique: "a thing exists as a natural purpose if it is ... both cause and effect of itself."[20] Kant describes this process with wonder: "The self-help of nature in case of injury in the vegetable creation, when the want of a part that is necessary for the maintenance of its neighbors is supplied by the remaining parts ... are among the most wonderful properties of organized creatures."[21] Kant's point is that we need to regard a natural phenomenon not only in terms of its mechanical causes, but also in terms of its purpose or final cause. Burke relies on the same metaphor to argue that the English constitution is superior to all others because it stands as proof of what both Burke and Kant conceive as *organized* nature.

Inheritance as an idea reconciles for Burke multiple contradictions: among them, self-directed and other-directed feelings, the two bases of the sublime and the beautiful. It even reconciles acquisitiveness and altruism. It is a "pattern of nature" that shapes how "we receive, we hold, we transmit our government and our privileges ... our property and our lives." Inheritance is the "spirit of philosophic analogy" (*Reflections*, 45–46) that unites public and private; legislative and domestic; political, economic, and genetic, Burke argues. That self, whose preservation is so memorably threatened in and through the sublime, here recognizes inheritance from "forefathers" as its own necessary condition. Inheritance can do all these things because Burke buries the concept of possession so deeply in it that it becomes almost invisible. He also distances it, of course, from any idea of color.

Yet even as Burke dematerializes it, inheritance comes back to the concept of "stock." In the case of King William, "the new line was derived from the same stock. It was still ... an hereditary descent in the same blood, though ... qualified with Protestantism" (*Reflections*, 34). In the second interruption, Princess Sophia (Figure 1.1) the Electress of Hanover, was named "for a stock and root of inheritance to our kings" because she was the granddaughter of James I: "through her it was to be connected with the old stock of inheritance in King James the First" (*Reflections*, 36). Race moves away from bodily morphology and back into the "flow of kinship across generations." Burke stipulates that "Upon that body and stock of inheritance we have taken care not to inoculate any cyon alien to the nature of the original plant. All the reformations we have hitherto made ... which may possibly be made

Figure 1.1 Princess Sophia, dressed as an American Indian, 1644. Painted by her sister, Louise Hollandine of the Palatinate. Oil on canvas. Museum Wasserburg Anholt. Photo credit: Art Collection 3/Alamy Stock Photo.

hereafter, will be carefully formed upon analogical precedent, authority, and example" (*Reflections*, 43). But Burke may be pressing too hard here on what inheritance can do, as an analogy or as a practice that creates inalienable wholeness. Parts can remain alien, refuse or resist assimilation to the original. Kant had noted,

> A bud of one tree engrafted on the twig of another produces in the alien stock a plant of its own kind, and so also a scion engrafted on a foreign stem. Hence we may regard each twig or leaf of the same tree as merely engrafted or inoculated into it, and so as an independent tree attached to another and parasitically nourished by it.[22]

Kant's very weird vision blurs the distinction between origin and alien, graft and birth, by seeing each leaf of a tree as an independent being "parasitically nourished by it." The single organism threatens to become a grotesque vision of conflicting ends, of struggle and domination and failure to cohere. A similar result could and did arise at the level of the social body through the cruel manipulation of inheritance. Some decades before Princess Sophia was named as "a stock and root of inheritance to our kings," the laws of the colony of Virginia declared "that all children borne [*sic*] in this country shall be held bond or free only according to the condition of the mother – *Partus Sequitur Ventrem*."[23] This statute was passed in response to a successful suit made by Elizabeth Keye, the child of an enslaved African woman and a white Englishman, who argued for her freedom in 1655.[24] Its source lies in English property law, where the phrase served "not as a rule that determined the status of someone, but as a rule that determined the ownership of something."[25]

Its effect, as Hortense Spillers has argued, was to create a situation in which "'kinship' loses meaning since it can be invaded at any given and arbitrary moment by the property relation."[26] Rather than securing conscious ties between ancestors and dependents or resolving the contradiction between necessity and choice, inheritance here only asserted the most violent of social divisions. The children of enslaved women of African descent counted as property that could be inherited by others, on the basis of a color that had to be ascribed where it could not be seen as the material sign of a legal condition. They became, in Jennifer Morgan's striking phrase, "vectors of kinlessness": kinlessness that became "the core of hereditary racial slavery."[27] Color thus became a line that demarcated kinlessness from inheritance. These developments occurred before, during, and after the period when Kant and Burke wrote their essays and treatises. Far from demonstrating "purposive suitability in an organized system" of nature ("Determination," 139), then, color is most important as a fiction brutally summoned into being through organized systems of laws of inheritance.

## Notes

1. Justin Smith, *Nature, Human Nature, and Human Difference* (Princeton: Princeton University Press, 2015), 240–41.
2. Henry Louis Gates, Jr. and Andrew S. Curran, *Who's Black and Why?* (Cambridge, MA: Harvard University Press, 2022), x.
3. Roxann Wheeler, *The Complexion of Race* (Philadelphia: University of Pennsylvania Press, 2000), 46.
4. David Harvey, "Cosmopolitanism in the Anthropology and Geography," in *Reading Kant's Geography*, ed. Stuart Elden and Eduardo Mendieta (Albany: State University of New York Press, 2011), 269.

5. Immanuel Kant, "Of the Different Human Races," in *Kant and the Concept of Race*, ed. Jon M. Mikkelsen (Albany: State University of New York Press, 2004), 41–54. Further references will be given in the text.
6. Smith, *Nature*, 148.
7. Smith, *Nature*, 146–47.
8. Smith, *Nature*, 148.
9. Smith, *Nature*, 22. Bernier posited four or five "Species or Races of men," characterized by morphological difference and geographical distribution (146–47).
10. Edmund Burke, *A Philosophical Enquiry into the Origin of Our Ideas of the Sublime and the Beautiful*, ed. James T. Boulton (Notre Dame: University of Notre Dame Press, 1986), 51–53. Further references will be given in the text.
11. Johann Blumenbach, "De generis humani varietate nativa" (1775), in *The Anthropological Treatises of Johann Friedrich Blumenbach*, trans. Thomas Bendyshe (London: Longman Green, 1865), 69–141, 107.
12. Blumenbach, "De generis humani varietate nativa," 112–13.
13. Blumenbach, "De generis humani varietate nativa," 111.
14. Immanuel Kant, "Determination of the Concept of a Human Race" (1785), in Mikkelsen, 128–41. Further references will be given in the text.
15. Immanuel Kant, *Critique of Judgment*, trans. J. H. Bernard (New York: Macmillan, 1951), 257.
16. Blumenbach, "De generis humani varietate nativa," 112.
17. Smith, *Nature*, 22.
18. Smith, *Nature*, 148.
19. Edmund Burke, *Reflections on the Revolution in France* (New York: Doubleday, 1989), 27. Further references will be given in the text.
20. Kant, *Critique*, 217.
21. Kant, *Critique*, 218.
22. Kant, *Critique*, 218.
23. Quoted in Jennifer Morgan, "Partus sequitur ventrem: Law, Race, and Reproduction in Colonial Slavery," *Small Axe* 55 (2018), 1.
24. Jennifer Morgan, *Reckoning with Slavery* (Durham: Duke University Press, 2021), 1–4.
25. Thomas Morris, *Southern Slavery and the Law, 1619–1860* (Chapel Hill: University of North Carolina Press, 1996), 45.
26. Hortense Spillers, "Mama's Baby, Papa's Maybe: An American Grammar Book," *Diacritics* 17/2 (1987), 74.
27. Morgan, *Reckoning*, 126.

CHAPTER 2

# Breathing Freedom in the Era of the Haitian Revolution

*Catherine R. Peters*

... when will we tire of breathing the air that they breathe?
[... quand nous lasserons-nous de respirer le même air qu'eux?]
– Haitian Declaration of Independence, January 1, 1804, CO 137/111/1

## Revolutionary Breathing

What is the relationship between breath and freedom? During the Age of Revolutions, the concept of atmosphere, initially understood as a vaporous envelope surrounding the earth, accumulated political and affective resonances. This semantic transition furthered its pluralization as specific atmospheres afforded specific possibilities and limitations. Romantic literature not only operated from an association between air and liberty but also furthered it: clouds inspired new horizons, spirits demanded accountability, and wind reverberated with revolutionary feeling. Pondering the atmosphere, Romantic writers intersected with white antislavery actors, who also drew upon the trope of unrestrained breath to gain sympathetic responses to the centuries-long enslavement of Afro-descendant peoples in the Atlantic world. However, even as they sought to end the Atlantic slave trade, and eventually African chattel slavery, such arguments presumed ongoing physical, reproductive, and literary labor from individuals of African descent. White antislavery genres, in other words, conceded little space for Black subjects to articulate their own relationships to breath and freedom, even when they wrote petitions, poetry, and constitutions.

The Haitian Revolution fundamentally transformed how European empires imagined the abolition of the Atlantic slave trade and African chattel slavery. What began as an insurrection of enslaved Africans, the majority of whom were born in West Central Africa, became an independent state whose armies had vanquished Spanish, British, and French troops. As hundreds of thousands of Afro-descendant residents revolted in Saint-Domingue, talk about revolution, often conveyed through the metaphor of wind/air/breath, inspired new alignments.[1] In 1804, Haitian leader Jean-Jacques Dessalines drew upon the trope of unencumbered breathing as he inaugurated the first Black sovereign state in the hemisphere. As part of the Haitian Declaration of Independence, he proclaimed "when will we tire of breathing the air that they [the French] breathe?"[2] Dessalines's rhetorical question articulated independence through demand for an atmosphere in which Haitian peoples could breathe their own air. His assertion inverted a common association between unfreedom and pestilential miasma that often typified European descriptions of Caribbean environments.

As tropes of constricted air animated antislavery discourse, unfree peoples of African – and Asian – descent labored through airborne infections, succumbing to respiratory diseases. In spite of exposure to environmental precarities, they forged political and intimate worlds for themselves, such as those conjured in the formerly enslaved Cuban poet Juan Francisco Manzano's "A Dream [Un Sueño]" (1838). Written for his younger brother who remained in bondage, the poem describes flying over the landscapes of Matanzas, Cuba, and becoming like wind: "I gather air and form / the columns of wind [aire recojo, y formo / las columnas de viento]."[3] Manzano's lived environment was shaped by Cuban planter advocacy for the Haitian Revolution to be leveraged into an economic opportunity. For example, in 1792, planter Francisco de Arango y Parreño wrote that "the insurrection of the blacks in Guarico [Haiti] has expanded the horizon of my ideas [la insurrección de los negros del Guarico ha agrandado el horizonte de mis ideas]."[4] Parreño's so-called horizon of ideas resulted in the arrival of hundreds of thousands of captive Africans, especially from West Central Africa, the Bight of Biafra, Sierra Leone, and the Bight of Benin. These diverse men and women coordinated frequent uprisings in nineteenth-century Cuba, some of which cited the example of Haiti.

White-authored writing during the period generally did not heed insurgent Black respiration, except as a threat to colonial control. Instead, their records attempted to mediate Afro-descendant voices as well as gradually reform slavery's stifling infrastructure. In contrast, formerly enslaved writers, such as Manzano and Haitian leader Toussaint Louverture, wrote for the immediate emancipation of themselves and loved ones. Manzano, in particular, called himself "already free; by the air [ya libre; por el aire]," as his imagined flight enabled unrestrained mobilities and familial visits in excess of particular conditions of enslavement.[5] Differentiated by its capacity to accommodate – rather than interrupt – the breathing of others, Manzano's poetry charts what it means to breathe through foreclosed presents toward imagined futures.[6] Extending the rhetorical question of early Haitian leaders, who yearned for atmospheres unstructured by French coloniality, this chapter traces divergent views of freedom expressed through attunement to wind/air/breath after the Haitian Revolution irrevocably altered the conditions of possibility for Black sovereignty in the Americas. As a point of departure, it elaborates upon William Wordsworth's sonnet to Louverture in order to establish how the "common wind" has been adapted to Caribbean fugitivities. Fundamentally, it argues that, in contrast to colonial writers who represented slavery through constricted air and the common through abstract atmosphere, Afro-descendant writers imagined freedom as breathing together with kin.

## The Common Wind

During the Age of Revolutions, Afro-diasporic words and intentions were often mediated by white interpreters and audiences, who sought to determine the significance of Black freedom struggle and, in particular, Haitian sovereignty. Wordsworth's 1803 sonnet "To Toussaint L'Ouverture" remains among the most-cited Romantic treatments of the capture, deportation, and incarceration of the eponymous Haitian revolutionary. First published for the British public on February 2nd in *The Morning Post*, the poem establishes an elegiac "breathing of the common wind" through the presumed death of Toussaint Louverture. It appeared alongside news regarding British transport of supplies to Saint-Domingue: material aid for its European rival against the Black majority.[7] At this time, the five-year British invasion of Saint-Domingue had concluded, although its history has been suppressed for its incompatibility with triumphalist narratives of white British antislavery. That the same page of the newspaper praised a deposed Haitian leader while also reporting upon continued efforts to undermine his fellow revolutionaries anticipates the appropriation of Louverture into British culture and the dissolution of his political legacy. Louverture's separation from other Haitians and incorporation into a common(s) transformed him into a symbol, rather than a man with a specific history.[8] Furthermore, disregard for Louverture's own writing, untranslated into English until 1863, severed him from nation and kin. Nevertheless, Louverture clearly testified to his own history while incarcerated in the Jura mountains. In fact, colonial letters suggest that he asked for writing materials immediately upon being detained inside five layers of fortifications.[9]

From August to September 1802, Louverture wrote nine letters and a twenty-one page *mémoire*. When nearly all his papers and notebooks were taken from him the following month, he sewed a concealed copy into a handkerchief that covered his head. Louverture's *mémoire*, penned concurrently with Wordsworth's poem, appeals to Napoleon for release in the manner of a bureaucratic petition.[10] Unlike Wordsworth's expansive sonnet, Louverture's *mémoire* articulates the feeling of being "covered" with censure. Where Wordsworth gestures toward a common(s), Louverture emphasizes his responsibilities to particular family members – his father, wife, and children:

> they try to cover me with opprobrium, infamy, and they make me the unhappiest man in the world by denying me my liberty and by separating me from what is dearest to me in the world, from a respectable father aged one hundred and five who needs my help, from a beloved wife who will probably not be able to bear the woes that will burden her, far from me, and from a cherished family that made my life happy.
>
> [on cherché a me couvrire d'aupprob, dinfamie, et on ne me rend les plus, mal heureux des homme, en me privant de la liberté, et en me separante de ce que jai de plus cher au monde, dun pere respectable agé de cent cienq ans qui a besoin de mes secoure; dun famme adorée qui ne poura san doute supporte les maux Dont elle séra a cablé, loin de moi; et dune famille cherix qui faisoit le bonheur de ma vix.][11]

While constrained by the fact that Napoleon, his jailer, was also his audience, Louverture describes his conditions of incarceration as suffocation. Moreover, French imperial silencing of Louverture as he fought for his life by offering "an exact account [un compte éxact]" of his "conduct [conduite]" contrasts with Wordsworth's celebration of the "miserable Chieftain."[12] The latter's triumphalist invocation of revolution through atmosphere reflects a structure of feeling legible within dominant narratives of the period. It was incompatible with the writing of a Black revolutionary who sought to shape the historical record by recording the human consequences of European dominance and suppression. Louverture, in other words, had learned the language and genres of the colonizer, but neither guaranteed he would be granted an audience.

Instead, Wordsworth's poem evokes a broad atmosphere of the "common wind" by its description of Louverture not as a writer, but as a listener, both in the original version, written in late 1802, and a revised version, drafted in 1807. The latter poem followed An Act for the Abolition of the Slave Trade, Parliament's abolition of British involvement in the transatlantic slave trade, a resolution impacted by fear of Haitian influence and precedent. As such, Wordsworth's use of wind/air/breath converged with white antislavery advocacy that Africans might breathe, if not freely, then under conditions of captivity.[13] This writing evinced a relationship between air and liberty through their respective absence: in other words, it described a lack of air to suggest a lack of liberty. For example, in 1788, Helen Maria Williams published "A Poem on the Bill Lately Passed for Regulating the Slave Trade," which marked Parliament's decision to limit the number of enslaved Africans on ships. Conveying the Middle Passage in the language of darkness and despair, the poem's early stanzas articulate tropes of wind and breath to affirm the need for regulatory reform: Williams describes the wind as "hollow" (1) and "howling" (11); death as "suffocating" (13); captives' breath as "stifled" (12) and "sinking" (14); air as "tainted" (22); and a child as "gasping" (26). Roughly one-third through the poem, she joins together "common" and "air" in her lines: "The mercy of the common air / The boon of larger space to breathe (102–3)."[14] Williams's phrase, the "common air," suggests that all those who respire share a collective need. During the period, this expression could also be found in scientific tracts as a means of describing the composition of air that arises naturally out of the atmosphere, the properties of which could be manipulated by containment, heat, and pressure. To Williams's suggestion that access to air was a charity that should be extended to captive Africans confined on ships, Wordsworth added wind, or the impression of revolutionary change, that sustained an unspecified public.

What did Wordsworth mean by breathing held in common(s)? In the early nineteenth century, the common(s) served to distinguish the majority of peoples from nobility. It could refer to community, the public, shared inheritances, and open land in England before enclosures. Although the term has often been associated with land or the formation of working classes in Europe, scientists also used it as a modifier to describe air that had not been manipulated through experimentation. Through quantifying and studying the attributes of gases, they developed modern meteorology, which was predicated upon Robert Boyle's seventeenth-century separation of air from ether. In 1622, he published what is now called Boyle's law, which, in today's parlance, states that the pressure of a gas increases as the volume of its container decreases. Nineteenth-century social theorists took up the concept of enclosed and agitated air particles in order to theorize the conditions of revolution through the concept of the safety valve, discussed by writers such as Karl Marx, Friedrich Engels, and Leon Trotsky. Yet, their ideas had been anticipated by wind's metonymic relation to social transformation, as when William Wilberforce described Haitian revolutionaries in the language of revolutionary currents during parliamentary debate in 1797: "They [Haitians] were no longer ... too low for the storm that was passing over them; they stood erect, and influenced its direction."[15] These resonances were not lost in the twentieth century when scholars of Atlantic Africa interpreted the common wind from the vantage of the Caribbean's own revolutionary geographies.

## Interlude: Caribbean Currents

In 1986, Julius S. Scott III finished a dissertation called "The Common Wind: Currents of Afro-American Communication in the Era of the Haitian Revolution," which circulated informally among scholars of the Atlantic and the Caribbean over the ensuing three decades. In the project, Scott reframed Wordsworth's common wind as communication, particularly in port cities, where runaways, sailors, and ex-soldiers conveyed insurrectionary ideas around the Haitian Revolution. His work centered on what he called the "masterless class": fugitive peoples throughout the Caribbean who sought autonomy despite conditions of enslavement, indenture, and impressment. Like the connective approach of the Atlantic field literalized through oceangoing, Scott described Caribbean geographies as linked through water – what he called Black peoples' orientation toward "the world of the sea."[16] His narrative simultaneously embraced the affective charge of wind, which he used as a flexible signifier for communication, environmental conditions, and the spirit of revolution. In Scott's rendering, the common wind was the critical speech of fugitive peoples who, by their self-emancipation, constituted a network.

In the circum-Caribbean that Scott describes, Black mobilities were predicated upon knowledge of daily and seasonal wind patterns. For example, Black seafarers navigating dugouts could not sail directly into the wind because their vessels did not have keels. Instead, they employed quick paddle strokes to travel with the wind. Furthermore, dugouts often demanded the collaboration of eight to twenty individuals, about a quarter of whom needed experience, in order to move through water.[17] Such collectives first selected trees and hollowed them out, drawing upon African traditions in the Bight of Biafra, Senegambia, and Angola. In fact, Scott notes that colonial authorities in Jamaica sought to limit boat size, thereby barring the landing of self-liberated peoples.[18] In other words, intracolonial movement during the Haitian Revolution also generated colonial attempts at bordering throughout the circum-Caribbean.

During the 1790s, British and Spanish administrators banned free and self-liberated Black peoples from landing in their port cities.[19] Colonial records indicate that the Jamaican assembly closely followed the war in Haiti, with regular reports on the activities of Louverture.[20] This securitization of colonial borders against Haiti – and Black peoples ascribed insurrectionary motives – continued into the early nineteenth century. For example, in 1802, Trinidadian Governor Thomas Picton wrote to London that French free people of color were "a dangerous Class which must gradually be got rid of."[21] In 1803, his successor affirmed a commitment "to refuse admittance, almost to all Description of French men."[22] In fact, Scott notes that British administrators described the task of colonial security as the prevention of communication between Afro-descendant peoples in Haiti and the rest of the Caribbean.[23] These moves to thwart Black revolution, which eventually included abolition of the Atlantic slave trade, appear not to have heeded Haiti's clear promise, articulated in its 1804 Declaration of Independence, that it would not interfere with other polities in the region: "let us allow our neighbors to breathe in peace [laissons en paix respirer nos voisins]."[24]

By establishing a common wind around Haiti, Scott demonstrates the foundational nature of its early nineteenth-century independence for all Caribbean peoples. In fact, several prominent leaders in Saint-Domingue hailed from elsewhere in the region, such as Mackandal, a rebel leader in the 1760s, and Boukman, a vodou priest credited with the ceremony which inaugurated the revolution, both of whom arrived from Jamaica; and the Haitian leader Henri Christophe, who was born in St. Kitts.[25] Furthermore, Caribbean identification with the Haitian Revolution nuances the paradigm of its "silencing," the critique that Haitian anthropologist Michel-Rolph Trouillot directed at decades of writing in North American and European attempting to erase Haiti from history.[26] Since the nineteenth century, Caribbean writers have, by contrast, claimed the Haitian Revolution as foundational to Caribbean history. Yet, unlike C. L. R. James's *The Black Jacobins* (1938), which centers on Toussaint Louverture, Scott's monograph follows no singular person. Instead, *The Common Wind* offers glimpses into the fugitivities of self-emancipated peoples, who challenged their domination by colonial powers, in part, by sharing atmospheres of vital communication. The final section of this essay returns to Juan Francisco Manzano's dream poem, which enacts an appeal for his brother's release. What

Wordsworth conjures as revolutionary feeling and Scott describes as fugitive geographies becomes, in Manzano's poetry, actual flight. In other words, Manzano writes atmosphere as the conditions that enable the reunion of family members.

### "Already Free; By the Air"

In November 1838, Manzano published the forty-seven stanza "A Dream [Un Sueño]" with the subtitle "to my second brother." After fleeing enslavement, Manzano had entered into an informal agreement three years prior with planter and cultural arbiter Domingo del Monte, who was supposed to arrange for Manzano's legal emancipation upon the completion of his autobiography. At the time, Del Monte held around 100 enslaved persons in bondage upon a 900-acre estate in Cuba. As a supporter of the abolition of the slave trade, he hoped that the colony might achieve white self-governance when captive Africans no longer arrived upon its shores. As Toussaint Louverture had written to Napoleon in 1803, so too did Manzano write to Del Monte from 1834–35, explaining the urgent need for his kin to be emancipated. Although both men wrote under duress, their manuscripts had divergent receptions: while Louverture's *mémoire* was buried in colonial documentation, Manzano's autobiography became utilized as source material for subsequent Cuban slave narratives, usually penned by white authors.[27] This appropriation of Manzano's work by a white intelligentsia reinforced white antislavery narratives of Black abjection while eliding how enslaved peoples instigated and enacted their own emancipation.

Although Manzano's corpus of work remained unpublished in Cuba until 1937, his edited writing was printed immediately in London after its presentation to the 1840 World Anti-Slavery Convention. In the same year, colonial administrator R. R. Madden published *Poems by a Slave in the Island of Cuba*, in which he translated and partially anonymized Manzano, calling him "a slave recently liberated in the Island of Cuba" who "was presented to me in the year 1838."[28] Madden's passive phrasing erased both phases of Manzano's self-emancipation: his fugitivity and his penning of an autobiography in exchange for legal freedom. The text reads as a curious amalgamation of the colonial administrator's poetry alongside writing by Manzano. It begins with Madden's poem "The Slave-Trade Merchant," which, like Williams's 1788 poem on slave trade regulation, articulates the deadly conditions aboard slave ships: "How many beings gasp and pant for air / How many creatures draw infected breath … To breathe that horrid atmosphere, and dwell / But for one moment in that human hell!"[29] As a medical doctor, Madden emphasized airborne disease, which, as in broader European writing on Caribbean colonies, metonymically implied slavery. Finally, despite the volume's broader goal of featuring an Afro-Cuban poet, its stanzas reduced African voices to "shrieks and groans."[30]

According to narratives of white British antislavery, Madden's presence in Cuba reflected decades of reform that compelled other European empires to end their involvement in the Atlantic slave trade. Shortly after an Anglo-Spanish treaty in 1835, Madden arrived in Havana, where his position was Superintendent of Liberated Africans for the next three years. Charged with overseeing the litigation of ships alleged to be carrying captives, Madden was to serve as paternalist guardian of African peoples and ensure they were transferred to the imperial government whose cruisers had apprehended them. While resident in Cuba, Madden grew concerned with the health of captive Africans awaiting adjudication before the Mixed Commission Court, particularly as the Cuban government had refused to build them living quarters out of fear that they would incite insurrection once landed.[31] Drawing upon an earlier association between bondage and disease, Governor Miguel Tacón described Africans as disease-prone and likely to provoke the "combustion" of already disaffected populations, deploying the language of explosive chemical reaction to describe what, in other terms, implied Black freedom struggle.[32] Cuban officials had long been driven by anti-Black logics that sought to minimize Afro-descendance in the colony, in part because of the possibilities enacted by Haiti. Their eugenicist ideas included an 1816 proposal that white and Black people should marry so as to eliminate the latter. As a consequence, liberated Africans inhabited a retrofitted slave ship called the *Romney*, docked in the Havana harbor, awaiting the outcome of their trials. In other words, white antislavery's mechanism of "liberation" actually reproduced the conditions of the Middle Passage with the objective of political containment.

In contrast to decades of white antislavery reform, which yielded ongoing unfreedom for Afro-descendant peoples, and its genres of writing, which featured their belabored breath, Manzano seized his own political freedom, in part through real and imagined atmospheres. His poem "A Dream [Un Sueño]" rewrites the urgent plea for his brother's emancipation that he had previously articulated to Domingo del Monte in an October 1835 letter. Structured by a dream sequence, the poem conjures shared moments with his younger brother, Florencio, and marks their lived geographies as they fly over the landscapes of Matanzas. In the opening verses, Manzano remembers Florencio as the person who used to soothe his suffering, particularly when they cried together.³³ He describes following the path of other fugitives to a forested hill, where he falls asleep and feels himself sprout wings. Soaring high, he picks up his wings, inclines his chest downward, and descends in slow spirals to view the graves of his parents in Matanzas. The site again reminds him of being with his brother when they were children, and, for a second time, these memories cause him to weep and locate a palenque, or maroon community, nestled in the mountains. Flying to the plantation where his brother continues to be enslaved, Manzano finds Florencio and embraces him. He suggests that they escape together, writing:

> "let us flee, dear brother
> let us leave by wind
> let us abandon forever
> our enemy the ground"
>
> ["huyamos, caro hermano
> partamos por el viento
> por siempre abandonemos
> nuestro enemigo suelo"]³⁴

Manzano takes his brother into his arms and, flapping his wings, gathers air and becomes like wind himself. He describes happiness in being with Florencio and viewing diverse features of the landscape, such as the wide sea. Drawing upon spiritual vocabularies, he feels free through immersion in air. Finally, a storm approaches, and he awakens to thunder and lightning, sounds which conclude the poem.

The stanzas of "A Dream [Un Sueño]" convey the feeling of traveling through air and the poetic voice's merging with atmosphere, a freer state of matter than the soil, which he calls his enemy ("enemigo suelo"). Upon rescuing his brother, he exclaims: "already free; by the air / I sublimate and exalt [ya libre; por el aire / me sublimo y excelso]" (148). Importantly, the air liberates Manzano in two senses: he expresses a sensation of awe, gesturing to poetic traditions of the sublime, and he transforms into air, like the chemical process of sublimation wherein solids become gas. Through his encounters with air, his sorrows morph into an experience of freedom. Initially, the wind's enormity bolsters his courage to escape the earth: "the contrasting air / from the earth I rise / self-assured and daring / by such a vast element [el aire contrastando / de la tierra me elevo / presumido y osado / por tan vasto elemento]" (145). Subsequently, after rescuing Florencio, he finds himself wielding the power of wind: "I gather air and form / the columns of wind / with the ether travel / the light birds [aire recojo, y formo / las columnas de viento / con que el éter recorren / los pájaros ligeros]" (148). Exceeding the earth, Manzano finds the wind a medium expansive enough to dissolve his painful past. It is as though he has become a vast lung, his tender feelings reflected in his newfound sensitivity to the environment.

Recent scholarship on breath has turned to rituals for living through environmental catastrophe.[35] Unlike white antislavery precedents, which consolidated unfreedom through anti-Black reform, Manzano's approach to air offers insight into living within circumscribed environs. His writing draws upon the experience of plantation ecologies, which he addressed in verses unpublished during his lifetime. In a fifty-two stanza poem called "The poet's vision composed on a sugar mill [La visión del poeta compuesta en un Ingenio de fabricar azúcar]," Manzano imagines bathing in his parents' ashes; becoming a bird; traversing a hellscape; and, finally, discovering a vast garden. He characterizes the countryside as scorched and describes a massive sugar mill with a hundred bronze teeth. It is a scene of imprisonment with red flames, sparks, fury, and tongues of fire, in which an overseer's hellish cries make his surroundings tremble.[36] Manzano's commentary reflects the real transformation of Cuban atmospheres due to ascendant industrial sugarcane production after the Haitian Revolution. In fact, during the nineteenth century, half of all trees on the island were removed in order to build plantations and steam mills. Scientists attempted to document what laboring peoples already knew through lived experience: sugar mills established toxic microclimates where the air was thick with smoke and particulate matter. In the mid-century, they established a post in the region where Manzano was born for the simultaneous documentation of weather measurements around the island.

From March to November 1843, enslaved collectives in western Cuba, as well as prominent people of color in Havana and Matanzas, coordinated several rebellions, which have become known as La Escalera for the way suspects were bound when interrogated by the colonial government. Madden learned about these uprisings and believed Manzano to have been killed. Writing from Lisbon, he expressed his sadness to a friend: "I cannot tell you how grieved I am about poor Manzano the Cuban poet. Many a time the poor fellow came to my house and talked over his troubles and those of his unfortunate tribe with me."[37] Madden's information was incorrect: although detained during colonial interrogations, Manzano had not been executed by the Cuban government. Nevertheless, his letter reveals an attachment to Manzano and concludes with an elegy, which calls to mind Wordsworth's celebration of Louverture in his final months.

As with Wordsworth's poem, Madden describes Manzano as a hero, repeating the term "Martyr," a person who attains freedom in death. Like Wordsworth's sonnet, which asks an unspecified collective to breathe for Louverture, it calls upon those who read the elegy to "[m]ake Manzano's life your aim." As with Romantic tropes within broader antislavery writing, both poems foreground Black vitality only when eclipsed by death. However, unlike Wordsworth's sonnet, which holds no one responsible for Louverture's incarceration, Madden's elegy denounces the Cuban governor as a "tyrant" whose "deeds of murder" and "torture" will only cease when he "breathes no more."[38]

## Conclusion

In spite of his invocation of collective breath, Wordsworth wrote during a revolutionary period in which atmospheres – whether environmental, affective, or political – were not held in common. Like histories written during the ensuing decades, his poem cleaves Louverture from the Black insurrectionaries who forged Haitian independence through fire, fight, and fugitivity. These approaches to the Haitian Revolution have generally failed to acknowledge that its independence has held different meanings according to different interpreters. Although Haiti formally declared its intention to allow its neighbors to breathe in peace, European and US empires actively sought to manipulate the new state for their own economic gain. Haitian leaders faced the challenge of advancing Black sovereignty in an Atlantic world that continued to traffic in captive Africans. For example, in 1819 Henri Christophe noted that it caused him "the greatest grief" to witness the slave trade upon Spanish shores but that he nevertheless had no intention to mobilize ships of war.[39] In the same letter, he requested reassurance from British abolitionists that their government would recognize Haiti's independence. Here the rhetoric of security, often invoked by white actors seeking to mitigate against the example of Black insurrection, assumes a rather different significance as an appeal for European empires not to harass independent Haiti.

Manzano, who lived in a colony shaped by white planters both skeptical and fearful of Black sovereignty, never explicitly mentioned Haiti in his work. This omission may be attributable to widespread censorship in colonial Cuba. It was also likely for this reason that he wrote about fugitivity through the premise of a dream poem. In contrast, white antislavery poetry in the early nineteenth century advocated reform of slavery's infrastructure, rather than immediate emancipation. In fact, both pro- and antislavery writers weaponized Black breath by considering it principally within the context of the slave ship or the plantation. Furthermore, writing in the vein of Wordsworth's and Madden's respective elegies invoked breathing in the stead of detained Black men, as though such a gesture would ameliorate violence. Manzano, having delivered his personal history in exchange for legal emancipation, was familiar with the vagaries of white antislavery. For example, in a September 1835 letter to Del Monte, he notes that liberty, once promised, could be "carried away by the wind [se la va llevando el viento]."[40] In other words, Manzano knew that legal freedom, bestowed transactionally, could be manipulated by both enslavers and antislavery actors in the Caribbean. His dream poem uses the language of wind, not to characterize the caprices of liberal freedom, but to describe the vulnerable, intimate, and transcendent qualities of respiration. In contrast to Wordsworth's 1803 sonnet, which conjures an atmosphere of abstract relationships ("Thou hast great allies / Thy friends are exultations, agonies / And love, and man's unconquerable mind"), Manzano breathes freedom through the air, refiguring the common as that which is shared with kin.

## Notes

1. Haitian Declaration of Independence, January 1, 1804, The National Archives of the United Kingdom, Colonial Office (hereafter CO) 137/111/1. Printed in *Slave Revolution in the Caribbean, 1789–1804: A Brief History with Documents*, ed. Laurent Dubois and John D. Garrigus (New York: Palgrave Macmillan, 2006), 188–91. The 1804 declaration invokes breath three times. It concludes with a resolution to fight until the "last breath for the independence of our country [dernier soupir pour l'indépendance de notre pays]." See also Lorgia García-Peña, *The Borders of Dominicanidad: Race, Nation, and Archives of Contradiction* (Durham: Duke University Press, 2016), 4; Marlene L. Daut, *Tropics of Haiti: Race and the Literary History of the Haitian Revolution in the Atlantic World, 1789–1865* (Liverpool: Liverpool University Press, 2015), 2.
2. Dubois and Garrigus, *Slave Revolution*, 189. For the relationship between early Haitian historical traditions and global Romanticism, see Marlene L. Daut, "'Nothing in Nature is Mute': Reading Revolutionary Romanticism in *L'Haïtiade* and Hérard Dumesle's *Voyage dans le nord d'Hayti* (1824)," *New Literary History* 49/4 (2018): 493–520.
3. There are several versions of this poem. I draw from Juan Francisco Manzano, *Autobiografía del esclavo poeta y otros escritos*, ed. William Luis (Madrid: Iberoamericana, 2016), 148. All translations, unless otherwise specified, are my own.

4. Francisco de Arango y Parreño, *Obras, Tomo I* (Habana: De Howson y Heinen, 1888), 96. See also Ada Ferrer, *Freedom's Mirror: Cuba and Haiti in the Age of Revolution* (Cambridge: Cambridge University Press, 2014), 213–70.
5. Manzano, *Autobiografía*, 148.
6. Ashon T. Crawley, *Blackpentecostal Breath* (New York: Fordham University Press, 2016), 3, 69; Jean-Thomas Tremblay, *Breathing Aesthetics* (Durham: Duke University Press, 2022), 32.
7. "Original Poetry," *The Morning Post* (London), February 2, 1803, British Library Newspapers. See also an anonymously published poem on insurrection in Saint-Domingue during the height of the British invasion: "Ode on the Insurrection of the Slaves at St. Domingo (1796)," in *Haitian Revolutionary Fictions: An Anthology*, ed. Marlene L. Daut, Grégory Pierrot, and Marion C. Rohrleitner (Charlottesville: University of Virginia Press, 2022), 52–54.
8. Grégory Pierrot, "'Our Hero': Toussaint Louverture in British Representations," *Criticism* 50/4 (2008), 582; 602.
9. Toussaint Louverture, *The Memoir of General Toussaint Louverture*, trans. Philippe R. Girard (Oxford: Oxford University Press, 2014), 11.
10. I follow Chelsea Stieber's decision to keep *mémoire* in French, given that the term can, as her work argues, mean "'memorial,' 'memorandum,' 'record,' 'report,' 'bill,' 'petition,' 'request,' 'proposal,' 'paper,' 'exposition,' 'note,' 'statement,' and 'account,' among others." See "*Mémoire* and Vindicationism in Revolutionary Saint-Domingue," *Small Axe* 26/1 (2022): 33.
11. Louverture, *Memoir*, 152–55.
12. Louverture, *Memoir*, 52–53. He uses the term fourteen times in the document.
13. Thank you to Dr. Lauren Dembowitz for bringing Helen Maria Williams's poem to my attention as well as for continuous feedback on this chapter. On the overlap between pro- and antislavery discourse in late eighteenth-century England, see Lauren Dembowitz's chapter in this volume (Ch. 12).
14. Helen Maria Williams, *A Poem on the Bill Lately Passed for Regulating the Slave Trade* (London: T. Cadell, 1788), 1–7.
15. David Geggus, "British Opinion and the Emergence of Haiti, 1791–1805," in *Slavery and British Society, 1776–1846*, ed. James Walvin (Baton Rouge: Louisiana State University Press, 1982), 128.
16. Julius S. Scott, *The Common Wind: Afro-American Currents in the Age of the Haitian Revolution* (London: Verso, 2018), 44. In a 2018 conversation at the University of Pittsburgh, Scott noted that he wished his text would have spent more time with the many meanings of the common wind. See "The Common Wind," March 12, 2018, 1:01:00–1:03:00, www.youtube.com/watch?v=BlSXrxFXSsw.
17. Kevin Dawson, "A Sea of Caribbean Islands: Maritime Maroons in the Greater Caribbean," *Slavery & Abolition* 42/3 (2021), 433–434.
18. Scott, *Common Wind*, 67.

19. Scott, *Common Wind*, 145–54; 170.
20. See, for example, CO 137/107/294.
21. CO 295/2/9; CO 296/1/61–62. See also Bridget Brereton, "Haiti and the Haitian Revolution in the Political Discourse of Nineteenth-Century Trinidad," in *Reinterpreting the Haitian Revolution and its Cultural Aftershocks*, ed. Martin Munro and Elizabeth Walcott-Hackshaw (Kingston: University of the West Indies Press, 2006), 127–28.
22. CO 295/4/63.
23. Scott, *Common Wind*, 205–6.
24. Dubois and Garrigus, *Slave Revolution*, 190.
25. Scott, *Common Wind*, 53.
26. See also Michel-Rolph Trouillot, *Silencing the Past: Power and the Production of History* (Boston: Beacon Press, 1995), 27; Marlene L. Daut, "Beyond Trouillot: Unsettling Genealogies of Historical Thought," *Small Axe* 25/1 (2021), 135; Matthew J. Smith, "'To Place Ourselves in History': The Haitian Revolution in British West Indian Thought before *The Black Jacobins*," in *The Black Jacobins Reader*, ed. Charles Forsdick and Christian Høgsbjerg (Durham: Duke University Press, 2017), 179.
27. William Luis, *Literary Bondage: Slavery in Cuban Narrative* (Austin: University of Texas Press, 1990), 38–39; Matthew Pettway, *Cuban Literature in the Age of Black Insurrection: Manzano, Plácido, and Afro-Latino Religion* (Jackson: University Press of Mississippi, 2020), 6–12; 33.
28. R. R. Madden, *Poems by a Slave in the Island of Cuba* (London: Thomas Ward, 1840), i.
29. Madden, *Poems*, 13.
30. Madden, *Poems*, 13.
31. R. R. Madden, *The Island of Cuba: Its Resources, Progress, and Prospects* (London: Charles Gilpin, 1849), 48–49.
32. *Correspondencia reservada del Capitán General Don Miguel Tacón con el gobierno de Madrid, 1834–1836*, ed. Juan Pérez de la Riva (Havana: Consejo Nacional de Cultura, 1963), 253. See also Jennifer Louise Nelson, "Slavery, Race, and Conspiracy: The HMS *Romney* in Nineteenth-Century Cuba," *Atlantic Studies* 14/2 (2017), 178; Manuel Barcia, *The Yellow Demon of Fever: Fighting Disease in the Nineteenth-Century Transatlantic Slave Trade* (New Haven: Yale University Press, 2020), 7.
33. Manzano, *Autobiografía*, 144. A translated version of this poem was also included after Manzano's autobiography in Madden's 1840 publication.
34. Manzano, *Autobiografía*, 148. Further references will be given in the text.
35. Jean-Thomas Tremblay, "Feminist Breathing," *Differences: A Journal of Feminist Cultural Studies* 30/3 (2019), 94.
36. Manzano, *Autobiografía*, 178–79.
37. British Library (hereafter BL) Add MS 41071/77.
38. BL Add MS 41071/78.
39. BL Add MS 41266, "Christophe to Clarkson, March 20, 1817."
40. Manzano, *Autobiografía*, 127.

CHAPTER 3

# Afropessimism, Queer Negativity, and the Limits of Romanticism

*Deanna P. Koretsky*

In 2019, Talia Vestri rightly asked, "where's queer?" in Romantic studies. Following a welcome embrace of queer studies' promise to disrupt "dominant heuristics" in the early aughts, Vestri calls attention to the problem of queer methodologies fading from the study of Romanticism even as "feminist critics and #Bigger6 advocates [work] to demasculinize and decolonize the period".[1] Certainly, Romantic studies, like all academic fields built on epistemologies of white supremacist imperialist domination, must constantly and vigorously interrogate its historically white heteropatriarchal pasts. It is not clear, however, whether the projects of disruption promised by feminist, decolonial, and queer methodologies (among others) are commensurate with *each other* – as well as, ultimately, with Romanticism itself. This is a substantial question, and one that cannot be answered in a single essay, nor by a single scholar. What follows is thus a necessarily incomplete effort – one which offers no definitive answers but will, I hope, serve as a catalyst and invitation for further discussion.

This essay re-examines the figure of the Romantic vampire, a critical darling of gender and queer studies, through an Afropessimist lens that reveals the figure's constitutive antiblackness. Within and beyond Romanticism studies, queer and gender theorists have long been interested in the vampire's disruptive potential. Arguably, it is precisely because he seduces readers with a veneer of subversive energy that the vampire remains one of Romanticism's most enduring cultural legacies. While it was John Polidori, Lord Byron's one-time physician, who fully developed the character in his 1819 short story "The Vampyre," the inspiration that Polidori took from Byron's life and work ties the figure to Byron's 1812 narrative poem *The Giaour*, as well as one of the poet's rare forays into prose, the 1816 "Augustus Darvell" (alternately called "Fragment of a Novel"). Thus, as the contemporary novelist and scholar Tom Holland observes, "even today, vampires remain recognizably Lord Byron's descendants."[2] But one does not have to look to the present to see the limits of the Romantic vampire's disruptive potential. An 1819 novella written in response to Byron and Polidori, *The Black Vampyre: A Legend of St. Domingo*, by the pseudonymous US author Uriah Derick D'Arcy, brings into focus how antiblackness structures the earliest Romantic vampire tales. In this way, it offers a counterpoint to critical framings of the Romantic vampire as consonant with marginalized subjectivities and freedom struggles.

Such readings have tended to emphasize the fact that both Byron's and Polidori's tales are partially set in Greece under Ottoman rule. This setting, as Jeffrey L. Schneider explains, "inherently creates a space ... for non-normative desires to be expressed [because] in the British collective imagination, sexual excess and the Orient were inextricable terms."[3] Stuart Curran has demonstrated the extent to which "the role of women in this world is to be abused by masculine dominance."[4] This pattern of misogyny is also unambiguously racialized: as Joseph Lew observes, "Western heroines tend to survive, while orientalized women die or disappear."[5] On one hand, then, the Romantic vampire has been said to uphold white heteropatriarchal dominance through racialized misogyny, while, on the other, he has been read as pushing against it, to a degree, by engaging in interracial homoeroticism. This essay argues that the Romantic vampire's widely acknowledged and broadly defined imbrications with discourses of "otherness" are underwritten by antiblackness. As João H. Costa Vargas and Moon-Kie Jung clarify, antiblackness differs from racism, the latter defined as "a set of social and institutional practices." Antiblackness foregrounds "the uniqueness of Black positionality and experience relative to those of nonblack social groups," which, as many scholars have demonstrated, is most clearly visible and enacted at the level of political ontology – those processes by which social and institutional practices, including racism, create and maintain societies and demarcate inclusion.[6] In the post-Enlightenment Western world order, political ontology turns on racialized conceptions of who does and does not count as "human," with blackness marking that category's outermost limit. In other words, Western modernity coheres around notions of "the human" that are constitutively antiblack.

Understood in this frame, the Romantic vampire is a deeply normative, "human" figure through and through. Recognizing how antiblackness constitutes the Romantic vampire undoes any disruptive potential that has been claimed for this figure in the name of queerness. The vampire's capacity for social critique, such as it is, does not approach the degree or kind of disruption necessary to begin to confront antiblackness in

Romantic literature (to say nothing of the institutionalized study of Romanticism). For, while eradicating forms of inequality such as homophobia, sexism, and racism requires, as Vargas and Jung put it, "deep transformations in social practices and structures," eliminating antiblackness "necessitates an entirely new conception of the social, which is to say a radically different world altogether."[7]

## The Social Life of the Undead

Within what Frank Wilderson calls the "symbiosis between the political ontology of Humanity and the social death of Blacks," the Romantic vampires of Byron and Polidori move comfortably through the social world and thus fit squarely within the category of human.[8] For Wilderson, blackness is the "position against which Humanity establishes, maintains, and renews its coherence, its corporeal integrity."[9] In other words, the existence of "the human" hinges on black death – both the social death of black (non)subjects in civil society and black people's increased proximity to literal death through that society's policies and conditions:

> Chattel slavery ... created the Human out of culturally disparate entities from Europe and the East ... The race of Humanism (White, Asian, South Asian, and Arab) could not have produced itself without the simultaneous production of that walking destruction which became known as the Black. Put another way, through chattel slavery the world gave birth and coherence to both its joys of domesticity and to its struggles of political discontent; and with these joys and struggles the Human was born.[10]

Sylvia Wynter comes to a similar conclusion, though her timeline begins well before chattel slavery. For Wynter, the Abrahamic religions in Europe and the Middle East all occupy the "human" position to varying degrees insofar as they all cohere through antiblackness via the curse of Ham, wherein sub-Saharan Africans come to function as subhuman for all three.[11] In this sense, the orientalist settings of the early vampire tales, while certainly marking and negotiating boundaries within what Wynter calls intra-European genres of the human, are all structured by what Wilderson calls the libidinal economy of antiblackness. Foundationally, then, the black (non)subject makes possible the constitution of the Romantic vampire, even as characters we might recognize to be racially black are absent from the earliest vampire texts. *The Black Vampyre* brings this unconscious register to the fore.

Published in New York in June of 1819, the author's introduction to *The Black Vampyre* explicitly calls Polidori's character "The White Vampyre." The novella itself likewise goes to great lengths to differentiate between black and white vampires. One could go so far as to argue that the black African figure referenced in the story's title is not a vampire at all – certainly not in the Romantic sense that, in 1819, had already begun to take hold of the Western popular imaginary. The exact nature of the title figure's so-called vampirism is never explained. Though he draws power from an ill-defined amalgam of Hellenistic and Caribbean mythologies, he does not behave like any vampiric figure in European or Afrodiasporic folklore. The author's inability or refusal to coherently depict his title character is telling. As Calvin Warren has argued, "[t]he violence of captivity expelled the African from Difference, or the Symbolic ... and relegated it to the vacuous space of undifferentiation."[12] In other words, the racializing logics of transatlantic slavery transformed, in the Western mind, the people and cultures of the African continent – people and cultures previously recognized as such in relation to other people and cultures of the world – into the broad category of "black." This is a category apart from that of "human," against which self-proclaimed "humans" would then define themselves in relation to other, nonblack racialized groups. Modern racialization itself, then, proceeds from this foundational antiblackness. Understood in these terms, the contrast between the novella's demarcation of white vampirism within the hegemonic discourse of Romantic individualism and its lack of clarity around what, if anything, makes the title figure (whose name we never learn) a vampire is part of the point. Throughout *The Black Vampyre*, the title figure's presence inscribes other characters' legibility within the novella's social world, while he remains indecipherable.

The novella opens with a French ship that has brought enslaved Africans as "mere skeletons" from Guinea to Haiti. They "all died shortly after their arrival," except for one ten-year-old boy. This boy is purchased by a planter, the aptly named M. Personne, who thinks it "charitabl[e]" to kill him.[13] At this point, the narrative proceeds through several pages of gratuitous violence to show that the boy cannot be killed. The narrative also rhetorically aligns him with death, describing him as "a little corpse" whose "complexion was a dead black" (16). While his apparent indestructability may indicate vampirism, notably the boy grows up and later returns in the guise of a "Moorish Prince" (20). Thus, while there is certainly something supernatural at work that makes him hard to kill, the fact that his body continues to develop into adulthood suggests that he is something

*Afropessimism, Queer Negativity, and Romanticism* 41

other than a reanimated corpse – the mode by which the prince will later create the monsters he calls vampires.

When we meet him as an adult, the prince is attended by Zembo, a "pale European boy, in an Asiatic dress," perhaps a wink to Byron's infamous Albanian portrait of 1813 (20). The prince marries Personne's widow, Euphemia. On their wedding night, he takes her to the graveyard where Personne and her other two husbands are buried and resurrects them. While there is plenty of magic in this scene, the only hints of vampirism are manifested in Euphemia and Zembo, who, we find out later, is the Personnes' long-lost son. Euphemia drinks from a chalice of blood, while Zembo attempts to feed on the blood of one of the reanimated husbands before eventually feeding on his mother and turning her into a vampire. The closest link between the prince and what Western readers would then, or now, associate with vampirism is the oath he forces Euphemia to take: "you will never disclose in any manner, aught of what you have seen and shall see this night" (25). This closely echoes the oath that Lord Ruthven, Polidori's vampire, demands of Aubrey, his English companion: "Swear by all your soul reveres . . . that you will not impart knowledge of my crimes or death to any living being in any way, whatever may happen, or whatever you may see."[14] This oath, in turn, echoes Byron's tale, in which Augustus Darvell demands a similar oath from his equally unwitting English attendant: "I have no hopes, nor wishes, but this – conceal my death from every human being . . . Swear it . . . you must swear."[15]

Notably, in *The Black Vampyre*, the corporeal violence associated with vampirism is carried out exclusively by white bodies. During the episode in the graveyard, the prince oversees a ridiculous farce of "civility" wherein the resurrected husbands fight each other. All three are naked, one is armed with a thigh bone, yet they still go out of their way to observe gentlemanly manners "to show their mutual good-will" (28). Eventually, Zembo stakes husbands two and three and, at this point, Personne's veneer of civility vanishes as he turns his attention to the prince, "saying, 'Don't be too familiar, Blackey;' and renewing his threats of cracking him over the noddle with the thigh-bone" (29). The prince ignores the threat and instead chooses this moment to reveal not only the truth of Zembo's parentage, but also that he is the one responsible for turning his parents into vampires: "To his exertions last night you are indebted for your revivification" (30). Having reunited the monstrous family, he banishes them to Europe:

> Amiable and virtuous VAMPYRES! May you long enjoy that tranquility and contentment, which your merit and accomplishments so eminently deserve! A vessel lies in the port, ready to sail for Europe... The Island is no longer a place for you. Here is money to pay your passages, and all I have to say, is, that the sooner you're off the better. (30)

But the Personnes don't comply. Instead, they follow him to an undersea cavern, where they observe the prince and others like him preparing a group of enslaved men for revolt. There, the interlopers learn of a potion that "belongs to the Obeah mysteries," which can restore one "to the plight, in which he was previous to his death, or his becoming a Vampyre" (35). The prince's compatriots – who are revealed to be demigods descended from Prometheus – mean to use this potion on their fighters during the revolt.[16] However, they are thwarted when Euphemia steals it as French soldiers ambush the meeting. As black bodies, including the prince's, fall around them, the white vampires steal a potion created by Afrodiasporic knowledges, escape, drink it, and are restored to live out their days as an emblematic white bourgeois heteropatriarchal family unit.

These are the true vampires, D'Arcy tells us in the "Moral" that follows the narrative: "In this happy land of liberty and equality, we are free from all traditional superstitions... Yet in a figurative sense... our climate is perhaps more prolific than any other, in... Vampyres" (41). D'Arcy names vampirism as the thread that holds together the Western world order, from the "accomplished dandy who... absorbs the life-blood of that which his prudent Sire had accumulated" to the work of lawyers, businessmen, physicians, professors, and even himself, who "'have spun this discourse out of my bowels,' and made as free with those of others – I am a Vampyre!" (42). Predating Karl Marx's famed analogy between vampirism and capitalism by nearly half a century, D'Arcy's "Moral" presents a sweeping indictment of a world that profits from the blood and labor of others; and, as Wilderson has argued, blackness marks the absolute limit point of that world.

Per Wilderson, "civil society is held together by a structural prohibition against recognizing and incorporating a being that is dead, despite the fact that this being is sentient and so appears to be very much alive."[17] Wilderson refers here to the social death of black people in the Western world order, a notion drawn from Orlando Patterson's 1985 study, *Slavery and Social Death*, which describe how societies are organized to prohibit some people – in this case, people of African descent – from accessing the rights and privileges that come from being recognized as fully human.

Without such access, according to Patterson, one lives in a state of social death. Wilderson takes Patterson's claims further, positing that liberal modernity is organized by that prohibition. For Wilderson, black freedom does not depend on accessing the rights and privileges of civil society, but on recognizing that civil society requires certain people – black people – to be shut out in order for others to thrive. Thus, it matters that the earliest literary vampires are emphatically socially alive.

Byron's Darvell is introduced as "a man of considerable fortune and ancient family" who "had been deeply initiated into what is called the world" (247). Likewise, even as Polidori's Ruthven works to systematically destroy English society's potential for reproductive futurity by laying waste to its women, he still finds himself "invited to every house" (3). At the level of representation, Byron's and Polidori's narratives are undoubtedly early manifestations of the now-commonplace association of vampirism with homoerotic desire, as many scholars have thoroughly demonstrated. Since the end of the last century, Romantic vampires have often been read as "queer," variably and broadly defined – signaling everything from sexual desire between men to more elastic explorations of experiences, drives, and forms of being and belonging beyond the bounds of Western notions of sexuality and binary gender. However, when understood in terms of the social death and political nonbeing of blackness, the Romantic vampire is precisely *not* exterior to civil society, but rather its ultimate insider: an incarnation of a monstrous world order that holds itself together by doling out violence and death. A parasite who demands the deaths of others to stay alive, what is he if not quintessentially "human"?

## Undead Futures

The Romantic vampire's obsession with reproductive futurity further underscores his belonging within the politico-ontological category of "the human." Insofar as he is motivated by securing his own futurity – and moreover, insofar as he can reasonably expect to have a future at all – the Romantic vampire operates within a normative frame. As Lee Edelman has taught us, the Western social order turns on an endlessly deferred fantasy of the future. In "the era of the universal subject" (which Edelman denotes by quoting from Wordsworth), this has been organized around the figure of "the Child" to whom that future is promised.[18] Modernity's emphasis on the figural Child is, according to Edelman, both a symptom of and a catalyst for the insistent privileging of sexual reproduction as the defining capacity to productively engage in the social. The Romantic vampire's decidedly nonheteronormative relation to futurity has thus been reasonably read as signaling his revolutionary queerness. Reassessing the Romantic vampire's interest in futurity within a framework of antiblackness, however, puts pressure on interpretations of the vampire as a queer figure. This is not to deny the figure's obvious homoeroticism, but rather to suggest that homoeroticism does not make him queer, where queerness is understood "less in the assertion of an oppositional political identity than in opposition to politics as the governing fantasy of realizing ... an always indefinite future." That is, as Edelman famously states, "queerness can never define an identity; it can only ever disturb one."[19] Reading futurity in Byron's and Polidori's tales against the same theme in D'Arcy's illuminates how the Romantic vampire upholds and reproduces the world as such. In particular, it highlights how white heteropatriarchal notions of masculinity and femininity undergird the figure's earliest incarnations. Thus, even as the Romantic vampire nominally challenges heteronormativity, the structuring logics of the social remain unexamined; indeed, many are embraced.

Although there no actual children in either Byron's or Polidori's narratives, reproductive futurity looms large over both. In Byron's "Augustus Darvell," the vampire's relationship to futurity manifests in the perpetual return of the vampiric figure himself. The narrative's main conflict arises when Darvell mysteriously begins to decay "without the intervention of any apparent disease" (248). He instructs the English narrator to bring him to a Turkish cemetery and gives him detailed directions for his burial. As he lays dying in the narrator's arms, the narrator observes "a stork, with a snake in her beak, perched near" (250). While the narrative remains unfinished, the strong implication is that the stork and snake foreshadow Darvell's revivification. As Mary Y. Hallab explains, these figures represent cycles of life and death: "Not only do storks appear to return to the same nest each summer, but they have long been associated with the arrival of babies in European folklore." Likewise, "because of its seeming ability to regenerate, the snake has been regarded as a symbol not only of fertility but of healing and immortality. The snake's ability to make its body into a circle is also an image of the cyclic return."[20] Darvell dies at the precise moment the stork flies away. He is buried, per his instructions, "exactly where that bird [was] perched" (251). As the earth is dug to create his grave, the narrator observes that it "easily gave way, having already received some Mahometan tenant" (251). The implication, then, is that Darvell has died before.

Polidori's "The Vampyre" expands on Byron's allusion to the vampire's eternal return by emphasizing the threat he poses to social reproduction.

## Afropessimism, Queer Negativity, and Romanticism 45

This is indicated primarily in the narrative's treatment of women. One by one, the eligible women of English high society succumb to Ruthven's bloodlust. Those whom he does not kill are "hurled from the pinnacle of unsullied virtue, down to the lowest abyss of infamy and degradation" (7). In other words, Ruthven chokes the marriage market, English society's primary means of ensuring its futurity through socially sanctioned family lineages. It is thus significant that the women he pursues are young and unmarried, as underscored by his adamant rejection of the widowed Lady Mercer, who takes an interest in him in the narrative's opening pages. His preferred victims, young women predestined by the traditions of their society to become the guarantors of England's future, are killed or corrupted so as to become, instead, the guarantors of Ruthven's eternal life.

More granularly, Polidori's narrative is driven by the crisis that Ruthven poses to Aubrey's capacity for socially sanctioned marriage and the reproduction of his already precarious family line: "he was an orphan left with an only sister in the possession of great wealth, by parents who died while he was yet in childhood" (4). Following his initial infatuation with and separation from Ruthven, Aubrey falls in love with the socially unsuitable Ianthe: "while he ridiculed the idea of a young man of English habits, marrying an uneducated Greek girl, still he found himself more and more attached to the almost fairy form before him" (10). When Ianthe is killed, Aubrey's grief mingles with his sublimated desire for Ruthven: "Aubrey being put to bed was seized with a most violent fever, and was often delirious; in these intervals he would call upon Lord Ruthven and upon Ianthe" (13). The full weight of the crisis erupts when Aubrey discovers that his sister is to marry "the monster who had so long influenced his life" (21). By this point, Aubrey has been reunited with Ruthven, watched him die, and promised not to speak to anyone "of [Ruthven's] crimes or death" (15). This promise leads to the family's decimation: Aubrey dies from a burst blood vessel brought on by the stress and trauma of keeping Ruthven's secret (as well as, implicitly, the distress of his thwarted desire), while his sister's corpse is found to have "glutted the thirst of a VAMPYRE!" (23).

Clearly, there is anxiety around the project of heterosexual reproduction in Byron's image of the stork eating the snake and in Polidori's rejection of heteronormative domesticity. Both narratives may even be said to bristle against heteronormative sociality by offering, in the figure of the male vampire who reanimates himself with the help of a male companion, an alternative modality of (homo)sociality. However, in neither narrative does that alternative challenge the broader social world their characters inhabit. Rather, the Romantic vampire remakes himself to conform to that world – so much so, in fact, that in Polidori's narrative, he comes to belong more than Aubrey, whose mental state marks him as outcast. The Romantic vampire, to borrow Warren's phraseology, offers little more than "a reconstitution of the liberal subject – a liberal subject that *divests* [some of] its privilege" but "neither provides ethical relief nor emancipatory transformations."[21] Both Byron's "Augustus Darvell" and Polidori's "The Vampyre" ultimately advance proto-homonationalist fantasies that exacerbate existing structures of gender and racial inequity in the interest of reforming the world into one dominated by white men who do not require white women to reproduce themselves.[22] In this way, as Warren argues, the "repertoire of non-normative sexualities" such as those presented by Byron and Polidori, while undoubtedly belonging to "an extreme position of unfreedom," exist within and maintain the ontological bounds of the modern world and thus represent "a particular humanism" – one that "denies itself only to reconstitute itself in the final outcome."[23] *The Black Vampyre* illuminates how the Romantic vampire's sociality is maintained against and through blackness.

In *The Black Vampyre*, the promise of futurity moves from the narcissistic frame of white proto-homonationalist self-reproduction to the decidedly heteronormative figure of the (white) child. *The Black Vampyre*'s investment in futurity precisely epitomizes Edelman's elucidation of the fantasy of "the Child" as "the telos of the social order ... the one for whom that order is held in perpetual trust."[24] Most obviously, the figural Child's role in preserving the social order is realized in the return of Zembo and the reinstatement of the Personne family unit. But the narrative's concern with preserving white heteropatriarchal futurity is felt as early as the opening sequence of gratuitous antiblack violence.

The boy who grows up to be the prince is introduced as a "small negro, of a very slender constitution, and fit for no work whatever" (16). Because he is not "fit" for the role for which he had been forcibly brought to the colony, Personne moves to eradicate him from the social order by murdering him. As the boy repeatedly defies death, Personne's agitation grows: he is "in considerable alarm" and "ashamed that a little negro of ten years old, should put him in bodily fear" (16–17). These strong emotions reflect Personne's astonishment at the possibility of black futurity beyond the bounds of white sociality. Personne's shame, moreover, suggests that his belief in his right to dominate is exposed in this moment as a fabrication that can be undone by those whom he subjugates.

Notably, however, when the boy kills the patriarch and appears to kill his son, the narrative shifts to Euphemia's point of view. In this way, rather

*Afropessimism, Queer Negativity, and Romanticism* 47

than engaging narrative space to explore black agency, *The Black Vampyre* posits a slippage between two differently subjugated positions – the black boy and the white woman:

> The amiable, but unfortunate Euphemia, was thrown into several hysterical convulsions; as well she might be, poor woman! When her husband had been made a holocaust, and served up like a broiled and peppered chicken, to feed the grim maw of death; and her interesting infant, the first pledge of her pure and perfect love, had been precociously sucked like an unripe orange, and nothing left but its beautiful and tender skin. (19)

The tongue-in-cheek imagery of Personne as main course and his child as garnish gestures to the role of domesticity in the maintenance of the social. As Edelman contends, it is the assumed product of (white) heteronormative domestic relations that "alone embodies the citizen as an ideal, entitled to claim full rights to its future share in the nation's good." Thus, "the social order exists to preserve for this universalized subject, this fantasmatic Child, a notional freedom more highly valued than the actuality of freedom itself."[25] *The Black Vampyre*'s opening episode rehearses the extent to which Edelman's figural Child is necessarily white and male: where the black child's many deaths are treated as points of personal frustration and embarrassment for the white patriarch, the dual losses of that patriarch and his white son destabilize the possibility of the entire social order's futurity. In other words, just as the titular black vampire is not actually legible *as* a vampire in this narrative, the black child is not a Child. Rather than an assumed inheritor of the world, his role in the narrative is to throw it, temporarily, off its axis.

The crisis introduced by the black non-Child is borne out in the threat that the deaths of the white patriarch and son pose to Euphemia's "true womanhood." As the sole remaining Personne, Euphemia is left in the vexed position of needing to remarry in order to produce more socially sanctioned children. Because she remains on the same estate throughout her successive marriages, we can infer that she inherits Personne's plantation and, with it, access to considerable patriarchal power. In a suggestive concurrence, a Jamaican folk legend of the era offers a window into the complexities of Euphemia's position.

Annie Palmer, better known as the "white witch of Rose Hall," was a Creole woman of British descent who was raised, in most versions of the tale, in Haiti and came to Jamaica to marry the planter Robert Palmer – the first of three husbands, all of whom she is said to have killed. She practiced an Afrodiasporic religion (either voodoo or obeah, depending on the source) and developed a reputation for torturing and sexually abusing the people she enslaved. The precise details of the legend and its veracity are beyond the scope of this essay to address.[26] Of interest here are two points. First, the broad strokes of Palmer's story bear similarities to Euphemia's. Both women bury multiple white husbands, which directly enables them to exercise forms of power traditionally reserved for white men. Moreover, as examined later in the chapter, they engage in sexual acts with black men and perform Africanist blood rites. As a result of these perceived transgressions, both women's stories yield associations with vampirism. Monika Mueller has shown how the most famous literary treatment of the Jamaican legend, Herbert G. de Lisser's 1929 novel *The White Witch of Rose Hall*, echoes J. Sheridan le Fanu's 1872 lesbian vampire romance, *Carmilla*. Jennifer Donahue has drawn connections between Palmer and the Afro-Caribbean figure of the soucouyant, a vampire-like female shape shifter whose explicit sensuality runs counter to colonial fantasies of white women as chaste and sexually submissive. These are stories of women whose sexual, economic, and political agency threatened the dominant order, and who were demonized as a result.

Of course, these women also consciously upheld unjust and cruel social hierarchies, which complicates, but does not erase, the fact of their denigration by a misogynistic society. As Natalie Zacek has argued, when compared with their white male contemporaries, women like Annie Palmer are much less exceptional than cultural memory would have us believe. For Zacek, Palmer's legendary status obfuscates the routineness of the violence that maintained the institution of slavery by redirecting the focus to how a white woman's assertion of the same abusive authority regularly exercised by white men posed a threat to the patriarchal order. Rather than condemning the institution of slavery as such, cultural narratives like the "white witch" legend reify the idea "that the true offenders were females who had gained too much independence from male authority, and who tried to mask their innate physical and emotional frailty through appalling abuse of the enslaved."[27]

If Euphemia is represented as less overtly cruel than Palmer, her position is nevertheless fully determined by her role as an enslaver. What's more, it is the prince's entanglement with the same institution that prompts Euphemia's interest in him. The first thing she learns about him is that he "had brought out a cargo of slaves, whom his subjects had lately taken prisoners of war; and whom he had resolved to dispose of himself; as he was desirous of seeing the world" (20). This knowledge intermingles with her physical attraction to him, prompting her to conclude: "This was a man!"

When he, in turn, renounces black women in favor of her love, she marries him the very same day despite "many remonstrances ... on the impropriety of marrying a negro" (21, 23).

On one hand, the prince's status as an enslaver ostensibly places them on similar social and political ground: both hold power usually reserved for white men. Yet, on the other hand, the prince wins her affection not because he is her equal, but by renouncing women of his own race:

> He said that the flat-nosed beauties of Zara; the scarred, squab figures of the golden coast; the well proportioned Zilias, Calypsos, and Zamas on the banks of the Niger; and even the great Hottentot Venus herself, had never for a moment made the least impression on his heart! His passion was a mystery to himself; its origin secret as the sources of the Nile; but full and impetuous as its ample channel, when replenished from the celestial fountains of Abyssinia; while if [Euphemia] would shine upon its waves, its enlivened currents would fertilize his vast dominions, in the luxuriant realms of central Africa; making them to fructify yet more abundantly, with burning gold, and radiant diamonds!!! (22–23)

This speech, as the narrative is careful to emphasize, appeals to Euphemia's "female heart," thereby neutralizing any claim to gender parity through a paternalistic avowal of the implicitly feminine vice of vanity. This is underscored by the prince's twofold display of antiblack patriarchal authority – that is, his enslavement of other Africans and his refusal of African women as suitable love interests. Even so, the prince's hold on power is mediated by white femininity insofar as it requires his ascription to white patriarchal ideals of feminine beauty. His lengthy proclamation of misogynoir, the narrative's only mention of black women, not only catalyzes the interracial union but gives it an unmistakably erotic charge.

When next we see the couple, the "bride was hanging on his arm, in an enchanting dishabille; and did not seem to be in perfect possession of her right senses" (23–24). While this may, at first blush, read like familiar handwringing about the supposed threat black men pose to white women's "virtue," the text suggests that because Euphemia is already an aberrant figure, and, moreover, because they are married, this is more accurately read as a description of postcoital ecstasy. To put it plainly, she is half naked and incoherent because the prince has fucked her senseless. The couple's reappearance in this state serves primarily to indicate the changed nature of Euphemia's social position. Although she is returned to the subservient role of wife, as the wife of a black man she remains deviant, as indicated by the state of her dress and unconcealed enjoyment of their recent sexual congress. By contrast, Euphemia's reunion with her first husband just a few pages later is far less charged. The relationship of this "fond couple" is characterized not by physical needs – "They forgot even their hunger and thirst" – but by gentle comfort and care. As they "tenderly inquir[e] into the state of each other's health," the narrator interjects that these "family concerns, might not be as interesting to the reader as they were to the parties concerned" (27–28). With the prince, Euphemia finds sexual gratification, which the narrative voyeuristically broadcasts; with Personne, she finds "proper" womanhood, which the narrative treats with self-conscious reserve.

Notably, the eroticized language of the wedding night episode gives no indication as to the prince's pleasure. That is, the narrative betrays its capacity to imagine, however obtusely, the sexual agency of a white woman but not that of a black man. This discrepancy, coupled with the differing presentations of Euphemia's relations with the prince and Personne, reflect what Sharon Patricia Holland has argued is the necessarily racial grammar of sexuality in our post-Enlightenment world. For Holland, blackness "not only produces 'erotic value' for whiteness, but it holds the very impossibility of its own pleasure through becoming the sexualized surrogate of another. In a sense, *blackness can never possess its own erotic life*."[28] Warren similarly posits that "We do not have a proper grammar outside of humanism to describe the domain of 'pleasure,' 'desire,' 'sexuality,' and 'gender' for the socially dead object." For Warren, and implicitly for Holland, sexuality "belongs to the human,"[29] even as (or indeed, precisely because) it is relentlessly repressed within civil society. Thus, in the wider arc of D'Arcy's narrative, sexuality yields to the humanist fantasy of heteronormative futurity: Euphemia returns to her socially sanctioned place as wife to a white man and mother to a white son, while the prince and his compatriots are destroyed. However, in a final twist, the novella introduces an interracial child.

After the three Personnes drink the potion and return to their prevampiric states, Euphemia is horrified to learn that she is pregnant, and later gives birth to a black child "of Vampyrish propensities" (39). Thus, even as society is set "straight" with the destruction of the prince and his abolitionist plans, a piece of his legacy remains in a distant descendant – one Anthony Gibbons of New Jersey, who inherits the family tale as recorded by Zembo and, as the narrative concludes, begins to show signs of "vampirism" himself.

We might thus return to the question of what exactly makes the prince a vampire: insofar as D'Arcy titles his story *The Black Vampyre*, he frames the figure in terms of a predefined monster – one that pushes some boundaries but ultimately belongs squarely to the ontological category of "the human." If, as D'Arcy's "Moral" argues, vampirism is the norm of the modern world order, what makes the black vampire a monster – that is, a threat to the social – is his blackness. His "vampirism" asserts itself in those moments where he can mime the "human" position – for instance, in his capacity to speak the language of civility, as well as in his seduction of Euphemia through the shared language of antiblackness. However, insofar as blackness maintains the bounds of the human, he can never truly inhabit that position: as Wilderson reminds us, "even when Blackness is deployed to stretch the elasticity of civil society ... that expansion is never elastic enough to embrace the very Black who catalyzed [it]."[30] What makes Anthony Gibbons a threat, however, is the white fear that blackness can be folded into vampirism – which is to say, the human position. *The Black Vampyre*'s final horror, then, is the suggestion that someday, in the distant future, the boundaries between blackness and the human will become so blurred that the world defined by liberal modernity – the ontological coordinates of which are secured by the nonbeing of blackness – will end.

## Conclusion

Despite a history of reading the Romantic vampire as a queer figure, I have argued here that he is decidedly normative, and that his normativity comes into focus through an analysis of his constitution through antiblackness. Reading this figure in this way will, I hope, encourage readers to examine how other facets of Romanticism uphold hegemonic norms even as they may appear to adopt counterhegemonic positions. Returning, then, to Vestri's important question – "where's queer" in Romantic studies? – I want to conclude by suggesting that perhaps it is lacking for good reason. Not two decades ago, the queer theory net was cast so wide that, for some scholars, the term "queer" served to describe Romanticism itself. For instance, per Michael O'Rourke and David Collings, "Like queer, Romanticism is always messy, excessive, overspilling historical and corporeal boundaries ... Romanticism and queer theory alike favour the indefinite and the boundless."[31] Before that, white feminist interventions sought to challenge, per Anne K. Mellor, "traditional prejudices" upheld by the canonical white male Romantics through "tales of shared rather than solitary experience" and, together with postcolonial approaches, facilitated, in the words of Elizabeth Bohls, a "gradual broadening of that narrow canon."[32] As the field grapples with the racist epistemes that make the study of Romanticism possible in the first place, the Romantic vampire's so-called queerness (to say nothing of Romanticism's supposed boundlessness) requires reassessment.

As one of its most enduring legacies, the Romantic vampire has been something of a mascot for Romanticism itself. Like the vampire, Romanticism was nothing if not a literature of self-fashioning against death: from the Wordsworthian cult of "original Genius ... creating the taste by which he is to be [posthumously] enjoyed" to the myth of the neglected artist who dies tragically young cultivated by Chatterton, Keats, and their disciples, Romantic writers walked a tenuous line between embracing and railing against the bounds of mortality in the name of legacy.[33] Also like the vampire, the field of Romantic studies has persistently resurrected itself, often by reinventing itself through other critical idioms, from white feminist and postcolonial moves toward "inclusion" at the end of the twentieth century, to the revolutionary promise of queer theory in the early aughts, to efforts to "decolonize" a Western European, male-driven aesthetic movement that was explicitly used to subjugate nonwhite peoples in the name of empire. Such moves have driven the fantasy that Romanticism has the capacity to contain and speak to, if not for, multitudes. Centering (anti)blackness establishes that it does not.

If antiblackness is the condition of possibility for what is variably called the modern, Western, or liberal world order, it follows that antiblackness is foundational to the literary, aesthetic, and historical projects that have been gathered under the rubric of Romanticism. Even as Romantic writers and Romanticist scholars have labored to make Romanticism commensurate with the principles of equality and freedom that, for some, defined the turn of the nineteenth century, the point is that those principles are, themselves, antiblack. Antiblackness gives the intellectual and aesthetic projects of Romanticism coherence. To put a finer point on it, Romanticism is antiblack, and this fundamental antiblackness will not be overcome by antiracist critical methods because antiblackness, as noted at the beginning of this essay, is not racism. Neither do the field's turns to queer theory, white feminism, or other humanist discourses hold the potential to remake Romanticism into an emancipatory project. White feminism, as Euphemia and Annie Palmer remind us, is not liberatory; homonationalism, as Darvell and Ruthven illustrate, is not queer. These projects have, as Wilderson puts it, "Human resonance [that] would lend itself to very Human answers to the question, What is to be done?"[34] This is why, even as *The Black Vampyre* rightly concludes that the monster is modernity itself, by presenting modernity's destruction as threatening rather than promising, the narrative admits the fundamental incompatibility of humanism with black liberation. "The end of [black] suffering," Wilderson teaches us, is only possible after "the end of the Human, the end of the world."[35] As such, there is no methodological reorientation, no antiracist praxis that will remake Romanticism into something other than a pedagogy of antiblackness. The only ethical choice is its abolition.

**Notes**

1. Talia M Vestri, "Where's Queer?" *Keats–Shelley Journal* 68 (2019), 186.
2. Tom Holland, "Undead Byron," in *Byromania: Portraits of the Artist in Nineteenth- and Twentieth-Century Culture*, ed. Frances Wilson (New York: Palgrave Macmillan, 1999), 154–65 (at 154).
3. Jeffrey L. Schneider, "Secret Sins of the Orient: Creating a (Homo)Textual Context for Reading Byron's *The Giaour*," *College English* 65/1 (September 2002), 93.
4. Stuart Curran, *Poetic Form and British Romanticism* (Oxford: Oxford University Press, 1986), 143.
5. Joseph Lew, "The Necessary Orientalist? *The Giaour* and Nineteenth-Century Imperial Misogyny," in *Romanticism, Race, and Imperial Culture*, ed. Alan Richardson and Sonia Hofkosh (Bloomington: Indiana University Press, 1996), 177.
6. João H. Costa Vargas and Moon-Kie Jung, "Introduction," in *Antiblackness*, ed. Moon-Kie Jung and João H. Costa Vargas (Durham: Duke University Press, 2020), 7–8.
7. Vargas and Jung, "Introduction," 7.
8. Frank B. Wilderson III, *Red, White, and Black: Cinema and the Structure of US Antagonisms* (Durham: Duke University Press, 2010), 21.
9. Wilderson, *Red, White, and Black*, 11.
10. Wilderson, *Red, White, and Black*, 20–21.
11. Sylvia Wynter, "Unsettling the Coloniality of Being/Power/Truth/Freedom: Towards the Human, After Man, Its Overrepresentation – An Argument," *CR: The New Centennial Review* 3/3 (Fall 2003), 257–337.
12. Calvin Warren, *Onticide: Afropessimism, Queer Theory, and Ethics* (Victoria: Camas Books, 2018), 9.
13. Uriah Derick D'Arcy, *The Black Vampyre: A Tale of St. Domingo*, ed. Duncan Faherty and Ed White, *Just Teach One*, https://jto.americanantiquarian.org/just-teach-one-homepage/the-black-vampyre/ (accessed May 27, 2022), 16. Further references will be given in the text.
14. John Polidori, "The Vampyre," in *The Vampyre and Other Tales of the Macabre*, ed. Nick Groom (Oxford: Oxford University Press, 2008), 15. Further references will be given in the text.
15. Lord Byron, "Augustus Darvell," in *The Vampyre and Other Tales of the Macabre*, ed. Nick Groom (Oxford: Oxford University Press, 2008), 250. Further references will be given in the text.

16. Although it is beyond the scope of this essay, it is worth noting that D'Arcy's engagement with the Prometheus myth is part of a tradition of allusions to Prometheus in nineteenth-century discussions of slavery, as Jared Hickman demonstrates in *Black Prometheus: Race and Radicalism in the Age of Atlantic Slavery* (Oxford: Oxford University Press, 2018).
17. Wilderson, *Red, White, and Black*, 41.
18. Lee Edelman, *No Future: Queer Theory and the Death Drive* (Durham: Duke University Press, 2004), 10.
19. Edelman, *No Future*, 17.
20. Mary Y. Hallab, *Vampire God: The Allure of the Undead in Western Culture* (Albany: State University of New York Press, 2009), 75.
21. Warren, *Onticide*, 8–9.
22. Jasbir Puar introduced the term "homonationalism" in 2007 to explain how liberal rights discourses are deployed to accord white gay and lesbian populations access to citizenship as part of the post-9/11 US militant anti-Arab nationalism. In 2013, Puar clarified that the term "is not simply a synonym for gay racism" but "rather a facet of modernity and a historical shift marked by the entrance of (some) homosexual bodies as worthy of protection by nation-states, a constitutive and fundamental reorientation of the relationship between the state, capitalism, and sexuality" (337). See *Terrorist Assemblages: Homonationalism in Queer Times* (Durham: Duke University Press, 2007) and "Rethinking Homonationalism," *International Journal of Middle East Studies* 45 (2013), 336–39.
23. Warren, *Onticide*, 8.
24. Edelman, *No Future*, 11.
25. Edelman, *No Future*, 11.
26. For more, see particularly Celia E. Naylor, *Unsilencing Slavery: Telling the Truths About Rose Hall Plantation, Jamaica* (Athens: University of Georgia Press, 2022). Naylor's study is uniquely significant among the body of work related to the "white witch" legend because it offers a history of the grounds that Annie Palmer is said to haunt with a focus on the people who were enslaved there. In so doing, Naylor contextualizes the legend in a wider frame than studies that focus solely on the legacies of white women enslavers.
27. Natalie Zacek, "Holding the Whip-Hand: The Female Slaveholder in Myth and Reality," *Journal of Global Slavery* 6 (2021), 64.
28. Sharon Patricia Holland, *The Erotic Life of Racism* (Durham: Duke University Press, 2012), 46, italics original.
29. Warren, *Onticide*, 20–21. Holland similarly argues that "claims to some universal humanity, though laudable, do not quite capture the kind of complex and often pernicious work that a 'black-white polarity' does for us both critically and in everyday practice ... [T]here is no 'raceless' course of desire"; *Erotic Life*, 43.
30. Wilderson, *Red, White, and Black*, 22.
31. Michael O'Rourke and David Collings, "Introduction: Queer Romanticisms, Past and Present," *Romanticism on the Net* no. 36–37 (November 2004).

32. See, respectively: Anne K. Mellor, "On Romanticism and Feminism," in *Romanticism and Feminism*, ed. Anne K. Mellor (Bloomington: Indiana University Press, 1988), 8; Elizabeth A. Bohls, "Introduction: Romantic Literature from the Margins," in *Romantic Literature and Postcolonial Studies*, ed. Elizabeth A. Bohls (Edinburgh: Edinburgh University Press, 2013), 1–2.
33. William Wordsworth, "Essay, Supplementary to the Preface to Poems," in *William Wordsworth: The Major Works, Including The Prelude*, ed. Stephen Gill (Oxford: Oxford University Press, 2008), 640–63 (at 657).
34. Frank B. Wilderson III, *Afropessimism* (New York: W. W. Norton, 2020), 331.
35. Wilderson, *Afropessimism*, 331.

CHAPTER 4

# Samuel Taylor Coleridge's Racial Imaginary

## Mathelinda Nabugodi

Samuel Taylor Coleridge is the only major Romantic poet who engaged with the subject of race at length. His attempts to divide humanity into distinct races and define their respective characteristics amounts to what we may term a "racial imaginary," a concept introduced by Claudia Rankine and Beth Offreda to describe "the scene of race taking up residence in the creative act."[1] This chapter explores not only Coleridge's ideas about race, but also how his racial thinking affected his literary work. In other words, it studies how Coleridge's hardening racism came to inhabit his creative imagination. The focus is on his representations of Black people and how these representations change over time: from his youthful abolitionism to his embrace of white supremacist ideas and imperialist politics later in life. The evolution of his thought is symptomatic of the ways in which Romantic-era abolitionism could coexist with anti-Black racism: like Coleridge, many abolitionists opposed the trade in human beings, but few of them asserted or even envisaged racial equality.

The chapter begins with an examination of Coleridge's prize-winning 1792 Greek Ode on the horrors of slavery and his 1795 lecture against the slave trade, which provide the historical context for a reading of the first version of *The Rime of the Ancyent Marinere* (1798). It then moves forward to his encounter with racial science pioneer Johann Friedrich Blumenbach during his 1798–99 stay in Germany. The second half of the chapter discusses the traces that Blumenbach's work left on a number of Coleridge's later writings, including his review of Thomas Clarkson's *The History of the Abolition of the Slave Trade* (1808), his lectures on Shakespeare's *Othello* (1813; 1819), and a selection of fragments from his notebooks and "table talk" (1799–1828). In the closing section, Coleridge's views on the African race are brought to bear on some of the revisions that he made when preparing the republication of *The Rime of the Ancient Mariner* in his poetry collection *Sibylline Leaves* (1817). These revisions erase the abolitionist energy that animated the 1798 version even as they reveal the entanglements between Romantic aesthetics and pseudoscientific racism.

## Coleridge's Student Abolitionism

Coleridge began his undergraduate studies at Jesus College, Cambridge, in the Michaelmas term of 1791. He most likely chose this college because he was attracted by the prospect of a Rustat scholarship. These scholarships, worth approximately £30 per year, had been endowed a century earlier by Tobias Rustat, a courtier and diplomat in the court of Charles II. In 1672, Charles II granted a Royal Charter to establish the Royal African Company, which in the course of its existence would come to traffic more Africans across the Atlantic than any other institution. For almost thirty years, Rustat was actively involved in the Royal African Company, both as an investor and as a member of its governance structures. This means that Coleridge's studies were, in part, paid for by a key figure in the development of Britain's leading role in the transatlantic slave system.

Yet, despite his generous Rustat scholarship, young Coleridge often found himself broke. In one of his first letters from university to his elder brother George, written in early November 1791, he describes his new student lifestyle as follows:

> After Tea – (N. b. / Sugar is very dear) I read Classics till I go to bed – viz – eleven o'clock. If I were to read on as I do now – there is not the least doubt, that I should be a Classical Medallist ... I am reading Pindar, and composing Greek verse, like a mad dog. I am very fond of Greek verse, and shall try hard for the Brown's Prize ode.[2]

The complaint about the price of sugar is of a piece with Coleridge's financial difficulties, but it is also important to remember that virtually all sugar consumed in Great Britain in the late eighteenth century was produced by enslaved Africans in the British West Indies. While the transatlantic slave system is most often associated with the two major slaving ports of Bristol and Liverpool, by the end of the eighteenth century the products and profits of this system had permeated the British economy to such an extent that they were also an integral part of daily life in the landlocked university town of Cambridge. While Coleridge was to become an outspoken abolitionist, he nonetheless enjoyed the proceeds of transatlantic chattel slavery through the food he ate and the scholarships he received.

The letter to George also testifies to Coleridge's intellectual ambitions. The Browne Medal was a prize awarded annually in three categories: the best ode in Sapphic Greek, in Horatian Latin, and composition of epigrams. The two odes were to be on a set subject, which was announced in the *Cambridge Chronicle* on January 28, 1792: *Sors misera servorum in insulis*

*Indiæ occidentalis*. "The unhappy fate of the slaves in the West Indian Islands." The subject was politically explosive and indicates something of the political climate in Cambridge. William Wilberforce and Thomas Clarkson had been educated a decade earlier at St. John's College, Cambridge, and the town was frequently visited by Olaudah Equiano, whose wife, Susannah Cullen, came from the Cambridgeshire village of Soham. As the 1792 Browne Prize subject was set, Wilberforce was preparing to present a bill for the Abolition of the Slave Trade for the third time. When Coleridge set off to compete for the Browne Medal, he entered a national conversation on abolition, and he did so in an environment that embraced abolitionist sentiments.

In April, he wrote a letter to his brother George in which he apologizes for not having written sooner, and explains that: "I have been writing for *all* the prizes – namely the Greek Ode, the Latin Ode, and the Epigrams. ... My Greek Ode is, I think, my chef d'œuvre in poetical composition."[3] Coleridge's confidence was not misplaced: a couple of months later he was proclaimed the winner of the Browne Medal for the Greek Ode. Contemporary assessments tend to agree that there are flaws in the Greek, but that Coleridge succeeded in representing sublime sentiments. For example, Samuel Butler, who won that year's Browne Medal for a Latin Ode on the same subject, would later recall that Coleridge's piece "contained some highly spirited and poetical passages, tinged with a deep feeling of melancholy, and moral pathos."[4]

In line with contemporary conventions for Greek composition, Coleridge composed the Ode by going through volumes of Aeschylus, Pindar, Sappho, Sophocles, and other Greek poets in order to find expressions to use. As his friend George Bellas Goodenough described it, Coleridge "first conceived the idea and afterwards hunted thro' the several poets for words in which to cloth[e] those ideas."[5] This mode of composition gives his ode a somewhat bookish flavor. Here are the opening four stanzas, in Coleridge's own "literal" translation:

> Leaving the gates of Darkness, O Death! hasten thou to a Race yoked to Misery! Thou wilt not be received with lacerations of Cheeks, nor with funeral Ululation – but with circling Dances and the joy of Songs. Thou art terrible indeed, yet thou dwellest with LIBERTY, stern GENIUS! Borne on thy dark pinions over swelling of Ocean they return to their native Country. There by the side of fountains beneath Citron Groves the Lovers tell to their Beloved, what horrors being MEN they had endured from MEN![6]

That final line is straight out of Aeschylus' *Prometheus Bound*, where Prometheus, recently strung up on a rock in the Caucasus, complains of what he "a god, has endured from gods." Anyone well versed in Greek poetry would recognize that the ode is a patchwork of citations. But this is not mere plagiarism: adopting found material to express his own ideas is a creative challenge – and, taken together, Coleridge's citations express ideas not found in his classical sources. The formulation "yoked to misery," for example, is borrowed from Sophocles *Philoctetes* l. 1025, but the idea that Afro-Caribbeans will receive Death with "circling dances and the joy of songs" is modern. To dramatize the suffering of the enslaved, abolitionists promoted the idea that Africans welcomed death because they expected to return to their homeland in the afterlife. "The slaves in the West-Indies consider death as a passport to their native country," as Coleridge himself explained it.[7]

Coleridge most likely borrowed the idea from his then-favorite poet William Bowles, who refers to it in a 1791 poem called "The African" (later renamed "The Dying Slave"). The poem opens with a dying man who is surrounded by his companions. Rather than mourning his impending death, they are "rejoicing" as he expires. The bulk of the poem is devoted to imagining the man's posthumous return to Africa: his crossing of the Atlantic, reunion with people and places remembered from childhood, "the fragrant citron's shade," the "embow'ring orange grove," "the dance, the festive song / Of many a friend divided long," and a chance to "Tell to thy long-forsaken love, / The wounds, the agony severe / Thy patient spirit suffered here!"[8] All these are elements that become transfused into Coleridge's Greek Ode which describes how dead Africans will return to their native land where they will rest by "the side of fountains beneath citron groves" and "tell their beloved what kind of horrors, being men, they had endured from men."

Coleridge's achievement lies in dressing contemporary abolitionist imagery in the language of the Ancient Greek poets. But it also serves to distance his work from the plight that he discusses: it is a virtuoso assemblage of book-knowledge that shows little emotional engagement with living Africans. This distance is amplified as the Ode unfolds. After attacking the profiteers who "revel in the ills of Slavery, O feeders on the groans of the wretched, insolent sons of Excess, shedders of own brothers' blood," Coleridge turns to anticipate the abolition of slavery.[9] Doing so, he turns away from the enslaved and toward their white savior, William Wilberforce. "Lo! I see a Herald of Pity, his head as it were shaded with boughs of olive! Lo! I hear the golden gladness of thy words, Wilberforce!"

(p. 77, ll. 61–4) The final third of the Ode is given over to an oration by Wilberforce, whose words are described as being "more pleasing than the shouts of countless voices round the delayed chariot of Victory." (p. 77, ll. 89–92) Those shouts belong to the formerly enslaved, represented as an anonymous, thronging, threatening mass. This image strikingly reveals the self-congratulatory outlook of white abolitionism. No sooner does Wilberforce appear on the scene than he absorbs all the attention, overshadowing the people whom he seeks to liberate – and the ode closes with a celebration of his name and his name alone. Bearing in mind that this is written in 1792, more than a decade before the passage of the Act for the Abolition of the Slave Trade in 1807, more than forty years before the Slavery Abolition Act of 1833–34, and almost half a century before the abolition of the apprenticeship system that replaced chattel slavery (under which the "freed" slaves were forced to continue to labor for their former enslavers as unpaid apprentices), Coleridge's decision to pre-emptively commemorate the anticipated success of Wilberforce while limiting his representation of Africans to stereotypes about dancing and ululation effectively discounts past, present, and future emancipatory struggles waged by the enslaved themselves: his ode leaves no space to imagine Black historical agency or capacity for self-determination. Sadly, this outlook is still widespread today: the historiography of abolition is centered around the successes of a handful of white men in Britain, letting them overwrite the sometimes violent, sometimes subtle, acts of resistance performed by Black rebels in the Caribbean as well as Black political activists on both sides of the Atlantic.

### Coleridge's Lecture on the Slave Trade (1795)

Coleridge met Robert Southey in the summer of 1794. A native of the slave-trading port of Bristol, the young radical Southey had just completed a series of sonnets against the slave trade. No doubt, Coleridge wanted to buoy up his abolitionist credentials in front of his new friend. He contributed a number of passages to *Joan of Arc*, a historical epic that Southey was then working on. Coleridge's contributions include a section on enslaved Africans, to which he appended a footnote containing the opening of his Greek Ode and his own literal translation (discussed earlier). For the two poets, abolitionism was part of a wider radical agenda that encompassed the politics of private property, marriage, and class relations.

Almost immediately after meeting, Coleridge and Southey made plans for "Pantisocracy," a utopian community to be founded on the banks of the Susquehanna River in Pennsylvania. They did not pause to consider that their utopia would be built on land expropriated from the Indigenous population; on the contrary, Coleridge advocated for Susquehanna as location for their utopia on account of "its excessive Beauty, & it's security from hostile Indians."[10] To make money for the scheme, they presented a series of lectures on theological and political subjects. On June 16, 1795, Coleridge delivered a lecture on the Slave Trade at the Assembly Coffee-House on the Quay in Bristol. He published a revised version of the lecture in *The Watchman* no. IV, March 25, 1796. His grandson Ernst Hartley Coleridge prepared a separate edition of the lecture, based on a manuscript that was written in part by Coleridge and in part by Southey. This manuscript, which formed the basis of Coleridge's delivery of the lecture, is now lost, so it is impossible to tell with certainty who contributed what to the lecture.

In either case, as with the Greek Ode, the lecture's composition method involved the deft use of sources. On the day before the lecture, Coleridge went to the library and borrowed Thomas Clarkson's *On the Impolicy of the Slave Trade* and a book called *On Colonization* by Carl Bernhard Wadström. Wadström was a Swede who had travelled to Africa to explore prospects for colonizing the continent. He argued that the transatlantic slave trade was wrong because it was so inefficient; instead, he promoted the establishment of sugar plantations on the African continent. This would not only offer a more effective exploitation of African labor and natural resources, but also, just as importantly, contribute to "civilizing" the African population – which in turn would increase African demand for European goods and thus promote further mercantile expansion.

The second book that Coleridge borrowed in preparation for the lecture, Clarkson's *On the Impolicy of the Slave Trade*, makes a similar case in favor of the colonization of Africa, though the heart of Clarkson's argument concerns the conditions on slave ships: he represents it as an example of bad policymaking that fails to make rational business sense. An important proslavery argument that he had to contend with was that the transatlantic trade was the "cradle" of British seamen, thus linking it to national pride in Britain's maritime ascendancy. A slave ship – or Guineaman, as they were commonly called – would aim to depart Britain with a crew at least 50 percent larger than that of a comparable merchant ship trading on other routes. Slavers would argue that this need for manpower made the slave trade into an ideal training ground for sailors who could go on to work elsewhere in the global machinery of shipping. But even on its own terms, this should raise suspicions. *Why* did slavers require such large crews? Above all, the surplus manning was a precaution against the extremely high mortality on slaving voyages – slave merchants calculated on a disproportionately large number of their crews dying en route. Sailors were well aware of this, and this is one reason why they shunned this particular trade.

This is where Coleridge launches his attack on the slave trade proper, beginning with "a brief History of a slave-vessel and its contents – and first the manning." Citing Clarkson's *On the Impolicy of the Slave Trade*, he notes that "the great Bulk of the Cargo are procured (according to Clarkson) by the most infamous allurements."[11] From the context, it is clear that the word "Cargo" is a slip for "Crew" and while it is impossible to know whether it originated with Coleridge or his editor, it indicates that many common sailors were also captives and victims in the machinery of transatlantic slavery. Few men signed up voluntarily; instead, most of them ended up on slave trips though a practice known as "crimping." Coleridge accurately describes the practice as follows:

> There are certain Landlords, who allured by the high Wages given them in this trade, the advance-money of two months, and the promises of the merchant, open houses for their reception. These, having a general knowledge of the Ships and Seamen in the Port and being always on the look out entice such as are more unwary or in greater distress than the rest into their houses. They entertain them with Music and Dancing, and keep them in an intoxicated state for some Time. In the interim the Slave-merchant comes and makes his application – the unfortunate men are singled out – their Bill is immediately brought them – they are *said* to be more in debt than even two months' advance money will discharge. They have therefore the alternative made them of a Slave-vessel or a Gaol.[12]

Faced with this choice, most preferred the Slave-vessel, though there are also stories of sailors being brought to a state of drunken stupor only to wake up onboard a slaver with the coastline already receding on the horizon. This is true for the common sailors, who received a fixed day rate that, albeit higher than wages in other trades, was not sufficient to compensate for the risk to life that the voyage implied, not to mention the dehumanizing violence involved in managing a human "cargo." The ship officers, in contrast, were recruited with the prospect of large profits as they were allowed to traffic a certain number of captives on their own account. However, both officers and crew were equally exposed to the particular dangers of a slaving voyage, which for many proved to be a death sentence. Coleridge repeats Clarkson's calculation that "every Slave Vessel from the Port of Bristol loses on an average almost a fourth of the whole Crew," adding that even those who survive "are rather shadows in their appearance than men and frequently perish in Hospitals after the completion of the Voyage."[13]

The excess mortality aboard Guineamen was caused, in part, by staying for long stretches off the coast of Africa: it would take several months to assemble a "complete" cargo of several hundred captives, during which time many sailors fell ill from lack of immunity to local diseases. Slaver captains were also famed for their cruelty toward crews, which abolitionists ascribed to the brutalizing nature of the trade. But the worst threat to health came from the unsanitary conditions on ships once underway, where captives were crammed together without any facilities to attend to even basic hygiene. Late eighteenth-century abolitionists placed crew mortality at between 20–25 percent, but these averages hide the uneven distribution of deaths. On some voyages, so many sailors died that some of the captive Africans were taken out of their chains and taught how to sail the ship; in other cases, both crew and captives were wiped out by the contagious diseases that could spread like wildfire through the ship's crowded and confined spaces. Newspapers on both sides of the Atlantic printed reports of ghost ships discovered along the Atlantic routes – decaying hulls floating on the waves, sometimes with a handful of emaciated survivors that appeared more dead than alive to their rescuers. Of course, such occurrences were bound to be magnified as legends and sailor's yarns, told and retold to terrify landbound auditors.

Given the detailed knowledge of slaving that Coleridge displays in his slave trade lecture, it is notable that he is completely silent on the second major cause of excess mortality for slave trade sailors: insurrection. From the moment of the first captive being brought on board until they are all disembarked at their destination, the sailor lives with the risk of a violent uprising. Drawing on first-hand experience, John Newton captures some of a sailor's paranoid state of mind. On the subject of insurrections, he writes:

> These I believe, are always meditated; for the Men Slaves are not, easily, reconciled to their confinement, and treatment; and if attempted, they are seldom suppressed without considerable loss; and sometimes they succeed, to the destruction of a whole ship's company at once. Seldom a year passes, but we hear of one or more such catastrophes: and we likewise hear, sometimes, of Whites and Blacks involved, in one moment, in one common ruin, by the gunpowder taking fire, and blowing up the ship.[14]

Historians now calculate that insurrections occurred on around 10 percent of transatlantic crossings, but the fear of them was a universal constant on all slave ships. This means that sailors worked in a state of constant vigilance. "One unguarded hour, or minute, is sufficient to give the Slaves the opportunity they are always waiting for," Newton recalls, adding that "when they are once in motion, they are desperate; and where they do not conquer, they are seldom quelled without much mischief and bloodshed."[15] Living in constant fear of being killed by the people they are set to guard must have contributed to the mental and physical strain of a slave ship sailor.

Less popular with abolitionists who sought to represent Africans as infantile victims, sensationalist accounts of Black insurrections found an eager audience among newspaper readers. By allowing them to revel in scenes of violence, such accounts anticipate later war and horror films (and there is a direct lineage from eighteenth-century accounts of slave rebellions to present-day zombie films), but they also indirectly supported the proslavery argument that Africans are inherently brutal and barbarous. This may be one reason why abolitionists avoided them, yet in so doing they also turned a blind eye to the significance of Black resistance in bringing an end to the transatlantic slave system.

For sailors, unlike for landbound readers, accounts of shipboard insurrections were not a source of vicarious thrills; on the contrary, they represented a very real prospect of violent death. Moreover, they would encounter the aftermath of successful insurrections first-hand while cruising along the African coast or during the Middle Passage. The saddest accounts concern ships found adrift with only a handful of survivors aboard, such as the case of a schooner that was reported in the *American Mercury* in January 1785. A year after leaving Newport, Rhode Island, on a slaving exhibition to Africa, the ship was discovered without sails, without crew, and with only fifteen Africans in a "very emaciated and wretched condition."[16] Most likely, they had risen and killed the crew, but without the navigational skills to sail the ship back to Africa, they must have drifted with the winds and tides, slowly starving to death. Coming face to face with ships whose crews had been killed must have seemed an uncanny premonition for any sailor.

### *The Rime of the Ancyent Marinere* (1798)

Coleridge's familiarity with conditions in the slave trade inform the nightmare voyage depicted in *The Rime of the Ancient Mariner*. The first version of the poem was completed in 1798, though Coleridge revised it several times in his lifetime; the final version of 1834 is the most widely printed one today. Yet it is worth returning to the 1798 version, not least because it embodies aspects of Coleridge's early abolitionism that he edited out of later versions as his views on Black people changed. This section traces the influence of the information that Coleridge gathered in preparation for the slave trade lecture on the poem.

The Mariner's ship sets sail with a suspiciously large crew – "Four times fifty living men" – whose size alone suggests a slaver.[17] Throughout the poem, Coleridge's representation of the crew's decay recalls his earlier representation of returning slave-ship sailors as "shadows in their appearance" on the verge of death. "With heavy thump, a lifeless lump / They dropp'd down one by one," Coleridge's Mariner recalls, probably capturing something of the psychic experience of a sailor (p. 388, ll. 218–19). While the majority of sailors (unlike the Mariner's shipmates) did not die, they nonetheless returned home having witnessed many of their mates waste away, one by one, their dead bodies being summarily thrown overboard where they would be instantly devoured by the sharks that followed in the wake of a Guineaman. In Coleridge's poem, these sharks are transfused into "a million million slimy things" milling around the ship:

> The many men so beautiful,
>     And they all dead did lie!
> And a million million slimy things
>     Liv'd on – and so did I.
>
> I look'd upon the rotting Sea,
>     And drew my eyes away;
> I look'd upon the eldritch deck,
>     And there the dead men lay. (p. 390, ll. 236–43)

Malcolm Ware has linked the image of the "rotting Sea" to a passage from the slave trade lecture in which Coleridge describes the "hold of a ship ironed with so many fellow victims so closely crammed together that the heat and stench arising from [their] diseased bodies should rot the very planks of the Ship."[18] The passage has some factual basis: the press of human bodies in the slave ship hold did rot the very planks from inside. The verbal echo also indicates that Coleridge was not only drawing on accounts of slave ship crews; he was also incorporating his knowledge of conditions for their captives.

The crew of the Mariner's ship dies, but this is not the end of their labors. Their lifeless lumps are resurrected by some unknown force to continue sailing the ship:

> Beneath the lightning and the moon
>    The dead men gave a groan.
>
> They groan'd, they stirr'd, they all uprose,
>    Ne spake, ne mov'd their eyes:
> It had been strange, even in a dream
>    To have seen those dead men rise.
>
> The helmsman steerd, the ship mov'd on;
>    Yet never a breeze up-blew;
> The Marineres all 'gan work the ropes,
>    Where they were wont to do:
> They rais'd their limbs like lifeless tools –
>    We were a ghastly crew. (p. 396, ll. 329–40)

This crew of ghosts sails the ship back to England. Their "groans" rhetorically link the resurrected sailors to abolitionist representations of Africans groaning under the weight of enslavement (one may recall Coleridge's own depiction of slavers as "feeders on the groans of the wretched"). Just like the slip substituting "Cargo" for "Crew" in the slave trade lecture, the ship filled with groaning dead men enacts a slippage between sailor and captive. While explicitly referencing contemporary depictions of slave ship sailors as living dead, Coleridge here imagines a form of labor-in-death that anticipates the fate that awaited Africans on the other side of the Atlantic. The trope can be read as a premonition of present-day theorizations of chattel slavery as a state of social death.[19] For Africans who survived it, the Middle Passage was a transformation from being human to becoming a commodity, occupying the same legal status as a lifeless tool.

But if Coleridge's representation of the Ancient Mariner's shipmates provisionally undermines racial boundaries, such boundaries are violently reinforced in his encounter with a "Spectre-ship." The encounter takes place shortly after the Mariner has shot the albatross: suddenly a ship appears on the horizon, sailing straight toward them. Ware locates the inspiration for this passage in a late eighteenth-century "superstition of mariners" recorded by Nathan Drake, namely

> that, in the southern latitude of the coast of Africa, hurricanes are frequently ushered in, by the appearance of a spectre-ship. At the dead of night, the

luminous form of a ship glides rapidly, with topsails flying, and sailing straight in the wind's eye. The crew of this vessel are supposed to have been guilty of some dreadful crime in the infancy of navigation.

This crime, Drake clarifies, was "that of first being [*sic*] a freight of bartered captives."[20]

The parallels between Coleridge's "Spectre-ship" and a Guineaman are heightened by the two passengers it carries: "are those two all, all the crew, / That woman and her fleshless Pheere?" the Mariner wonders as the ship draws near (p. 386, ll. 187–88). A ship with two passengers is not as fantastic as may appear at first sight. As noted earlier, slaving was characterized by excessive mortality rates, and whoever was sailing along the Atlantic triangular route would sooner or later come face to face with abandoned or near-abandoned Guineamen whose crews and captives had been decimated by either disease or insurrection.

Coleridge develops this allusion to experiences in the slave trade through the racialized depictions that he provides of the "woman and her fleshless Pheere" (an archaic word for companion or partner) in the stanzas that follow. The companion is described first:

> *His* bones were black with many a crack,
>     All black and bare, I ween;
> Jet-black and bare, save where with rust
> Of mouldy damps and charnel crust
>     They're patch'd with purple and green. (p. 386, ll. 190–94)

The jet-black, skinny, naked, and wounded man resembles an enslaved African, covered with open sores from his confinement in the hold. In the next stanza, the Pheere's Blackness is used to set off his companion's whiteness:

> *Her* lips are red, *her* looks are free,
>     *Her* locks are yellow as gold:
> Her skin is as white as leprosy,
> And she is far liker Death than he;
>     Her flesh makes the still air cold. (p. 386, ll. 195–99)

The golden blond hair and rosy lips emphasize her whiteness. Coleridge furthermore links these racial characteristics to freedom: "her looks are free." In an age where Blackness was being increasingly identified with enslavability, to be Black meant to be enslaved. And the reverse holds true: to be white is to be free. But whereas whiteness, in addition to freedom, usually denotes fairness, with the attendant virtues of purity and innocence, here the woman's whiteness signals disease – her leprosy is at once a metaphor for the moral stain of slavers as well as the bodily disfigurements of slave trade crews, who were often victims of malnourishment and tropical diseases.

*The Rime of the Ancient Mariner* contains multiple references to the transatlantic slave trade that would have been legible to its early readers, not least to Southey. While he published a scathing review of the poem, lambasting it for being "absurd or unintelligible," he also adapted its plot and ballad stanza to write his own "The Sailor, Who Had Served in the Slave Trade" (1799).[21] Southey's poem pares back Coleridge's metaphysical obscurities to deliver a piece of straightforward abolitionist propaganda; for example, whereas Coleridge's Mariner is punished for the inexplicable crime of shooting an albatross, Southey's sailor commits the much more forthright crime of flogging an African woman to death. This was clearly modelled on the real-life case of slave ship captain John Kimber, who was put on trial in 1792 for flogging a fifteen-year-old African girl to death during an Atlantic crossing. While Kimber was acquitted, his trial became a *cause célèbre* among abolitionists. This suggests that Southey's issue with the *Ancient Mariner* was that the poem's metaphysics obscured its abolitionist politics. Coleridge himself was on the opposite trajectory: in the coming decades he became attracted to the racial science of his day. The following section discusses Coleridge's changing attitudes toward Africans, before returning to the revisions that he made to *The Rime of the Ancient Mariner* when he was preparing it for republication in 1817.

## Discovering Racial "Science": Blumenbach and Beyond

In late 1798, with the *Ancient Mariner* hot off the press, Coleridge set off for Germany with William and Dorothy Wordsworth. He spent a period studying at the University of Göttingen, where he attended lectures with Johann Friedrich Blumenbach, a pioneer in developing racial science. Blumenbach's work intervened in taxonomic debates about the nature of mankind ignited by Carl Linnaeus (Carl von Linné) in the tenth edition of *Systema Naturae* (1758–59). Scientists attempted to subdivide humanity into different species, kinds, races, or varieties: The biological terminology was still in flux, but ultimately the debate boiled down to whether all humans were descended from the same origin (*monogenesis*) or from several separate points of origin (*polygenesis*). As a monogenist, Blumenbach postulated that all of humanity, which he divided into five races, had the same point of origin – an original "Caucasian" race now embodied in white Europeans. He used skull-measurements to prove that the other four races ("Mongolian," "Ethiopian," "American," and "Malay"), had "degenerated" from this origin to varying degrees; a degeneration caused by diet, climate, and environment. What he called "Ethiopians" (Black Africans) and "Mongolians" (East Asians) were the most "degenerated" races. For Blumenbach, degeneration was merely aesthetic: degenerated races were ugly, but they were not impaired in intellectual or moral capability. To prove that Africans were capable of intelligence, he collected works by Black writers – a collection that he would also use as an argument against slavery. While Blumenbach himself spoke out against slavery, his work nonetheless provided a crucial impetus for the emergence of racial science and served to justify white supremacism.

Coleridge must have made a good impression on the German professor. Blumenbach invited him to view both his collection of skulls and his library of African authors, and he also organized a goodbye party on Coleridge's departure. Coleridge was likewise impressed: "Nothing can be conce[ived more] delightful than Blumenbach's lectures / & in conversation he is indeed a most i[nteresting] man," Coleridge enthused to his friend Thomas Poole.[22] On his return from Germany, Coleridge begins to collect various "anecdotes" about Black people in his notebooks. "Tribes of Negroes who take for the deity of the day the first thing they see might have originated in a sublime conception" he writes in a note from autumn 1799;[23] the sentence is cited almost verbatim in another note of late summer 1802, where he adds "sublime conception possible – & a ludicrous one of a Narcissus, himself his Fetisch."[24] If there is something sublime about this conception, this would be the sublimity of primitive religions. Coleridge's remarks about Africans make it clear that he regarded them as barbarians in the classical sense of people living outside of civilization, but he also drew on Enlightenment notions of historical progress to locate them on a temporal axis. His Africans did not just live in a distant place but also in a distant time, being stuck in a precivilized state that Europeans had long since surpassed. That is what makes them such an appealing subject for philosophical speculation.

Two entries from June 1805 linger on another racist caricature which they present as "fact":

> Curious fact mentioned to me <by Mr Dennison> the Negroes often console themselves in their cruel punishments, that their wounds will become *white*/ and looking on this as a grand Progression on their rank of Nature, spite of their abhorrence of the cruelty of white men. Their Love of *white*, their belief that superior Beings are white, even in the inmost parts of Africa where they have seen no White men/it is a color beloved by their good Deities & by the Supreme of all, the Immense, to whom they do not pray, but whose existence they confess. This among so many others in favor of permanent Principles of *Beauty* as distinguishable from Association or the Agreeable[.][25]

Beauty is a universal and permanent principle, and it is white. It follows that different races stand in different degrees of proximity to beauty depending on the color of their skin. Coleridge's spurious claim that Black people enjoy their white scars because they bring them closer to whiteness accords with Blumenbach's theory of racial variety as degeneration from a white "Caucasian" origin that sets the standard of beauty. But this is not merely an aesthetic claim. In associating whiteness with "superior Beings" and even God himself ("the Supreme of all"), Coleridge ensures that the aesthetic category of beauty becomes inextricably entangled with the racial outlook of white supremacy.

The Act for the Abolition of the Slave Trade passed by British Parliament in 1807 can be seen as a turning point in Coleridge's engagement with Africans. Shortly after its passing, Thomas Clarkson published *The History of the Abolition of the Slave Trade*, which became the basis for the received account of abolition. Coleridge received it enthusiastically. He wrote to Clarkson in terms that flaunted his own abolitionist credentials, bragging that "my first public effort was a Greek Ode against the Slave Trade, for which I had a Gold Medal" and that "at Bristol I gave an especial Lecture against the falling off of the zeal in the friends of the Abolition," before going on to mention his acquaintance with Blumenbach and his works.[26] This indicates how the political question of abolition had become supplanted by the pseudoscientific question of African racial characteristics in Coleridge's mind.

Coleridge's embrace of pseudoscientific racism pivots him from his youthful abolitionism toward a politics of white supremacist imperialism, representing colonial conquest as a civilizing mission. This shift is evident in his review of Clarkson's *History*. After praising Clarkson and his fellow abolitionists (singling out Wilberforce, Granville Sharp, and the community of Quakers, but not making a single mention of the

Black insurrectionaries and rebels who broke down the plantation system from within), Coleridge veers into an extended discussion of the racial abilities of Africans. Echoing the arguments of Clarkson's *Essay on the Impolicy of the Slave Trade* and Wadström's treatise *On Colonization*, Coleridge promotes the colonization of Africa as the logical next step after abolition. The review amply demonstrates how white abolitionism can exist in a perverse symbiosis with anti-Black racism. The condemnation of the slave trade that Coleridge offers here rests on the conviction that free and civilized Europeans are bound to act better toward their inferiors.

Coleridge further suggests that the cultural and intellectual backwardness of Africans makes them ideally suitable for European civilizing efforts. "The Africans are more versatile, more easily modified than perhaps any other known race," he states. The claim is rooted in his racist speculations, such as the idea that Africans "take for the deity of the day the first thing they see" in the morning. While such impressionability may be infantile and unworthy of an Englishman, it is ideal in a colonized subject; "the facility with which the Africans are impressed, the rapidity with which they take the colours of surrounding objects, oftentimes place them in a degrading light, as men, but are most auspicious symptoms of what they may hereafter become, as citizens."[27] In other words, because Coleridge does not consider Africans to have a developed culture of their own, he believes that they will easily absorb the culture of their colonizers.

But his arguments about the versatility of the African "race" are also entangled with economic considerations. Coleridge envisages that the former slave factories and barracoons, where people had been imprisoned prior to being forced onto ships to take them across the Atlantic, would be replaced with "commercial magazines" to act as centers of British trade on the continent: "each fort, instead of being, as hitherto, a magazine of death and depravity, would finally become a centre of civilization" he suggests, further surmising that living in proximity to "a race confessedly so superior to them" will prompt the "most intelligent of the African tribes" to adopt the religion and habits of English settlers.[28] Coleridge's confidence that Black Africans will recognize White Europeans as a superior race resonates with his notion that Black Africans consider white skin to be more beautiful than their own color. He takes his own sense of white superiority and makes it into a universal principle of human perception.

Coleridge continued his attempts to incorporate the purported characteristics of various races into a greater philosophical scheme throughout the 1820s. Henry Nelson Coleridge (the poet's nephew) reproduces an 1827 diagram visualizing what Coleridge terms "Blumenbach's scale of dignity." It has the shape of an equilateral triangle: the apex is labelled "1. Caucasian or European," along the sides he places "2. Malay = 2. American," while the triangle's base is marked "3. Negro. = 3. Mongolian = Asiatic."[29] Blumenbach had somewhat disingenuously insisted that racial degeneration only affected appearance, not intellect. In recasting his taxonomy into a "scale of dignity," Coleridge infuses it with a white supremacist sense of racial superiority.

This sense of superiority also runs through a series of lectures on race that Coleridge's contributed to a course at the Royal College of Surgeons on the invitation of its Professor of Anatomy, Joseph Henry Green. Here Coleridge argues "that the Human Species consists of ONE *historic Race*, and of *several* others."[30] His conception of a "historic" race is inspired by Blumenbach's definition of Caucasians, but the change of terminology indicates Coleridge's ambition to reconcile Blumenbach's taxonomy with the Biblical account of man's origin: the term "historic" harks back to the original race at the center of divine creation. The main thrust of his lecture is to explain how and why the four other races have degenerated from the historic race: "the formation of the Races," he conjectures, "involv[es] an <intellectual, and tho' less perfectly a moral & social> separation of the infirm Races from the central or ruling ONE."[31]

Coleridge's explanation of racial degeneration repeatedly conflates physical differences (e.g. of skin tone) with moral, intellectual, social, and cultural factors. This is part of a deliberate attempt to get beyond Blumenbach's physiological focus to gain moral insights. "Blumenbach has clearly and with classical neatness given the distinctive Characters of the 5 Races, in respect of countenance, and bodily form," Coleridge writes in a notebook entry of 1828. "But where shall I find any similar diagnosis of their hereditary character, ~~of~~ in respect of intellectual faculties, and moral predispositions?"[32] He surmises that the question could only be answered by placing an English child with a Senegambian community and comparing their development to that of an African child given an English education, admitting that the "difficulty" of so doing is "an insuperable obstacle to any decisive conclusions."[33] Notwithstanding the difficulties of empirically testing his hypotheses, Coleridge was confident in the superiority of white Europeans, whom he identifies as the "Historic Race." He calls them "the Masters of the world" and argues that through his definition of "the *idea* of the Historic Race we have presented a Vision of Glory – the very capability of which & the fact that its realization is the final cause of our existence in this world cannot but wonderfully ~~elevate our~~ raise and ennoble our nature & the Race to which we belong in our own eyes – and in the eye of Reason."[34]

Coleridge never developed a coherent statement on race, and, taken together, his various remarks on Africans occupy a relatively small proportion of his complete output. Nonetheless, the fact that he returns to the subject again and again over several decades indicates that attempts to determine racial character were an integral component of his worldview. While few of his contemporaries paused to interrogate their own prejudices about race, Coleridge was actively building a racial imaginary. This, in turn, infuses all aspects of his thought, including his conception of literature. The closing section discusses how his racial ideas affects Coleridge's interpretation of Shakespeare's *Othello*, as well as his revisions of *The Rime of the Ancient Mariner* (1817).

## Coleridge's Lectures on *Othello* and *The Rime of the Ancient Mariner* (1817)

In the 1810s, Coleridge delivered several series of lectures on Shakespeare in London and Bristol. He extemporized from notes and marginal annotations, which makes it hard to reconstruct exactly what he said, but there is clear evidence of how Coleridge's racial thinking affected his interpretation of *Othello* in published accounts of his lectures. A report in the *Bristol Gazette* of November 11, 1813, states that "Mr. C. ridiculed the idea of making Othello a negro, he was a gallant Moor, of royal blood, combining a high sense of Spanish and Italian feeling."[35] The word "Moor" could refer to North Africans of Arab and Berber heritage as well as Black Africans from the sub-Saharan regions. Although stage tradition ever since Shakespeare's time had represented Othello as a Black African, Coleridge argued that Shakespeare must have imagined him as either Arab or Berber in origin. The sentiment is repeated in the opening entry, dated December 29, 1822, of Henry Nelson Coleridge's edition of Coleridge's *Table Talk*: "OTHELLO must not be conceived as a negro, but a high and chivalrous Moorish chief."[36]

Henry Nelson Coleridge also published a summary of a lecture on *Othello* that Coleridge delivered at the Crown and Anchor pub in

London in January 1819. The edition is based on Coleridge's own notes; although some of these are now lost, it appears that Coleridge used the lecture to expand the argument that Shakespeare could not have intended Othello as a Black African:

> Can we imagine him [Shakespeare] so utterly ignorant as to make a barbarous negro plead royal birth, – at a time, too, when negroes were not known except as slaves? ... No doubt Desdemona saw Othello's visage in his mind; yet, as we are constituted, and most surely as an English audience was disposed in the beginning of the seventeenth century, it would be something monstrous to conceive this beautiful Venetian girl falling in love with a veritable negro. It would argue a disproportionateness, a want of balance, in Desdemona, which Shakespeare does not appear to have in the least contemplated.[37]

In this comment, the identification of Blackness with enslavement comes full circle: Africans can only be known "as slaves" in Coleridge's imaginary. But, ultimately, his issue with the color of Othello's skin does not rest on historical accuracy but on his conflation of racist ideas and aesthetic principles. In evoking a disproportionate "want of balance" in the very notion of a love affair between a beautiful white woman and a Black man, Coleridge treats the sociocultural politics of interracial relations as an aesthetic flaw inadmissible in Shakespearean drama.

The *Othello* lectures indicate that, by the 1810s, Coleridge's views on literature had become infected by his evolving racism. This throws light on Coleridge's revision of the "Spectre-ship" passage in *The Rime of the Ancyent Marinere* in which a white woman appeared together with a Black companion. Preparing the poem for republication in *Sibylline Leaves* (1817), Coleridge removes the stanza containing a graphic description of the man's "Jet-black and bare" body and makes several changes to the surrounding lines that serve to eradicate his race and gender. Whereas the 1798 encounter with the ghost ship makes the Mariner wonder "are those two all, all the crew, / That woman and her fleshless Pheere?" (p. 386, ll. 188–89), in 1817 and subsequent versions the Mariner asks: "And is that Woman all her crew? / Is that a DEATH? And are there two? / Is DEATH that woman's mate?"[38] The revision replaces the "Jet-black and bare" companion with a disembodied and epistemically uncertain figure whose very existence is immediately put into question; "Is that a DEATH? And are there two?"

And whereas the following stanza originally ended on a contrast between the leper-white woman and her jet-black companion, the revised version closes with an assertion identifying her as the "Night-Mair LIFE-IN-DEATH."

| | |
|---|---|
| And are those two all, all the crew, / That woman and her fleshless Pheere? / *His* bones were black with many a crack, / All black and bare, I ween; / Jet-black and bare, save where with rust / Of mouldy damps and charnel crust / They're patch'd with purple and green / *Her* lips are red, *her* looks are free, / *Her* locks are yellow as gold: / Her skin is as white as leprosy, / And she is far liker Death than he; / Her flesh makes the still air cold. / (*The Ancyent Marinere* [1798], p. 386, ll. 188–99) | And is that Woman all her crew? / Is that a DEATH? and are there two? / Is DEATH that woman's mate? / *Her* lips were red, *her* looks were free, / Her locks were yellow as gold: / Her skin was as white as leprosy, / The Night-Mair LIFE-IN-DEATH was she, / Who thicks man's blood with cold. / (*The Ancient Mariner* [1817], p. 14, ll. 187–94) |

    Coleridge also removes a later stanza that appears in the 1798 version, describing how the wind "whistled thro' [the companion's] bones; / Thro' the holes of his eyes and the hole of his mouth / Half-whistles and half-groans" (p. 388, ll. 204–5). Here the bodily imagery is substituted by a generic description of the sea: "The Sun's rim dips; the stars rush out: / At one stride comes the dark." (1817 edition, p. 15, ll. 199–200). When revising *The Rime of the Ancyent Marinere*, Coleridge additionally added marginal prose notes to elucidate the poem's content. The note accompanying this passage states: "The spectre-woman and her death-mate, and no other on board the skeleton-ship." This clarification does not clarify the status of the companion, but it does reveal Coleridge working through whether the Black "Pheere" is to be counted as a fellow passenger or discounted as a spectral presence, a "DEATH" or "death-mate" whose epistemically uncertain existence points to the social invisibility of Black subjects.

    Coleridge's various revisions add up to a revisionist process that obscures the poem's original anchoring in the context of the transatlantic slave trade even as they accord with the increasingly racist tenor of his thought. In his lecture on *Othello*, Coleridge rejected the idea of a white woman with a Black companion – and he applied the same racial logic to his own poem by editing out the Jet-black Pheere. His revisionary process is emblematic of how the realities of slavery were written out of British cultural memory even as racism and racial science was solidifying in the decades after emancipation.

## Notes

1. Claudia Rankine and Beth Offreda, 'On Whiteness and the Racial Imaginary: Where Writers go Wrong in Imagining the Lives of Others', *Literary Hub*, April 9, 2015. https://lithub.com/on-whiteness-and-the-racial-imaginary/. Accessed 21 Nov 2023.
2. Samuel Taylor Coleridge, *Collected Letters of Samuel Taylor Coleridge*, ed. Earl Leslie Griggs, 6 vols. (Oxford: Clarendon Press, 1956), 1: 16–17.
3. Coleridge, *Collected Letters*, 1:34.
4. Samuel Butler, "To the Editor of the Analyst," *The Analyst* 1/3 (1834), 227.
5. George Bellas Goodenough, "Coleridge in Germany (1799)," ed. Edith J. Morley, in *Wordsworth and Coleridge: Essays in Honor of George McLean Harper*, ed. Earl Leslie Griggs (New York: Russell & Russell, 1962), 231.
6. Coleridge, 'Literal Translation', in Robert Southey, *Joan of Arc, An Epic Poem* (Bristol: Joseph Cottle, 1796), 64n.
7. Cited in Anthea Morrison, "Samuel Taylor Coleridge's Greek Prize Ode on the Slave Trade," *An Infinite Complexity: Essays in Romanticism*, ed. J. R. Watson (Edinburgh: Edinburgh University Press, 1983), 157.
8. William Bowles, "The African," *Monody, Written at Matlock, October 1791* (London: Dilly and Cruttwell, 1791), 15–16.
9. Samuel Taylor Coleridge, *Sors Misera Servorum in Insulis Indiæ Occidentalis* in *Poetical Works Part I*, ed. J. C. C. Mays, vol. 16 of *Collected Works of Samuel Taylor Coleridge* (Princeton: Princeton University Press, 2001), page 77, lines 45–8. Further references will be given in the text.
10. Coleridge, *Collected Letters*, 1:99.
11. Samuel Taylor Coleridge, *Lectures 1795: On Politics and Religion*, ed. Lewis Patton and Peter Mann, vol. 1 of *The Collected Works of Samuel Taylor Coleridge*, Bollingen Series LXXV (Princeton: Princeton University Press, 1971), 327.
12. Coleridge, *Lectures 1795*, 237.
13. Coleridge, *Lectures 1795*, 238.
14. John Newton, *Thoughts upon the African Slave Trade* (London: Printed for J. Buckland, in Pater-noser Row; and J. Johnson, in St. Paul's Churchyard, 1788), 12–13.
15. Newton, *Thoughts*, 15–16.
16. *American Mercury*, Jan. 31, 1785; cited in Marcus Rediker, *The Slave Ship: A Human History* (New York: Viking, 2007), 298.
17. Coleridge, *The Rime of the Ancyent Marinere* (1798), in *Poetical Works Part I*, ed. J. C. C. Mays, vol. 16 of *Collected Works of Samuel Taylor Coleridge* (Princeton: Princeton University Press, 2001), page 388, line 216. Further references will be given in the text.
18. Malcolm Ware, "Coleridge's 'Spectre Bark': A Slave Ship?," *Philological Quarterly* 40/4 (1961), 591; Coleridge, *Lectures 1795*, 247–48.
19. Orlando Patterson, *Slavery and Social Death: A Comparative Study* (Cambridge, MA: Harvard University Press, 1982).

20. Cited in Ware, "Coleridge's 'Spectre Bark,'" 589. Presumably "being" is meant to be "bearing."
21. Robert Southey, "Review of Lyrical Ballads," *Critical Review* 24 (1798), 200.
22. Coleridge, *Collected Letters*, 1:494.
23. Samuel Taylor Coleridge, *The Notebooks of Samuel Taylor Coleridge*, ed. Kathleen Coburn, vol. 1, *1794–1804* (London: Routledge & Kegan Paul, 1957), entry 464.
24. Coleridge, *Notebooks*, vol. 1, entry 1232.
25. Coleridge, *Notebooks*, vol. 2, *1804–1808*, entry 2604.
26. Coleridge, *Collected Letters*, 1:78.
27. Samuel Taylor Coleridge, "Review of *The History of the Abolition of the Slave Trade* by T. Clarkson," *The Edinburgh Review* 12 (1808), 378.
28. Coleridge, "Review," 377, 378.
29. Samuel Taylor Coleridge, *Specimens of the Table Talk of the Late Samuel Taylor Coleridge*, ed. Henry Nelson Coleridge, 2 vols. (London: John Murray, 1835), 1:56.
30. Samuel Taylor Coleridge, *Shorter Works and Fragments*, ed. H. J. Jackson and J. R. de J. Jackson, vol. 11 of *Collected Works of Samuel Taylor Coleridge* (Princeton: Princeton University Press, 1995), 2:1402.
31. Coleridge, *Shorter Works and Fragments*, 2:1404.
32. Coleridge, *Notebooks*, vol. V, entry 5742.
33. Coleridge, *Notebooks*, vol. V, entry 5742.
34. Coleridge, *Shorter Works and Fragments*, 2:1404, 1405–6.
35. Samuel Taylor Coleridge, *Collected Works: 5. Lectures 1808–1819: On Literature*, ed. R. A. Foakes, vol. 5 of *Collected Works of Samuel Taylor Coleridge* (Princeton: Princeton University Press, 1987), 1:555.
36. Coleridge, *Table Talk*, 1:1.
37. Samuel Taylor Coleridge, *The Literary Remains of Samuel Taylor Coleridge*, ed. Henry Nelson Coleridge, 4 vols. (London: Pickering, 1836), 2:257–58. This passage is contested by A. Roberts in his edition of *Coleridge: Lectures on Shakespeare (1811–1819)* (Edinburgh: Edinburgh University Press, 2016), 163n370. Roberts appeals to Foakes's Bollingen edition of the surviving text and – without any evidence – implies that the editor Henry Nelson Coleridge "concocted" the passage himself. This shows the lengths to which scholars will go to obfuscate the history of racism. The text of all Coleridge's lectures is problematic since they were oral performances in part improvised in the moment, but there is no evidence to suggest that H. N. Coleridge would have invented only this one racist passage; in fact, the racist remark is quite in keeping with Coleridge's opinions stated elsewhere.
38. Compare these lines from *The Rime of the Ancyent Marinere* (1798) with *The Rime of the Ancient Mariner* (1834) printed on the facing page in Coleridge, *Poetical Works Part 1*, as well as the same passage in the version published in his *Sibylline Leaves: A Collection of Poems* (London: Rest Fenner, 23, Paternoster Row, 1817), 14.

CHAPTER 5

# (Not)freedom

## DJ Lee and Aaron Ngozi Oforlea

### "a quire of paper"

On June 1, 1797, Boston King wrote a letter from Freetown, Sierra Leone, Africa, to John Clarkson in London. Clarkson had been the governor of Freetown, a colony for African Americas like King who had fought for the British during the American Revolutionary War. They were referred to as Black Loyalists. King's letter warned Clarkson of trouble in the colony. The dishonorable British were forcing Loyalists to pay rent, stripping them of the freedoms they'd been promised. The Loyalists refused to pay, and now people were leaving the colony, dispersing into the dense Sierra Leonian jungle, some disappearing entirely. King signed off by asking Clarkson to send him a "quire of paper" and a few pens.[1] Perhaps King wanted to chronicle his life in Sierra Leone, as he had his enslavement in the American South.

A world away, the poet Samuel Taylor Coleridge sat in the seaside town of Watchet, England, dreaming up ghost ships, slime fish, and diseased seamen stalled in the Atlantic Ocean under a nightmarish sun. These images would become *The Rime of the Ancient Mariner*, one of the most influential literary works of the English language. Although Coleridge's poem doesn't mention individuals like King, and to our knowledge he didn't reference Black Loyalists among his writings, the *Rime* mirrors the sea journeys Loyalists made. It also speaks to how white writers of the Romantic period processed their country's complicity with slavery by focusing on the metaphor of disease. The poem imagines how the ocean's "deep did rot" and the awful symptoms that "plagued" the crew: "parched" throats, "glazed" eyes, and "black lips baked."[2]

Coleridge was right. Britain was elbow deep in moral disease, having built its economy on the transatlantic slave trade. Sickness festered because slave plantations existed far from British shores, in the Caribbean and the Americas. The physical remove gave ordinary Britons the illusion of ethical distance with a repressed sense of guilt. They may not have been aware of the magnitude of the trade: that between 1525 and 1866, some 12.5 million people were transported from their African homelands to work on British-owned plantations in the Americas. But they would have known some things. England abounded with famous court cases about enslavement as well as abolitionist societies. Allusions to slave trafficking appeared in poetry, plays, musicals, art, novels, and nonfiction by white writers and artists. Black-authored histories, poetry, memoirs, and polemics by poets like Phillis Wheatley and nonfiction writers like Olaudah Equiano and Mary Prince also proliferated. But what about Black Loyalists? Although their stories have been given scant attention by Romantic scholars, it is clear to us these individuals live at the center of the period as surely as Romantic poets.

## On Freedom

When we began researching this chapter, we knew we wanted to focus on the Black Loyalists, men and women who moved with incredible dexterity and personal danger throughout the Atlantic in the late eighteenth and early nineteenth centuries, hoping to better their situations. A white American writer and scholar of Romanticism (Lee), and a Nigerian American scholar of African American literature and folklore (Oforlea), we were drawn to the Loyalists' intricate personal stories, as told through their letters and memoirs. Especially powerful were how they used their rhetorical skills to "signify" on beliefs about race, ideas about religion, and notions of liberty. As our inquiry progressed, we weren't surprised to find Black Loyalist writings entangled with the rhetoric of freedom. After all, questions of emancipation preoccupied them. Furthermore, scholars have long studied how discourses of "freedom," "liberty," and "deliverance" drove Romantic-era writings. What did surprise us was how, the deeper we dug, the more nuanced freedom became to our inquiry. Thus, it is the focus of our chapter.

For us, it's crucial to unpack the term's history in the Atlantic world, where liberty was defined for one group of people through bondage of another. In that task, we've been guided by the brilliance of postcolonial theorists like Homi K. Bhabha, who provides analyses of American–European power and the ways colonial subjects pursued liberation. We've also looked to scholars of the Black Radical Tradition, like Fred Moten, Cedrick J. Robinson, and George Lipsitz, who articulate the development of "a collective consciousness informed by the historical struggles for liberation" and point out that "the greatest achievement of the Black community was itself, its emergence as an aggrieved and insurgent polity committed to social justice."[3] Finally, we've benefited from the work of writer-critic Maggie Nelson in her 2021 book *On Freedom* and her multivalent discussion of the concept. Above all, it is Black Loyalists who speak most powerfully and poetically about freedom. Thus, our major argument is that the voices of the Sierra Leone settlers must have a place in the Romantic literary canon alongside white poets.

## Discoursing Freedom

"Liberty to Slaves." This phrase was printed on a sash worn by the all-Black Ethiopian Regiment of the American Revolutionary War. The phrase became a motto for Britain's entire war policy between 1775 and 1782.[4] It was shorthand for the proclamation made by Virginia's colonial governor Lord Dunmore to "free" all "negroes" who joined British troops to "bear arms."[5] Yet Dunmore's liberty was anything but humanitarian. The idea was to enlist the entire population of African Americans to bolster struggling British forces and destroy the slaveholding South.[6] This strategy was Britain's only hope to hold onto the colonies, so much so that authorities further declared that "every NEGRO who shall desert the Rebel Standard... [will have] any occupation which he shall think proper."[7] Cynically, "Rebel Standard," as poet C. S. Giscombe notes, meant that planters like Dunmore, loyal to the crown, intended to keep their slaves.[8] Historians estimate that 50,000–100,000 Black people joined the British war effort in hopes of liberation.[9]

Boston King, who lived in South Carolina, enlisted. So did David George, who was born in Virginia to parents captured in Africa. We know this because George later wrote *An Account of the Life of Mr. David George, from Sierra Leone in Africa*.[10] One important aspect of George's narrative is how he became one of the most powerful orators of the day, delivering a message of future freedom for Black audiences. As George tells it, in 1775, on the brink of the American war, he discovered his talent by listening to the Black preacher David Liele, who had visited the plantation and trading post in Silver Bluff, on the South Carolina side of the Savannah River, where George was enslaved. George became so committed to preaching that he founded the first African American church in the United States: the Silver Bluff Church.[11] He faced difficulties as a pastor, yet he continued to preach, even as Virginia's colonial status collapsed on July 4, 1776, when the Second Continental Congress issued the Declaration of Independence. He led services until the British took Savannah in 1778.

George's *Account* often displays the Biblical rhetoric of deliverance. In fact, many enslaved people harnessed Christian rhetoric for liberatory purposes – but that rhetoric was under surveillance by white authorities. Though George was permitted to realize personal religious freedom after the war, he was prohibited from introducing ideas that encouraged the Black population to see themselves as equal to whites. The British allowed religious practices that taught Black Loyalists they were not physically enslaved, but they were downright hostile to teachings that encouraged psychological freedom.

In his *Account*, George is clear about where he wants readers to focus: on the idea of discourse. George related that when he heard Liele preach, "[h]is sermon was very suitable on *Come unto me all ye that labour and are heavy laden, and I will give you rest*. When it was ended, I went to him and told him I was so; That I was weary and heavy laden; and that the grace of God had given me rest. Indeed, his whole discourse seemed for me."[12] George calls preaching "discourse," a shapeshifting term that has grown in importance in twentieth- and twenty-first-century cultural criticism. Thinkers like Michel Foucault have helped us understand that discourse reaches beyond words. In fact, discourse means a strongly bounded area of social knowledge within which the world is known. In this expanded sense, discourse not only gave George language to express his "heavy" feelings but also brought the racial dynamics of America and Britain into being. Through what was spoken and written, speakers and listeners, writers and readers, understood themselves, their relationships, and their places in a racialized world. Prominent white men of this era – such as David Hume, Immanuel Kant, Thomas Jefferson, and Georg Wilhelm Friedrich Hegel – built this racialized world when they wrote about Africans' ability to imagine powerful art and take a few giant steps up the Great Chain of Being.[13] For Black Loyalists like George and King, the laws – or discourses – governing slavery protected white people. At the same time, Black Loyalists' freedom through their writings and physical actions threatened white domination.

Is freedom the right word? Our inquiry into slavery of the Romantic period makes us wonder, since scholars use different iterations of the word. Instead of freedom, historian Jared Ross Hardesty examines "unfreedom," arguing that enslaved people in America inhabited a hierarchical world where they nonetheless decoded their new homeland, shaped the terms of their bondage, and used personal actions to weave themselves into the fabric of colonial society.[14] From the perspective of work alone, the opportunity to enjoy the fruits of their labor was more important to these individuals than abstract notions of freedom. Moreover, these less dramatic forms of influencing their fates helped enslaved people defy legal unfreedom while not openly challenging the so-called master class.

Perhaps freedom is not one univocal force but a set of practices – fragmentary, specific, never-quite-finished actions riven with daily complexities. Practices of freedom – according to Nelson – matter more than moments of revolution, a notion that seems vital in understanding Black Loyalists.[15] Nelson says revolutionary days – July 4, 1776, for instance – happen in a flash, whereas practices of freedom are ongoing engagements, liberations continually energized by inventive new ways of being. Certainly, the Black Radical Tradition of the Romantic period was bursting with literary, communal, and bodily practices of freedom, which have been understudied, according to Moten in his essay "Knowledge of Freedom." Moten turns to Romantic-era Black writers Olaudah Equiano and Mary Prince, calling Prince's refusal of the colonial lord, but acceptance of the Lord, the paradox at the heart of her text that raises questions such as "what is the relation between the knowledge of God (so deeply bound to heaven, the faint idea of a future state) and the knowledge of freedom (another, and one would hope more material, future state)?"[16]

We are interested in where Black Loyalists fit into discussions of freedom and unfreedom. To begin with, we offer a change in terminology. Rather than "freedom" or "unfreedom," we suggest that "(not)freedom" characterizes Black Loyalists' experiences and writings. We place parentheses around the word "not" to stress the contradictions in the binary freedom/unfreedom. (Not)freedom also captures the fragmentation, resistance, and transgression with which Black Loyalists lived. (Not)freedom furthermore highlights the forms of performative freedom Black Loyalists employed to get what they wanted. Most importantly, (not)freedom is our way of challenging conventional scholarly assumptions, a way to capture our readers' eyes, to make them think again about experiences of freedom that they take for granted.

Our touchstone for (not)freedom comes from nineteenth-century African American intellectuals who described how white Europeans and Americans refused to acknowledge how they used Africans to define themselves and build their economies. Indeed, African American Studies scholars like Moten would argue that this is still the case: Americans and Anglo-Americans to this day refuse to acknowledge the role enslaved Africans played in the building of their countries. Centuries of abuse created an internal struggle in African Americans that W. E. B. Dubois called "twoness – an American, a Negro; two souls; two thoughts, two unreconciled strivings; two warring ideals in one dark body, whose dogged strength alone keep it from being torn asunder."[17] This twoness is apparent in the absurdity of the national holiday established to celebrate freedom – Independence Day – as Frederick Douglass and Henry McNeal Turner make clear: "I shall see, this day, and its popular characteristics, from the slave's point of view," said Douglass in 1852. "Standing, there, identified with the American bondman, making his wrongs mine, I do not hesitate to declare, with all my soul, that the character and conduct of this nation never looked blacker to me than on this Fourth of July!"[18] "The Fourth of July – memorable in the history of our nation as the great day of independence to its countrymen – had no claim upon our sympathies," wrote Turner in 1866. "They made a flag and threw it to the heavens and bid it float forever; But every star in it was against us."[19] Turner's and Douglas's point is: Don't expect Africans – enslaved or free – to be excited about American and European "liberty" that is conceptualized on the subjugation of black bodies. Scholar Saidiya Hartman further nuances this sentiment, saying that white people used discourses of freedom to re-enslave Africans and other marginalized people.[20]

### Spectral Dwelling

Coleridge was a student at Cambridge in 1792 when he won a medal for his poem "Ode on the Slave Trade." Was he aware that European slave ships regularly arrived in and departed from Sierra Leone, a major slave-trading factory?[21] Had he heard about Black Loyalists? No one knows. What we do know is Coleridge was young, without direction, in debt, and suffering from depression that would plague his life. He was seeing ghosts and hearing voices – phenomena that would inhabit his writings from this period, especially *The Rime of the Ancient Mariner*. The *Rime* is filled with oceanic feelings even as it set among death, zombies, and phantoms, the murderous and the lost at sea. Scholars have robustly interpreted the *Rime* as a poem about slavery. Others point out the poem is about revolution in a time of slavery.[22] The French and American Revolutions stirred the Romantic world. So did revolts in Jamaica, South America, and, importantly, Haiti. The Haitian Revolution notably established the world's first Black republic, with its own Declaration of Independence abolishing the French colony and reinstating the original Taino name, Hayti. The point is that while slavery obsessed Romantic poets, they were also aware of the

Haitian Revolution, as William Wordsworth's sonnet "To Toussaint L'Overture," the great Haitian leader, acknowledges. Even so, most Romantic poets wrote about slavery more often than they versified about acts of Black self-liberation.

Coleridge's "Ode" is a case in point. Filled with pestilence, groans, cries, blood, roars, and death, the "Ode" recycles tired discourses of freedom circulating throughout Britain in the 1790s, a high point in antislavery rhetoric. Yet Coleridge's "Ode" is striking for how he imagines liberty as a return to Africa, the exact journey Black Loyalists would soon make. He has them flying on "murky wings" to "their fatherland," picturing how they will "dwellest with Liberty" ("spectral dwelling," in some translations) as they tell their loved ones "what terrible things . . . they suffered."[23] More than anything, the young Coleridge's rhetoric of freedom is eerie, as disembodied souls journey to Africa with the crashing waves of the transatlantic trade. Freedom as spectral dwelling is thus an infinite process of returning without ever arriving, an always unsettled trauma, never a true homecoming. (Not)freedom indeed.

## Unhomeliness

Freedom, as Nelson observes, is often cast as "freedom of movement," the ability to travel beyond intolerable living conditions, to find a better mode of dwelling.[24] Certainly, King practiced his (not)freedom on the move.[25] "I began to feel the happiness, liberty, of which I knew nothing before," writes King, referring to when he escaped his plantation and threw himself "into the hands of the English" (212). In fact, King lived between multiple lines of constraint. His memoirs are filled with stories of treacherous travel. Before he joined a British regiment, he'd journeyed throughout the American South by water, on foot, and on a saddled horse. He crossed rivers, sheltered with farmers, darted into thickets, stowed away on whaleboats, and had fearful dreams that "the world was on fire" (211). Still, King seized the chaotic times to assert his (not) freedom, the "lawless freedom and the struggle for freedom in unfreedom," to use Moten's words.[26]

That struggle meant eluding slave holders. After the war, plantation owners, George Washington foremost among them, tried to recapture people who had joined the British. Stories abounded of people who had "escaped from slavery and taken refuge in the English army" and then were "delivered up to their masters," according to King. He describes the "inexpressible anguish and terror" Loyalists felt, "especially when we saw our old masters coming from Virginia, North Carolina, and other parts, and seizing upon their slaves in the streets of New York, or even dragging them out of their beds" (217).

Nonetheless, King moved to New York City, where tens of thousands of Black Loyalists occupied tenement housing until the British made good on their promises. Some were transported to the Caribbean, others to England. More than 5,000 made a 22-day voyage to Halifax, Nova Scotia, in 1782, George and King among them. Once there, George became an itinerant minister, attracting both black and white audiences to camp meetings and mass baptisms. But freedom in this new land was even more fraught than before. One early historian wrote of white Loyalists: "They had not changed their views, in regard to the rights of Negroes, by being removed from a land where the two races had hitherto sustained the relation of master and slave."[27] Even so, George built a church on the banks of a river and led his followers, as he had in Silver Bluff, with emotionally potent discourse. George's church would have provided a unique opportunity for self-governance, mutual assistance, leadership development, and education for Black Loyalists. His church also undoubtedly generated competing understandings of displacement, racism, and emancipation, making it a threat to colonial administrators.[28] Almost inevitably, George's church on the riverbank was burned down by rioting whites.

Coleridge wrote dwelling as ghostly trauma in his "Ode," but George and his congregation, who lived out practices of (not)freedom, represented dwelling differently. The Christian rhetoric he and King used was in part a performance. They likely employed religious imagery slantwise, especially since both of their narratives were mediated through religious institutions – Baptist and Methodist. The postcolonial theory of Bhabha offers one way to think through the complexity of this (not)freedom predicament. Bhabha's concept of unhomeliness helps explain prominent rhetorical moves Black Loyalists made as they navigated their material conditions.[29] Unhomeliness, a negative twist on Coleridge's spectral dwelling, captures the sense of uncertainty these people experienced as they adjusted to new cultures. They had to decide which customs to adopt and which ones to avoid as they adapted to British, American, and then African contexts. Their sense of uncertainty must have intensified as they spread the Christian gospel to other Africans who were forced to accept second class citizenship or adopt subservient roles to survive. How free is one when freedom is contingent upon how well one acquiesces to the dominant discourses that oppress them?

As Bhabha further argues, colonial discourse – the Christian rhetoric King and George used in their memoirs – demands compliant subjects who reproduce its assumptions, beliefs, and values. That is, discourse that mimics the colonizer. Instead, colonial discourse produces ambivalent subjects whose mimicry is never far from mockery. Ambivalence describes the fluctuating relationship between mimicry and mockery. Bhabha contends that colonial discourse is compelled to be ambivalent because it never really wants colonial subjects to be exact replicas of the colonizer. This would be too threatening. In this respect, it's not necessarily disempowering for colonial subjects. Thus, ambivalence is akin to Black Loyalists's (not)freedom. When George writes: "the Lord took away my distress. I was sure that the Lord took it away, because I had such pleasure and joy in my soul, that no man could give me," and when King says, "All tormenting and slavish fear, and all the guilt and weight of sin were done away. I was so exceedingly blessed, that I could no longer conceal my happiness," they were likely mimicking freedom.[30] They became proficient at speaking the colonizer's language, adept at dramatizing its concerns, expert at acting within the ambivalent boundary marked off by colonial discourse: the liminal space of (not)freedom, like a dream of the world on fire.

## Utopian Dreams

As King and George were relocating to Nova Scotia, Coleridge was staging his own mimicry. In 1793, he left Cambridge depressed and in debt, and enlisted in the 15th Light Dragoons under a fabricated identity: Silas Tomkyn Comberbache. Whereas King and George joined the British military to gain a modicum of freedom, Coleridge found military service oppressive. Even under a false identity, military action disturbed him so much that he was unable to resume life at Cambridge. In June 1794, he made a walking tour of north Wales, where he met the poet Robert Southey. The two men spent a couple of weeks talking about the sorry state of Western civilization. When Coleridge returned to Cambridge, the poets wrote letters to one another where they developed a scheme called "Pantisocracy," based on their understanding of freedom. The word comes from the Greek meaning "government by all equally."

Coleridge and Southey originally planned to use land in Kentucky for an egalitarian community, but they quickly decided to emigrate instead to Pennsylvania, incidentally just 100 miles from New York City, the very place from which Black Loyalists were trying to escape. Coleridge and Southey finally settled on establishing their colony on the banks of the

Susquehanna River. They imagined twelve couples, men and women, who would raise their children apart from the corruptions of Europe. This would ensure a better future generation – seeds that would grow a healthy new crop of enlightened humans. Private property would be banned. The poets naively planned to have the men work a few hours per day to support the colony. The rest of the time they would read and write. Perhaps they intended to translate Ovid. The Pantisocracy scheme started to break down when Southey wanted to bring a servant along. Coleridge vehemently protested, abandoned Pantisocracy, and left Cambridge without a degree.

While some scholars argue that Pantisocracy was for Coleridge a literary experiment and never meant to be translated into action, we disagree. Coleridge married Sara Fricker specifically to emigrate to America, a union he would regret for the rest of his life and may not have agreed to if he thought the scheme was imaginary. But if Pantisocracy was more literary than literal, it stands in even greater contrast to the colonies of Nova Scotia and Sierra Leone. In these places, Black Loyalists made real wagers with their bodies and minds, moving through in-between spaces, swapping identities as they went, shapeshifting, improvising, surviving. Coleridge and Southey could "play" with emigrating to a utopian colony while Black Loyalists undertook treacherous voyages of emigration in order to survive, and, when they did, they found even more difficult living conditions.

## Translating Ovid

Coleridge was more vocally antislavery than most white writers, at least in his early work. Evidence suggests he may well have relied heavily on the poetry of African American poet Phillis Wheatley.[31] In fact, Wheatley provides crucial insight into Black social life for free Africans in the West as well as the influence of white Romantic rhetoric on freedmen and women like the Black Loyalists. Phillis Wheatley wrote before, during, and after the Revolutionary War. Literary historians speculate that she was about seven years old when she traveled the Middle Passage from Africa. Since she was transported after 1750, she probably traveled in the hull of the ship. Densely packed Africans in a slave ship was the trend as captains figured that the high mortality rate caused by the overcrowding was offset by the large number of people they could carry.

Her biographers speculate about Wheatley's experience in America based on historical accounts and documents about other enslaved Africans. She arrived on the Boston Dock shivering and near naked with only a piece of dirty rug around her, to be sold. What kind of indelible mark would this experience leave on such an extraordinarily perceptive and sensitive mind? Obviously too frail for labor and too young for breeding, she was bought because her mind was malleable. Many colonial ladies preferred such slaves so that they could be cast in the image of a Puritan New England domestic and companion. She learned English with the alacrity that bespeaks of genius. By age twelve, she took up the study of Latin, translating Ovid into English, and encountered the work of Alexander Pope, whose forms she used as a model for her poetry. Her accomplishments are all the more remarkable since there's no evidence that her instructor, eighteen-year-old Mary Wheatley, was any more proficient than most New England women, who possessed few books except the Bible, and weren't expected to read, far less to write. At fourteen Wheatley was a full-fledged poet, who some years later, as the colony's most esteemed slave, was granted an audience with its most esteemed slaveholder, George Washington. Despite Thomas Jefferson's explicit racism, he wrote: "Among the blacks is misery enough, God knows, but no poetry. Love is the peculiar oestrum of the poet. Their love is ardent, but it kindles the sense only, not the imagination. Religion indeed has produced a Phillis Wheatley; but it could not produce a poem."[32]

Besides being a precursor to the Black Radical Tradition, Wheatley enacts (not)freedom. In the gradations of place, she was in the cruelest situation. She was not allowed to mingle with enslaved Africans or consider them as equals, nor could she engage whites in conversations on equal terms, since many regarded her as the Wheatleys' servant. She inhabited a strange, ambiguous twilight zone between enslaved, freed Black, and white stepchild, cut off from any normal human contact with either community, denied the sustenance of group identity, doomed to a loneliness that, being particular and peculiar, was more tragic than the existentialist generalizations about the human condition.

Perceptive as she was, the poet probably knew she was at least equal, and most often superior, to the Boston Brahmins in intellectual accomplishment. But she was not their social equal at the dinner table. She could break bread with neither the white masters nor the enslaved Blacks. Even in this elemental nourishment she was alone.

While scholars have read Wheatley's poems for their subversiveness, we want to highlight her difficult position to enlarge the context for the writings of Black Loyalists and suggest their location in the Black Radical Tradition. Like Wheatley, Black Loyalists aligned themselves with the dominant culture to explore their (not)freedom. Their writings demonstrate an awareness of their political context and the implications of what they wrote. For Wheatley and Black Loyalists alike, their nuanced grasp of Biblical rhetoric was a conducive vehicle for making subtle yet effective statements against slavery. Rather than dodge the issue of slavery, they used their writing talent to wage war against racialized discourses about Black humanity and intellect. Thus, their methodology in this war included Biblical language and allusion whose implications were meant to turn from the practice of slavery the biblically aligned audiences of their day.

It's difficult to imagine that the irony implicit in the metaphor of slavery so often shouted from pulpits and splashed across newspapers was lost on Wheatley or the Loyalists. For her part, Wheatley drew explicit attention to it. In one of her earliest poems, "To the Right Honorable William, of Earl od Dartmouth," she refers to the "wrongs, and grievance unredress'd hand," attempts "t'enslave" the citizens of another "land" by depriving them of the rights that God and nature entitled them to. She prays "America" might never again experience "the iron chain" of such an outrageous injustice. In what was perhaps her strongest poetic comment on slavery, she recalls her own experiences while she was a child in Africa, when she:

> Was snatch'd from Afric's fancy'd happy seat:
> What pangs excruciating must molest,
> What sorrows labour in my parent's breast?
> Steel'd was that soul and by no misery mov'd
> That from a father seiz'd his babe belov'd
> Such, such my case. And can I then but pray
> Others may never feel tyrannic sway?[33]

## (Not)Freedom

Most Black Loyalists in Nova Scotia did not secure the land they'd been promised. Interest in emigrating to Sierra Leone materialized partly because of this continued (not)freedom, and partly because of the hardships of surviving in a landscape of cold winds and racial prejudice. In 1791, the frustrated settlers appointed Black Loyalist Thomas Peters as their representative. Peters traveled to England to petition the government for help. He returned with news that the Sierra Leone Company was offering to send willing Black Loyalists to the African colony called Freetown.

Freetown was conceived by white abolitionist Granville Sharp in 1786 as a self-governing community of former enslaved people resettled in their West African homeland – a real-life version of Coleridge's "Ode." However, that first colony failed. Peters's voyage to London to seek redress for Black Loyalists gave the Sierra Leone Company a second chance. John Clarkson, a naval officer and brother to the philanthropist and antislavery agitator Thomas Clarkson, was selected as governor. But David George was even more instrumental in establishing the African colony. Just as he had founded a church in the US to promote discourses of freedom, he activated his Nova Scotia congregation for African resettlement. Both George and King became fast friends with Clarkson. Nearly 2,000 Nova Scotian Black Loyalists sailed to Sierra Leone in 1792. King entered Freetown as a Methodist pastor in January. George arrived a few months later, where he preached the first Baptist sermon in Africa, walking ashore with his congregation singing hymns and celebrating deliverance.

Clarkson had assured the Black Loyalists free title to a piece of land in Africa. In fact, such a promise was outside the scope of his authority. The Sierra Leone Company was not offering land, which became a major point of contention for the Loyalists. Instead, the company charged annual rental fees on farmland worked by the new settlers. This exploitation, along with Clarkson's unfulfilled promise of land, turned the Loyalists' hope into bitter disappointment. Shortly after they moved in and built huts, heavy rains began. Malaria and dysentery broke out, and about ten Black Loyalists died. Two-thirds of the accompanying whites also died, while others returned to England. Clarkson became ill. That, coupled with the insubordination of his white colleagues and the lack of provisions, ignited emotional distress in the Black Loyalists. The letters they wrote him as he lived among them and after he returned to England register their escalating sense of betrayal.

Yet the letters are more than emotional missives. They are literary artifacts in their own right, especially because they were written by the settlers without the heavy editing done to George's and King's memoirs by white Baptists and Methodists. For example, one man, Andrew Moor, wrote to Clarkson shortly after arriving, telling him about his wife who had just delivered a daughter. Moor asked for "Some Nourishmen Such as Oat meal Molassis or Shugger a Little Wine and Spirits and Some Nut mig," adding "NB and one lb Candles for Light" (25). This simple, material ask – for spices, spirits, and, most importantly, the spiritual sustenance of candlelight – is powerful in its poignancy and poetic in its specificity, even as it exposes Black Loyalists' threadbare lives. As linguist Geneva

Smitherman asserts, "African slaves in America initially developed a pidgin, a language of transaction, that was used in communication between themselves and whites."[34] She points out that this "lingo ... developed without benefit of any formal instruction" and "involved the substitution of English for West African words, but with the same basic structure and idiom that characterized West African language patterns."

At the same time, it's clear that Black Loyalists used their "lingo" not just for transactions. They also employed it poetically. In another example, one hidden in plain sight, the Black Loyalist Susane Smith writes herself into history through the powerful symbolism of "sope." The original page written by Smith, housed in the Sierra Leone Collection at the University of Illinois at Chicago, reads:

> Sierra Leone May 12th 1792
> Sir I your hum bel Servent begs the faver of your Excelence to See if you will Pleas to Let me hav Som Sope for I am in great want of Some I hav not had aney Since I have bin to this plais I have bin Sick and I want to git Som Sope verry much to wash my famely Close for we ar not fit to be Sean for dirt –
> 
> Your hum             Susane Smith
> Bel Servet[35]

On the one hand, Smith's request is striking because it is one of the few letters in the Sierra Leone collection authored by a woman. But its real power is how raw and visceral it is. The letter works as metaphor or symbol partly because of its concreteness, and partly because of the cultural significance of soap as a commodity. Soap, at this juncture in British and American history, had become a fetishistic consumer item. Although daily washing was a routine domestic action, in the global economy soap was being bought and sold (not unlike enslaved people themselves), and that fact helped establish Britain's imperial superiority. That is, soap captured the odd conjunction between cleanliness, empire, and domesticity. The cleansing agent was a sign of the middle-class domestic space as well as a metaphor for the perceived difference between black and white skin. At the same time, white British imperial policy was anything but morally clean. Furthermore, as a material object, Susane Smith's letter is powerful. She penned her letter in sky-blue ink on a scrap of dirty parchment, which may be why one can't help notice how she repeats the need for soap several times. Smith reasons that she wants her family "fit to be Sean." Practically, she must keep them disease-free, but soap is also symbolic because it is a liquid object – a thing in transition from a plain household tool to a sign of maternal fitness in a culture that was morally unfit. Just as Coleridge's common seafaring images, such as the lighthouse and the albatross, became symbolically significant in his poem, Smith's letter proves what nuance an extended metaphor, and a mother, can hold.

In December 1792, Clarkson left Sierra Leone for England. He had intended to marry and return to the colony but never did. Two white men took charge during his absence, which the settlers found upsetting. In 1793, George sailed to England to visit Clarkson as discontent reigned in the colony. The following year, the settlers sent a group letter to Clarkson expressing the (not)freedom they labored under: "In Your Being here We wance did call it Free town but since your Absense – We have A Reason to call it A Town Of Slavery" (43). In desperation, the settlers then sent two representatives, Cato Perkins and Isaac Anderson, to London to speak to the Sierra Leone Company directors and beg Clarkson to return. But the directors had become increasingly suspicious of Clarkson, and they fired him. Perkins and Anderson were not even allowed to see their former governor, and they returned to Sierra Leone empty handed. Trouble grew. When Britain went to war with France in 1793, the French sacked Freetown. The settlers' discontent solidified over the following years and they came to interpret the French attack as the event that brought British rule to an end. Intense fights broke out between the Black Loyalists and the white authorities. "We are willing to shew that we cannot get justice from the White people," wrote Loyalist Nathaniel Wansey in 1800 (61). Thomas Ludlum, the white governor, and Isaac Anderson, a rebel leader, disagreed violently over the future of the colony. Some of the rebel Loyalists were thrown in prison.

### Mariners in the Middle Passage

When King wrote to Clarkson asking for a quire of paper in 1797, the governor sent the paper along with a reply in which he patronizingly advised King: "you must not quarrel with each other, or with your Rulers, but put up with little inconveniences to insure the future happiness of your posterity" (75). At the same moment as King's and Clarkson's letters crossed the Atlantic, Coleridge was contemplating the transatlantic trade. Struggling with chronic pain and opium addiction, he had moved to the Lake District, and in this bucolic landscape his life and work intersected explicitly with that of Black Loyalists. There Coleridge befriended Thomas Clarkson, brother of John Clarkson, the governor of Freetown. He most certainly would have learned about the Black Loyalists through this association. One day in 1797, Coleridge walked from his home in Nether Stowey, over the Quantock Hills, to the seaside town of Watchet, where he penned his haunted *Rime*.

Reading the *Rime* against the discourse of slavery is logical, especially given that Coleridge had a few years earlier, in 1795, delivered a seething lecture against the slave trade in Bristol, one of Britain's major slave-trading ports. He asked listeners to imagine themselves as bodies in the hull of a ship: "Would you choose to be sold? to have the hot iron hiss upon your breasts, after having been crammed into the hold of a Ship with so many fellow-victims, that the heat and stench arising from your diseased bodies, should rot the very planks?"[36] Coleridge was also concerned with slavery's opposite: freedom. In his 1798 poem "France: An Ode," he used "freedom," "liberty," and slavery to describe the errant French revolutionaries: "Slaves by their own compulsion! In mad game / They burst their manacles and wear the name / Of freedom, graven on a heavier chain!"[37] Shortly afterward, he reviewed a detailed tome written by Thomas Clarkson, *The History of the… Abolition of the African Slave-Trade*, for *The Edinburgh Review*.

Questions of freedom also plague the *Rime*, though no one in the poem has liberty. The mariner holds captive with his "glittering eye" and his "skinny hand, so brown" those to whom he tells of the crimes he committed at sea.[38] Furthermore, the spectral dwelling the poet imagined in his 1792 "Ode" is visited on the mariner himself. The ghostly flying back to Africa for the enslaved is not an option in the 1798 *Rime*. Instead, spectral dwelling permeates the mariner, his crew, and the ships they encounter. The crew drop dead and live ghoulishly as dead men. The mariner is zombie-like because, as much as he wants to, he cannot die. The other ship he meets is a "spectre-bark" helmed by "Night-mare Life-in-Death."[39] Even the hermit the mariner encounters at the poem's end is passing from one world to the next. He is the living dead, compared to leaves decaying in the forest. There is no home, no peace, no freedom, no dwelling, no declaration of independence for anyone in this apparitional world. It is the realm of uncertainty, alienation, and unhomeliness that Bhabha invokes.

## "Turn out the womans and Chill Dren"

We conclude this inquiry with the words of Black Loyalists, since our major argument is that, from the perspective of (not)freedom that pervaded the Romantic period, the voices of the Sierra Leone settlers must have a place alongside canonical white poets. We call attention to the final dispatch in the collection of forty-one letters from Isaac Anderson to Governor Ludlum. Anderson demands that Ludlum either release Black Loyalists being held captive, or send the women and children out of the fort in anticipation of a rebel attack: "September Sunday [1800] Mr Ludlow Sir we de sire to now wether you will let our Mends out if not turn out the womans and Chill Dren." This phrase "turn out the womans and Chill Dren" (65), a truly chilling utterance, is a way of saying "prepare for a bloody war". Here, Peters embodies, in a way canonical Romantics cannot, Black Atlantic identity, as he lives as immigrant and refugee, as he speaks out and against, throwing himself into liminal spaces even as he creates them, enacting (not)freedom at all costs. Previously, the form of the letter was reserved for legal redress. Now, it was direct resistance. Sending such a letter was a capital crime for which Isaac Anderson was duly tried, convicted, and hanged.

When David George was in England in 1792, he spent some time raising funds among Baptists for missionary activities in Africa. A year later, in 1793, he was back in Sierra Leone. He died there in 1810. Boston King journeyed to England in 1794, where he was mentored at a Methodist school near Bristol. When he sailed back to Sierra Leone in 1796, he went south to minister among the Sherbro people. He died there in 1802.[40] Still, George's and King's words live on. We hope the letters of the Sierra Leone settlers, and the mediated texts of George and King, can be more widely discussed in Romantic scholarship.

In sum, to broaden and deepen discussions about race and slavery in the context of Romanticism, the period can be viewed through practices of (not)freedom pioneered by those carving out the Black Radical Tradition. Because feelings of (not)freedom have continued beyond Romanticism. Mary Prince, after moving to England from the Caribbean, wrote grimly in her 1831 *History*: "I was free in England, and I might go and try what freedom would do for me, and be d – – d."[41] Across the Atlantic, (not) freedom was the response to enslavement, according to Harriet Tubman, who said "I freed thousands of slaves, I could have freed thousands more, if they had known they were slaves."[42] James Baldwin provides the best explanation of (not)freedom when he writes that "to be born in a free society and not be Born Free is to be born into a lie. To people told by co-citizens and co-Christians that you have no value, no history, have never done anything that is worthy of human respect destroys you because in the beginning you believe it."[43] (Not)freedom continues into the twentieth century, as Toni Morrison remarks in her neoslave narrative *Beloved* on the predicament of newly freed slaves: "Freeing yourself was one thing, claiming ownership of that freed self was another."[44] Morrison's words powerfully articulate the continuing struggle for black lives in a world of (not) freedom.

## Notes

1. *"Our Children Free and Happy": Letters from Black Settlers in Africa in the 1790s*, ed. Christopher Fyfe (Edinburgh: Edinburgh University Press, 1991), 54. All letters from the Black Loyalists quoted in this chapter come from this book, and further references will be given in the text.
2. Samuel Taylor Coleridge, *The Rime of the Ancient Mariner*, in *A Critical Edition of the Major Works*, ed. H. J. Jackson (Oxford: Oxford University Press, 1985), 51, 54.
3. Cedric J. Robinson, *Black Marxism: The Making of the Black Radical Tradition* (Chapel Hill: University of North Carolina Press, 2000), 245–46; George Lipstiz, "What Is This Black in the Black Radical Tradition," *Verso*, June 24, 2020, versobooks.com/blogs/4766-what-is-this-black-in-the-black-radical-tradition (accessed October 23, 2022).
4. James W. St. G. Walker, *The Search for the Promised Land in Nova Scotia and Sierra Leone 1783–1870* (Toronto: University of Toronto Press, 2017), 2; Mary Louise Clifford, *From Slavery to Freetown, Black Loyalists After the American Revolution* (Jefferson: McFarland, 1999), 191.
5. Walker, *The Search for the Promised Land*, 1.
6. Joanna Brooks and John Saillant, "Introduction," in *Face Zion Forward: First Writers of the Black Atlantic, 1785–1798*, ed. Joanna Brooks and John Saillant (Lebanon: Northeastern University Press, 2002), 6.
7. Walker, *The Search for the Promised Land*, 1.
8. C. S. Giscombe, "Our Variousness," in *Race, Romanticism and the Atlantic*, ed. Paul Youngquist (Farnham: Ashgate, 2013), 59–77.
9. See Benjamin Quarles, *The Negro in the American Revolution* (Chapel Hill: University of North Carolina Press, 1961), 119, and Sylvia R. Frey, *Water from the Rock: Black Resistance in a Revolutionary Age* (Princeton: Princeton University Press, 1991), 211.
10. David George, *An Account of the Life of Mr. David George, from Sierra Leone in Africa*, in *Face Zion Forward*, ed. Brooks and Saillant, 178–90.
11. Ruth Holmes Whitehead, *Black Loyalists: Southern Settlers of Nova Scotia's First Free Black Community* (Halifax: Nimbus Publishing, 2013).
12. George, *An Account of the Life*, 180.
13. Gates, *The Signifying Monkey*, 27.
14. Jared Ross Hardesty, *Unfreedom: Slavery and Dependence in Eighteenth-Century Boston* (New York: New York University Press, 2016).
15. Maggie Nelson, *On Freedom: Four Songs of Care and Constraint* (Minneapolis: Graywolf Press, 2021), 63.

16. Fred Moten, "Knowledge of Freedom," *CR: The New Centennial Review* 4/2 (2004), 301.
17. W. E. B. Debois, *The Souls of Black Folk* (Oxford: Oxford University Press, 2007), 8.
18. Frederick Douglass, *The Speeches of Frederick Douglass: A Critical Edition*, ed. John R. McKivigan, Julie Husband, and Heather L. Kaufman (New Haven: Yale University Press, 2018), 69.
19. Quoted in Mitchell Snay, *Fenians, Freedmen, and Southern Whites: Race and Nationality in the Era of Reconstruction* (Baton Rouge: Louisiana State University, 2010), 145.
20. Saidiya Hartman, *Scenes of Subjection: Terror, Slavery, and Self-Making in Nineteenth-Century America* (Oxford: Oxford University Press, 1997), 115.
21. Cassandra Pybus, *Epic Journeys of Freedom: Runaway Slaves of the American Revolution and Their Global Quest for Liberty* (Boston: Beacon Press, 2006), 140.
22. See Md. Monirul Islam, "Coleridge and 'Slavery's Spectres,'" *International Journal of Language and Linguistics* 1/2 (2014), 18; Malcolm Ware, "Coleridge's 'Spectre-Bark': A Slave Ship?" *Philological Quarterly* 40 (1961), 589.
23. Samuel Taylor Coleridge "Greek Prize Ode," trans. Anthea Morrison, "Samuel Taylor Coleridge's Greek Prize Ode on the Slave Trade," in *An Infinite Complexity: Essays in Romanticism*, ed. J. R. Watson (Edinburgh: Edinburgh University Press, 1983), 145–60.
24. Nelson, *On Freedom*, 187.
25. Boston King, *Memoirs of the Life of Boston King, a Black Preacher, Written by Himself, during his Residence at Kingswood-School*, in *Face Zion Forward*, eds. Brooks and Saillant, 210–32. Further references will be given in the text.
26. Fred Moten, *Stolen Life (Consent Not to Be a Single Being)* (Durham, NC: Duke University Press, 2018), 55–56.
27. Walter H. Brooks, D. D., *The Silver Bluff Church: A History of Negro Baptist Churches in America* (Washington, DC: Press of R. L. Pendleton, 1910), 22.
28. Brooks and Saillant, "Introduction," 12; Barbara Ransby, *Making All Black Lives Matter: Reimagining Freedom in the Twenty-First Century* (Los Angeles: University of California Press, 2018), 195–96.
29. Homi K. Bhabha, *The Location of Culture* (London: Routledge, 1994), 25–107.
30. George, *An Account of the Life*, 180; King, *Memoirs*, 221.
31. John C. Shields, *Phillis Wheatley and the Romantics* (Knoxville: University of Tennessee Press, 2010).
32. Thomas Jefferson, *Notes on the State of Virginia* (London: John Stockdale, 1786), 267.
33. Phillis Wheatley, *The Poems of Phillis Wheatley with Letters and Memoir* (Mineola: Dover Publications, 2010), 33–34.
34. Geneva Smitherman, *Talkin and Testifyin: The Language of Black America* (Detroit, MI: Wayne State University Press, 1986), 5.

35. Susane Smith to John Clarkson, May 12, 1792, SLEO_0001_0005_0001, Sierra Leone Collection, University of Illinois at Chicago Library, https://collections.carli.illinois.edu/digital/collection/uic_sierra/id/91/.
36. Samuel Taylor Coleridge, "Lecture on the Slave Trade," *Lectures 1795: On Politics and Religion*, ed. Lewis Patton and Peter Mann (London: Routledge & Kegan Paul, 1971), 249.
37. Samuel Taylor Coleridge, "France: An Ode," in *A Critical Edition of the Major Works*, ed. H. J. Jackson (Oxford: Oxford University Press, 1985), 92.
38. Coleridge, *Rime*, 54.
39. Coleridge, *Rime*, 52–53, 57.
40. Vincent Carretta, *Unchained Voices: An Anthology of Black Authors in the English-Speaking World of the Eighteenth Century* (Lexington: University Press of Kentucky, 2003), 392, 395.
41. Mary Prince, *The History of Mary Prince, A West Indian Slave, Related by Herself* (London: F. Westley and A. H. Davis, 1931), 19.
42. Alonford James Robinson, "Free Blacks in the United States," in *Africana: The Encyclopedia of the African and African American Experience*, ed. Kwame Anthony Appiah and Henry Louis Gates Jr. (Oxford: Oxford University Press, 1999), 710.
43. James Baldwin, "James Baldwin … In Conversation," prepared by Dan Georgakas, *Arts in Society* 3/1 (1966), 555.
44. Toni Morrison, *Beloved* (New York: Knopf Doubleday, 2004), 111.

CHAPTER 6

# Disability and Race

*Essaka Joshua*

When Henry Highland Garnet gave his influential "Call to Rebellion" speech before the National Negro Convention in Buffalo, New York, in 1843, he employed an important set of abolitionist tropes relating to disability. The first called attention to the injury done to a race: "Two hundred and twenty-seven years ago the first of our injured race were brought to the shores of America."[1] Here, he alludes to a moral injury while evoking the physical, mental, and emotional injuries that are caused by or symbolize enslavement. The second trope refers to intellectual abilities that were used to define racial hierarchy. Addressing the convention, Garnet warns: "your intellect has been destroyed as much as possible, and every ray of light they have attempted to shut out from your minds" (281). In this way, Garnet holds intellectual enlightenment as an ideal of citizenship. Denying education to enslaved people harms them, he argues, and causes their "oppressors themselves" ruination, as they "become weak, sensual, and rapacious" (281). The third trope references the irrationality, strength, and savagery of animals. The dehumanizing oppressors, Garnet says, "endeavor to make you as much like brutes as possible ... They buy and sell you as though you were brute beasts" (281–83). As these examples show, the rhetoric of racial politics is deeply concerned with notions of intellectual ability as a qualifier for humanity and citizenship, and the injured body is a shorthand for the harm caused by the violence of slavery.

Recent debates over injury rhetoric and visual imagery associated with physical suffering have highlighted some of the problematic aspects of this usage in the context of race. For example, Courtney R. Baker notices the resistance to talking about the vulnerability of Black people in a way that could be misconstrued as sentimental. Baker cites Debra Walker King's compelling statement about the problematic paradox of continuing to use this kind of visual and verbal image: "black people disappear while their bodies are constantly renewed as memorials to suffering."[2] Importantly, Baker switches our attention to how we look at images of Black bodies in pain. While the injured African is a powerful image for promoting change, Baker suggests that this kind of rhetoric does not seem to halt the dehumanizing of Black people. The pain of the sufferers, the trauma of those who witness it, and the narrowing of the Black cultural presence to violent imagery are important concerns for anyone who engages with this material, as modern perspectives on race acknowledge. The implications for understanding the cultural presence or copresence of disability in these contexts is also a matter of concern. While the rhetoric of injury and pain are powerful signifiers of moral, physical, and mental harm, disability studies perspectives invite us to think about ability and aesthetic difference as politicized concepts that have consequences for disabled people. The injured African trope connects race with disability oppression and social systems that privilege able-bodied and able-minded norms, raising questions about how we talk about race and disability together.

Although we might think of a disability as a biological reality, the term 'disability' references a category whose meaning undergoes complex shifts and variations throughout history. The earliest definitions of "disability" refer solely to incapacity in general, and not specifically to people. According to the *Oxford English Dictionary*, this remains its primary meaning: the "want of ability (to discharge any office or function); inability, incapacity, impotence" (earliest source 1580). The use of the word to describe a range of people with different kinds of impairments does not begin to emerge until the 1830s, with the administrative systems established by the British Poor Laws. In this context, disability describes an inability to work. In general usage, our modern definition of "disability," when specifically applied to people, refers both to the cause of the inability (the disabling condition) and the inability resulting from the condition: the effect. Identifying disability as the effect of one's impairments is known in disability studies as the medical model of disability. The medical model supposes that disability is determined solely by a person's bodily or mental condition. This is challenged by the social model, or a relational understanding of disability. The social model uses 'impairment' for a bodily or mental condition and 'disability' for the disadvantages that arise from the interaction between a condition and its surrounding context. Describing what people can do is different from describing how they look. The aesthetic evaluations of an impairment are often understood in the Romantic period as a separate issue from ability. For instance, some conditions that we would now refer to as function impairments, such as scoliosis, would previously have been thought of in aesthetic terms, as deformities. Aesthetic differences were often subject to social disablement.

The *Oxford English Dictionary* (3rd ed.) defines race in the following manner: "According to various more or less formal attempted systems of classification: any of the (putative) major groupings of humankind, usually defined in terms of distinct physical features or shared ethnicity, and sometimes (more controversially) considered to encompass common biological or genetic characteristics." The earliest usage is 1735. This definition of race is grounded in the eighteenth-century philosophical, anthropological, and physiological studies that sought to taxonomize race. There are, of course, earlier forms of racialization, such as blackness as a stigmatized characteristic or marker of difference. Like disability, race is a heterogeneous group term that encompasses diverse subgroups, and that is commonly understood to be constructed from socially determined and biologically based identifiers.

While definitions of disability and race are important, much of the modern discussion of disability and race focuses on what we mean when we say *and*. When we start thinking about how disability relates to race, we might ask, for instance: What is our understanding of disability when it is used as a marker of race? Does the use of ability concepts in taxonomies of race mean that race and disability are interrelated social constructs? Is disability-based discrimination like race-based discrimination? Can we talk about racialized disabled people in ways that separate race and disability?

My discussion will also focus on this relationality. The first part is organized around two modes of comparison between disability and race in literature: *similarity* and *combination*. By 'similarity' I mean that disability and race function in ways that are analogous. 'Combination' refers to a range of closer relationships, such as the characteristics of one being used to describe the other, or the idea that the two are inseparable or mutually constitutive. This framework (similarity and combination) includes but is not restricted to racialized disabled people and characters. I shall end with a discussion of disability and race as *different*. This is an important element in abolitionist debates, where writers and campaigners argue for the acceptance of Black people as human beings with intellectual and emotional capacities equal to those of whites by distancing the conflation of blackness and disability. It is worth acknowledging that, while discussions of disability and race may not always overtly acknowledge gender, sexuality, class, financial status, or other attributes, these attributes are nevertheless also relevant.

## Disability and Race: Similarities

The central issue in this approach to disability and race is that the injustices that face people who are disabled are like those that face racialized people, and vice versa. For example, a person excluded from mainstream education because of race and a person prohibited because of a disability are possibly rejected on the basis of perceived biological differences or assumptions about intelligence. Encounters with *institutional* racism (within organizations) or *systemic* racism (across society and institutions more broadly) may be akin to experiences of institutional or systemic ableism. For example, disability theorist Fiona Kumari Campbell compares internalized racism with internalized ableism.[3] Campbell argues that internalized ableism involves consciously or unconsciously disavowing one's disability, passing, and emulating ableist norms. Infantilization is a further experience shared by disabled people and racialized people.[4] Approaching disability and race through similarities usually involves setting aside as a separate consideration the discussion of people who are both racialized and disabled (e.g., a Black African blind person) and assuming that the categories of disability and race are distinct or can be discussed separately.

Discussions of the similarities between disability and race involve comparisons of experiences of discrimination, disenfranchisement, and stigma, but they also include attempts to understand the emergence of group identities and shared pride. In his provocatively titled article "Uncle Tom and Tiny Tim," Leonard Kriegel proposes that the situation of African Americans in the 1960s is an analogy for people with mobility impairments who sought to discover a positive personal and group identity and a way to resist social oppression.[5] Kriegel's article is partly a personal memoir and partly a sociological reflection on acquiring a mobility impairment in his youth. Influenced by Goffmanian sociology, Kriegel argues that the social difficulties encountered by people with mobility impairments are analogous to the bias against Black people in white-dominated societies. He writes, "my crutches are as visible as a black man's skin, and they form a significant element, probably the most significant element, in the way in which I measure myself against the demands of the world" (414). Kriegel concludes that the situation of disabled people in the 1960s is more fraught than that of African Americans, because he thinks that any sense of collective identity for disabled people is based on shame rather than pride, and that the absence of social and political organizations leaves disabled people isolated. Importantly, it is likeness, but not sameness, that is emphasized in this kind of approach to the relationality of disability and race.

In the Romantic period, such race analogies are prominent in the debates about deaf education and deaf cultural separateness. For example, "Progress of the Deaf" (1838), an article in *The Monthly Chronicle*, observes that "deaf-mutes ... have peculiarities not less striking than what often constitutes the characteristics of a remote tribe, or a distinct race."[6] The anonymous author asserts that it is not necessary to search for exotic objects of study abroad, when the deaf "may be studied with an interest not less lively, with advantages not less important" (154). A deaf person in the nineteenth century, as the disability studies historian Douglas Baynton observes, was often perceived to be an outsider: "not an Englishman, a German, a Frenchman, or a member of any nationality, but ... a man without a country."[7] Race is evoked in other ways, too, in connection with deafness. Affinity between Native Americans and deaf signers was often alluded to in the periodical press. Native American sign language was believed by some commentators to be "employed by many savage tribes to supply the paucity of expression in their language, or to communicate with other tribes."[8] The naturalness and primitiveness, as well as the utility, of sign language paradoxically linked deaf people both to the idea of the noble savage and to the intellectual advances associated with the enlightenment. The systematization of deaf sign in the eighteenth century was considered to be a triumph of enlightenment thinking.

The injury rhetoric that we see in Garnet's rebellion speech is present in Anglophone literature concerning the inaccessibility of deaf education. Deaf people are spoken about in the poetry of the early nineteenth century as an injured race, incarcerated or chained by their condition, with intellects that have been destroyed. In his narrative poem "Emma," in *Tales of the Deaf* (1835), the deaf American poet John Robertson Burnet describes deaf education as emancipatory in the sense that it is a release from imprisonment. Addressing education, he opines,

> Thousands, – nay millions, heaven born minds to keep
> Of ignorance the lowest – darkest deep,
> Where prejudice clinch'd fast the chains of fate,
> And barr'd their dungeon with a mountain's weight;
> Thou com'st! the mountain's weight is roll'd away,
> The dungeon is unbarr'd, the chains give way,
> And thy hand leads the rescu'd captives forth
> To light and life and happiness on earth;
> Nay more, – thou sett'st their footsteps on the road
> Which leads them to their father and their God![9]

For Burnet, to be uneducated and deaf is to be bereft of language, "lock'd up" in an "intellectual night" (189). Like Garnet, Burnet also uses the rhetoric of brutishness. The uneducated deaf are "link'd with the brutes" and are "savages with minds more all debas'd" and "hearts a wild uncultivated waste" (189, 190). To educate the deaf is "To lift the savage to the rank of man / And cultivate the moral wild" (190). Burnet's attitude toward deaf education is reminiscent of colonial missionaries enlightening the "heathen darkness" (190). Imagining a world where there is wider access to deaf education, Burnet asserts that the injury of "this smitten, once degraded race" will be "In mind and feeling, to *themselves* restor'd" (192). The deaf New York poet James Nack offers similar sentiments in "The Minstrel Boy" (1827). Here, a lack of education means that deaf people are "Denied the rights of man, as to employ / Those rights incapable." Both poems echo sentiments seen in the wider campaigns for deaf education, such as Charles Orpen's *The Contrast* (1829), which uses emancipation and salvation claims grounded in Christian theology, the abolitionist movement, and the enlightenment principle of "the progress of humanity."[10]

Romantic-era discussions of madness also use race analogies in the context of forced incarceration in asylums. John Thomas Perceval, a son of the prime minister, Spencer Perceval, in his account of surviving the psychiatric system of the early nineteenth century, regards the treatment he received at Edward Long Fox's lunatic asylum, Brislington House, as a form of enslavement. He comments that "the lunatic doctor treats his patient as a slave driver does his slave."[11] It was, however, a confusing form of slavery, he remarks. John Thomas Perceval is outraged that he is under the control of base keepers who do not acknowledge his situation: "Let me, if I am to be a slave, be at least the slave of men of enlightened and liberal minds – and let me know it – let me understand my position – do not call slavery a benefit – my slave-kennel an asylum" (214). Although he evokes the humanitarian arguments put forward in the antislavery campaigns, Perceval nevertheless distances himself from this alliance.

These accounts of Romantic-era deafness and madness reveal the racialized discourse surrounding disability and deafness. Injustices and discrimination are found to be similar in the case of race and disability, because of the comparable situations regarding educational exclusion, cultural difference, and the curtailment of liberty. Injury rhetoric and ideas about intellectual enlightenment and brutishness connect the racialized and disabled subject, providing the cause of disabled and deaf people, who are not given the opportunity to flourish, with a sense of urgency. As scholars such as Anna Mollow have pointed out, however, "if race and disability are conceived of as discrete categories to be compared, contrasted, or arranged in order of priority, it becomes impossible to think through complex intersections of racism and ableism in the lives of disabled people of color."[12]

## Disability and Race: Combinations

Most modern scholarship treats disability and race as a combined category. Much of the discussion of disability and race has centered on the reasons for their inseparability and on understanding how they combine. When disability and race are considered together, there is a range of different ways of approaching these combinations. We may see disability and race as in some sense overlapping or intersecting (joining with other traits), or as "mutually constitutive" (i.e., coconstructed). The concept of the mutual constitution of disability and race is quite malleable. Sometimes, multiple approaches to the idea of combination operate at the same time in the same discussion. Using intersectionality and mutual constitution, for example, Liat Ben-Moshe introduces the term "race-ability" (a play on "dis-ability") to conceptualize "race and ability, and racism, sanism, and ableism as intersecting oppressions" that "are mutually constitutive and cannot be separated." Feminist scholars of color, such as Kimberlé Crenshaw and Nirmala Erevelles, have theorized extensively about intersectionality, questioning theories of identity that privilege one characteristic (e.g., race, class, disability, gender), or place characteristics in a hierarchy, or in "separate systems of oppression."[13]

The idea of the mutual constitution of disability and race has a relatively long history in disability studies. Rosemarie Garland Thomson argues that disability helps explain how "other systems of representation ... intersect and mutually constitute each other." Building on this idea, Sharon Snyder and David Mitchell suggest that disability is a "keystone" in different systems of bodily disqualification. Ellen Samuels uses the metaphor of a shadow to suggest that disability is often an unacknowledged element in the background when systems of oppression are evoked.[14] For Samuels, disability and race are "deeply connected, mutually constituted, and entangled" (24). More recently, Alison M. Parker's comments give an idea of the theoretical trajectory of this concept, when she advises that we can no longer treat disability, race, and gender as separate identities; these are, Parker observes, interrelated "systems of power." Moving away from the idea of disability and race being in some sense built together, Paul Lawrie argues that the categories of disability and race are "mutually reinforcing" in the way that they place value on certain kinds of bodies. Therí Pickens similarly sets aside the idea of coconstruction, employing the metaphor of focal differentiation. She suggests that disability and race come into view at different times, even as they are "interrelated and simultaneously present." Pickens reminds us to think about the disability part when we think of disability and race as mutually constitutive.[15]

One prominent example of disability and race as coconstructed in the nineteenth century is John Langdon Down's 1866 "classification of the feeble minded by arranging them around various ethnic standards." Down uses terms such as Malay, Mongol, and Ethiopian to describe different forms of idiocy that he sees as genetic throwbacks from supposedly less evolved races. Down racializes disability to prove that different types of intellectual impairment are indicative of the possibility of racial regression, and that this means that there is one human species. Here disability and race are not merely similar, but are understood to be inseparable. Treating disability as a characteristic of race has a long history, however. Early anthropological or medicalized accounts of racial characteristics and hierarchies make judgments about the intellectual and physical capacities of races that play a significant role in the justifications for slavery and colonialism. Discourses of racial hierarchy also persist in the colonial setting, with opium addiction, indolence, and alcoholism associated with racial othering. For example, in Maria Edgeworth's "The Grateful Negro" (*Popular Tales*, 1804), "Mr. Jefferies considered the negroes as an inferior species, incapable of gratitude, disposed to treachery, and to be roused from their natural indolence only by force: he treated his slaves, or rather suffered his overseer to treat them, with the greatest severity." Furthermore, travel accounts associated non-European peoples with idiotism. Scientific discussions often present some races as lacking in intellectual capacity and unable to self-govern, and thus treat racialized people as disabled.[16]

Some claims for the intellectual inferiority of the enslavable were based on ideologies that maintained that one's capacity for physical work made one nonhuman, or "brutish" (animal-like) and uncivilized. The term "brute" was commonly used of people with intellectual disabilities, of people supposed incapable of rational thought, and of "uncivilized" people. For example, in "On the Phrenology of Hindostan" (1824), the Scottish physician George Murray Paterson describes his visit to a lunatic asylum in Calcutta. Observing the inhabitants, he is "struck by the truncated foreheads of the idiots" and by "a Malay girl ... who had no more regard for her person and habits than a brute." In this case, the girl's lunacy is also elided with how her race is viewed. Gayatri Chakravorty Spivak views Bertha Mason, in *Jane Eyre* (1847), similarly as a "figure produced by the axiomatics of imperialism" that "renders the human/animal frontier as acceptably indeterminate." This indeterminacy is just as much a product of empire as it is an instance of ableism. Bertha's "madness" and proximity to Blackness aligns her with the nonhuman and with racialized ableism.[17]

Racializing disability in this way is, of course, distinct from another way of combining disability and race: the case of people who, for instance, are both blind and of African descent. It is different again if we add sexuality or gender. As Sami Schalk defines it, "Black disability studies scholarship traces how disability has appeared among Black people, how disability has been treated and understood within Black communities, and how Blackness and disability have been – and continue to be – discursively linked in various cultures."[18] In the Romantic period, the testimonies of enslaved people include many emotive accounts of the disfigurements and disablements acquired through violence. Torture, starvation, overwork, and injury all affected enslaved and colonized people. Slavery required mental and physical endurance at a level that was inhumane, disabling, and often fatal. Trauma, depression, suicide, and despair appear frequently.

For example, in his 1789 memoir, the formerly enslaved writer Olaudah Equiano recalls being "brought ... very low; so that I became a burden to myself, and viewed all things around me as emptiness and vanity, which could give no satisfaction to a troubled conscience."[19] In 1831, Mary Prince describes the condition of her feet and legs while being forced to work on a salt farm in Turks Island (Grand Turk, Turks and Caicos). Prince was made to stand "in the salt water for so many hours" that her limbs "soon became full of dreadful boils, which eat down in some cases to the very bone."[20] She laments that no allowances were made for illness: "my tasks were never ended. Sick or well it was work – work – work" (21)! Poor old Daniel, she recalls, "was lame in the hip" and unable to keep up to the expected pace, and was punished for it. Sarah, who was "almost past work" and had "several bodily infirmities" and "was not right in the head," is killed by her master once she is no longer productive. Prince herself became physically disabled by rheumatism ("became quite a cripple") and used a stick (25). She describes being left without medical care: "For several months I could not lift the limb. I had to lie in a little old out-house, that was swarming with bugs and other vermin, which tormented me greatly;

but I had no other place to lie in" (25). Eventually, a neighbor is moved to "send an old slave woman to help me, who sometimes brought me a little soup" (25). Memoirs of enslaved people reveal that impairments (bodily and mental conditions) and disabilities (disabling contexts) occur because of race, and the evidence that these accounts provide of the "injured race" signals disability's importance in the abolitionist context.

The interconnections between racialized and disabled bodies are particularly apparent where racialized bodies are on display. William Earle's account of a slave revolt in *Obi; or, The History of Three-Fingered Jack* (1800), for example, uses enfreakment to signal the emblematic and religious power of its title character. The novel takes the form of letters written from Jamaica by an abolitionist, George Stanford, to his friend, Charles, in England. The correspondence is initiated by the concerns on the island about an imminent slave revolt led by Jack. Stanford describes Jack as "nearly seven feet in height," hinting at the giants of the fairs.[21] Jack's hand impairment is mentioned three times in the first five paragraphs: "Jack!!! And his cursed three fingers!!!"; "Jack, his three fingers and his Obi, and all that belongs to him"; "the three-fingered one" (69). Ironically, Stanford is conscious of the injury to his own hands caused by his excessive writing, creating echoes of Jack in himself: "—fingers cramped—and my little finger wears as fine a polish as an agate" (82).

Symbolic uses of Black disability that evoke traditional practices are a powerful mode of simultaneously othering and enabling. *Hamel, The Obeah Man* (1827), by Cynric R. Williams, destabilizes race, gender, and disability through its multiple characters who fake each category. In this novel, an unnamed blind African man possesses an uncanny quality, and vanishes inexplicably into a lagoon, which we later discover has a secret underwater exit. We are told that the lagoon must be "bewitched: if such a creature as this is once seen gliding about in this fashion."[22] He is, however, faking blindness, having been taught by Roland, a corrupt and hypocritical Methodist missionary. Although "he walks as if he were blind," he seems to be able to "dissolve himself into the elements" (185). The inconsistency of the abilities of the "strange blind man" reinforces the idea of his collusion with Obeah practices (184). The man is forced to mimic blindness, however, because he is a witness to Roland's killing of a child. The blind man's appearances in the novel are brief, but his physical similarity to Hamel makes him emblematic of the novel's mysterious and defiant hero who wields power via his knowledge of other characters' secrets. Disabled witnesses, such as nonspeaking, idiot, or blind characters, were a staple of melodrama on the stage. Here the disabled impostor figure gains advantage from the combination of Black and disabled identities that imply that he is otherworldly.

The display of Saartje Bartman (as "the Hottentot Venus"; see Chapter 12) and Chang and Eng Bunker (as "the Siamese Twins") has received much scholarly attention. Their celebrity focused as much on their racial othering as on the exhibition of their bodies for their aesthetic differences. Nadja Durbach observes that the exhibition of Bartman "ultimately collapsed the categories of the ethnographic type and the freak of nature and discouraged audiences from distinguishing between a body that was anomalous in relation to the human species and one that merely diverged from the white British 'norm.'" Paul Youngquist observes similar connections between enfreakment and racialization in his exploration of monstrosity. Youngquist presents the Romantic era as a time when "singular bodies become subject to regulatory norms in liberal society."[23] Youngquist centers the idea of "the proper body" as normative (xv). For him, Bartman's "remarkable buttocks and genitalia came to identify deviant sexuality with blackness" (57).

Political opinions about slavery were also associated with disablement. For example, support for abolition could be diagnosed as a psychological impairment. In his *An Appeal to the Earl Bathurst* (1828), Joseph Clayton Jennyns, a white English former magistrate in the united colonies of Demerara and Essequibo, uses the term "negro-mania" to characterize white support of abolition. Enraged by movements toward the abolition of slavery in the colonies (which was eventually abolished in 1833), Jennyns describes support for abolition as a "phrenzied enthusiasm."[24] He asks for protection "against the contagion of wild and impracticable politics" (9). The symptoms included "real insensibility," "dangerous absurdities," and "loud harangues on the pretended oppression of strangers they have never seen" (7–8). Such usages of disability reinforce a narrow sense of normative behavior, stigmatizing madness and diagnosing it through symptoms that have currency in political contexts. Here, white sympathy with Black subjugation disables whiteness, demonstrating the ideological power of disability in racialized systems of oppression.

### Disability and Race: Differences

Douglas Baynton reveals the centrality of disability to the great "citizenship debates of the nineteenth and early twentieth centuries: women's suffrage, African American freedom and civil rights, and the restriction of immigration."[25] Disability is evoked in the egalitarian debates of the

Romantic era, too, where enslaved people are deemed qualified for or deserving of freedom, on account of their abilities. For example, Mary Wollstonecraft explores at length the apparent physical and intellectual weakness of women as a form of enslavement, arguing that women are potentially physically and intellectually strong and therefore qualified for rights. The differences between disability and race are often evoked in abolitionist debates, where enslaved people are deemed to be qualified for, or deserving of, freedom based on their abilities. Abolitionists emphasized intellectual capacity and the capacity for refined emotions (or, as I shall term it, Black sensibility) to raise the status of Black people. Here disability is assumed to be a disqualifier for equality. Abolitionism involved reminding the public of the suffering of people subjected to enslavement; it also involved advocating for the intellectual capacity of enslaved people. Dissociating racial classification from intellectual inferiority was an important response to early accounts of racial hierarchies. The work of the enslaved African American poet Phillis Wheatley, for example, was published with a signed declaration by educated white men that she had "been examined by some of the best Judges, and is thought qualified to write them."[26]

The anonymously written novel *The Woman of Colour* (1808) challenges both gender and racial norms through emphasizing the physical and mental strength of its heroine, Miss Olivia Fairfield. Olivia is the daughter and heiress of a white Jamaican planter and an enslaved African woman. While the novel keeps in place many of the common stereotypes about slavery, Olivia's liminal status as a biracial woman challenges the status quo. The novel is unusual in that it shares more with novels of sensibility than it does with dominant narratives of enslavement and escape that we see elsewhere in the cultural archive pertaining to people of color. Olivia is imagined in a normative situation, and even as a paragon. Her "mind and form," for instance, "were cast in no common mould," as "her understanding and capacity" and her "energy" raise her "above the standard of her sex."[27] *The Woman of Colour* counters the suggestion that Olivia is intellectually and physically inferior but demonstrates that her context is disabling by placing her in a white courtship narrative that deems her deformed. Treating racialized bodies as deformed is a significant aspect of othering in the Romantic era. Abolitionist literature, however, occasionally challenges the idea of associating Africans with deformity. Equiano, for example, begins *The Interesting Narrative* with memories of his African childhood, characterizing his people as without any kind of deformity: "Deformity is indeed unknown amongst us, I mean that of shape" (38).

Being free of deformities, he suggests, marks his people as deserving of dignity, setting them apart from the white people who enslaved them.

While abolitionists emphasized the able-mindedness of enslaved people and their ability to suffer, by contrast, the arguments in favor of slavery emphasize able-bodiedness to the extent that bodies are commodified via their capacities. In antislavery contexts, the connections between animal-like strength or savagery (brutishness) and enslavability are often dissociated. Equiano, for example, protests against the cruelty of "these human butchers who cut and mangle the slaves in a shocking manner on the most trifling occasions, and altogether treat them in every respect like brutes" (109). In "The Sorrows of Yamba" (1795), Hannah More refers to enslaved people being "driven like cattle to a fair." William Cowper's "The Negro's Complaint" (1788) rejects brutishness as a reason for enslavement:

> Deem our nation brutes no longer,
> Till some reason ye shall find
> Worthier of regard and stronger
> Than the colour of our kind.[28]

William Lloyd Garrison, writing in his preface to *Narrative of the Life of Frederick Douglass, An American Slave* (1845), likewise complains that according to the slave code a Black man is "adjudged to be as incompetent to testify against a white man, as though they were indeed a part of the brute creation."[29] When he hears Douglass give his first speech, Garrison is awestruck by Douglass's physical and intellectual capacities: "There stood one, in physical proportion and stature commanding and exact – in intellect richly endowed – in natural eloquence a prodigy – in soul manifestly 'created but a little lower than the angels' – yet a slave, ay, a fugitive slave, – trembling for his safety" (3–4). Here Garrison rehearses the abolitionist argument that separates disability and race by disavowing supposed limited capacities. He argues that Douglass is "capable of high attainments as an intellectual and moral being" and would be "an ornament to society and a blessing to his race," if he were not treated as "a piece of property, a beast of burden, a chattel personal" (4). Brutishness is, instead, rescripted onto the personas of oppressors. The Creole planter, in James Montgomery's poem *The West Indies* (1807), for instance, possesses "the vague brute instinct of an idiot mind."[30]

Ideological justifications for slavery drew on capacity-based arguments to provide support. The enslavable were deemed to be inferior according to intellectual, aesthetic, and cultural value systems. People of color were positioned as having superior physical abilities, but inferior intellectual abilities, when compared with whites. Widening ideas about who could express refined feeling (Black sensibility) is an important element in dissociating enslaved and racialized people from conventions about defects. Dissociating concepts of disability and deformity from race was a powerful rhetorical response to their use as justifications for oppression.

## Conclusion

The government-sanctioned mass enslavement of people of African descent is one of the most prominent arenas in which disability and race are considered together in the Romantic period, due to the scale, brutality, and economic impact of slavery. Slavery was based on exploiting the abilities of human beings by limiting their education, controlling their migration and imprisoning them in a biopolitical system that removed their autonomy. There are many contexts in which ideas about disability and race come into contact. For example, organizations, scientists, and state machineries treated racialized people in ways that some writers of the period regarded as comparable to disabled people. Both groups were subjected to incarceration without criminal convictions. Moreover, anthropological and medical classification systems, beginning in the early eighteenth century, trace the interconnectedness of disability and race through ability hierarchies and aesthetic evaluation. Even the use of sophisticated language as a marker of humanity (and of one's rights to autonomy or citizenship) is as important in the case of enslaved people as it is for disabled people, as cultural capital is generated by the right kind of communication. The socioeconomic position of enslaved Black people and free white disabled people, while different, is connected by the exceptionality of both groups. This exceptionality within social structures is important for discussions of disability and race. Early accounts in disability studies of the evolution of disabled people in Britain as a recognizable group argue that disability emerged as a product of industrialized labor. These accounts, however, usually do not mention the dependence of the economy on slave labor. Enslaved and disabled bodies are, nevertheless, caught up in the biopolitics of a capitalist commodification of the body.

In outlining three central approaches to the relationship between disability and race (treating them as *similar*, *combined*, and *different*), my intention has not been to close off other ways of thinking about the relevance of these categories for each other, but to provide a starting place for organizing a body of conceptual work. There are underdiscussed aspects of this relationship that do not fit easily into this framework. For example, Edmund Burke uses the case of a blind boy gaining his sight for the first time to support his claim that the association between Blackness and terror is natural. He comments that the boy, "upon accidentally seeing a negro woman . . . was struck with great horror at the sight. The horror, in this case, can scarcely be supposed to arise from any association," Burke suggests.[31] Burke positions the formerly blind boy as a neutral observer who can corroborate the supposed naturalness of anti-Black bias, conveniently setting aside the boy's immersion in ideas embedded discursively in his culture. Here, ableist assumptions about blindness are justifications for racism. Burke's example contrasts with Edward Rushton's vigorous campaigning against anti-Blackness. Rushton, who does not use his blindness as a justification for neutrality, argues on religious grounds that "to imagine that the wise Framer of the Universe is partial to this or that particular colour . . . is, in my opinion, to degrade Omnipotence."[32] Rushton's is an important voice, in that he imagines racial division as person made, and, more specifically, as a problem caused by sighted people. Burke should be part of the discussion of disability and race because he shows that ableist assumptions about blindness can be used as a justification for racism; Rushton is significant because he disavows this racism as ableist. The contrast between Burke and Rushton demonstrates that disability is an expansive concept for understanding racialization and serves as an important reminder that any discussion of race that excludes disabled voices is incomplete.

## Notes

1. Henry Highland Garnet, "An Address to the Slaves of the United States of America," in *The Norton Anthology of African American Literature*, ed. Henry Louis Gates Jr. and Nellie Y. McKay (New York: W.W. Norton, 1997), 279–85 (at 280); subsequent citations will be given in the text, for this and later references. For other examples of racial injury, see Thomas Clarkson, *The History of the Rise, Progress, and Accomplishment of the Abolition of the African Slave-Trade by The British Parliament*, 2 vols. (London: Longman, Hurst, Rees, and Orme, 1808), vol I, 191; Henry Sipkins, *Oration on the Abolition of the Slave Trade; Delivered in The African Church, in The City of New-York, January 2, 1809* (New York: John C. Totten, 1809), 18.
2. Courtney R. Baker, *Humane Insight: Looking at Images of African American Suffering and Death* (Chicago: University of Illinois Press, 2015), 6.
3. Fiona A. Kumari Campbell, "Exploring Internalized Ableism Using Critical Race Theory," *Disability & Society* 23/2 (2008): 151–62.

4. I am grateful to Dr. Nicholas Perkins, St Hugh's College, Oxford, for a reminder of this connection.
5. Leonard Kriegel, "Uncle Tom and Tiny Tim: Some Reflections on the Cripple as Negro," *The American Scholar* (Summer 1969): 412–30 (at 416).
6. Anonymous, "Progress of the Deaf," *The Monthly Chronicle* (July–December 1838): 154–60 (at 154). Deafness is not always regarded as a disability. As Carol Padden and Tom Humphries point out, "'Disabled' is a label that historically has not belonged to Deaf people." Carol Padden and Tom Humphries, "Deaf People: A Different Center," *The Disability Studies Reader*, ed. Lennard J. Davis, 3rd ed. (New York: Routledge, 2010), 393–402 (at 396). The upper-case D in the word Deaf refers to people who identify as culturally deaf and communicate via sign language. The use of deaf with a lowercase d refers to the audiological condition of deafness. To signal both, d/Deaf is used.
7. Douglas Baynton, "'A Silent Exile on this Earth': The Metaphorical Construction of Deafness in the Nineteenth Century," *American Quarterly* 44/2 (1992): 216–43 (at 230).
8. *Encyclopædia Americana: A Popular Dictionary of Arts, Sciences, Literature, History, Politics, and Biography*, ed. Francis Lieber, Edward Wigglesworth, and Thomas G. Bradford (Philadelphia: Desilver, Thomas, 1836), 4: 329–37 (at 332).
9. John Robertson Burnet, *Tales of the Deaf and Dumb, with Miscellaneous Poems* (Newark: Benjamin Olds, 1835), 191.
10. James Nack, *The Legend of the Rocks, and Other Poems* (New York: E. Conrad, 1827), 60; Charles Edward Herbert Orpen, *The Contrast between Atheism, Paganism and Christianity, Illustrated; or, the Uneducated Deaf and Dumb, as Heathens, Compared with those who have been Instructed in Language and Revelation, and Taught by the Holy Spirit, as Christians* (Dublin: Thomas Collins, 1828), 29.
11. John Perceval, *A Narrative of the Treatment Experienced by A Gentleman, During a State of Mental Derangement; Designed to Explain the Causes and the Nature of Insanity, And to Expose the Injudicious Conduct Pursued Towards Many Unfortunate Sufferers Under that Calamity* (London: Effingham Wilson, 1840), 214. First published 1838.
12. Anna Mollow, "'When *Black* Women Start Going on Prozac': Race, Gender, and Mental Illness in Meri Nana-Ama Danquah's *Willow Weep for Me*," *MELUS* 31/3 (2006): 67–99 (at 69).
13. Liat Ben-Moshe, *Decarcerating Disability: Deinstitutionalization and Prison Abolition* (Minneapolis: University of Minnesota Press, 2020), 4–5; Patricia Hill Collins, "It's All in the Family: Intersections of Gender, Race, and Nation," *Hypatia* 13/3 (1998): 62–82 (at 63); Kimberlé Crenshaw, "Mapping the Margins: Intersectionality, Identity Politics, and Violence Against Women of Color," *Stanford Law Review* 43/6 (1991): 1241–99; Nirmala Erevelles, "Unspeakable Offenses: Untangling Race and Disability

in Discourses of Intersectionality," *Journal of Literary and Cultural Disability Studies* 4/2 (2010): 127–45.
14. Rosemarie Garland Thomson, "Integrating Disability, Transforming Feminist Theory," *National Women's Studies Association Journal* 14/3 (2002): 1–32 (at 9); Sharon L. Snyder and David T. Mitchell, *Cultural Locations of Disability* (Chicago: University of Chicago Press, 2006), 12; Ellen Samuels, "'A Complication of Complaints': Untangling Disability, Race, and Gender in William and Ellen Craft's *Running a Thousand Miles for Freedom*," *MELUS* 31/3 (Fall 2006): 15–47 (at 24).
15. Alison M. Parker, "Intersecting Histories of Gender, Race, and Disability," *Journal of Women's History* 27/1 (Spring 2015): 178–86 (at 186); Paul Lawrie, "Race, Work, and Disability in Progressive Era United States," in *The Oxford Handbook of Disability History*, ed. Michael Rembis, Catherine Kudlick, and Kim E. Nielsen (New York: Oxford University Press, 2018), 229–46 (at 229); Therí Alyce Pickens, *Black Madness:: Mad Blackness* (Durham: Duke University Press, 2019), 24.
16. J. Langdon H. Down, "Observations on an Ethnic Classification of Idiots," *Heredity* 21/4 (1866), 695. Maria Edgeworth, "The Grateful Negro," *Popular Tales*, 3 vols., 2nd ed. (London: J. Johnson, 1805), 3, 193–240 (193).
17. George Murray Paterson, "On the Phrenology of Hindostan," *Transactions of the Phrenological Society, Instituted 22nd February 1820* (Edinburgh: John Anderson, 1824), 448. Gayatri Chakravorty Spivak, "Three Women's Texts and a Critique of Imperialism," *Critical Inquiry* 12/1 (Autumn 1985), 247.
18. Sami Schalk, *Black Disability Politics* (Durham: Duke University Press, 2022), 5.
19. Olaudah Equiano, *The Interesting Narrative and Other Writings*, ed. Vincent Carretta (New York: Penguin, 1995), 181.
20. Mary Prince, *The History of Mary Prince*, ed. Sara Salih (London: Penguin, 2004), 19.
21. William Earle, *Obi; Or, The History of Three-Fingered Jack*, ed. Srinivas Aravamudan (Peterborough: Broadview, 2005), 172.
22. Cynric R. Williams, *Hamel, The Obeah Man*, ed. Tim Watson and Candace Ward (Peterborough: Broadview, 2010), 184.
23. Nadja Durbach, *Spectacle of Deformity: Freak Shows and Modern British Culture* (Berkeley: University of California Press, 2010), 32; Paul Youngquist, *Monstrosities: Bodies and British Romanticism* (Minneapolis: University of Minnesota Press, 2003), xiv.
24. J. Clayton Jennyns, *An Appeal to the Earl Bathurst, When Colonial Minster, On the Unconstitutional Continuance of Foreign Laws in the Colonies Ceded to Great Britain with A Preface on the Direful Revolution Projected in England and Excited in the British Antilles, by the Advocates of Negro-Mania* (London: Sams, 1828), 12.
25. Douglas C. Baynton, "Disability and the Justification of Inequality in American History," in *The New Disability History: American Perspectives*,

ed. Paul K. Longmore and Lauri Umanski (New York: New York University Press, 2001), 33–57 (at 33).
26. Anonymous, "To the Publick," in *The Collected Works of Phillis Wheatley*, ed. John C. Shields (Oxford: Oxford University Press, 1988), n. p.
27. Anonymous, *The Woman of Colour: A Tale*, ed. Lyndon J. Dominique (Peterborough: Broadview, 2008), 102.
28. Hannah More, "The Sorrows of Yamba; or The Negro Woman's Lamentation," in *Cheap Repository Tracts; Entertaining, Moral and Religious* (London: F. and C. Rivington, 1795), l: 424; William Cowper, "The Negro's Complaint," in *The Lansdowne Poets: The Poetical Works of William Cowper* (London: Frederick Warne, n.d.), 408.
29. Frederick Douglass, *Narrative of the Life of Frederick Douglass, An American Slave*, ed. Deborah E. McDowell (Oxford: Oxford University Press, 2009), 10.
30. James Montgomery, *The Poetical Works of James Montgomery. Collected by Himself*, 4 vols. (London: Longman, Orme, Brown, Green, and Longmans, 1841), 1, 161.
31. Edmund Burke, *A Philosophical Enquiry into the Sublime and Beautiful* (Oxford: Oxford University Press, 2015), 116. I am grateful to Professor Francisco Robles, University of Notre Dame, for reminding me of this reference.
32. Edward Rushton, *The Collected Writings of Edward Rushton (1756–1814)*, ed. Paul Baines (Liverpool: Liverpool University Press, 2014), 208. I am grateful to St. Hugh's College, Oxford University, for inviting me to present this research as the 2022 Lady Ademola Lecture. This chapter went to press as the *Disability Studies Quarterly* vol 43.1 (Fall 2023) special edition on race and disability was published.

CHAPTER 7

# *The Crip Foundations of Romantic Medicine*

*Travis Chi Wing Lau*

## Romantic Medicine

Historians of medicine have long grappled with the difficulties of characterizing and periodizing medicine during the Romantic period, which has been so often "considered to be an historical indiscretion which is better forgotten and forgiven, than brought up again and studied anew."[1] Because the Romantic period witnessed forms of medical practice now viewed as alternative or pseudoscientific, Romantic medicine remains a slippery critical object for how it frustrates attempts at periodization, in terms of literary and medical history. A consequence of periodization, both literary and medical, has overdetermined how Romanticism tends to be historicized as a "reaction from rationalism" toward "irrationality."[2] More traditional medical historians have tended to overlook Romanticism because of its quirks that undermine the progress narrative of heroic, erudite physicians and technological innovation that culminated in hospital medicine in the nineteenth century. Preceding the later professionalization of medicine, which created and licensed a class of practicing physicians trained in increasingly specialized scientific fields like chemistry and psychology, Romantic medicine embodied the intense contestation over what constituted medicine, who practiced it, and how it was to be legitimately practiced.

At first treated exclusively as a facet of the German Romantic movement in the late eighteenth century, Romantic medicine has since been revised by literary and medical historians to reflect the myriad of transformations in medical theory and practice that coincided with the social, cultural, and political changes across multiple geographic locations during the Age of Revolution. Rather than glossing over Romantic medicine's eccentricities, scholars of Romanticism have since reinvested attention in the period's transitional quality between older humoral medicine at the bedside – a patient-as-patron model that framed health as the balance of the four humors of black bile, yellow bile, blood, and phlegm – and professionalized hospital medicine. This transition was hardly clean or linear, but rather messy and recursive: humoral medicine and alternative approaches coexisted with increasingly scientific and regulated medical practices. More carefully historicized accounts of Romantic-era medicine challenges earlier medical histories that exceptionalized physicians as the key agents of medicine's advancement. Such medical triumphalism began to give way to what Roy Porter has called "doing medical history from below" – a methodological shift toward more capacious histories of medicine that emphasize medicine as a social experience and shaped by social conditions and values.[3] "Medical history from below" has typically involved displacing physician-centered accounts and instead focusing on the experience of the sick and disabled themselves, many of whom were unnamed and unrecognized in their engagement with healthcare institutions or were forced to seek other forms of care due to socioeconomic barriers to medicine. Such a reorientation has not only raised questions about the forms of hierarchy within medicine itself (i.e., between physicians and other caregivers like surgeons, nurses, pharmacists, and chaplains), but has also challenged the presumed divide between the humanities and the sciences by tracing how physicians (many of them also poets and novelists) participated in the projects of Romanticism by shaping and being shaped by literary and philosophical discourse.

The return to Romantic medicine has also been part of a larger scholarly reassessment of Romanticism in terms of disability history and theory. Romantic medicine, more recently characterized by its qualities of "open-minded experiment, flexible definition, and distributed authority," has become of great interest to scholars of disability, who find in Romantic medicine an unexpected openness to bodily difference and a radical contingency at a cultural moment when the terms of the normative body were being increasingly codified.[4] The resituating of Romanticism in terms of disability has not only helped to recover Romantic writers as disabled but also to understand Romantic writing as shaped by disabled experience centuries prior to disability's becoming a politicized identity category. "A disabling of a Romantic text is a new reading, but can also be a form of un-reading," write Michael Bradshaw and Essaka Joshua of the nascent project of "disabling Romanticism" that seeks to undo long-standing narratives of Romanticism as transcending the material or the bodily.[5] This project takes to task Romantic studies' neglect of disability's influence on Romantic cultural production despite how many canonical Romantic writers were themselves disabled. If disability is invoked at all, it has tended to be for its supposedly transgressive implications or to justify Romantic genius – claims which no longer bear the same critical purchase, as disability studies has come to question the ableism and ahistoricism of these fundamental claims.

Though scholars of disability have rightly pushed back against a teleological narrative of disability history as inevitably moving toward disability's reification into "the master trope of human disqualification," this chapter contributes to the ongoing excavation of the manifold ways disability has and continues to underpin race and racialization.[6] Disability's role in the production of race in the Romantic imagination remains understudied despite its afterlives in contemporary race-based medicine. In conjunction with slavery as itself a mass disabling event, Romantic racial science depended upon ableist ideologies and ableist violence that would come to animate later nineteenth-century eugenic movements framed around racial hygiene and national health. Recent intersectional histories of eighteenth- and nineteenth-century medicine, race, and transatlantic slavery have not only revealed the brutal objectification of nonwhite people by science and medicine, but have also interrogated who gets centered in medicine and medical historiography, as well as charted the dual extraction and erasure of Black and Indigenous labor and knowledge systems by Western medicine's imperial projects. Drawing on the insights of Black critical disability scholars such as Jenifer Barclay, Dea Boster, Stefanie Hunt-Kennedy, and Cristina Visperas who have theorized the inextricable relationship between slavery and disability allows us to attend to disability's formative role in the development of Romantic science and medicine. To reframe Romantic medicine in terms of disability and slavery helps historicize the underpinnings of contemporary healthcare inequities that have had lethal consequences for patients of color already marginalized in their navigation of the medical industrial complex.

## Disability and the Dependencies of Racial Science

Examining the historical development of scientific racism reveals how disability and race have long been imbricated in Western scientific and medical epistemologies. Across the taxonomic thinking of eighteenth-century naturalists – from Carolus Linnaeus to Georges-Louis Leclerc, Comte de Buffon, and Johann Blumenbach – disability provided the unspoken, unacknowledged foundation for philosophies of racial thinking and the vocabulary for racial difference as bodily weakness or inferiority. From the "deformed" to the "idiot" to the "cripple" to the "feebleminded," disabled figures were historically the substrate on which thinking about embodiment and the human grew, yet disabled people were consistently excluded from participation in that knowledge-making on the grounds that they were incapable of doing so. Disability as a concept was simultaneously deployed as part of cutting-edge, experimental methodologies yet unworthy of being understood on its own terms as it became attached to forms of racial and gender difference taxonomized and pathologized *as* deformed versions of white, able-bodied, "ideal typology."[7] By the nineteenth century, race science had come to justify anti-Black racism and white supremacy by anatomizing racial difference, while race medicine reinforced such difference by pathologizing those physiological differences. This medicalization of Blackness "defined blackness as a surrogate marker of difference to stabilize and reify racial differences," themselves contingent and unstable.[8] Much of the medical knowledge production in the Atlantic world thus involved the deliberate production of disability in racialized subjects for the purposes of "knowing" race at the level of tissues and organs. Phrased differently, *to know difference was to disable*.

The early science of skin color enfleshed racial difference by the disabling of bodies of color through the acts of direct experimentation, anatomical dissection, or even vivisection, which involved operations performed upon live subjects. This incisive work upon Black flesh is both literal and, as it was deployed in the work of French *anatomie*, figurative: to anatomize was to operate based upon the necessity that "to understand a complex whole, one is obliged to extract, dissect, and consider the viscera that compose it."[9] This scientific "obligation" justified some of the earliest work in the anatomy of Blackness, such as Jean Riolan's attempt to boil skin from an "Ethiopian" cadaver to separate its layers. Because the layers did not separate, Riolan relied upon an older dissection technique of putrefaction, which involved the deliberate decomposing of a small tissue sample. Riolan's anatomical research in the *Encheridium anatomicum et pathologicum* (1649) and his later *Manuel anatomique et pathologique* (1661) perpetuated the belief that Blackness was localized to the skin (and that skin "color" referred to dark skin only): in the case of the "Ethiopian" subject, the skin bore an outer "black" layer and an inner "white" layer, which proved that race was climatological rather than innate.[10] Paralleling this fascination with Black skin, Marcello Malpighi's identification in 1665 of a third layer of "African" skin between the outer and inner layers, called the *reticulum mucosum* or *rete mucosum* (later referred to as the "Malpighian layer" or "Malpighian mucus"), revealed "a measurable and readily identifiable 'racial' feature" unique to 'African' skin structure."[11]

Using both optical technologies like microscopes and violent instruments like the scalpel, other anatomists, such as Johann Nicolas Pechlin, "confirmed" the physical cause of dark skin in the *rete mucosum* through invasive "explorations of the macro- and microanatomy" of Black skin.[12] These skin-deep experiments, even as they left lasting imprints on their subjects, "proved" that Blackness could be identified, isolated, and therefore contained. In terms of disability, not only did these anatomists objectify Black bodies as scientific "anomalies" that merited violent deconstruction to understand, but they also framed their findings like the *rete mucosum* as the sources of disabling Blackness in Africans. By proxy, these findings provided the convenient justifications for enslavement, as Black skin meant Black people were biologically predisposed for physical labor. By contrast, white bodies did not bear the blackening taint of the Malpighian fluid that quite literally deformed Black bodies beyond recognition. This helps to explain the virality of Blackness-as-disability as a philosophical and scientific belief: As much as it helped to describe and classify Black people, it defined whiteness as a natural, superior state of health and well-being in direct contrast to debilitated and debilitating Blackness.

Malpighi's findings sparked a generation of eighteenth-century thinkers eager to replicate and expand upon the study of the *reticulum* through the abuse of African cadavers, as knowledge could still be extracted from these bodies even in death. Pierre Barrère, whose *Dissertation sur la cause physique de la couleur des nègres* (1741) claimed the black pigment in African skin was derived from black bile that tainted the skin, depended entirely on violent dissections of Afro-Guyanese cadavers.[13] Similarly, Johann Freidrich Meckel identified Blackness within the interiors of African bodies by claiming Africans had distinctly bluish-black brains and, therefore, implied differences in cognition and capacity for reason.[14] The expansion of the claim of innate Blackness beyond skin to organ and organ systems provoked Claude-Nicolas Le Cat to revise humoral theories of black bile "staining" Black skin through his 1765 "discovery" of an inky, acidic fluid called *ethiops* that supposedly flowed throughout Black bodies.[15] The suffusion of *ethiops* throughout the African body reached even the sperm, which became the object of Dutch geographer Cornelius de Pauw's *Recherches philosophiques sur les Americains* (1768) that framed it as uniquely "active and violent."[16] Unsurprisingly, de Pauw's theories reached a eugenic pitch when he determined that the primary method of eradicating Blackness was the purification of the black gel circulating throughout African physiology.

Attempts at such purgation involved not only the violent extraction of the fluid, which he already achieved in his preliminary experiments, but also protoeugenic attempts at racial bleaching via the deliberate introduction of white sperm and selective racial mixture. Heightening cultural anxieties surrounding miscegenation, De Pauw's seemingly benevolent rhetoric of "cure" reinscribed Blackness as a hereditary disability that could only be eliminated through generations of selective reproduction while also lamenting it as an indelible disability intrinsic to Black people. Each of these studies reaffirmed the notion that whiteness was structurally superior in its purity of form uncontaminated by *ethiops*, which was constantly imagined as permeating the entirety of the Black body and entirely defining the person by its suffusion. Romantic medicine originated a pernicious tautology that endures in race-based medicine: the Black body was disabled because it was Black, and was Black because it was disabled.

This proliferation of anatomical studies underscores the extent to which white naturalists depended upon the replication of disabling experiments as part of their scientific method. Be it live experimentation or dissection, these naturalists wanted to witness the physiological causes of Blackness in situ. Participating in the scarring, maiming, or dismembering of Black bodies – alive or dead – thus became a prerequisite for inclusion within these larger networks of knowledge and power that circulated racist views of Blackness as a form of monstrosity and deformity. Membership within these communities of knowledge demanded a fluency in the explicitly ableist rhetoric of Blackness-as-disability and replication in experimental research. Comparative anatomist and naturalist Georges Cuvier composed in the early 1800s both *Leçons d'anatomie comparée* and *Memoires du Museum d'Histoire Naturelle*, which featured his infamous account of Saartjie Baartman (or Sara Baartman): the "Hottentot Venus."[17] Born in South Africa in 1789 as a member of the Khoisan peoples, Baartman was forced into labor during Dutch colonization. Without her consent or knowledge, Hendrick Cezar, a freed Black man, and Alexander Dunlop, a former Scottish surgeon and medical superintendent of the Slave Lodge in Cape Town, contracted to have her brought to London for circus, salon, and museum exhibitions because of her exotic appearance. The darkness of her skin, the elongated shape of her labia (referred to as the "*tablier*" or "apron"), and the size of her buttocks (or steatopygia, a protruding condition understood by Western naturalists as "disabling") – all framed within a spectacular presentation of her eroticized primitivism that attempted to pseudoethnographically reproduce her in her "native African setting" – became objects of public fascination to the extent that she was transported again from

England to France after being sold to an animal handler named S. Reaux. Because she was so frequently exhibited and reproduced in cartoons and drawings, George Cuvier took interest in her as the "missing link" between primates and humans, which he organized hierarchically in terms of the "complexity and location of the nervous system in the body."[18] Yet, despite his fascination, he was also disgusted by what he perceived to be animal traits in her features, or the hideous mixture of features from two inferior species like the orangutan and the mongoloid. What emerged was a biology grounded in what he understood to be undeniable anatomical evidence amassed over decades – a biology that naturalized his racism. This biology, however, was hardly new: Carolus Linnaeus, sixty years earlier, had expressed the very same scientific fascination for a fourteen-year-old girl from Jamaica, whom he also saw as the intermediate species between *Homo sapiens* and apes.

Perversely, even after Baartman's death in 1815, Cuvier requisitioned her remains from the coroner to posthumously dissect and preserve parts of her body, specifically her genitals and brain, which were all later exhibited. After decades of dehumanizing exhibition that reinforced the stereotyping of her Africanness and Blackness as subhuman and lascivious, Baartman never gained autonomy over her own body despite her remains being returned to South Africa for burial in 2002. Cuvier's abuse of her body, both in life and in death, was not only expected but lauded by his contemporaries, for Baartman "was relegated to the world of brute flesh" within the naturalist imagination desperately trying to make sense of her form.[19] Baartman's body became the surface for Cuvier and other naturalists' to project their fantasies of what constituted Black womanhood and sexuality – she was, for all intents and purposes, figuratively disabled because she was a Black woman, but also literally disabled by her de facto enslavement as she was trafficked between showmen and naturalists for profit.

As Baartman's spectacular though hardly anomalous history reveals, the colonies would become not only the source of experimental subjects but also the grotesque theater of scientific medicine during the late eighteenth and nineteenth centuries because they provided the convenient, "safe" proving grounds for testing the efficacy of new experimental treatments and cures. Given the history of the term "disability" and its relationship to the capacity to perform work, those who could no longer work – typically enslaved peoples who became disabled by their work or who became too old and infirm to continue working – were made again to "work" as the experimental subjects that could sustain the life of those who could continue to have labor extracted from them. West Indian medical men like Colin Chisholm, Donald Monro, John Quier, James Thomson, and William Wright contributed to ongoing continental research with their own experiments on enslaved people, who could neither consent nor even know how they would be abused for research.[20] Like Riolan before him, James Thomson detailed in his "numerous dissections" (really autopsies) how he "blistered" the skin with boiling water to properly detach the "plexus of vessels" that circulated the Malpighian fluid blackening the skin. Because he believed African skin surfaces to be particularly sensitive and active in their secretions, Thomson "deemed perspiration the plantation physician's greatest diagnostic tool" because it signaled the potential imbalances of the cutaneous system.[21] While anatomy exceeded his work as a physician, he understood it to be essential for proper diagnosis and treatment of African patients under his care. In fact, his dissections revealed to him that African people tended to be exceedingly healthy in the perfection of their viscera. From a disability perspective, Thomson's claims are paradoxical and contradictory. On one hand, they valorized African people as inherently hyper-ablebodied and healthy (and, thus, structurally predisposed for inhumane amounts of manual labor). On the other hand, they pathologized Africans for their skin's structure, which rendered them susceptible to highly communicable tropical diseases that impacted their capacity to labor and threatened the well-being of planters no less vulnerable (or perhaps even more vulnerable) to diseases endemic to the colonies. Thomson's faulty logics exemplify some of the cruel ironies of white medical men attempting to universalize notions of health and disease from the idiosyncrasies of racialized bodies whose differences they pathologized. Thomson also provided one of the earliest justifications for race-based medicine: that it allowed physicians to better treat people of color.

Physicians working in plantation hospitals – spaces themselves often hastily constructed, poorly attended, and completely unregulated – disabled as much as they attempted to cure – or, more accurately, they *disabled in order to cure*. In terms of preventative medicine, John Quier and James Thomson regularly used enslaved people for their experiments in smallpox and yaws inoculation. Quier's inoculation studies began in 1768 and took the form of mass inoculations, where some procedures were done repeatedly on the same subject to confirm an immune response.[22] Despite warnings by leading inoculation authorities about its risks, Quier inoculated numerous pregnant women and enslaved children, many of whom were nursing infants, for the "sole purpose of "observing the phenomena, which might be produced." Following Quier's work, James Thomson sought to practice a radical experimental approach to inoculation that could combat yaws, a painful chronic skin infection that debilitated primarily slave populations. In his own experimental trials, Thomson ordered the injection of pus and blood to induce yaws in otherwise healthy young children. Neither physician offered significant accounts of long-term impairment or extensive deaths caused by these experiments, yet this absence in the historical record does not preclude the possibility of widespread disability due to botched inoculations, which often caused debilitating cases of smallpox and yaws that could leave individuals blind or scarred. While these inoculation experiments "were not aimed primarily at identifying racial differences . . . they were aimed at developing plantation medicine that could better cope with the ravages of tropical disease that Europeans poorly understood."[23] The advancement of colonial medicine necessitated the continuous and widespread disabling of enslaved people, even those who were already sick and disabled. This was justified as necessary to preserve the health of the planters and the enslaved, who could still be used for labor even as "slaves with disabilities threatened the delicate illusion of control and stability that white authority figures had constructed but also forced them to confront their own deeply-held assumptions about race, deviance, and defect."[24] Put in these terms, slavery was itself "an inherently disabling institution producing conditions of mental and physical injury, as well as ideological notions of inferiority" and a long-term project of mass disablement perversely used to better diagnose and treat disease and disability.[25]

## #DisabilityTooWhite

Redefining racial science *as* ableist science helps to underscore how every historical account of race is also a historical account of disability. Rather than conflate racism and ableism, this chapter has sought to delineate how the science of race always depended on disability to advance even while disavowing that dependency. From the seventeenth century onward, racism frequently justified violent medical experimentation as an attempt to diagnose and cure Blackness as disability. Ableist ideologies of the inherent able-bodiedness of white subjects allowed for the disabling of enslaved people at a massive scale purely on the basis of objective scientific inquiry. Yet, the question remains: *Whose good does this science serve? Who benefits from this science that so often presents itself as value-neutral and objective?* Considering this history, research debacles like the Tuskegee Syphilis Study in fact follow a much longer genealogy of unethical experimentation framed as medical necessity and innovation even at the expense of Black well-being. This legacy of ableism and medical abuse powerfully contextualizes what Harriet Washington calls "black iatrophobia," which is actually a "situational hypervigilance [that] is neither a *baseless* fear of harm nor a fear of imaginary harms."[26] Tying this racial history to the histories of disabled incarceration and sterilization only underscores why both groups have tended to be deeply skeptical of and resistant to medicalization. The historical traumas of racism and ableism are by no means imaginary but lived out painfully in the present by many disabled people of color. The critical stakes of such historical work lies in "exposing the symbiosis between racism and ableism and the deeply troubling history of pitting the categories of disability and race against one another" rather than thinking about them as mutually constitutive and in solidarity.[27] The Romantic period witnessed the concurrent formation of this "symbiosis" across multiple institutions, from professional medicine to the legal system to the slave trade.

Given the dearth of contemporaneous literary representations of figures such as Saartjie Baartman and their histories or works thematizing the experimental exploitation of the enslaved, archival traces of slave disability instead exist in the forms of various published and unpublished documents, like "plantation journals and worklogs, slave sale records and auction advertisements, warranties and bills of sale, as well as personal correspondence."[28] The recovery of these sources, alongside the rhetorics on both sides of the slave debates about what Andrea Stone has called "black well-being," have helped to reinforce how expressions of Black selfhood foregrounded a range of embodied experiences of pain, ill health, debility, and impairment that coalesced into a "nineteenth-century politics of well-being opposed to as well as independent of medically and legally informed systems of subjugation."[29] To that end, a critical disability studies approach that "sees value in vulnerability and the instability of the body" exposes how the disease and disability of racialized subjects were so often juxtaposed against fictions of healthiness and sovereignty afforded only to white subjects.[30] If such accounts of disability in the historical record "disrupt[ed] distinctions between human and nonhuman and demonstrate the danger of the ideal of the whole, pure, autonomous self not only for the Black and enslaved but for the white and free, too," it only makes sense that they tend to frustrate literary analysis that has itself tended to be ableist in its approach to what even merits analysis in the first place, let alone how it grapples with the deeply discomforting, layered experiences of suffering.[31] What would it mean, then, to read adaptations of

Saartjie Baartman's life, such as Elizabeth Alexander's poem "The Venus Hottentot (1825)" (1990), Suzan-Lori Parks's play *Venus* (1996), or Barbara Chase-Riboud's novel *Hottentot Venus* (2003), in the context of Cuvier's own anatomical case studies or the scientific debates about the Malpighian layer's debilitating effects on the body?[32] How do these works undo her pathology and dehumanization by investing her with a subjectivity that exceeds that of a scientific specimen and by revealing the social construction of her Blackness as defect or disability?

Lastly, attending to the interconnected historical formations of disability and race has also helped to forward long-standing critiques of disability studies as still a primarily presentist, Anglo-American field of study. Christopher Bell's condemnation of early disability studies' "tenuous relationship with race and ethnicity" and "glaring dearth of disability-related scholarship by and about disabled people of color" raised serious questions about what constituted the field's objects of study, who disability scholarship is for, and who was allowed to do it, especially as disability studies was becoming increasingly legitimized in the academy as a field of study.[33] Bell's naming of the field's whiteness underscored the consequences of an ableist and racist forgetting of race and disability's coconstitution even as the field of disability studies was finally becoming institutionalized in centers and programs all over the US and the UK. Despite the activist origins and commitments of the field, disability studies has yet to fully reckon with its connections to white supremacy and global imperialism. Scholars of color interrogating the formation of disability studies as a field through crip of color critique, Mad studies approaches, and critical disability frameworks have rightly called out how disability scholarship without engagements with race, especially in Global South contexts, risks reifying a hierarchy of disabled people and a complicity with imperializing projects of disabling. If disability studies is to have a future, it must lie in the intersectional engagements with the histories of race and disability that reveal the shared oppressions of racialized and disabled people and their opportunities for collective solidarity.

## Notes

1. Iago Galdston, "The Romantic Period in Medicine," *Bulletin of the New York Academy of Medicine* 32/5 (1956), 346.
2. George Rosen, "Romantic Medicine: A Problem in Historical Periodization," *Bulletin of the History of Medicine* 25/2 (1951), 151.

3. Roy Porter, "The Patient's View: Doing Medical History from Below," *Theory and Society* 14/2 (1985), 175–98.
4. Fuson Wang, "Romantic Disease Discourse: Disability, Immunity, and Literature," *Nineteenth-Century Contexts* 33/5 (2011), 477.
5. Michael Bradshaw and Essaka Joshua, "Introduction," in *Disabling Romanticism: Body, Mind, and Text*, ed. Michael Bradshaw (Basingstoke: Palgrave Macmillan, 2016), 1–2.
6. David T. Mitchell and Sharon L. Snyder, *Narrative Prosthesis: Disability and the Dependencies of Discourse* (Ann Arbor: University of Michigan Press, 2000), 3.
7. David Bindman, *Ape to Apollo: Aesthetics and the Idea of Race in the Eighteenth Century* (Ithaca: Cornell University Press 2002), 224.
8. Rana Hogarth, *Medicalizing Blackness: Making Racial Difference in the Atlantic World, 1780–1840* (Chapel Hill: University of North Carolina Press, 2017), 2.
9. Andrew Curran, *The Anatomy of Blackness: Science and Slavery in an Age of Enlightenment* (Baltimore: Johns Hopkins University Press, 2011), 28.
10. *Encheridium anatomicum et pathologicum. In qvo ex naturali constitutione partium, recessus à naturali statu demonstrator* (Livro impresso, latim, 1649); *Manuel anatomique et pathologique, ou abregè de toute l'anatomie, et des usages que l'on en peut tirer pour la connoissance, et pour la guerison des maladies ...* (Paris: Meturas, Gaspard, 1661).
11. Curran, *The Anatomy of Blackness*, 121. Marcello Malpighi, *De externo tactus organo anatomica observatio* (Neapoli: apud Aegidium Longum, 1665).
12. Craig Koslofsky, "Superficial Blackness? Johann Nicholas Pechlin's *De Habitu et Colore Aethiopum Qui Vulgo Nigritae* (1677)," *The Journal for Early Modern Cultural Studies* 18/1 (2018), 140.
13. *Dissertation sur la cause physique de la couleur des nègres* (Paris: P.-G. Simon, 1741).
14. "Recherches anatomiques, sur la nature de l'épiderme, et du réseau, qu'on appelle Malpighien"; "Sur la diversité de couleur dans la substance médullaire du cerveau des négres"; "Description d'une maladie particulière du péritoine." In *Mémoires de l'Académie royale des sciences et des belles lettres de Berlin*, 79–113. (Berlin: Ambroise Haude, 1755).
15. *Traité des sens* (Paris: G. Cavalier, 1742); *Traité de la couleur de la peau humaine en général, de celle des nègres en particulier, et de la métamorphose d'une de ces couleurs en l'autre, soit de naissance, soit accidentellement: ouvrage divisé en trois parties* (Amsterdam: n.p., 1765).
16. *Recherches philosophiques sur les Américains, our Mémoires intéressans pour server à l'histoire de l'espèce humaine* (Berlin: G. J. Decker, 1768).
17. *Lecons d'anatomie compare* (Paris: C. Duméril, 1805); *Memoires du Museum d'Histoire Naturelle* (Paris: G. Dufour, 1815).
18. Matthew Senior, "Classify and Display: Human and Animal Species in Linnaeus and Cuvier," in *Animals, Animality and Literature*, ed. Bruce Boehrer, Molly Hand, and Brian Massumi (Cambridge: Cambridge University Press, 2018), 168.

19. Londa Schiebinger, *Nature's Body: Gender in the Making of Modern Science* (New Brunswick: Rutgers University Press, 2004), 172.
20. Colin Chisholm, *An Essay on the Malignant Pestilential Fever Introduced into the West Indian Islands from Boullam, on the Coast of Guinea, as it Appeared in 1793 and 1794*, 2 vols. (London: C. Dilly, 1795); Donald Monro (ed.), *Letters and Essays on the Small Pox and Inoculation, the Measles, the Dry Belly Ache, the Yellow, and Remitting, and Intermitting Fevers of the West Indies: To Which are Added, Thoughts on the Hydrocephalus Internus, and Observations on Hydatides in the Heads Of Cattle / By Different Practitioners* (London: J. Murray, 1778); Donald Monro, *Observations on the Means of Preserving the Health of Soldiers: And of Conducting Military Hospitals. And on the Diseases Incident to Soldiers in the Time of Service, and on the Same Diseases as They Have Appeared in London*, 2 vols. (London: J. Murray, 1780); Donald Monro, *A Treatise on Medical and Pharmaceutical Chymistry, and the Materia Medica: To which is Added, an English Translation of the New Edition of the Pharmacopoeia of the Royal College of Physicians of London*, 3 vols. (London: T. Cadell, 1788); James Thomson, "Dissections in Convulsive Diseases," *Edinburgh Medical and Surgical Journal* 14 (1818), 614–18; James Thomson, *A Treatise on the Diseases of Negroes, as They Occur in the Island of Jamaica; with Observations on the Country Remedies* (Jamaica: A. Aikman, 1820); and works by William Wright, such as *Memoir of the Late William Wright, MD: With Extracts from his Correspondence, and a Selection of his Papers on Medical and Botanical Subjects* (Edinburgh: W. Blackwood, 1828), "On the External Use of Cold Water in the Cure of Fever," *London Medical Journal* 7, pt. 2 (1786), 109–15, "On the Use of Cold Bathing in the Locked Jaw," *Medical Observations and Inquiries* 6 (1784), 143–62, and "Remarks on Malignant Fevers; and Their Cure by Cold Water and Fresh Air," *London Medical Journal* 7, pt. 2 (1786), 109–14.
21. Londa Schiebinger, *Secret Cures of Slaves: People, Plants, and Medicine in the Eighteenth-Century Atlantic World* (Palo Alto: Stanford University Press, 2017), 34.
22. Schiebinger, *Secret Cures of Slaves*, 95.
23. Schiebinger, *Secret Cures of Slaves*, 115.
24. Dea Boster, *African American Slavery and Disability: Bodies, Property and Power in the Antebellum South, 1800–1860* (New York: Routledge, 2013), 3.
25. Cristina Visperas, "The Able-Bodied Slave," *Journal of Literary & Cultural Disability Studies* 13/1 (2019), 93.
26. Harriet Washington, *Medical Apartheid: The Dark History of Medical Experimentation on Black Americans from Colonial Times to the Present* (New York: Harlem Moon, 2006), 21.
27. Jenifer Barclay, *The Mark of Slavery: Disability, Race, and Gender in Antebellum America* (Champaign: University of Illinois Press, 2021), 8.
28. Boster, *African American Slavery and Disability*, 12.
29. Andrea Stone, *Black Well-Being: Health and Selfhood in Antebellum Black Literature* (Gainesville: University Press of Florida, 2016), 13.

30. Stone, *Black Well-Being*, 18.
31. Stone, *Black Well-Being*, 18.
32. Elizabeth Alexander, *The Venus Hottentot* (Minneapolis: Graywolf Press, 2004); Suzan-Lori Parks, *Venus* (New York: Theatre Communications Group, 1997); Barbara Chase-Ribout, *Hottentot Venus* (New York: Anchor Books, 2003).
33. Christopher Bell, "Introducing White Disability Studies: A Modest Proposal," *The Disability Studies Reader*, ed. Lennard J. Davis, 2nd ed. (New York: Routledge, 2006), 275–82.

CHAPTER 8

# *The Voice of Complaint*

*Joseph Albernaz*

> I must yet say, although it is not for me to determine the manner, that the voice of our complaint implies a vengeance.
> —Ottobah Cugoano, *Thoughts and Sentiments on the Evil of Slavery* (1787)

## Introduction: Poetic Complaint

What kinds of complaint can a poem register? How can a poet or poem complain about an injury or injustice in the world, or, even, an injustice having to do with the very constitution of the world itself? Who could hear and adjudicate such a complaint? Who – what voice – could speak or sing it, and how?

The complaint as a subgenre of the lyric poem has a long and venerable tradition. The first and only complete poem in the surviving corpus of the archaic Greek poet Sappho is a lovelorn complaint to the gods, and perhaps also to the deceiving lover who may (over)hear the poem, a song sung to a lyre (hence *lyric*). In English, the complaint poem was especially prominent in the early modern period, taken up by no less than Spenser and Shakespeare (the latter's "The Lover's Complaint" was printed alongside his sonnets in 1609). The typical conceit of the early modern complaint lyric found a male poet writing in the persona and voice of a dejected female lover; in this way, complaint's play of pitched voices, especially when taken up in Romanticism, presents a particularly important poetic mode through which to explore some of the elemental components of lyric poetry, such as emotion, address (or apostrophe), speaker, and especially *voice*. Indeed, the literary theorist Jonathan Culler summarizes a common view, attributed here to Paul de Man, that voice is the "fundamental aspect" of lyric.[1]

In the British Romantic period, the complaint poem frequently surfaces in abolitionist literature, where, typically, a white poet assumes the "I" of an

## The Voice of Complaint

enslaved Black speaker to lament the injustices of slavery and present them to a potentially sympathetic audience. This political subgenre of Romantic lyric poetry thus foregrounds important questions of racialization and lyric voice – of the racialization *of* the lyric voice – that shed light on the conventions of lyric at this crucial moment of modern lyric form's consolidation. The most widely circulated and celebrated of these complaint poems was William Cowper's "The Negro's Complaint" (1788), but instances of the complaint genre were widespread, and Cowper had many imitators in his wake. In fact, we find the racialized complaint trope at the heart of the book often taken to embody the essence of Romantic lyric: Wordsworth's *Lyrical Ballads* (1798), which contains a poem entitled "The Complaint of the Forsaken Indian Woman."

This chapter examines how poetic complaint was negotiated by both white and Black writers across the Romantic period and its legacies. While the genre conventionally turns on the "sentimental ventriloquism" of white writers that often makes a spectacle of Black suffering and mutes the voices of the enslaved at the moment of claiming to let them speak, the more interesting variations offer valuable glimpses into how poetic forms can both solidify and dissolve a lyric speaker's relation to ordering terms like identity, justice, law, and God, and ultimately gesture toward a reckoning with the constitution of the world itself.[2] In attempting to represent poetically what Nicole Aljoe refers to as "this thing that we understand or call 'the slave voice,'" a number of difficulties, tensions, and subterranean rumbles emerge.[3] These irruptive moments arise from confrontations with the racial institutions that form the bedrock of the modern world, shaping openings that let another voice speak – or sing. Several of these Romantic complaint poems feature a prosopopoeia (the trope of giving voice or face) that attributes speech to the wind, though not as the "correspondent breeze" that M. H. Abrams once identified in major Romantic lyrics, but as an irreconcilable voice from the whirlwind.[4]

Marc Redfield argues that the particular mode of Romantic lyric poetry, especially in its "associat[ion] with voice," has since its inception tended to stand in "for the essence of poetry, and ultimately, by extension, [for] literature or literariness itself."[5] If Romantic lyric has often been cast as a paradigmatic form of modern literature, then the antislavery complaint poem can be a lens through which to investigate the ways that the modern category of lyric voice is entangled with processes of racialization. Complaint lyric brings to the fore issues such as voice, speaker, sentiment, and (in)authentic individual expression in ways that render visible how these concepts can shore up or question the racial order of the world. Close attention to these and related poems can shape the way we understand and read Romantic lyric – and so many of the critical categories that derive from it – both in terms of its explicit and implicit crossings with the institution of racial slavery that permeated socioeconomic life in Romantic-era Britain, and also in terms of reading for and amplifying a more antagonistic voice, an (im)possible "No," throughout Romantic literature and its variegated legacies.

## Complaint, Justice, Negation

The term "complaint" has several meanings, all of which are important for thinking about it as a genre of poetry and as a racialized lyric form in Romanticism. While a complaint can be any utterance of pain, frustration, unhappiness, injury, unfairness, and so forth, the term also has a narrower legal meaning: to file a complaint with a judge, court, magistrate, or other authority, to be a *plaint*iff (a word that derives from the same root as "complaint"), and seek redress. As Matt Sandler notes, the intertwining of complaint and poetry can be traced back to the Book of Job in the Hebrew Bible.[6] Nearer to British Romanticism, Edward Young wrote a poetic paraphrase of Job before publishing his influential theological complaint poem *The Complaint, or Night Thoughts* (1742–45), and the two were often printed together. Even in Job, which is composed largely in poetic verse, the modality of complaint is not simply a lamentation or declaration of wrong, but takes on a specifically legal character, for readers of Job have long noted the thread of legal metaphor and imagery (witness, judge, umpire, court, judgment, guilt, etc.) that is woven throughout the text. Job, a loyal servant of God whose life is suddenly upended by horrific calamities in order to test his faith, complains to friends around him and to God: "I will speak in the anguish of my spirit; I will complain in the bitterness of my soul" (Job 7:11). Essential to this grievance is Job's express wish to take God himself to court in a lawsuit, but as he realizes: "For [God] is not a man, as I am, that . . . we should come together in judgment" (9:32). Job raises a question that resonates with the predicament of the enslaved's complaint: how is it possible to register a complaint when positions of power are so radically unequal?

As readers of the Book of Job realize (perhaps to their surprise), while Job does sometimes complain about the specific miseries that have been inflicted on his own life, the majority of his complaints are about the very constitution of the cosmos, the transience of mortality, the distance and negligence of God, and the seemingly unjustifiable nature of all human existence. Job's problem, his complaint, is with the *world as a whole*, not simply a particular unjust situation *in* the world – this is why the Book of Job is considered as one of the earliest instances of the discourse of theodicy: that is, the inquiry into how God could be just despite creating a world filled with evil and suffering. When Job finishes his long complaint, much of which is conducted in the interrogative mode, God finally responds with his own thundering series of questions, each of which dismisses the attempts of a mere mortal to understand, much less to question or complain about, the creation of the almighty being. God does not appear visually, but only speaks – his voice, as the text notes twice, comes from "out of the whirlwind" (38:1; 40:6). From the dark heart of the whirlwind, then, emerges a voice to say there is no answer regarding the brokenness of the world. While Job ultimately does attain a kind of (dubious) redress for his own personal pain at the book's conclusion, the voice of his complaint about the world as such lingers in the windy air. As we will see, Job's poetic complaint will be important for the antislavery complaint poem in Romanticism, both for understanding the genre's thematic stakes and formal conventions and as a directly invoked precursor. While the tradition of the lover's complaint usually remains situational, remarking upon a contingent and particular injury, pain, or injustice caused by another, the tradition of Job's complaint can be differentiated by its *totality*: it questions the very foundations of the unjust world itself.

Before turning to some antislavery complaint poems from the Romantic era, it is helpful to note the particular resonance the word "complaint" would have then had in relation to race, slavery, and the law. The situation of being unable to have one's complaints heard in a court of equals was the order of the day for those were enslaved (and additionally, though often differently, for those who were free and Black). However, a number of archives have documented complaints filed by enslaved people in the situations where this was possible, such as in the colony of Berbice (modern-day Guyana) starting in 1819. The documentation of actual complaints, like those compiled by historian Trevor Burnard in *Hearing Slaves Speak*, remains one of the main archival sources of enslaved people in the Caribbean speaking in something close to their own voice – though, as Burnard cautions, these are still official government documents registered by the dominant power and as such "do not provide such unmediated reflections by slaves upon their condition."[7] The archival record of complaints by the enslaved therefore raises questions of voice (thematized even in the title Burnard chose for the anthology) that are also at issue in the prolific Romantic genre of complaint poems by white British poets assuming another's voice. These records manifest particular complaints about concrete issues, but the particular complaints carry within them a more total complaint, a "No," as Debbie Lee and Peter Kitson note, toward the world that created and sustains the horrors of racial slavery. Reading the repetition of the word "No" in one complaint recorded from Berbice, Lee and Kitson write that "the triple repetition of the word 'No'" is a "complicated and subtle" gesture that "seem[s] to say to white audiences in England who claimed to know the sufferings of the slave, 'No, you cannot grieve deeply for me unless you have endured what I have.'"[8] Romantic complaint poems similarly bear out the impossibility of crossing the chasm of experience to speak as and for the enslaved, but also, often against their own current, find themselves punctured by a destabilizing negativity, a voice that breaks through the words of poet and speaker.

### Abolitionist Lyric, Race, and the Problem of Voice: Cowper's "The Negro's Complaint"

William Cowper's "The Negro's Complaint" (1788) was perhaps the most successful of the antislavery poems of the period. Cowper writes this lyric poem with an instruction to the reader to sing the words to the melody of a popular ballad, making "The Negro's Complaint" a lyrical ballad avant la lettre. Cowper's poem, even before the actual verses start, invites its (mostly white) readers not only to read in the persona and voice of a suffering enslaved person, but to actually vocalize this voice, to *sing*, to a certain ballad tune they would know. This note on the melody foregrounds and even literalizes the question of voice in its relation to race. Ivan Ortiz deciphers the complicated, "polyphonic" layering of voices in "The Negro's Complaint" (alongside another poem set to the same tune) in relation to the history of the ballad's melody, which is taken from a patriotic song named "Admiral Hosier's Ghost" that praises a British military hero who fought to expand slavery: "Their enslaved speakers do achieve a political voice, but it is a British voice that reverberates the very imperial history that contributed to their enslavement."[9] With hopes to stir up abolitionist sentiment, the poet's voice attempts to inhabit the voice of a suffering slave, the poem's speaker and "I," and asks readers (as singers) to perform an act of sympathetic identification with the speaker, and consequently with the plight of the enslaved more generally – to feel the complaint and work to answer it with succor and redress.

While the poem is laden with what would become the stock tropes of antislavery literature (like affirming the freedom of thought despite physical chains), the speaker also questions "England's rights" to practice slavery and invokes "Nature's claim" to racial equality, thus introducing the first bit of juridical language in the poem after the title; the claim of nature (as in, e.g., a claims court) aligns with the legal resonance of the titular "complaint" to begin building a case against slavery (the etymology of "claim," from Old French *clamer*, has to do with summoning someone to the law or to court) (10, 14).[10] After establishing a kind of poetic courtroom, the speaker then proceeds to cross-examine white England in a flurry of interrogatives, ultimately demanding proof: "*Prove that you* have human feelings" (55). The series of questions are formally like those posed by Job in his quasi-legal poetic complaint and culminate in an "answer" that bears a direct allusion to the Book of Job:

> Why did all-creating Nature
>     Make the plant for which we toil?
> . . .
> Is there, as ye sometimes tell us,
>     Is there One who reigns on high?
> Has He bid you buy and sell us,
>     Speaking from his throne the sky?
> . . .
> Hark – He answers. Wild tornadoes
>     Strewing yonder floods with wrecks,
> Wasting Towns, Plantations, Meadows,
>     Are the voice with which he speaks.
> He foreseeing what vexations
>     Afric's sons should undergo,
> Fix'd their Tyrants' habitations
>     Where his whirlwinds answer – No.
> (17–18, 25–28, 33–40)

The most powerful moment in Cowper's poem is when the impersonation seems to stop, and a voice reverberates through that is neither the poet's, nor exactly the enslaved voice the poet is imitating, but a third voice – a voice attributed indirectly to God, by way of a cosmic voice in the "whirlwinds['] answer," recalling precisely the voice answering "out of the whirlwind" at the end of Job. This voice says only a single syllable: "*No.*" The *No*, the negation of the entire slave world, is the sole utterance adequate to the slave's complaint. Like in Job, the complaint here corresponding with the *No* is total and cosmic, as suggested by the questioning not just of a particular wrong, but the deposition of "all-creating nature." Despite Cowper's white ventriloquism and appeal to a defanged "pity" ("Pity for Poor Africans" is the title of another antislavery poem by Cowper), which has been rightly critiqued, the core of the poem's energy is this *No*. The "No" is not only a refusal of the world, but carries a destructive negativity within it, a material force embodied in the storms that rip through plantations and shatter the societies around them, that wreck ships and devastate shores. While Cowper cannot properly speak (or write) the "No" of the enslaved, his poem gives the voice of this "No" to a whirlwind, rather than to his own poetic voice or to his appropriated one. Whatever Cowper's express political beliefs as an individual person, which tended toward the view that the British Empire could serve as a potential force for moral good if it could expurgate the stain of slavery (as Ortiz shows), the material event of this poem's language prompts him, consciously or not, toward a reckoning with the totality that involves himself and his readers intimately.

Since the "oral metaphor" of voice is, arguably, the constitutive formal element of modern lyric poetry, when the manifest content of a poem explicitly thematizes voice and vocalization, it demands especial attention.[11] In Cowper's "The Negro's Complaint," these moments are the note on the poem's ballad melody, and the voice in the whirlwind, the "No." The speaker enjoins the audience to "Hark!" and listen to another voice: "Hark! He answers! – Wild tornadoes / . . . are the voice with which he speaks." In this dramatic prosopopoeia – the trope of attributing a voice or face to something absent, disembodied, or inanimate (the Greek *prosopopoeia* literally translates to "making a face") – drawn from Job, a third voice breaks in, one that has little to do with sympathy or identification (indeed, it might even momentarily break the paradigm of sympathetic identification otherwise operative in this poem); the express aim of Cowper's poem is to make the slave's complaint legible, but its real illegibility (its *refusal* of legibility) breaks through instead, as the rumble of this third voice harbors a complaint that reaches the entirety of "all-creating nature," to curse the world that the British Empire has forged. Indeed, this world could not hear and address this complaint without itself crumbling. If voice is fundamental to lyric, and to how lyric voicing "masks" the author, more specifically it is prosopopoeia that, in de Man's influential conception, is the "master trope" in the procedure of every lyric poem.[12] In this view, all modern lyric poetry is a kind of imitation or prosopopoeia – but the whole of Cowper's poem, and the other complaint poems by white authors, raise important questions about lyric voice and racialization at the very moment of modern lyric's formation in Romanticism. What faces can be made or given poetically, by whom, and how, and why? In a world riven by slavery and antiblackness, what color is the face that seems to speak, and with whose voice? If prosopopoeia as "making face" is constitutive of all lyric voice(ing), what happens when the face made is made in blackface?

This remains a live issue in Cowper's "The Negro's Complaint," and even more so in other antislavery (or otherwise racialized) complaint poems in the Romantic period. For his part, Cowper refrains from attempting to imitate an enslaved person's diction and pronunciation, but poems from British magazines that continue the complaint subgenre, such as "The Poor Negro Beggar's Petition and Complaint" (1791, attributed to "M.H.") and "The African's Complaint on Board a Slave Ship" (1793, anonymous), are written in an embarrassing and patronizing attempt at the dialect of an enslaved person that make them nearly unreadable and unteachable today. This is especially true for the latter poem, about which Marcus Wood writes: "The voice in this poem has nothing to do with black suffering and everything to do with white sentimental fictions of black suffering."[13]

"The African's Complaint," however, bears mention for being included by the radical Black activist Robert Wedderburn in his abolitionist periodical *The Axe Laid to the Root* (1817), where the poem is inserted between Wedderburn's own prose sections of fiery antislavery rhetoric and prophetic denunciation. Wedderburn, the son of an enslaved Black woman and a Scottish planter who grew up free in Jamaica (born into slavery but manumitted as an infant) before arriving on the London ultra-radical scene, has a significantly different relation to the dialect voicing of this otherwise insufferable complaint poem than the (almost certainly) white author. Wedderburn's editorial gesture of including the piece in *Axe* seems to wager that a different force of complaint might surge through the words when placed in a different textual site – that is, in an abolitionist periodical that proudly declares itself to be edited and mostly written by someone with intimate experience with the horrors of Caribbean slavery. Particularly notable is that this poem appears in Wedderburn's *Axe* with no attribution (not even to "Anonymous"), as if to prompt readers to consider that it might have come from his hand (indeed, even until a few years ago, scholars mistakenly attributed a number of the poems anthologized in *Axe* to Wedderburn). Moreover, "The African's Complaint" poem ends issue two of *Axe*, and the following issue immediately begins with more dialect writing – this time in prose, and by Wedderburn himself, leading into a discussion about an unjust legal case in which a British jury failed to convict sailors for the murder of enslaved people, yet another unanswered and unanswerable complaint in the court of the world.

Wedderburn sees something in the genre of the complaint poem, even the dubious dialect versions, whose voice he can redirect and turn to his own radical abolitionist ends. Lyric voice is not only an operation of poet and speaker, but a force that inheres in the materiality of its local, textual site, and is entangled with worldly antagonisms that flow variously through it. By writing his own Patois dialect passage immediately following the dialect poem, Wedderburn is both showing a more "authentic" voice of the enslaved, but also placing in question such a paradigm of authenticity; he does so without legitimating the bathos of white sympathetic imitation, instead performing an indifference to it and a reappropriation of its material. For Wedderburn's own complaint, which he roots in the complaint of the enslaved, his "countrymen and relatives yet in bondage," is total – his program is a complete uprooting of this unjustifiable world, moving from the abolition of slavery to the abolition of private property and a "generalized rebellion" for an entirely new society.[14] Unlike Cowper and other polite abolitionists, Wedderburn wants from his audience not sympathy, pity, and reform, but for them to join in a revolutionary movement that would sweep across the Atlantic and attack the totality of the racial capitalist world-system.

## Sympathy and the Forsaken Voice: Opie and Wordsworth

Authors in the Romantic period continued to produce antislavery complaint poems in droves. A poem like "The Black Man's Lament" (1826), by the prominent abolitionist author Amelia Opie (and included in a publication addressed to children), is noteworthy for its self-conscious thematization of the question of voice and appropriation through multiple speakers. The poem's first speaker, who seems to align with the positionality of the poet (white, middle-class, British, woman), enjoins the audience to "listen to my plaintive ditty," thus with the word "plaintive" reminding the reader of the complaint subgenre and of the suffering slave as a "plaintiff" who registers wrongs and injuries (1).[15] As with so much British antislavery literature, the clichés of sympathy and pity are deployed ("should it move your souls to pity"), and the device of a white poet impersonating a Black voice is at work (3). Opie's poem, however, seems to acknowledge the need to let the enslaved speak in their own voice by shifting speakers mid-poem, even as this new speaker is just as much (or even more) the creation of the white poet and is shorn of all singularity, being referred to only as "Negro" or "Negro slave." The passing of the microphone between speakers reads as follows:

> But, Negro slave! *thyself* shall tell,
> Of past and present wrongs the story;
> And would all British hearts could feel,
> To *end* those wrongs were *Britain's glory*.
>
> *Negro speaks.*
>
> "First to our own dear Negro land,
>     His ships the cruel White man sends
> And there contrives, by armed band,
> To tear us from our homes and friends["] (13–21)

The poem thus frets over the authenticity of poetic voice – implying that only the enslaved themselves can recount their own suffering ("*thyself* shall tell") – while enfolding this very fretting into an even deeper racial appropriation. In indicating to readers that a new vocalization interjects, the poem doubles or even triples down on the constitutive lyric fiction of voice. But what exactly is the poetic, or lyric, status of the interstanzaic words "*Negro speaks*," the vestibular utterance that accompanies and trumpets the change of speaker and voice? Who speaks "*Negro speaks*," and who could verify this? The poem's tangle of voices gets even more complicated as yet another voice enters: a white skeptic of abolition who questions the enslaved speaker as if cross-examining him in a courtroom. The enslaved speaker responds with a list of complaints, detailing to the skeptic the horrendous injustices and brutalities of slavery, but the poem does not approach the total complaint except perhaps in the hint of "rage" ("I burn with rage!") in the enslaved speaker's final lines (168). After these lines, however, the initial white speaker returns to close out the poem with a concluding quatrain, which ends: "Alas! it rends my heart to know / He only told a *tale of truth*" (173). The sentimental last lines work both to pacify the boiling "rage" of the enslaved speaker for white audiences fearful of Black revolt and vengeance, and to confer authority, legitimacy, and legibility on the "truth" of the (fictional) testimony and complaint provided in the poem. Holding the last word, the first speaker returns and ultimately unifies the fragmented voices of the poem back into the calm, white voice that is associated with the author, Amelia Opie, whose name appears after these final lines but before an exergue stating "The End."

Abolition, she avers, would not cause too much upheaval and would even redound to "Britain's glory."

The anxiety about the plurality of speakers' voices and the fiction of authenticity that riddles Opie's poem is far from an anomaly. Romantic lyric poems, which are already formally constituted by the fiction of a speaking voice, seem to betray an added self-consciousness in complaint poems that impersonate the voices of the subaltern, a reflexivity that often takes the form of a nonhuman or cosmic voice. This is especially visible in a complaint lyric from the primal scene of British Romanticism: Wordsworth and Coleridge's *Lyrical Ballads*. Although not explicitly a poem dealing with slavery, Wordsworth's "The Complaint of a Forsaken Indian Woman" warrants mention in a discussion of the antislavery complaint genre for its treatment of voice and its use of the prosopopoeia of the speaking wind. Besides its title announcing its affiliation with the tradition of complaint poems, this poem finds Wordsworth impersonating the voice of a racialized (and gendered) subject to register a complaint of calamitous mistreatment, in this case writing in the lyric voice of an Indigenous North American woman. While the poem cannot be divorced from its context of British settler colonialism in North America (specifically in this poem, present-day Canada), including the histories of indigenous petition and complaint, it also evokes the context of slavery in several ways, tying it to the more explicitly abolitionist complaint poems discussed in this essay. Wordsworth's appended prose note explains the context of an "Indian" woman in the Americas who was left behind to die of sickness by her travelling companions, but since "Indian" could also refer to "West Indian," and nothing in the poem itself specifies the exact setting, it is not unreasonable to assume the poem would have also had the resonance of Caribbean slavery for readers; in addition to the title, the central episode of "The Complaint of a Forsaken Indian Woman" recounted by the speaker is the tearing of her child from her arms, a ubiquitous motif in abolitionist literature to illustrate the concrete evils and fundamental immorality of slavery.

While the speaker laments the injustice of being abandoned to die and the wretched sorrow of having her child ripped away, the fifth stanza (of seven) shifts the complaint into a reflexive mode, where the speaker's complaint is about how her power of utterance – her voice of complaint – has been foreclosed: "Too soon, my friends, you went away; / For I had many things to say" (49–50).[16] Wordsworth's poem, written by a white male poet, assumes a racialized and gendered lyric voice to register a complaint about this voice (Indigenous, female) being unheard. And at this very moment of lyric appropriation and racialized (meta)complaint, the desire for another, third voice irrupts through the poem's language. This comes in the form of another prosopopoeia, a voice in the wind:

> Oh wind that o'er my head art flying,
> The way my friends their course did bend,
> I should not feel the pain of dying,
> Could I with thee a message send.
> Too soon, my friends, you went away;
> For I had many things to say. (45–50)

Just as in Job and Cowper, a speaking wind is invoked in relation to complaint.[17] The wind is the subject of an apostrophe, a direct address ("Oh wind"), and is given voice in being asked to a carry "a message" to her companions. The content of this message is not disclosed – only that the speaker wishes to say more, to continue speaking in her own voice in a complaint that has no possible redress. In the voiced desire for voice, a deeper estrangement between the poem's own authorial voice (Wordsworth) and fictional speaker (the forsaken Indian woman) is both occasioned and figured by the imagined merging of a voice with the flying, whirling wind. This is less either to castigate Wordsworth for appropriation or to defend him as someone concerned with the plight of Indian women (whether American Indigenous or enslaved West Indian), but instead to notice something about the historical and social pressures that shape poetic form vis-à-vis race.

## Complaint and Conviction in Equiano's Poetry

The most prominent Black writer of the Romantic era in Britain, Olaudah Equiano, takes up the complaint poem genre in a way that lays bare its most radical stakes: the complaint's ability to call the entire world, with its apparatus of justice and law, into question.[18] Equiano's abolitionist autobiography *The Interesting Narrative of the Life of Olaudah Equiano, Or Gustavus Vassa, The African* (1789), published in London one year after Cowper's "The Negro's Complaint," in fact contains several original poems, though his verse is often overlooked. I wish to focus on the extended poem that concludes chapter 10 of *The Interesting Narrative*, entitled "Miscellaneous Verses." This complex poem takes on yet further dimensions when situated alongside the instances of actual complaint in the life narrative in which it is enmeshed, and when seen in the mode of poetic complaint discussed in this essay, especially in the poem's signaled relation to the total complaint voiced in Job. Equiano's poem is rarely seen in the complaint tradition that it proleptically scrambles, but doing so allows one to discern aspects of an abolitionist and political-theological idiom that are more latent in Equiano's prose autobiographical voice.

The poetic complaint voiced in *The Interesting Narrative* must be read in the context of two earlier instances in the text where Equiano – once as an enslaved man and once after having purchased his freedom – describes bringing a complaint of mistreatment or injustice to a higher authority, only to have his complaint dismissed out of hand, completely illegible to the white world. The first occurs in chapter 6, when Equiano and another enslaved companion have their bags of goods stolen from them by two white men who threatened to beat them. The two wronged men complain to the superior of the malefactors, but their commanding officer threatens to beat them further, responding to their "complaint" with a whip: "But we obtained not the least redress: he answered our complaints only by a volley of imprecations against us, and immediately took a horse-whip, in order to chastise us."[19] Later in the same chapter, Equiano reflects on the impossibility of justice for Black people in the West Indies, whether enslaved or free, there being no court in which they could appear and no judge to adjudicate their complaints (97).[20] Indeed, it is at this very moment in chapter 6, at the threshold of impossible complaint, that Equiano's narrative breaks out into poetry. In chapter 9, Equiano experiences precisely this injustice after his freedom is obtained, when he is cheated in a business deal by a white man and seeks legal redress as a plaintiff. Going "to complain to one Mr. M'Intosh, a justice of the peace; we told his worship of the man's villainous tricks, and begged that he would be kind enough to see us redressed: but being negroes, although free, we could not get any remedy" (141).

Like his recourse to verse after an unheard – in fact, unhearable – complaint in chapter 6, Equiano's poem "Miscellaneous Verses" occurs in the chapter immediately following the denied complaint of chapter 9. While a personal theological experience is integral to the poem, part of the larger narrative of religious conversion that is central to the arc of *The Interesting Narrative*, the specific theological context of complaint surrounding the poem orients its critique of slavery. In London, Equiano hears a sermon preached on a single verse from the book of Lamentations – a verse about *complaint*: "Wherefore doth a living man complain, a man for the punishment of his sins?" (Lamentations 3:39). He is struck, and, in a moment of spiritual agony, decides to give himself over to God. Even though the verse advises the sinner *not* to complain, it is specifically a "living man" who is discouraged from complaint: What might this injunction against complaint mean for one who has experienced the living death of slavery? This question is what the poem works through, before arriving at which Equiano cites several biblical verses, among them notably Job 33:30. In fact, the final words before the text abruptly switches from prose narrative to lyric outcry are yet another quote from Job (14:14, "appointed time"), though this time the citation is hidden. This means that the words directly leading into Equiano's own poem of complaint are not exactly in his own voice, but a quotation of another, earlier plaintiff: the cosmic and total complaint of Job. Just as Job can find no court of equal justice with God, Equiano finds no possibility of justice for his complaint in the demiurgic white world.

The full title of Equiano's poem contains a juridical pun on the word "convictions," affiliating it further with the thread of legal language in Job and the legal resonance of "complaint," both of which Equiano makes clear he is well aware of.[21] The verses commence immediately in a plaintive register, lamenting Equiano's life of "sorrow and of pain" as an enslaved man, and the complaint mode is explicitly invoked when the speaker later describes himself as being "compelled ... to complain" (160). At several points, the poem's speaker enunciates not only the intensity but the *totality* of his being wronged, emphasizing his total separation from the world, and thus the force of his total complaint against its injustice. He has been left in "an orphan state ... forsook by all," and "unknown / to all"; he finds himself so abandoned that "*all things* added to my pain"; and he refers to himself, simply, as "lost in the world" (160, 161, 162).

It is to song that the speaker tells of turning in his grief, even as in his song (or lyric poem) he recognizes song's inadequacy to find redress for his complaint or an end to torment: "I sung, and utter'd sighs between" (160). With a voice in the syncopated rhythm between song and sigh, the speaker names woes that blend the misery of slavery with the misery of sin, making the poem a mix of social critique and inward-looking Protestant theology. But in Equiano's feeling of his "orphan state," his being severed from community and lost in the world, there is also a special resonance with the sense of orphanhood and cosmic complaint that Nathaniel Mackey sounds in Black music and literature: "The quintessential source of music is the orphan's ordeal – an orphan being anyone denied kinship, social sustenance, anyone who suffers, to use Orlando Patterson's phrase, 'social death' ... Song is both a complaint and a consolation dialectically tied to that ordeal."[22] Despite the proscription (or at least discouragement) of complaint in Lamentations 3:39, the verse that sparks his conversion to

Christianity, Equiano turns to composing poetry to complain both in chapter 6 and especially here in chapter 10. There is something, then, in the complaint of song and the song of complaint, that resists this conversion narrative, that resists the conviction from the Lamentations verse that his sufferings in the world are the punishments of his sins other than the "sin" of being Black, of which the world convicts and condemns him without a hearing. When complaint in or to the world is impossible, poetry grants Equiano a voice to complain about the world as such. A voice from elsewhere, from nowhere, a voice that is at odds with the entirety of the world and that says "No."[23] No court can summon the world itself to judgment – but perhaps a poem, that unacknowledged legislation (to paraphrase Percy Shelley), can.

This negating edge of lyric voice, which according to Marshall Brown may be inherent in all lyric, takes on an additional sharpness in the context of a formerly enslaved poet.[24] The voice even demands that Equiano negate himself, provoking a movement of self-tension and self-estrangement expressed especially in the legal language of the poem, and given a certain formal and spiritual resolution by the turn to Christianity. The phrase "my ... Convictions" in the full title of "Miscellaneous Verses" obviously first means "my beliefs," but the double meaning of a legal conviction of guilt is evoked when the same word occurs in the body of the poem, now paired with "guilt": "Conviction still my vileness shew'd; / How great my guilt" (160). The motif of legal metaphor and the question of guilt culminate in a moment of crisis, when the speaker, "lost in the world," calls to Christ:

> Like some poor pris'ner at the bar,
> Conscious of guilt, of sin and fear,
> Arraign'd, and self-condemn'd, I stood –
> 'Lost in the world and in my blood!'
>
> Yet here, 'midst blackest clouds confin'd,
> A beam from Christ, the day-star shin'd;
> Surely, thought I, if Jesus please,
> He can at once sign my release. (162)

Similar to Job, Equiano's speaker here is both plaintiff and defendant. Indeed, he is "self-condemned," a priori convicted by a world that degrades him, and destitute before God. Christ is figured as a legal authority that can "sign [the] release" of the speaker (tantamount to manumission papers), but, at the same time, the force of Christ's name is what releases the speaker from the entire apparatus of the law. The legal language of the poem ends with just such a dissolution of the court of the world, as the penultimate couplet deactivates all worldly law that denies a hearing to those who are Black: "He dy'd for all who ever saw / No help ... by the law" (162). No help is in the law, and no redress is possible in the world for this complaint, but the poem resounds before and beneath the law, opening the space where the voice beyond the law can sing, whether to call to God or to anything, anywhere out of this world.[25] While embracing Christianity is the way out of this zone of absolute negation, a conventional move in the genre of spiritual autobiography, the complaint against the world from one utterly lost in it is what lingers in the poem's language. Moreover, the context of the total complaint of the enslaved suggests that this abolitionist Christianity should have nothing to do with the world, nor with "the law." It longs to abolish the court of the world as part of its refusal or "No" to theodicy – that is, its refusal to justify the world and the system of slavery that is its foundation.

Unlike so many other Romantic-era complaint poems that turn on a racial appropriation and impersonation, Equiano's verses are presented by a Black writer in his own voice (as it were). A poem nestled inside an autobiography indeed raises an interesting question about lyric speaker and voice, for if there were ever a justification for identifying poet and speaker, it would be in such a case. Yet this poem's voice of complaint emerges from an impossibility of voicing a complaint in the world of racial slavery that Equiano finds himself (lost) in, as is narrated in the prose sections, and this vocal disjunction also occurs within the poem's self-estrangement of voice, in the speaker's being "self-condemned" and unable to be heard. This is particularly what distinguishes it from white impersonation complaint poems, which tend to emphasize a complaint about the state of affairs within the world that, however egregious or horrific, can be remedied or ameliorated, with the world (and the British Empire's glory) intact – except, as we saw, in brief flashes of negativity otherwise largely unsolicited by white writers. Equiano's lived experience of blackness, his experience of total dispossession and being "lost in the world," affects the material formation of the words, forms, and grooves of the poem. Rather than only finding in Equiano the proper (as opposed to appropriative) poet for an antislavery complaint speaker, we might also consider how he forges and inhabits a literary form that draws closer to the third voice of negation that inheres, perhaps, in every lyric poem, the collective undersong of *No*, the depthless well of non-sense from which all sense springs. Without losing sight of the question of positionality in the racialization of lyric voice, this protocol of reading would shift the focus from improper imperson*ation* to the improper and impers*onal*, thus revising the close association of lyric with individualized personality and inner subjectivity. The "person" is, after all, a fictive legal construct – a white mask.

## Voices in the Wind: Afterlives of Black Complaint

Complaint can complain *to* the world or *of* the world. Though such a division is rarely a neat one, the antislavery complaint poems of the Romantic period allow this tension to come into view in a way that also illuminates some of the fundamental mechanisms of Romantic lyric. The conjuncture of Romanticism and complaint has continued to occupy Black poets up to the present, providing an occasion and a form for engaging the legacies of slavery and the forms of racial exclusion that still govern the order of things. The enslaved African American poet George Moses Horton, who, as Matt Sandler demonstrates, "took up the aesthetic prerogatives of Romanticism" to reimagine them, wrote a poem in the subgenre entitled "The Slave's Complaint" in 1829.[26] Here Horton depicts himself as suspended in "slavery's night," "cast aside" and radically excluded from "the world," which cannot hear his total complaint calling this very world into question.[27] More recently, the labyrinthine corpus of Nathaniel Mackey has explored the lineaments of Black poetic complaint taken to cosmic extreme, mobilizing music and mythology against the world as such, bearing "a grudge against the cosmos," where "complaint [is] a condition of / soul."[28]

The Caribbean-Canadian poet M. NourbeSe Philip's *Zong!* (2008) performs a radical inversion of the Romantic antislavery complaint poem. Whereas the latter usually finds a white poet complaining in the imagined voice of an enslaved person, Philip takes the actual legal text of a Romantic-era complaint in which the plaintiffs were not slaves but *slavers* – the owners of the slave ship *Zong* who attempted to recoup insurance money after the captain murdered more than 130 enslaved people by throwing them overboard – as the material of her poem. By "explod-[ing] the words" of the 1783 legal case and rearranging them in staggeringly evocative and haunting ways, as Philip herself explains in the book's afterword, the poem turns the voice of the law into a collective voice of total complaint, a chorus of voices "*outside* of the law" that calls the entire constitution of the world to judgment: "*Zong!* bears witness to the 'resurfacing of the drowned and the oppressed' and transforms the desiccated legal report into a cacophony of voices – wails, cries, moans, and shouts that had earlier been banned from the text."[29]

Philip, who worked as a lawyer before taking up writing full time, probes the linguistic power of both poetry and law to cancel out or acknowledge being by taking or "*giving voice*" (194). In both inhabiting and resisting the operations of lyric poetry – Philip admits wrestling with the poem's "apparent lyric form" – *Zong!* expresses the cry of a fragmented reality that is 'multiple and 'many-voiced'" (203, 205). Part 3 of the book is named "Ventus" (Latin for "wind"), and at one point later in the text the prosopopoeia of voices in the wind that occurs so often in the tradition of poetic complaint surfaces, or rather submerges, once again: "*sub voce*   the   voi   ces…in the wind."[30] *Sub voce*, a Latin phrase typically used in reference works, literally translates to "under the voice," but we might also hear it as the breaking through, and the undertow, of an "undervoice." In *Zong!*, the voice from the whirlwind on high has become the drowned voices from under the sea, voices that sing the everything and nothing stowed in their *No*.

## Notes

1. Jonathan Culler, "Changes in the Study of Lyric," in *Lyric Poetry: Beyond New Criticism*, ed. Chaviva Hosêk and Patricia Parker (Ithaca: Cornell University Press, 1985), 50.
2. Peter Kitson, "'Bales of Living Anguish': Representations of Race and the Slave in Romantic Writing," *ELH* 67/2 (Summer 2000), 522.
3. Nicole Aljoe, "Testimonies of the Enslaved in the Caribbean Literary History," in *Literary Histories of the Early Anglophone Caribbean*, ed. Nicole Aljoe, Brycchan Carey, and Thomas Krise (London: Palgrave, 2018), 108.
4. M. H. Abrams, "The Correspondent Breeze: A Romantic Metaphor," *The Kenyon Review* 19/1 (Winter 1957), 113–30.
5. Marc Redfield, *Theory at Yale: The Strange Case of Deconstruction in America* (New York: Fordham University Press, 2015), 62.
6. See Matt Sandler, *The Black Romantic Revolution: Abolitionist Poets at the End of Slavery* (London: Verso, 2020), 68.
7. Trevor Burnard, "Introduction," *Hearing Slaves Speak* (Guyana: The Caribbean Press, 2010), ix.
8. Debbie Lee and Peter Kitson, "General Introduction," *Slavery, Abolition and Emancipation*, ed. Peter J. Kitson and Debbie Lee, 8 vols. (London: Routledge, 1999), 1:x.
9. Ivan Ortiz, "Lyric Possession in the Abolition Ballad," *Eighteenth-Century Studies* 51/2 (2018), 203.
10. William Cowper, "The Negro's Complaint," *The Poems of William Cowper*, vol. III, ed. John D. Baird and Charles Ryskamp (Oxford: Clarendon Press, 1996), 13–14. Line numbers cited in text.

11. Eliza Richards, "Voice," in *Princeton Encyclopedia of Poetry and Poetics*, ed. Roland Greene and Stephen Cushman (Princeton: Princeton University Press, 2012), 1525.
12. "In the lyric poem, the author masks his or her expression by speaking through an objectified figure of voice." Richards, "Voice," 1525. Paul de Man, *The Resistance to Theory* (Minneapolis: University of Minnesota Press, 1986), 48. De Man's own metaphor of "master[y]," so bound up with the paradigm of slavery, bears noticing.
13. *The Poetry of Slavery: An Anglo-American Anthology, 1764–1865*, ed. Marcus Wood (Oxford: Oxford University Press: 2004), 211.
14. Robert Wedderburn, *The Horrors of Slavery and Other Writings*, ed. Iain McCalman (Princeton: Markus Wiener, 1991), 83, 61.
15. Amelia Opie, "The Black Man's Lament," in *The Collected Poems of Amelia Alderson Opie*, ed. Shelley King and John B. Pierce (Oxford: Oxford University Press, 2010), 318–23. Line numbers cited in text.
16. Cited from *Lyrical Ballads*, ed. R. L. Brett and A. R. Jones (London: Routledge, 2005), 151–53.
17. Regarding race and the prosopopoeia of wind in Wordsworth and beyond, see Chapter 2 in this volume.
18. I use "Romantic era" here as a general temporal marker signifying roughly 1780–1830; Equiano's critical position vis-à-vis the specific movement of Romanticism is more vexed, as discussed by Manu Chander and Patricia Matthew, "Abolitionist Interruptions: Romanticism, Slavery, and Genre," *European Romantic Review* 29/4 (2018), 431–34.
19. Olaudah Equiano, *The Interesting Narrative*, ed. Brycchan Carey (Oxford: Oxford University Press, 2018), 93. Further references will be given in the text; poems cited by page number.
20. "[Free Black people] are universally insulted and plundered without the possibility of redress; for such is the equity of the West Indian laws, that no free negro's evidence will be admitted in their courts of justice." Equiano, *The Interesting Narrative*, 97.
21. Full title: "MISCELLANEOUS VERSES, OR, Reflections on the State of my Mind during my first Convictions, of the Necessity of believing the Truth, and experiencing the inestimable Benefits of Christianity."
22. Nathaniel Mackey, "Sound and Sentiment, Sound and Symbol," *Callaloo* 30 (Winter 1987), 29.
23. On worldlessness, see Tyrone Palmer, "Otherwise than Blackness: Feeling, World, Sublimation," *Qui Parle* 29/2 (2020), 247–83.
24. See Marshall Brown, "Negative Poetics: On Skepticism and the Lyric Voice," *Representations* 86/1 (Spring 2004), 120–40.
25. On Equiano's negotiation of Lord and law, see the first chapter of Fred Moten's *Stolen Life* (Durham: Duke University Press, 2018).
26. Following James Weldon Johnson, Sandler places Horton in the long tradition of complaint from Job through Cowper, arguing: "Horton's complaints

*The Voice of Complaint* 149

give a picture of the consciousness of enslavement in a spiritually bankrupt world"; *Black Romantic*, 68, 69.
27. George Moses Horton, "The Slave's Complaint," in *The Poetry of Slavery*, ed. Wood, 462–63.
28. Nathaniel Mackey, *Moment's Omen* (Pittsboro: Selva Oscura Press, 2015), n. p.; Mackey, *Blue Fasa* (New York: New Directions, 2015).
29. M. Nourbese Philip, *Zong!* (Middletown: Wesleyan University Press, 2008), 200, 207, 203. Further references will be given in the text.
30. Philip, *Zong!*, 168. The typographical arrangement of *Zong!* is difficult to reproduce but is essential to the poem. Here is an approximation of this passage:

            can y                                ou not he
ar *sub voce*                  the voi                      ces *au*
            *di* of kin *a*                 *udi* in the wind

CHAPTER 9

# *Romantic Manscapes*

### Devin M. Garofalo

In his *Guide to the Lakes* – an introduction to the Lake District, that most iconic of Romantic stomping grounds – William Wordsworth draws an analogy between the arts of poetry and landscape design:

> Laying out the grounds, as it is called, may be considered as a liberal art, in some sort like poetry and painting; and its object ... is to assist Nature in moving the affections ... of those who have the deepest perception of the beauty of Nature; who have the most valuable feelings, that is, the most permanent, the most independent, the most ennobling, connected with Nature and human life. No liberal art aims merely at the gratification of an individual or a class ... [T]he true servants of the Arts pay homage to the human kind as impersonated in unwarped and enlightened minds.[1]

Here, Wordsworth triangulates poetry, nature, and humankind in ways typical of Romanticism at its most canonical and normative. Positing poetry and landscape as concomitant "liberal art[s]," he argues that their aspirations are universal: ranging beyond "individual" and "class," they "pay homage to human kind," broadly construed. And yet, Wordsworth also argues that the aesthetic "[l]aying of grounds" – whether in poetry or landscape – will "mov[e]" only select human communities on the basis of taste (or the capacity to discern "the beauty of Nature") and an "enlightened" quality of "min[d]." In Wordsworth's view, to be human is to be moved according to a culturally situated set of assumptions about aesthetic merit and a restrictive scheme of "enlighten[ment]." Wordsworth says as much when he proclaims that "a vivid perception of romantic scenery is neither inherent in mankind, nor a necessary consequence of even a comprehensive education" (151). Excluded from "human kind" are hardworking "artisans and labourers" (152), whom Wordsworth considered a threat to the Lake District's ecological purity, as well as "the humbler ranks of society" who – unlike those with "mo[re] valuable feelings" – do not stand "to gain material benefit from a more speedy access than they now have to this beautiful region" (157). Still others are voided from the world altogether. Advocating against the construction of railroads whose infrastructure and working-class passengers threaten the integrity of the Lake District as a "national property" (92), *Guide to the Lakes* obscures how the material and aesthetic infrastructures of some of the poet's most beloved English rural haunts (for instance, the Wye Valley, as envisioned in "Lines Composed a few miles above Tintern Abbey") were quite literally sponsored by enslavement and imperial enterprise. This begs the question: *whose* "national property"?

This essay explores the colonial whiteness at stake in Wordsworth's triangulation of poetry, nature, and humankind. While the Romantic Big Six – Wordsworth, William Blake, Samuel Taylor Coleridge, Percy Bysshe Shelley, Lord Byron, John Keats – are known today as quintessential nature boys, the ecologies in which they were enmeshed and the landscapes they envisioned are anything but neutral. As M. H. Abrams puts it in his foundational essay on the lyric: "Romantic writers, though nature poets, were humanists above all, for they dealt with the nonhuman only insofar as it is the occasion for the activity which defines man." In the context of, say, Coleridge's "Frost at Midnight" or Shelley's "Ode to the West Wind," the term "nature lyric" is therefore not just a misnomer but also "radically misleading."[2] This is because the representation of so-called nature says more about the contours of humankind – of who is or is not included in that category and who abjected from it as partially or wholly nonhuman – than a world rife with more-than-human animacies. So understood, Romanticism as normatively represented by the Bix Six is a venture in manscaping. I mean this in at least two senses: (1) it terraforms nature, reading a culturally specific conception of the human into the landscape such that it is invisibilized as the world's structuring principle; and (2) it anthropomorphizes the category of the human into conformity with white, European, bourgeois, colonial man such that the latter is asserted as the former's privileged archetype.

Lyric – a genre of poetry organized around a "bourgeois subject" or "private individual expressing himself to other private individuals who read in quiet contemplation" – looms especially large in this context because, as Anthony B. Reed demonstrates, for the likes of Wordsworth it "corresponds with and provides an aesthetic basis ... for the emergence of Man." It is in this way "a race project concerned with establishing and maintaining the boundaries of the human."[3] Here, boundaries are emphatically ecopolitical, foregrounding the intersections between the restrictively universal human fiction promulgated by the normative Romantic lyric, material processes of dehumanization (such as enslavement and dispossession), and the fantasy of a terraformed Earth available for the infinite taking. The violent ramifications of this restrictive universalism, environmental degradation, and race are manifest in Romantic-era science writing. For instance, the influential late eighteenth-century French natural historian the Comte de Buffon observes that "the entire face of the Earth today carries the imprint of the power of man." From Buffon's vantage, "man['s]" rise to geologic power is cause for celebration: "By his works, swamps were drained, the rivers contained, their cataracts smoothed, the forests cleared, the land cultivated. By his reflection, time was counted, space was measured ... Through his arts derived from science, the seas were traversed, mountains crossed, peoples brought closer, a new world discovered."[4]

Here, Buffon describes what some now call the Anthropocene: a new geologic epoch defined by humankind's indelible presence in the rock record and capacity to act at the scale of the planet. Invoking the European colonization of the Americas – wherein the genocide of some 61,000,000 Indigenous people and subsequent environmental "regeneration" produced a "dip in atmospheric $CO_2$," that "is the most prominent feature ... in pre-industrial atmospheric $CO_2$ records over the past 2,000 years" – Buffon, like Wordsworth, argues forcefully for the exclusively human prerogative of white colonial man.[5] Both thinkers in this way conflate man – which Sylvia Wynter theorizes as just one "genre" or cultural construction of the human among many – with the human as "natural organism" or species, thereby "absolutizing" whiteness as biologically prototypical and racializing nonwhite human communities as Other.[6] The remainder of this chapter explores the coconstitutive relationship between poetic and geologic, or anthropomorphic and anthropogenic, discourses of the human. Treating Wordsworth as the representative poet he claims to be shows how much the restrictively universal subjects of Romantic poems and planets have to tell us about the production of whiteness at the turn of the nineteenth century.

## Soil, Improvement, Taste

Often read as marking the emergence of an increasingly conservative, disillusioned, aggrieved poet, the Wordsworth of the 1815 "Essay, Supplementary to the Preface" is riddled with ugly feelings: envy, disdain, resentment, paranoia, violent ambition. These stem most immediately from Wordsworth's anger with his critics, whom he accuses of venerating second-rate poets, thereby lending credence to lay readers' undiscerning tastes. In support of his claims, Wordsworth sets his sights on the reception of James Thomson's long poem, *The Seasons*. Published initially in parts and then as a collected edition in 1730, *The Seasons* remained wildly popular at the time of Wordsworth's writing: it enjoyed a long life in print and occupied a formidable position of influence in the English literary canon. Less than impressed with *The Seasons*, Wordsworth asserts his unacknowledged right to canonization by taking swipes at Thomson and his readers (expert and otherwise). Declaring "Wonder" a "natural product of Ignorance" while drawing upon the language of cultivation and improvement, Wordsworth claims the metaphorical "soil was *in such good condition* at the time of the publication of the Seasons" that Thomson was serendipitously positioned to take unearned advantage of "the prepared sympathies of every one" (401, emphasis original).[7] The figurative land wherein Thomson's work would take healthy and enduring root, in other words, had been cleared prior to his arrival on the English literary scene.

But who are the bad agriculturalists that "prepared" the so-called "soil" such that readerly "sympathies" blossomed into a "crop" of indiscriminate wonder? Per the 1815 "Essay," critics are responsible for Thomson's bloated reputation. If *The Seasons* is marked by a "vicious style" and "title" whose cheap pandering to what we might now call relatability was contrived to "bring [the poem] home" to "the undiscerning," Thomson's expert readers should know better than to mistake smoke and mirrors for genius (401). That Wordsworth resorts to the language of soil, tillage, and harvest is important here. Taking *The Seasons* to task on its home turf – the georgic, a poetic mode distinguished by its didactic attention to rural laborers, cultivation, and best agricultural practices – Wordsworth figures the poem's devotees as failed agronomists. This becomes apparent in his emphases upon national taste and the critic's power to sow seeds of "enlighten[ment]" or "corrupt[ion]." Insofar as critics might "prepar[e]" (or deplete) readerly "sympathies," or the figurative "soil" of the nation, their vocation (like that of the English rural yeoman or West Indian plantocrat) is one of improvement. But whereas Wordsworth's agrarian metaphorics might seem strictly figurative, they are in fact "rooted in the earth," to borrow Edward Said's phrasing. Comprising "a vital part of the texture of linguistic and cultural practice" that Said understands as constituting "something like an imperial map of the world in English literature," the 1815 "Essay" is entangled with the material violence of enclosure whereby "[t]he old organic rural communities were dissolved and new ones forged under the impulse of parliamentary activity, industrialization, and demographic dislocation."[8]

This argument might seem counterintuitive insofar as Wordsworth railed forcefully and poignantly against the injustices of enclosure (see, for instance, *Salisbury Plain* or "Michael," among other poems). Even so, Wordsworth at the same time promulgates a program of taste that marshals the language and logics of improvement in service of both national purity (as theorized in the 1815 "Essay") and conservation. Hence, in the *Guide to the Lakes*, Wordsworth suggests that "every man has a right and interest" in the "national property" that is the Lake District, only to then argue repeatedly that "uneducated persons" are not "trained to a profitable intercourse with nature" (152), lack the "more susceptible taste [that] has been spreading among us for some years" (152), and are therefore unequipped to discern those ecological majesties which gratify the "perso[n] of pure taste" who possesses "an eye to perceive and a heart to enjoy" (92). Comprising a core part of his argument against the construction of railroads in and around the Lake District, the claim that "the humbler ranks of society are not, and cannot be, in a state to gain material benefit from a more speedy access than they now have to this beautiful region" (157) makes visible how Wordsworth's projects of taste and conservation (in an aesthetic as well as ecological sense) are conjoined – and how they are sponsored by the very forms of ecopolitical violence to which he elsewhere often vehemently objects. Here, an aesthetic sensibility (or lack thereof) affords the necessary grounds for a restrictive humanism that cordons off particular natures and forms of experience for a privileged few.

The 1815 "Essay," in particular, exposes how the restrictive humanism at stake in Wordsworth's aesthetic framework of readerly taste, arable land, and their corruption are consonant with Lockean ideals of individualism, cultivation, and property. As Brenna Bhandar demonstrates, these ideals are not only bound up with the project of enclosure but also emphatically racialized. In *Two Treatises of Government* (1689), John Locke, a so-called founding father of democratic thought, lays out the criteria by which a prodigiously fecund Earth "given to mankind in common" might be parceled into private property "without any express compact of all the commoners."[9] Positing nature as a "spontaneous" and inexhaustible resource, Locke observes "there must of necessity be a means to appropriate" the productions of Earth such that they are removed from their "natural state" in common and annexed for individual possession (111).

The "means" of appropriation for Locke lies in the possessive individual who "has a property" both "in his own person" and in "[t]he labour of his body" or "the work of his hands" (111). By working the land and so "mix[ing] his labour with, and join[ing] to it" the Earth, Locke's possessive individual "remove[s]" and so claims that which prior to his labour had existed in a "common state of nature." As Bhandar shows, he "gives rise to a right in that land that he has improved."[10]

The racial logic of Locke's framework becomes apparent in his assertions that "the grass my horse has bit; the turfs my servant has cut; and the ore I have digged in any place ... become my property, without the assignation or consent of any body" (112). Here, possessive individualism affords an alibi for the forcible abstraction of nonhuman and select human bodies into "stocks" (116) or inert resources. Only particular human beings possess a claim upon their own persons and labor. Or, to put it differently: some human beings' bodies and toils – "the work of [their] hands" – are not their own (111). Locke here gives voice to "economic visions of land" and "laws of property" that subtended not only the dispossession of the English rural poor, but also, as Bhandar argues, enslavement, plantation ecologies, and settler dispossession.[11] These material processes of dehumanization sustained the British Empire's world-building (and world-destroying) enterprise. Thus, on the basis of these culturally specific ideas about land use and property, Locke asserts Indigenous peoples in the Americas possess no claim upon their lands and, in a certain sense, do not even exist. Whereas "the civilized part of mankind" (112) refines the Earth by "till[ing], plant[ing], improv[ing], cultivat[ing]," and terraforming it for human use, "the wild Indian ... knows no enclosure" (111). Neither "subdu[ing]" nor "anne[xing]" to himself the fruits of nature, he possesses no property in his person or labor (113). But if "God gave the world to men in common," Locke contends "it cannot be supposed he meant it should always remain common and uncultivated" (114). A European, bourgeois, colonial, masculinist form of whiteness here asserts itself by and through an ethic of improvement whereby Earth is spiritually as well as materially revitalized and self-determination denied to those human communities who do not accommodate the "industrious and rational" ideals of "civilized" man (114).

If Locke's framework legitimizes enslavement as well as colonial dispossession and genocide, Wordsworth invokes it to cast his bad-agronomist critics as "corrupt" and corrupting on grounds of having abdicated those tenets of white liberal personhood and regimes of taste through which the English nation might achieve a coherent racial identity. So contextualized, Wordsworth's language of soil, enclosure, and improvement is inextricable from a white supremacist world order quite literally rooted in Earth – in land, property, and Englishness, as determined by what Yoon Sun Lee in Chapter 1 of this volume calls a "constitutional" (as opposed to "genetic" or phenotypic) "inheritance" (16–17). To be clear, in the early nineteenth century "race" did not yet refer to a stable hierarchy of categories of being. Rather, it was in active and contested formation. As Saree Makdisi has shown, in the 1790s and the decades that followed, the "white, Western self" – and, by extension, Englishness – did not exhibit the "continuity of form and practice," or "sense of security and consolidation," they so often appear to possess from our present vantage.[12] On the contrary, those "acts of demarcation" that would by the Victorian period solidify into "systematic" distinctions between, say, whiteness and blackness were only nascent in the Romantic period (5). They began to emerge, in this transitionary historical moment, out of a more dynamic discourse preoccupied with intra- as well as extranational difference. As Makdisi puts it, this discourse "did not operate simply along native/ foreigner or native/immigrant axes." Instead, it "cut across and among native indigenous English people," thereby interrogating forms of *internal* (not just external) heterogeneity that might unsettle the aspirational coherency of a national English "us" and an attendant "narrative of racial Anglo-Saxonism" (xiv). This discourse – which Makdisi describes as a "metropolitan Occidentalism" – worked to cast "common people" like the London poor "as ... cultural and racial Others," thereby "defus[ing] the sense of radical alterity at home" (108). Defining the possessive, self-sufficient, bourgeois individual in contradistinction to its domestic, collectivist, plebian Others, this early nineteenth-century Occidentalism asserted value-laden distinctions between different forms of Englishness, elevating one into and as whiteness while racializing others as uncivilized or savage. In so doing, it at one and the same time "ma[de] Africans, Arabs, Indians, and Muslims all the more Other to England" (108).

Subtending Wordsworth's tacitly racialized invocations of enclosure and harvest is the self-divided, messy, often elusive production of whiteness in action on the early nineteenth-century page. What at one moment remains largely implicit becomes referentially explicit when Wordsworth analogizes "the reader" in the absence of an adequate "leader" to "an Indian prince or general – stretched on his palanquin, and borne by his slaves ... like a dead weight" (410). In this moment, Makdisi argues, Wordsworth "creat[es] a new kind of reader as well as a new kind of author," both of which take shape over and against "a supine and unmanly Eastern other" (13). In contradistinction to the "dead weight" of recumbent brownness, whiteness for Wordsworth materializes by and through an upright "advance, or a conquest, made by the soul of the poet" (410). Restrictively iconizing humankind as he "invigorate[s]" his readers, Wordsworth's poet wields whiteness as a kind of galvanic force that, in contrast to the Indian prince's "dead weight," is supercharged and uniquely concomitant with life. "[C]*reating* the taste by which he is to be enjoyed" (408, emphasis original), the poet "call[s] forth and bestow[s] power" upon the reader so that he, too, "may exert himself" in supramaterial opposition to inhuman "quiescence" (410). Readers are thus "humbled and humanised" (408) in conformity with a world-vision that is superficially universal inasmuch as it seems to emphasize "those points wherein ... all men are alike" (408) and yet ultimately enshrines a "sublimated" or refined "humanity" coeval with Wordsworth's restrictively representative poet. Unspoken but evident is this: a reader's capacity for "humanis[ation]" depends on whether and to what degree they can accommodate themself to the likeness (which is to say, whiteness) that Poetry with a capital "P" naturalizes as human typology. In Wordsworth's eyes, some readers were necessarily and irredeemably less-than-human.

## Poetry, Anthropogenesis, Extinction

In confrontation with critics whose tastes are common (in the agrarian *and* lowly senses of the word), Wordsworth styles the unrecognized poet of genius in not just white colonial but also geologic terms. Forging taste and world in his own image, Wordsworth's poet must rise to planetary power in order to "*creat*[*e*] the taste by which he is to be enjoyed." For while his literary "predecessors ... will have smoothed the way for all that he [the poet] has in common with them," those elements of "original Genius" that are "peculiarly his own" – being of a new and unprecedentedly "high order" – will be enjoyed by readers only if the poet answers the "cal[l] to clear and often to shape his own road" (408). According to Wordsworth, then, a true poet is a terraformer of sorts, meaning (in the words of Amitav Ghosh) that he "coloniz[es] and subjugat[es] not just other humans but also planetary environments," clearing and shaping them on a large scale and at a rapid pace.[13] If, as Wordsworth claims, true poetry "humanise[s]" or, rather, speciates, this project is markedly anthropogenic: readers, like planets, constitute terrain available for the poet's "conquest" and "purifi[cation]," for his taking and reshaping. The operations of anthropomorphosis (a rhetorical figure) and anthropogenesis (a material terraforming enterprise) here go hand in hand. Ultimately, the 1815 "Essay" posits as coeval the white colonial poet's iconization as human prototype and the colonial European effort to transform a heterogeneity of planetary natures into what Ghosh calls neo-Europes. Clearing a unitary path through a wilderness of human difference to manscape the world in his own image, the poet is "in the condition of Hannibal among the Alps" (408). This comparison bears scrutiny.

Analogizing the poet to Hannibal – the Carthaginian general famous for launching an attack on Rome after crossing the Alps with some 30,000 soldiers, 15,000 horses, and 37 elephants in tow – Wordsworth positions himself as neither "in" (engulfed or subsumed by) nor "crossing" (athwart to or surpassing) but "*among*" – or in assemblage and even conspiracy with – the Alps. In other words, rather than conquering a mountain range per se, Wordsworth's Hannibal proceeds as its anthropomorphic analog and agentic equal. No supramaterial wanderer gazing down upon sublime vistas from on high, he at once assimilates and is assimilated into mountains. Figured as a so-called Hannibal *among* the Alps, or as one mountain among many, Wordsworth's poet posits man and Earth as coconstitutive. Crucially, poetry is the vehicle through which their concomitance is achieved, for the poet joins together "a history of the remote past" with "a prophetic annunciation of the remotest future" (412), thereby constituting the nexus between human shallows and planetary deeps. Here, Wordsworth's phrasing recalls the Romantic-era geologist James Hutton's infamous declaration that in deep time "we find no vestige of a beginning, – no prospect of an end."[14] The word "sublimated" does a lot of work in this context. On the one hand, it invokes the purportedly universal but whitewashed humankind that is the Wordsworthian poet's endgame: a distilled, refined, nobler species whose superior taste and restrictively anthropomorphic humanization "absolutizes" (Wynter's term) bourgeois colonial whiteness as *the* genre of the human. On the other hand, the language of sublimation works in tandem with that of depth and prophecy to collapse the distinction between human and planetary histories; to posit the latter as indelibly imprinted by and "annunciat[ing]" the duration of the former; to assert the anthropogenic synonymity of colonial man and Earth.

The synonymity of colonial man and Earth is similarly (though perhaps more subtly) proposed and naturalized in the preface to *Lyrical Ballads*, where Wordsworth first described (and defended) his poetic project at length. In the expanded version of the preface published in 1802, in particular, Wordsworth conceives the poet as a representative "man speaking to men" (85) who is "pleased with his own passions and volitions . . . delighting to contemplate similar volitions and passions as manifested in the goings-on of the Universe" – and, crucially, who "create[s]" said similitudes between man and nature "where he does not find them" (86). Poetry, per this line of thought, cosmologizes human and world into conformity with man. When Wordsworth purports to "convers[e] with general nature," he is therefore in actuality conversing with himself (88). A "rock of defence," he, like Hannibal before him, goes boulder: he is "an upholder and preserver" of a vast and enduring set of laws that uniformly encompass the planet – "[i]n spite of difference of soil and climate" – as well as "the vast empire of human society, as it is spread over the whole earth, and over all time" (88). To echo Shelley's *A Defence of Poetry*, Wordsworth's poet is a world-legislator: he "carr[ies] every where with him" a planetary, flattening, and decisively brutal form of "relationship and love" (88).

Wordsworth's racialized geo-poetry unsettles familiar notions of ecological relationality and responsibility, particularly as envisioned by the Romantics. Often, the Big Six are cast as radical animists, nonanthropocentric transcendentalists, stalwart environmentalists. So construed, their oeuvres seem to refute the anthropocentric, colonial, extractionist conception of nature advocated by thinkers like Locke. Likewise, they appear to straightforwardly recognize, anticipate, and mourn the long-nineteenth-century acceleration of exhaustive industrialism and the concretion of a planetary world order we might summarize crudely but illustratively as "man versus nature." Here, animist cosmologies – which, in a Romantic context, assert a universe rife with all manner of agentic beings, forces, and things; redistribute action, divinity, and meaning beyond the human; and assert a happy consummation of subject and world – superficially stand in corrective opposition to Anthropocene fantasies of an all-powerful, supramaterial, indomitable humankind who wrangles and subdues a malleable Earth. But such arguments overlook the subtle violence at stake in Wordsworth's poetic project. For Wordsworth articulates this project in all its colonial expansivity and white supremacy not in contradistinction to nature – not over and against Earth – but by and through it. The logic of this project, in other words, is animist: it envisions a world wherein poetry legislates the human (in the most restrictive sense of the word) *as* planet. Hence, the poet is not only a "man speaking to men" but also "a rock," a material effect of and synecdoche for geologic formation; an agent of

Earth process; "an upholder and preserver" of law in the most absolute because "natural" of senses. Colonial-anthropogenic whiteness is thereby invisibilized as cosmological neutrality or, rather, natural law. Where similitudes between man and "Universe" cannot be found, the poet is tasked with "creating" and concealing them as nature's mere "goings-on."

Wordsworth's formulation of the poet as a representative man among men and a Hannabalian mountain among mountains anticipates the logic by which geology would be co-opted in service of white supremacy in the Victorian period. Robert Knox's *The Races of Men* (1850) – a work of scientific racism that was influential on both sides of the Atlantic – exemplifies this co-optation.[15] Arguing that "man" is both "a part of Nature's plan" and a "perpetual antagonist" (459), Knox draws distinctions between the so-called races of men based on the degree to which they "differ in this antagonistic power" (460). He defines this power in emphatically geologic terms. For him, it is manifest in the anthropogenic extinctions of "[t]he Irish elk" and "the dodo" (among other species), which parallel the "climatic changes [that] destroyed the mammoth" (467) and thus make visible how "the Saxon man" acts in concert with, and even as, Earth (466). In contradistinction, "the feebly armed Indian" (460) and African "wild man" (461) are, according to Knox, supposedly incapable of exerting such influence upon nonhuman species like "the seal and walrus, the polar bear, the whale" (460), "the rhinoceros, the elephant, the lion" (464). On geologic grounds, select human communities are thereby essentialized as nonhuman. Likewise, they are posited as ripe for necessary "extermination" (466) in service of a "nature" that "dies not," but is "ever returning" and "ever reviving," her immutable "essence" coterminous with colonial whiteness (467). As we can see, Wordsworth's philosophy of poetry anticipates this racialized planetary regime, exposing its aesthetic (and not just scientific) grounds – its material basis in the human fantasy of the so-called lyric, particularly the restrictively anthropomorphic similitudes this poetry forges between man and nature.

## Specters of Napoleon and Toussaint

Wordsworth's Hannibalian poet carries with him the ghost of Napoleon Bonaparte: usurper of the French Revolution, imperial tyrant, and Alpine aspirant notorious for traversing the Great St Bernard Pass with his vast army. The intertwinement of Hannibal and Napoleon is perhaps nowhere more evident than in Jacques-Louis David's "Napoleon Crossing the Alps," an iconic painting of the (then) newly minted First Consul of France seated in placid repose on a cavalry horse mid-charge, his gaze steady, his hand beckoning toward mountains whose treacherous peaks dissipate into roiling mist and cloud. Lingering in the portrait's bottom-left corner is a set of boulders emblazoned with the names of three men distinguished for their military campaigns through the Alps: "Bonaparte," "Karolus Magnus" (Charlemagne), and "Hannibal."[16] Evident, here, is not only the inescapable co-involvement of Napoleon and Hannibal, but also the Romantic significance of the Alps as a long-historied manscape whose material forms are (for some) indelibly inscribed by white colonial masculinity. Like Wordsworth's poet, Napoleon is a prototypical man whose "master-spirit" – in the words of Romantic-era novelist, antiquarian, and Bonaparte stan, Walter Scott – blasts through "barrier[s] erected by Nature herself, on which she has inscribed in gigantic characters, 'Here let Ambition be staid.'"[17] He, too, calls select men to climatic and climactic greatness.

That Wordsworth – a self-identified sympathizer with the democratic ideals of the French Revolution – embraces Hannibal but bypasses Napoleon is less than surprising. Indeed, Napoleon often appears in Wordsworth's oeuvre as a harbinger of unbridled ruin for having quashed political reform and installed himself as "Consul for life" ("Calais, August 15th, 1802," 4). Nevertheless, in the 1815 "Essay" Napoleon is the colonial-anthropogenic poet's unacknowledged but near-perfect analog and, as such, *the* elephant in the room. Though the French Emperor might seem a supramaterial figure, he is (like Hannibal and Wordsworth's poet) construed in the Romantic period as a mountain among mountains, one geologic force among many. Thus, to create taste and so smooth one's own way is, per Scott's vision of Napoleon, to appear in the guise of atmospheric tumult: he strikes "like lightning" (303), "t[akes] the Alps" and human enemies alike "by storm" (309), and joins together "system[s] of natural tactics" practiced by "[n]ations in the savage state" with "power[s] of calculation" whereby "the greatest numbers of forces" might be ruthlessly maximized (302–3). So contextualized, Hannibal, Napoleon, and the Wordsworthian poet alike are representative men "among" and in strategic (racialized) relation with clouds, rocks, and trees. Whereas in "A slumber did my Spirit Seal" (1815) Lucy Gray is "Rolled" inertly "round in earth's diurnal course" (7), possessing "No motion" or "force" or sense (5–6) – and whereas in the 1815 "Essay" an "Indian general or prince" luxuriates in insensate and characteristically

Orientalist recline – Wordsworth's colonial poet-specimen possesses a geologic eye and wields planetary (which is to say, Hannibalian and Napoleonic) power. It is he, the poet, who does the rolling and moving, animating and envoicing, magnetizing and transmuting. As such, he appears in the guise of geologic process. If some humans are abjected as mere matter of Earth on the basis of difference, others (such as Wordsworth's colonial-anthropogenic poet) "absolutize" themselves by superseding Earth process – by approximating themselves to and invisibilizing themselves as planet. The human claim of poetry as theorized by Wordsworth thereby lies in its synonymizing of manscapes and Earthscapes, colonial whiteness and natural formation.

If it is impossible to think about Hannibal in the absence of Napoleon, it is equally difficult to think about Napoleon in the absence of his most formidable associate and rival: Toussaint Louverture – a man who was described by devotees and nemeses alike as, among other things, "the Bonaparte of the Caribbean" and "the Hannibal of Saint-Domingue."[18] Born into slavery and later manumitted, Toussaint was a shrewd political diplomat and military strategist who rose to power in Saint-Domingue (present-day Haiti) in the 1790s amidst the French Revolution, the white colonial humanism of which he rebuked in action as well as thought. C. L. R. James explicitly links Toussaint and Napoleon in his foundational account of the Haitian Revolution, writing: "between 1798 and 1815, with the single exception of Bonaparte himself, no single figure appeared on the historical stage more greatly gifted than this Negro."[19] That these two men perpetually shadow one another in the Romantic cultural imaginary is evident in the parallels between David's "Napoleon Crossing the Alps" and Denis Alexandre Volozan's "Equestrian Portrait of Toussaint Louverture on Bel-Argent," wherein the Haitian general raises his sword in defiance on rearing horseback, a backdrop of subtropical flora and billowing cloud just behind.[20] As Helen Weston observes, both men are depicted as "calm and fiery, prancing on white horses," similarly posed and styled. Likewise, each "adopts a well-worn formula for the heroic equestrian portrait." Assuming the earliest versions of both portraits appeared in 1800, Weston asserts it is possible Volozan's "might predate" David's – a potentiality that attests to the bidirectionality of the two men's entanglement.[21]

I emphasize this entanglement here to suggest that Wordsworth's elision of Napoleon in the 1815 "Essay" may have as much to do with antiblackness as with a rejection of antirevolutionary despotism in general. Insofar as Wordsworth detested Napoleon for "posing as the heir of the [French R]evolution" while destroying it from the inside out, his antipathy exposes a particular brand of bourgeois colonial whiteness that (1) failed to conceive revolution as a call for Black or interhuman freedom, (2) refused to recognize the achievement of the revolution's fullest potentiality in the fight for Haitian independence, and (3) aspired instead to redistribute personhood to a more expansive but still emphatically exclusionary community of representative men (James 294). Eliding Napoleon and so circumventing the specter of universal empire, Wordsworth at the same time all too conveniently gives the Haitian Revolution and the global project of Black freedom the slip. When he dodges Napoleon – who, as James forthrightly states, unequivocally "hated black people" and reinstantiated slavery in the French colonies prior to his defeat at the hands of the Black revolutionaries – Wordsworth obfuscates those material processes of dehumanization that sponsor and subtend the anthropogenic whiteness of his colonial poet and the restrictive humanism he embodies. Here and elsewhere in Wordsworth's oeuvre, Black people are, with rare exception, not in or of the world but voided from it. Failing to appear at the level of reference, they are a present absence.

In all its allusions and effacements, inclusions and exclusions, proclamations and silences, the 1815 "Essay" reveals how Wordsworth – a poet who, unlike many of his contemporaries, remained largely silent on the subject of abolition (his close friendship with the abolitionist Thomas Clarkson notwithstanding) – envisioned the revolutionary project, like his colonial-anthropogenic poet, as magnetizing an entire universe around the call of white bourgeois colonial man. Tracing Wordsworth's and Robert Southey's "attempts to separate Romantic poetry from the subject of abolition itself," Atesede Makonnen draws our attention to a letter wherein Wordsworth attests slavery "is in principle monstrous, but it is not the worst thing in human nature."[22] Significantly, this turn of phrase biologizes slaving as an innate human propensity. However "monstrous" or distasteful it might be, then, to enslave (per the logic of Wordsworth's phrasing) is to assert a purportedly intrinsic and proprietary human claim. This, I argue, is the racial architecture at stake in Wordsworth's colonial-anthropogenic regime of poetry and its violently "humanising" enterprise. Which brings this chapter, in its final turn, back to the Alps. James recounts how, on August 24, 1802, Napoleon imprisoned Toussaint "in the Jura mountains" – a portion of the French Alps located near the Swiss border – "at an altitude of over 3,000 feet" (363). Worried about the "repercussions" that would follow were Toussaint put on trial or executed, Napoleon "kill[ed] him by ill-treatment, cold and starvation" (363). Toussaint's incarcerators "reduced his allowance for wood" in the winter and left him to die "in a cell inadequately warmed, where the walls ran with moisture" (365). By April 7, 1803, Toussaint Louverture was dead. But the revolutionary effort was by no means crushed: "in Toussaint's last hours," James writes, "his comrades in arms, ignorant of his fate, were drafting the declaration of independence" (365).

Situated in this context, Wordsworth's seemingly laudatory sonnet "To Toussaint L'Ouverture" enshrines a restrictively universal conception of humankind from which Toussaint is excluded even as he comprises the necessary fodder for its assertion. Penned in late 1802 and published in February 1803 (a few months prior to Toussaint's assassination by incarceration and neglect), the poem is, as Makonnen observes, one of only three "about a black subject" in Wordsworth's oeuvre.[23] Calling out to an incarcerated "Toussaint, the most unhappy Man of Men" (1), the poem's speaker counsels the "miserable chieftain" (5) to "die not" (6) – to "Wear rather in thy bonds a chearful brow" (7) and "take comfort" (9) in "great allies" (12), among them "Man's unconquerable mind" (14). In the span of a short fourteen lines, Wordsworth directly addresses the subject of his poem numerous times: "Toussaint, the most unhappy Man of Men!" (1), "O miserable chieftain! where and when / Wilt thou find patience?" (5–6), "do thou / Wear rather in thy bonds a chearful brow" (7–8), "Thou hast left behind / Powers that will work for thee" (9–10), "thou hast great allies" (12). The sonnet thereby constitutes a single protracted and extravagant apostrophe: a figurative mode of address wherein the poem's speaker talks to (and so animates) someone or something absent or dead as though they were present and alive. Emblematic of lyric as a genre – thanks, in large part, to Romantic poetry, which is rife with calls to entities as varied as hermits, birds, marbles, affects, and clouds – apostrophe's fiction, according to Virginia Jackson, is "a communal horizon of shared sociality projected out of a radical privatization of experience" or, more succinctly, "an illusion of intersubjectivity" that seems to pantheistically conjoin addresser and addressee.[24] But whereas the apostrophic conjoining of a Romantic lyric speaker and, say, a nightingale might seem innocuous (perhaps even radical in its interweaving of human and nonhuman), the dynamics of apostrophe shift considerably when the poem's addressee is an enslaved African (as was often the case in Romantic abolitionist poetry) or, in Toussaint's case, an incarcerated Haitian revolutionary. Apostrophe, in other words, is racialized: it can function as a vocative blackface. And, insofar as it emblematizes the lyric genre, it elevates as prototypical the white colonial-anthropogenic poet.

So understood, apostrophe facilitates what Wordsworth advocates in his foundational essays on poetry: the transmutation of colonial man – a representative man speaking to men – into *the* human. To be clear, Wordsworth does not ventriloquize Toussaint in apostrophizing him. He does not, in other words, appropriate Toussaint's voice or put words in his mouth. Nevertheless, "To Toussaint L'Ouverture" vocatively absolutizes colonial man as universally human insofar as the poem's speaker constitutes a kind of centripetal force around which world and planet are organized. In "To Toussaint L'Ouverture," apostrophe's precondition is the impassive silence of the poem's addressee: Wordsworth's speaker cries out and "the rural Milk-maid by her Cow / Sing[s]" (2–3), but Toussaint – a man who spoke and wrote prolifically, in as well as out of prison – is uncharacteristically mute. His voicelessness corresponds to and is indicative of his inanimacy. Prostrate, he "liest now / Alone" (3–4) and "fallen" (8). In contradistinction, Wordsworth's speaker wields a planetary eye and speaks across vast swathes of space-time. Commanding Toussaint and Earth alike – counseling the one to "find patience" and the other never to "forget" – he insists the "air, earth, and skies" are remembrances of Toussaint (12), as is "Man's unconquerable mind." Whereas the sequencing of the poem – its opening with "Toussaint" and closing with "Man's unconquerable mind" – might seem to indicate the Haitian revolutionary has shaped or even reconstituted who or what counts as "Man," the racialized dynamics of apostrophe indicate it is "Man" – which is to say, Wordsworth's particular genre of being human – that preconditions and subtends the poem's otherwise seemingly originary call to Toussaint. Man, in other words, is the poem's alpha and Toussaint its omega: the latter is assimilated into the former's "accord of sublimated humanity" (to return to Wordsworth's 1815 "Essay"), thereby leaving the ideational and material infrastructures of Romantic antiblackness intact.

Significantly, even as he counsels Toussaint to "die not," Wordsworth presumes him already dead: "fallen . . . never to rise again" (8), he is insensate. The centripetality of the poem's whiteness and the planetarity of its language – its insistence "[t]here's not a breathing of the common wind / That will forget thee" (11–12) – voids Toussaint from the world, dislocating him to an "earless den" in "some deep dungeon" of nonexistence wherein blackness is collapsed into death. In the poem Toussaint lives on in some altered form, yes, but only as the apostrophic ground for the colonial-anthropogenic speaker's call. As Catherine R. Peters argues in Chapter 2 of this volume, Wordsworth's sonnet "foreground[s] Black vitality only when eclipsed by death" (33). What aspires to planetarize and reanimate Toussaint over and over again is Wordsworth's colonial-anthropogenic speaker – a speaker who forges "air, earth, and skies" in his image and then proffers this restrictive planetarity as the stuff of a "common" or interhuman "wind." The Romantic lyric fantasy of a terraformed, manscaped, ensouled Earth whose every object, force, and being materially bespeaks colonial man's vocative power here coincides with and affords a key substrate for what Christina Sharpe calls "anti-blackness as total climate" or a planet-cum-prison.[25] Whereas Wordsworth, Napoleon, and Hannibal move freely "among" and even *as* the Alps, Wordsworth's Toussaint is held captive in and subsumed by them, achieving freedom only through the colonial-anthropogenic poet's violent enterprise of vocative sublimation.

In Wordsworth's poem, we thus can see an instantiation of what contemporary artist Kehinde Wiley calls the "pictorial plane" wherein whiteness – which Wiley locates in the glittering ice and light of mountain-scapes – comprises "[a] kind of anywhere-but-nowherepresence that's ineffable and hard to pin down, but is nevertheless a unifying force that's rationally policing the movements and the comings and goings of people and their bodies," (Black people and their bodies in particular).[26] In Romantic landscape paintings, Wiley contends, "whiteness becomes a metaphor for a cage."[27] Something similar might be said about the project of lyric poetry as theorized by Wordsworth insofar as it aims to demetaphorize (which is to say, geologize) whiteness as planet, to sponsor the material collapse of colonial man into and as a kinetic, metamorphic, creative, but also selectively death-dealing and world-rending "common wind."

## Notes

1. William Wordsworth, *Guide to the Lakes* (1835), 5th ed. (London: Henry Frowde, 1906), 144. Further references will be given in the text.
2. M. H. Abrams, "Structure and Style in the Greater Romantic Lyric," in *The Correspondent Breeze* (New York: W.W. Norton, 1984), 77.
3. Anthony B. Reed, "The Erotics of Mourning in Recent Experimental Black Poetry," *The Black Scholar* 47/1 (2017), 25, 26.
4. Georges-Louis Leclerc, *Epochs of Nature*, trans. Jan Zalasiewicz, Anne-Sophie Milon, and Mateusz Zalasiewicz (Chicago: University of Chicago Press, 2018), 124.
5. Simon L. Lewis and Mark. A Maslin, "Defining the Anthropocene," *Nature* 519 (12 March 2015), 174–75.
6. Sylvia Wynter, "Unsettling the Coloniality of Being/Power/Truth/Freedom: Towards the Human, After Man, Its Overrepresentation – An Argument," *CR: The New Centennial Review* 3/3 (2003), 257–337.
7. All citations of this essay and other works by Wordsworth (excepting *Guide to the Lakes*) are taken from *Wordsworth's Poetry and Prose*, ed. Nicholas Halmi (New York: W. W. Norton, 2014).
8. Edward Said, *Culture and Imperialism* (New York: Vintage, 1993), 7, 82–83.

9. John Locke, *Two Treatises of Government and A Letter Concerning Toleration*, ed. Ian Shapiro (New Haven: Yale University Press, 2003), 111. Further references will be given in the text.
10. Brenna Bhandar, *Colonial Lives of Property: Law, Land, and Racial Regimes of Ownership* (Durham: Duke University Press, 2018), 48.
11. Bhandar, *Colonial Lives of Property*, 6.
12. Saree Makdisi, *Making England Western: Occidentalism, Race, and Imperial Culture* (Chicago: University of Chicago Press, 2014), 26, 4. Further references will be given in the text.
13. Amitav Ghosh, *The Nutmeg's Curse: Parables for a Planet in Crisis* (Chicago: University of Chicago Press, 2022), 54.
14. James Hutton, "Theory of the Earth; or an Investigation of the Laws observable in the Composition, Dissolution, and Restoration of Land upon the Globe," *Transactions of the Royal Society of Edinburgh* 1 (1788), 304.
15. Robert Knox, *The Races of Men*, 2nd ed. (London: Henry Renshaw, 1862). Further references will be given in the text.
16. Reproductions of this image abound in the public domain. See, for instance, https://en.wikipedia.org/wiki/File:David_-_Napoleon_crossing_the_Alps_-_Malmaison2.jpg.
17. Walter Scott, *The Life of Napoleon Buonaparte*, vol. I (Exeter: J. & B. Williams, 1827), 301. Further references will be given in the text.
18. Sudhir Hazareesingh, *Black Spartacus: The Epic Life of Toussaint Louverture* (New York: Farrar, Straus and Giroux, 2021), 2.
19. C. L. R. James, *The Black Jacobins: Toussaint L'Ouverture and the San Domingo Revolution* (New York: Vintage, 1989), x. Further references will be given in the text.
20. Reproductions of this image are somewhat more difficult to find. In addition to Hazareesingh (who discusses the similarities between it and David's equestrian portrait of Napoleon in *Black Spartacus*, 356), see https://commons.wikimedia.org/wiki/File:Volozan.-Portrait_équestre_de_Toussaint_Louverture_sur_son_cheval_Bel-Argent,_1800.png.
21. Helen Weston, "The Many Faces of Toussaint Louverture," in *Slave Portraiture in the Atlantic World*, ed. Agnes Lugo-Ortiz and Angela Rosenthal (Cambridge: Cambridge University Press, 2013), 356–57.
22. Atesede Makonnen, "'Even in the Best Minds': Romanticism and the Evolution of Anti-Blackness," *Studies in Romanticism* 61/1 (2022), 11, 12.
23. Makonnen, "'Even in the Best Minds,'" 12.
24. Virginia Jackson, "Apostrophe, Animation, and Racism," *Critical Inquiry* 48/4 (2022), 653, 660.
25. Christina Sharpe, *In the Wake: On Blackness and Being* (Durham: Duke University Press, 2016), 21.
26. Kehinde Wiley, as interviewed by Zoé Whitley, "Overcoming the Body," *Kehinde Wiley at the National Gallery: The Prelude* (London: National Gallery, 2021), 38, 35.
27. Wiley, interview, 38–39.

CHAPTER 10

# Romantic Poetry and Constructions of Indigeneity
## Nikki Hessell

When we lay out our sense of literary history – its established canons, its productive theories, and its future directions – we are setting out the genealogy in which we believe a body of work should be understood. We are manifesting our critical relations. This chapter attempts to remap those critical relations by attending to the methods by which we read, cite, and situate ourselves when we are considering Romantic poetry and Indigenous peoples. The only critics cited in the body of this essay are Indigenous scholars or scholars of color; there is work on Romanticism and indigeneity undertaken by settler and other white scholars, much of it very productive, but it will sit in the notes. It is time for us (and, as a white settler-scholar, I use this pronoun deliberately) to be marginal, to sit away from the central circle of critical seats.

It is apt, then, that I am writing this for a volume called a "Companion." Companionability suggests the possibility of writers, scholars, methods, and fields walking along side each other, on the same road but not necessarily heading to the same place, in company but not necessarily in agreement. My aim here is to show that Indigenous studies, at least for the time it takes to walk along the path set out by this chapter, can be a companion to Romantic studies, there to challenge us, to extend our thinking, and to develop what we might mean when we talk about "race and Romanticism."

There is a rich scholarly tradition that considers the interplay of race, indigeneity, and sovereignty. Joanne Barker (Delaware) points out, for example, that the "*making ethnic* or *ethnicization* of indigenous peoples has been a political strategy of the nation-state to erase the sovereign from the indigenous ... The erasure of the sovereign is the racialization of the 'Indian.'"[1] Any discussion of Indigenous peoples, race, and Romanticism thus needs to center sovereignty as the primary node of discussion, acknowledging that it is around questions of sovereignty and thus of land, resources, and knowledge extraction that Indigenous peoples have been forcibly racialized by colonial systems, including literary systems. This centering should not, however, be understood as a wedge between Black and Indigenous solidarities; while the contours of those communities' history and liberation are different, the common source of racialized injustice is colonization. Centering sovereignty simply means not losing sight of what racializing Indigenous peoples was ultimately intended to achieve.

In this chapter, I am guided by two important theories from Indigenous studies that together help link sovereignty and literature in ways that can inform work in Romantic studies. The first comes from Goenpul scholar Aileen Moreton-Robinson, whose phrase "constructions of Indigeneity" is borrowed for my title. I will return throughout this chapter to Moreton-Robinson's influential ideas of this construction and its relationship to settler colonialism.[2] The second is Dakota scholar Scott Richard Lyons's paralleled ideas of "rhetorical imperialism" and "rhetorical sovereignty," the latter defined as "the inherent right and ability of *peoples* to determine their own communicative needs and desires in this pursuit, to decide for themselves the goals, modes, styles, and languages of public discourse."[3] The chapter considers three ways in which these ideas might guide our understanding of Romantic literature: by examining the depiction of Indigenous peoples, and then of settler-Indigenous engagements, in canonical Romantic texts, and finally by reading two nineteenth-century Indigenous writers as part of the Romantic tradition.

## Inscribing Indigeneity

We can see how fundamentally Indigenous peoples shaped the British Romantic canon by examining the foundational Romantic text: William Wordsworth's and Samuel Taylor Coleridge's 1798 *Lyrical Ballads*.[4] The collection includes Wordsworth's "The Complaint of a Forsaken Indian Woman," a lament voiced in the first-person by an unnamed woman left to die by her people as they migrate. The poem is prefaced by an explanatory note, in which Wordsworth writes:

> When a Northern Indian, from sickness, is unable to continue his journey with his companions, he is left behind, covered over with deer-skins, and is supplied with water, food, and fuel, if the situation of the place will afford it. He is informed of the track which his companions intend to pursue, and if he be unable to follow, or overtake them, he perishes alone in the desert, unless he should have the good fortune to fall in with more, exposed to the same fate. See that very interesting work Hearne's "Journey from Hudson's

Bay to the Northern Ocean." In the high northern latitudes, as the same writer informs us, when the northern lights vary their position in the air, they make a rustling and a crackling noise, as alluded to in the following poem.[5]

Wordsworth's note is typical of canonical Romanticism's engagement with Indigenous lifeways. It claims authority from written Euro-American sources to solidify the authenticity of its claims, but simultaneously lacks specificity about individual and community identity (as we can see in the undifferentiated "Northern Indian" label). It is not alert to the human and nonhuman kinships that guided and continue to guide Indigenous communities in a process that Rarámuri scholar Enrique Salmón calls "kincentric ecology."[6] It also overlays the account of a practice or person with emotional and moral implications entirely divorced from an understanding of local practices and based on a sense that the dramatic possibility of these practices can be interpreted from within European cultural and emotional contexts. From the connotations of the adjective "forsaken" in the poem's title, through to the reimagining of the woman's thought processes and expression in the verses, Wordsworth insists that there is a universal standpoint from which to interpret such stories.

It is the interpretation of the emotional impact of this community practice that the poem works to exploit. Across seven stanzas, the woman oscillates between wishing for death ("Before I see another day, / Oh let my body die away!" [1–2]) and bemoaning the decisions made by her own people ("Alas! ye might have dragged me on / Another day, a single one! / Too soon I yielded to despair; / Why did ye listen to my prayer?" [21–4]). Details within the poem are filtered through European understandings of gender, family, individual, and community: at one point, the woman calls out "My Child! they gave thee to another, / A woman who was not thy mother" (31–2). The woman is understood to be operating within the frameworks set down by the *Lyrical Ballads* project: voiced in English, in ballad form, ostracized from her society, and in extreme emotional distress.

The presence of only one clearly identified Indigenous person in the *Lyrical Ballads* might make indigeneity seem like an afterthought in Wordsworth and Coleridge's project. But the *Lyrical Ballads* were closely linked to a less well-known collection of verse: Robert Southey's 1799 *Poems*, which featured a section titled "Songs of the American Indians."[7] In some respects, Southey's poems operate differently from Wordsworth's complaint. None of the five "Songs of the Indians" adopt a conventional English rhyme scheme, and each of them identifies a specific Indigenous

## Romantic Poetry and Constructions of Indigeneity 171

nation as the source of the story and the identity of the poem's speaker. But this group of five songs draws out some familiar themes in British writing about Indigenous peoples: an obsession with death customs, violence, understandings of the relationship between the human and the other-than-human, oral performance and rhetoric, and the supernatural and spirituality. Like Wordsworth's poem, Southey's songs focus on a state of heightened emotion, especially around ideas of death, violence, and revenge. In "Song of the Chickasah Widow," for example, the grieving woman declares "The stake is made ready, the captives shall die / To-morrow the song of their death shalt thou hear" (5–6), while in "The Old Chickasah to His Grandson," the grandfather tells his grandson that he is "ripe for the labours of war" (4) and urges him to take vengeance on the people who killed his father. The songs frequently attempt to interpret spiritual matters – "When the evil spirits seized thee, / Brother, we were sad at heart: / We bade the Jongler come, / And bring his magic aid" ("The Huron's Address to the Dead," 10–13) – with no underlying comprehension of what they purport to depict. The combination of Wordsworth's poem and Southey's songs demonstrates how fundamental the depiction of Indigenous peoples was to the formation of the first stages of canonical Romanticism, but also highlights the profound flaws in that depiction.

Second-generation Romantic authors replicated some of the first generation's approach to creating Indigenous characters, but there are also important lessons to be drawn from the specific decisions made by individual poets. Felicia Hemans wrote at least fourteen poems that include Indigenous characters, speakers, or references to Indigenous peoples, as part of her wide-ranging interest in both folk genres and marginalized speakers.[8] Like Wordsworth, Hemans used headnotes and other paratextual devices to authenticate her material for her readers. Poems such as "The Messenger Bird," "A Stranger in Louisiana," and "The Isle of Founts" (a three-poem sequence from "Lays of Many Lands" that assumes Indigenous voices or knowledges) include notes detailing the accounts from which Hemans draws her authority.[9] A similar note accompanies "The Indian Woman's Death Song," which, like another of her poems, "The Aged Indian," follows Wordsworth and Southey in its interest in the genre of the death song. The former poem begins, as does Wordsworth's "Complaint," with a scene-setting stanza that introduces and interprets the Indigenous-voiced stanzas that will follow, and likewise frames the emotional content of the poem within European sentimental norms. The woman, who is about to commit suicide and infanticide after being deserted by her partner, is depicted "Proudly, and dauntlessly, and all alone / Save that a babe lay sleeping at her breast" (7–8). This opening stanza establishes the Otherness of the imagined woman: "upon her Indian brow / Sat a strange gladness" (9–10) and she "lifted her sweet voice, that rose awhile / Above the sound of waters, high and clear, / Wafting a proud strain, her song of death" (13–15). The woman's song then addresses the river before turning to speak to the child: "And thou, my babe! though born, like me, for woman's weary lot, / Smile! – to that wasting of the heart, my own! I leave thee not" (36–7). The poem thus manages to suggest a sense of both mysteriousness and universality about the woman's behavior and decision; it is simultaneously "wild" or "strange," but also simply another example of "woman's weary lot."[10] In a pattern that continues to play out in the relationship between white and Indigenous feminisms today, the poem assumes a solidarity between Indigenous women and white women, but overwrites Indigenous experience with the needs and expressions of white femininity.

Byron undertook a related process in his long poem *The Island*, a narrative based around Fletcher Christian and the mutiny on the Bounty.[11] *The Island* draws on William Mariner's *Account of the Natives of the Tonga Islands*, and, like Wordsworth and Hemans, Byron is keen to inform his readers of the ethnographic writings that underpin and authenticate his poem. The opening of Canto II includes this author's note:

> The first three sections [of the canto] are taken from an actual song of the Tonga islanders, of which a prose translation is given in Mariner's Account of the Tonga islands. Toobonai is *not* however one of them; but was one of those where Christian and the mutineers took refuge. I have altered and added, but have retained as much as possible of the original.[12]

As in the case of the other Romantic poets discussed, Byron reveals a great deal about his attitude toward Indigenous peoples and knowledges here. His source is not, in fact, an Indigenous one, but rather a European traveller and author. The song is, then, not an "actual song," given that Mariner presents it in translation and in prose. Moreover, the real homelands of Pacific peoples, and the creative works that emanate from and relate to them, are treated as entirely portable and transferable; the poet simply picks up a song from one island and places it elsewhere. Finally, poetic license is both celebrated and, paradoxically, seen as harmonious with the implications of authenticity.

Byron was also, like other Romantic poets, fascinated by Indigenous women. His central Indigenous character in *The Island*, Neuha, is portrayed in troublingly sexualized terms:

> There sate the gentle savage of the wild,
> In growth a woman, though in years a child,
> ...
> The infant of an infant world, as pure
> From Nature – lovely, warm, and premature;
> Dusky like Night, but Night with all her stars;
> Or cavern sparkling with its native spars;
> With eyes that were a language and a spell,
> A form like Aphrodite's in her shell;
> With all her loves around her on the deep,
> Voluptuous as the first approach of sleep;
> Yet full of life – for through her tropic cheek
> The blush would makes its way, and all but speak;
> The sun-born blood suffus'd her neck, and threw
> O'er her nut-brown skin a lucid hue,
> Like coral reddening through the darkened wave,
> Which draws the diver to the crimson cave. (2:123–40)

The predatory and pedophiliac nature of these lines connects to a history of violent sexual offending against Indigenous women and children – one still evident in, for example, the cases of MMIWG (Missing and Murdered Indigenous Women and Girls) in North America. It is part also of a long-standing literary and artistic trope of the "dusky maiden"; as Māori scholar A. Marata Tamaira has written, "[a] central component of these early romantic constructions was the ubiquitous image of the sexually receptive and alluring Polynesian maiden."[13] While Wordsworth, Southey, and Hemans focused on loss and loneliness in their depictions of Indigenous women, Byron's poem offers another kind of stereotype in its focus on hypersexualization. But, in either form, all such depictions manifest exploitative colonial violence.

These poems by canonical authors operate as key Romantic examples of what Lyons has called "rhetorical imperialism": "the ability of dominant powers to assert control of others by setting the terms of debate."[14] Lyons's term should be a key framework for readers and scholars to apply to poems like these, since it helps explain the literary motivation behind the deployment of Indigenous voices and how we might read the verses they are made to speak. Poetic forms, especially the textual versions of oral forms such as songs and ballads, embolden the poet to channel voices, including those from other cultures, via the persona of a speaker or singer. These poems operate in a tense space between the possible benefits of a universalizing humanism and what Moreton-Robinson calls "the white possessive," a desire to own, define, and administer *everything*.[15] In this bleaker reading, the same universalizing impulse is not humanism but dehumanizing, refusing Indigenous sovereignty by claiming the poetic speaker's voice, a "militant universalism," as Red River Métis/Michif scholar Max Liboiron has described it.[16]

This literary dehumanizing is significant on its own terms; rhetorical imperialism virtually ensures that non-Indigenous poets will appropriate and deploy Indigenous voices to their own creative ends. But, as Lyons makes clear, it is also important to remember that such rhetorical imperialism underpinned and was reinforced by *actual* imperialism; both the source information and the impulses that lay behind poems such as "The Complaint of the Forsaken Indian Woman" and "The Huron's Address to the Dead" were derived explicitly from the seizure of Native land and the genocidal policies that accompanied that greed and acquisitiveness, as Romantic authors harvested knowledge from accounts written by the settler foot-soldiers of British imperialism and their journals, travelogues, and ethnographies. The adoption of Indigenous women's voices, especially, enacted a literary violence that paralleled the deep-seated and long-lasting physical, psychological, and sexual violence to which Indigenous women were and are subjected, while the focus on death songs as a genre only superficially concealed a fascination with exterminating Indigenous peoples and imagining them into extinction. White Earth Ojibwe scholar Jean O'Brien named these processes "firsting and lasting," with the former term outlining the technique by which settlers and white authors claimed Indigenous lands as their own, as if they were the first to find them, and the latter outlining the process of purifying the landscape of Indigenous presence.[17]

This dark assessment of poems like those of Wordsworth, Southey, Hemans, and Byron runs counter to some of the signature notes of British Romanticism, such as its philosophies of justice for the marginalized and rebellion against oppression. On the surface, these poems connect with the broader questions of social justice with which their authors were grappling; alongside the voices of other marginalized peoples (women, the poor, the disabled, refugees, Black communities and other peoples of color), Indigenous speakers could contribute to a coherent argument against injustice and harm by simply telling their story. Moreover, the presence of Indigenous voices as poetic, as fully human, and as worthy of both political and literary attention, might be regarded as a radical move in the conservative literary culture of late eighteenth-century Britain. But it is precisely that poetic occupation of the voice of the sovereign individual and their collective relations that readers can interrogate via Lyons's and

Moreton-Robinson's ideas. While in many of these poems the speakers or characters seem to act from within Indigenous worldviews, modern readers of these poems can sense the presiding poet's ignorance of the peoples they describe, their vague grasp of the kincentric ecologies they purport to depict, their distortion of modes of expression and value systems. All of the losses represented by these poetic depictions are sustained by Indigenous epistemologies, lifeways, and peoples, while all the extractive gains are accrued by British Romantic literature and culture.

## Becoming 'Indigenous'

Standing Rock Sioux scholar Philip J. Deloria has outlined the ways in which "playing Indian" has been central to the development of white settler American identity. In Deloria's formulation, the adoption of pseudo-Indigenous costumes, objects, identifiers, and practices helped solidify settler belonging and nationhood, at the same time as it violently dispossessed Indigenous peoples of land and lifeways.[18] The effects of this violent appropriation can be seen today in the white supremacist "sovereign citizen" movements in the settler colonies, but they manifested in the Romantic literary movement as well.

British Romanticism made its own contribution to the practice of "playing Indian." In Thomas Campbell's *Gertrude of Wyoming*, a fictional settler family becomes embroiled in the real-life conflict between British forces and American settlers in the Wyoming Valley.[19] Campbell, like Wordsworth, Southey, and Hemans, ventriloquizes Indigenous voices in his depiction of Outalassi, an Oneida man who brings the orphaned baby Henry to live with the family. Outalassi speaks in the studied diplomatic metaphors that were familiar to European audiences via famous examples such as the widely circulated speech by Logan, a Cayuga leader, and which were subsequently translated into poetic forms by Romantic authors. A speech like this by Outalassi demonstrates these co-opted tropes:

> "Christian! I am the foeman of thy foe;
> Our wampum league thy brethren did embrace:
> Upon the Michigan, three moons ago,
> We launched our pirogues for the bison chase;
> And with the Hurons planted for a space,
> With true and faithful hands, the olive-stalk;
> But snakes are in the bosoms of their race,
> And though they held with us a friendly talk,
> The hollow peace-tree fell beneath their tomahawk!" (127–35)[20]

But alongside these stereotyped depictions of an Indigenous person, Campbell emphasizes the ways in which his settler characters come to feel at home in the colonies by borrowing Indigenous tropes, especially in the relationship between Henry and Gertrude, the daughter of the settler family:

> Three little moons, how short! amidst the grove
> And pastoral savannas they consume!
> While she, beside her buskined youth to rove,
> Delights, in fancifully wild costume,
> Her lovely brow to shade with Indian plume;
> And forth in hunter-seeming vest they fare;
> But not to chase the deer in forest gloom;
> Tis but the breath of heaven – the blessed air –
> And interchange of hearts unknown, unseen to share. (487–95)

In these lines, the young lovers follow the model Deloria articulates, adopting Indigenous dress and a pretense of Indigenous practices for living on the land. None of the underlying kinship relationships with the non-human world or kincentric ecologies are manifested or even imagined in the poem; instead, the trappings of indigeneity are understood to authenticate the rights of settlement.[21] This process is complemented in the poem by metaphors of "lasting" the Indigenous inhabitants of the land. The final lines of the poem are spoken by Outalassi, as he contemplates the future beyond the battle. In this speech, Outalassi gives voice to a range of Romantic stereotypes about Indigenous people, imagining himself unable to return to his homelands, or to take up residence away from them, and concluding by labelling his own speech "The death-song of an Indian chief" (828).

What Campbell achieves here is what Eve Tuck (Unangax̂) and K. Wayne Yang describe as "settler adoption fantasies." These fantasies

> can mean the adoption of Indigenous practices and knowledge, but more, refer to those narratives in the settler colonial imagination in which the Native (understanding that he is becoming extinct) hands over his land, his claim to the land, his very Indian-ness to the settler for safe-keeping. This is a fantasy that is invested in a settler futurity and dependent on the foreclosure of an Indigenous futurity.[22]

Poems such as Campbell's helped to provide the literary ballast for actual settlements, securing the extraction and exploitation of Indigenous land within a fictional narrative of sovereignty surrendered willingly to settler communities and their descendants.

A different but related process can be seen in Byron's *The Island*, in which the emphasis is on indigenizing settlers who were British but not English. In his poem, Byron depicts his hero Torquil, Neuha's lover, as a sort of Scottish Indigene by drawing out the similarities between the two:

> Both children of the isles, though distant far;
> Both born beneath a sea-presiding star;
> Both nourish'd amidst Nature's native scenes,
> Lov'd to the last, whatever intervenes
> Between us and our childhood's sympathy,
> Which still reverts to what first caught the eye.
> He who first met the Highlands' swelling blue,
> Will love each peak that shows a kindred hue,
> Hail in each crag a friend's familiar face,
> And clasp the mountain in his mind's embrace. (2:274–83)

While it is possible to read this paralleling of Neuha and Torquil as an acknowledgment of equal status, the depiction flattens the colonial power imbalance and bolsters claims to settlement and occupation. In Byron's telling, the lovers are suited to one another by their paralleled Indigenous islander status, a point he repeatedly makes using the term "native." When the lovers are making their escape from the British sailors who are tracking the mutineers, for example, Byron notes that to Torquil, "the swimmer's skill / Was native" (4:65–6) because he is "the nursling of the northern seas" (4:113), just as Neuha's "track beneath her native sea / Was as a native's of the element" (4:106–7). These parallels shift, however, from being signs of a love match to advancing more straightforwardly imperialist ends. By the end of the poem, this sense of paralleled indigeneity has been replaced by a unified claim to Pacific land and genealogy:

> Again *their* own shore rises on the view,
> No more polluted with a hostile hue;
> . . .
> The Chiefs came down, around the People poured,
> And welcom'd Torquil as a son restored" (4:401–8, my italics).

Torquil is, by the conclusion of *The Island*, not simply a suitable partner for Neuha but able to claim the land and its people as his own.

"Playing Indian" also shapes some of the key characteristics of the version of canonical British Romanticism that does not stray from Britain's borders. Much of Wordsworth's poetic output adopts the rhetoric of indigeneity to make space for the speaker on the land. The term "native" appears frequently in Wordsworth's verse to underscore a particular affinity between his speakers and their lands; a survey of his use of the adjective shows it clinging to "regions," "mountains," "hills," "rock," "soil," and "fields." While it would have been common in the nineteenth century to apply such a term to British people and their lands without reference to global Indigenous populations, it is clear from Wordsworth's reading that he was deeply interested in the sovereignty and lifeways of the Indigenous peoples of North America. This reading helped inform the typical Wordsworthian speaker in his conceptualization of self and land and moves those speakers into the "playing Indian" framework. Thus, Wordsworth can describe "what I was when first / I came upon these hills; when like a roe / I bounded o'er the mountains" (*Tintern Abbey*, 66–8) by borrowing William Bartram's description of his Indigenous travelling companion in the southern United States, who "bounded off like a roebuck," or remember when his five-year-old self

> ... stood alone
> Beneath the sky, as if I had been born
> On Indian plains, and from my mother's hut
> Had run abroad in wantonness to sport,
> A naked savage in the thunder-shower. (*Prelude*, 1:296–300)[23]

This association between indigeneity and possession of the land partly reflects Wordsworth's uneasy sense of himself and his life in the Lake District. The poems composed around 1800, when he settled at Grasmere, are suffused with anxiety about his right to inhabit the place and a consequent overstating and overwriting in relation to his connections to the land.[24] Deloria's ideas are useful here because they help to concentrate our understanding on the political and historical processes behind this apparently personal and interior feeling, one that is vitally important to the characteristics of Romantic verse. Wordsworth casts himself as Indigenous to the Lake District in a manner that is not, in fact, consistent with Indigenous lifeways, but one that rather mirrors settler logics. The only way for the settler to imagine themselves as native to the land is to play Indian, and Wordsworth reveals himself as both a settler, and a model for other settlers in the global colonies, through this appropriative language and self-depiction.

In some of its key canonical texts, then, Romanticism not only engages indigeneity as a convenient metaphor, but drives the colonial misappropriations of Indigenous existence to fuel settler logics, and is in turn shaped by them. Rhetorical imperialism guides the appropriation of Indigenous voices and ideas in poems that range from Indigenous-voiced songs and laments, to narratives of encounter and settlement, and finally to British imaginings of their own relationship to the land. It is fundamental to how Romantic poetry was generated and produced.

## Indigenous Romanticism

How might we, instead, manifest a commitment to rhetorical sovereignty in Romantic studies? One approach is to facilitate what Scott Andrews (Cherokee) has dubbed "red readings," which involve "interpreting, re-interpreting, transposing, or deconstructing non-native texts from a native perspective, sometimes playfully, sometimes seriously."[25] Much of the success of such an approach will depend on making space for Indigenous scholars to work in Romantic studies, but Andrews is clear that, in a red reading, "The reader does not need to be native for this practice, but the reading should be native-centric; the reading process should be grounded in issues important to native communities and/or native histories or practices. Put more simply, a red reading produces an interpretation of a non-native text from a native perspective."[26] A complementary move would be to locate more Indigenous authors among the "Brown Romantics" of Manu Samriti Chander's formulation.[27] In what remains of this chapter, I want to consider two obvious candidates for such a role, although many other Indigenous authors might also be included.

Jane Johnston Schoolcraft/Bamewawagezhukaquay (Ojibwe) was a prolific poet writing in both English and Ojibwemowin in the Romantic period.[28] Her English-language poetry (some of which she composed in English and some of which was translated into English either by her or by her husband, the settler administrator Henry Rowe Schoolcraft) manifests all the hallmarks of Romantic poetry, while offering the perspective of an Indigenous woman poet. In "Lines written at Castle Island, Lake Superior," for example, Schoolcraft writes a Romantic lyric, moving between nature and her emotional state:

> Here in my native inland sea
> From pain and sickness would I flee
> And from its shores and island bright
> Gather a store of sweet delight.
> Lone island of the saltless sea!
> How wide, how sweet, how fresh and free
> How all transporting – is the view
> Of rocks and skies and waters blue
> Uniting, as a song's sweet strains

> To tell, here nature only reigns.
> Ah, nature! here forever sway
> Far from the haunts of men away
> For here, there are no sordid fears,
> No crimes, no misery, no tears
> No pride of wealth; the heart to fill,
> No laws to treat my people ill. (1–16)

There are conventions on display here, but also disruptions. The poet-speaker, inspired by a particular place and its natural beauty, to reflect on their melancholy but reaffirm their commitment to nature, manifests any number of Romantic tropes. But this poem is not composed in the Lake District. Schoolcraft's title places the poem in Anishinaabewaki, the homelands of the Anishinaabe people, while her final line locates the poem in her community and its experiences of colonization. She understands land and water within Ojibwe epistemologies, even if they are here expressed via the English language and British Romantic poetry's norms. In particular, she speaks of the injustices that the major Romantic authors also lamented from within the communities directly affected by them, with the anaphora of the last four lines insistently negating and rejecting colonial logics. Schoolcraft comprehends, as her final line attests, that settler-imperial laws directly shaped and distorted the possibilities of being nurtured and soothed by her own ancestral lands. She exercises rhetorical sovereignty in its strict sense, as an Indigenous author deciding what to say and how to express herself, but also weaves notions of sovereignty into Romantic rhetoric, asking the forms and tropes of Romantic poetry to be responsive and accountable to her people's sovereign rights.

"An Indian's Grave," by the Cherokee writer John Rollin Ridge (Cheesquat-a-law-ny/Yellow Bird), is likewise almost indistinguishable from the works of the major Romantic lyric poets.[29] The fifty-four-line poem begins with the establishment of a lyric speaker: "Far in a lonely wood I wandered once, / Where warbling birds of melancholy wing / And music sad, rehearsed their melancholy songs" (1–3). The speaker is continuing to wander and muse,

> When suddenly my footstep paused before
> A mound of moss-grown earth. I wondered,
> For a while, what mortal here hath found
> A resting place? But soon I minded me,
> That many years agone a noble race
> Had roamed these forest-wilds among, and made

> These mountain-fastnesses rebound to shouts
> Of liberty untamed, and happiness
> That knew no bounds. (13–21)

The speaker decides

> This must be the grave of one
> Who ranked among the warriors of the
> Wilderness! – And when he saw his country
> Doomed, ...
> . . .
> ... he here had dug his grave,
> And, singing wild his death-song to the wind,
> Sunk down and died! (26–36)

The speaker then insists to the reader:

> But no rude step, and no rude hand shall e'en
> Despoil the beauty of this silent spot,
> Or sacrilegiously disturb the rest
> Of *one* lone Indian form. Sleep on! (42–45, emphasis in the original)

Readers of canonical Romanticism will recognize any number of Romantic tropes and common-places here: the wandering, musing speaker; the symbolism of the single observed natural or manmade feature, associated with the death of an ordinary but typically marginalized person; the address to the deceased; and the injunction to both the reader and any imagined passer-by to respect the spiritual nature of the place. Many of Wordsworth's contributions to the *Lyrical Ballads*, as well as some of his later lyric poems, for example, can be read as possible intertexts for this poem. As in Schoolcraft's case, Ridge enacts rhetorical sovereignty in the simple act of writing the poem as he wishes, but he also interrogates the specifically Indigenous implications of these Romantic ideas, such as the violent distillation of Indigenous nations down to a single, anonymous figure, who, recognizing the disruption of relations with the land in a "country / Doomed," performs a death song and then dies, illegible even to other Indigenous people. Schoolcraft and Ridge both create poems that overlap with Romantic poetry but offer considerable complexity to its central ideas.

These overlaps should prompt us to ask two critical questions. First, what is the appropriate intertextual reading strategy for assessing a poem such as "An Indian's Grave" or "Lines written at Castle Island, Lake Superior"? At the very minimum, it requires us to be well versed in the work of Indigenous literary scholarship, including thinkers like Alice Te

Punga Somerville (Te Āti Awa, Taranaki), Daniel Heath Justice (Cherokee), Robert Warrior (Osage), Craig Womack (Creek, Cherokee), and Chadwick Allen (Chickasaw), among others. It should also prompt us to think about Indigenous theory more generally. How do these poems engage with Indigenous concepts of death? Of land and water? Of law? Of colonization? What other Indigenous intertexts are operating to shape these poems? And should an ethical reading also prioritize nation-specific understandings and methodologies (in Ridge's case, those that emerge from Cherokee epistemology, and, in Schoolcraft's, those that come from Ojibwe or wider Anishinaabe ideas)?

The second point we must consider is the tangled question of chronology. What comes first: Romanticism, in the British or European form that we recognize in the field of Romantic studies, or Indigenous knowledges and lifeways? At a literal level, it is clearly the latter; the epistemologies and traditions that Ridge and Schoolcraft descend from and embody have a far longer lineage than British Romanticism. At a political and ethical level, too, we must prioritize Indigenous knowledges in order to attempt the reparations and restorations necessary to undo some of the damage colonization has done to these knowledge systems and their durability. Moreover, as the early part of this chapter aimed to demonstrate, those epistemologies and traditions were always embedded in Romanticism, no matter how mediated and distorted the version produced by non-Indigenous poets might have been. But poets such as Ridge and Schoolcraft are demonstrably influenced by Romantic poetry in English, and thus operating in a confluence of traditions that have shaped their verse. British Romanticism is not the only key to understanding their poetry, but it is one of the prior threads that make up their work.

Perhaps, then, establishing who has a prior claim to the knowledge frameworks that might guide interpretations of these poems when we read them *within* Romantic studies is just one more version of "firsting." It might be preferable to think, instead, about how Romanticism and Indigenous peoples can be in good relations with each other, on the page but also in the past, present, and future. This approach will require some rethinking of what Romanticism is, and who gets to be a Romantic author. As Moreton-Robinson points out in the sentence from which I draw part of my title, "The possessive logics of patriarchal white sovereignty require the constructions of Indigeneity to be validated and measured through different regulatory mechanisms and disciplinary knowledges within modernity."[30] As readers and critics, we will need to understand not simply that Romanticism is one of the "disciplinary knowledges" that has contributed to racialized constructions of indigeneity that serve settler-imperial projects, but, more radically, that Romantic poetry itself is a "regulatory mechanism" for indigeneity in white eyes. Indigenous peoples are, in the poems by canonical British Romantic authors, measured against the regulatory mechanism of, say, Wordsworth's conceptions of land, peoples, and sympathies in the *Lyrical Ballads*, or Hemans's ideologies of global womanhood, or Byron's notions of revolutionary international freedoms, and found to be satisfactory. At the same time, real Indigenous authors are regulated out of the canon of Romanticism. There is a vital need to undo these regulatory mechanisms in Romantic studies, one which will be much more powerful when it is understood as part of the process of undoing all of the regulatory mechanisms of settler colonialism, many of which were themselves shaped by Romanticism.

## Notes

1. Joanne Barker, "For Whom Sovereignty Matters," in *Sovereignty Matters: Locations of Contestation and Possibility in Indigenous Struggles for Self-Determination*, ed. Joanne Barker (Lincoln: University of Nebraska Press, 2005), 16–17.
2. Aileen Moreton-Robinson, *The White Possessive: Property, Power, and Indigenous Sovereignty* (Minneapolis: University of Minnesota Press, 2015), 191.
3. Scott Richard Lyons, "Rhetorical Sovereignty: What Do American Indians Want from Writing?" *College Composition and Communication* 51/3 (2000), 449–50.
4. This point was established in Romantic studies by Tim Fulford, who noted that "It is not too much to say that Romanticism would not have taken the form it did without the complex and ambiguous image of Indians that so intrigued both the writers and their readers." See *Romantic Indians: Native Americans, British Literature, and Transatlantic Culture 1756–1830* (Oxford: Oxford University Press, 2006), 12.
5. William Wordsworth, *William Wordsworth: The Poems*, ed. John O. Hayden, 2 vols. (New Haven: Yale University Press, 1977), 1:275. All references to Wordsworth's poetry are to this edition unless otherwise specified.
6. Enrique Salmón, "Kincentric Ecology: Indigenous Perceptions of the Human–Nature Relationship," *Ecological Applications* 10/5 (2000), 1327–32.
7. References to Southey's poems are to *Joan of Arc, Ballads, Lyrics, and Minor Poems* (London: Routledge, 1894). For further discussion of these poems, see Fulford, *Romantic Indians*, 168–70.
8. An overview of this aspect of Hemans's work can be found in Nancy Moore Goslee, "Hemans's 'Red Indians': Reading Stereotypes," in *Romanticism, Race, and Imperial Culture, 1780–1834*, ed. Alan Richardson and Sonia Hofkosh (Bloomington: Indiana University Press, 1996), 237–61.

9. References to Hemans's poems are to *The Poetical Works of Mrs. Felicia Hemans* (Philadelphia: Thomas T. Ash, 1836).
10. Goslee has pointed out the particular work that this poem is doing in Hemans's conception of womanhood, in which Indigenous women are presented "as simultaneously alien, uncivilizable objects and universally-feeling subjects relates to interpretation of Hemans's own melancholy, a melancholy usually linked more exclusively to gender" (238).
11. References to *The Island* are to Lord Byron, *The Complete Poetical Works*, vol. 7, ed. Jerome J. McGann (Oxford: Clarendon Press, 1993).
12. Byron, *Complete Poetical Works*, 144.
13. A. Marata Tamaira, "From Full Dusk to Full Tusk: Reimagining the 'Dusky Maiden' through the Visual Arts," *The Contemporary Pacific* 22/1 (2010), 1.
14. Lyons, "Rhetorical Sovereignty," 452.
15. Moreton-Robinson, *The White Possessive*, xii.
16. Max Liboiron, *Pollution is Colonialism* (Durham: Duke University Press, 2021), 54.
17. Jean M. O'Brien, *Firsting and Lasting: Writing Indians Out of Existence in New England* (Minneapolis: University of Minnesota Press, 2010).
18. Philip J. Deloria, *Playing Indian* (New Haven: Yale University Press, 1998).
19. References to *Gertrude of Wyoming* are to *The Poetical Works of Thomas Campbell* (London: Frederick Warne, 1874).
20. Logan's speech was familiar to readers via Thomas Jefferson's *Notes on Virginia*. Campbell himself suggests that the speech was an influence on *Gertrude of Wyoming*, 352.
21. These questions are dealt with in detail in Fulford, *Romantic Indians*, 186–93; Kevin Hutchings, *Romantic Ecologies and Colonial Cultures in the British-Atlantic World 1770–1850* (Montreal: McGill-Queen's University Press, 2009), 134–53; Julia Hansen, "Viewless Scenes: Vividness and Nineteenth-Century Ideals of Reading in and through *Gertrude of Wyoming*," *English Literary History* 84/4 (2017), 943–77.
22. Eve Tuck and K. Wayne Yang, "Decolonization is Not a Metaphor," *Decolonization: Indigeneity, Education and Society* 1/1 (2012), 14.
23. References to *The Prelude* are to William Wordsworth, *The Prelude or Growth of a Poet's Mind*, ed. Helen Derbyshire and Ernest de Selincourt, 2nd ed. (Oxford: Clarendon Press, 1959); William Bartram, *Travels through North and South Carolina, Georgia, East and West Florida*, ed. Mark van Doren (New York: Dover, 1928), 113. For discussion of these lines and their implications for Wordsworth's self-depiction, see Fulford, *Romantic Indians*, 152–53. For the significance of Bartram in Romantic literature, see Alan Bewell, *Natures in Translation: Romanticism and Colonial Natural History* (Baltimore: Johns Hopkins University Press, 2017), 196–225.
24. Some of these ideas about Wordsworth's return to the Lake District are covered in James A. Butler, "Tourist or Native Son: Wordsworth's Homecomings of 1799–1800," *Nineteenth-Century Literature* 51/1 (1996), 1–15; Scott McEathron, "Stuck at Grasmere: Wordsworth and the Limits of

Native Authority," in *Romantic Generations: Essays in Honor of Robert F. Gleckner*, ed. Ghislaine McDayter, Guinn Batten, and Barry Milligan (Lewisburg: Bucknell University Press, 2001), 203–20; David Simpson, "Wordsworth and Empire – Just Joking," in *Land, Nation, Culture, 1740–1840: Thinking the Republic of Taste*, ed. Peter de Bolla, Nigel Leask, and David Simpson (New York: Palgrave, 2005), 188–201; Alan Bewell, *Wordsworth and the Enlightenment: Nature, Man, and Society in the Experimental Poetry* (New Haven: Yale University Press, 1989); Alison Hickey, "Dark Characters, Native Grounds: Wordsworth's Imagination of Imperialism," in *Romanticism, Race, and Imperial Culture, 1780–1834*, ed. Richardson and Hofkosh, 283–310.
25. Scott Andrews, "Red Readings: Decolonization through Native-centric Responses to Non-Native Film and Literature," *Transmotion* 4/1 (2018), ii.
26. Andrews, "Red Readings," i.
27. Manu Samriti Chander, *Brown Romantics: Poetry and Nationalism in the Global Nineteenth Century* (Lewisburg: Bucknell University Press, 2017).
28. References to Schoolcraft's poetry are to *The Sound the Stars Make Rushing Through the Sky: The Writings of Jane Johnston Schoolcraft*, ed. Robert Dale Parker (Philadelphia: University of Pennsylvania Press, 2007).
29. References to John Rollin Ridge's poem are to *Changing is Not Vanishing: A Collection of American Indian Poetry to 1930*, ed. Robert Dale Parker (Philadelphia: University of Pennsylvania Press, 2011).
30. Moreton-Robinson, *The White Possessive*, 191.

CHAPTER 11

# Romanticism and the Novel(ty) of Race

*Atesede Makonnen*

In *Pride and Prejudice* (1813), among the most enduring novels to come out of the Romantic period, Jane Austen includes the following brief exchange about dancing:

> "What a charming amusement for young people this is, Mr. Darcy! There is nothing like dancing after all. I consider it as one of the first refinements of polished societies."
>
> "Certainly, sir; and it has the advantage also of being in vogue amongst the less polished societies of the world. – Every savage can dance."[1]

Mr. Darcy's cutting rejoinder to Sir Lucas allows dance to be a universal trait of humanity but not an equalizing one: like people and societies, dancing can be both polished and unpolished. Darcy's comment on dancing echoes a wider trend of contemporary thought regarding cultural and artistic output. Editors of the novel have pointed to the sentiments as "a commonplace of Enlightenment thought. Darcy has perhaps been reading Hugh Blair's comments on the 'savage state.'"[2] Less frequently highlighted are the racial underpinnings of this commonplace. Blair himself refers to a sort of cultural climate theory, allowing a single source for humanity but one with distinctions, referring to "that current of human genius and manners, which descends originally from one spring. Diversity of climate and manner of living, will, however, occasion some diversity in the strain of the first Poetry of nations."[3] Cultural production, from dance to literature, features as a category of difference in racial philosophy, and, vice versa, racialism informs meditations on cultural production and the products themselves. These works, both primary and secondary, tend to feature a common thread: the expression of a belief in a cultural monogenism in which all have the capability for cultural production in some manner but with varying (and often racially determined) levels of quality and sophistication. As Vicesimus Knox states in 1778, "The productions of the mind, like those of the earth, are found to have different degrees of vigour and beauty in different climates."[4] He and others suggest that, while all nations/cultures/races might have the capability for something like poetry or dance, they do not necessarily possess the ability to develop higher forms of the genre. Cultural production might be universal, but there are racial limits on performance, composition, and even the forms and tools of production.

This cultural-racial philosophy emerges not only within novels but also in how the novel form was being thought of and written about during the Romantic period, from its supposed evolution away from "Eastern" and African origins to the beginning of its valorization as a pinnacle of literary output. Race was an important theme and device in the Romantic novel; however, equally important was how the novel itself was racialized. The late eighteenth century into the nineteenth was a moment in which advocates for the novel tried to cast it as less of a novelty and more of an established literary form; part of that work was to imbue the form with cultural and intellectual stature. Unsurprisingly, racial philosophy, itself a type of novelty in the sense of being "[a] new custom or practice; an innovation," provided an additional framework for validation.[5] While there were both novels and ideas about race before what is traditionally considered the Romantic period (1770s–1830s), the notion of race and, specifically, scientific and philosophical racism, was in many ways a flourishing novelty of the moment, a new "practice; an innovation" increasingly finding its way into discussion and evaluation of government, culture, music, art, and literature.

This chapter explores how that innovation crossed paths with literary histories of the novel, how both the "modern" novel and systemic constructions of race came of age during this time, and how writers were engaging with race in their novels and with the idea of the novel itself. It considers not necessarily an earlier "rise of the novel," or the concurrent rise of racialism, but rather the maturation and classification of both in the British literary landscape through the lens of two literary histories. Focusing on some of the ways that race gets wrapped up in the very definition of the novel itself, it examines Clara Reeve's 1785 *The Progress of Romance*, which uses the conversation of three friends to explain the difference between Romances and novels, and Anna Letitia Barbauld's 1810 introductory essay to her series *The British Novelists*, entitled "On the Origin and Progress of Novel Writing." In these works, Reeve and Barbauld attempt to define, categorize, and judge the "modern" novel, while also racializing, exoticizing, and distancing its origins as they create literary systems reminiscent of other taxonomies of the eighteenth and nineteenth centuries. The chapter ends by discussing how what we might call "the Romantic novel" complicates their attempts at generic categorization.

### "Sprung up out of its ruins"

As a novelist and literary critic, Clara Reeve (1729–1807) wrote across a variety of forms, from Gothic and epistolary novels to a history of the Romance in *The Progress of Romance* (1785). Early in *Progress*, Reeve acknowledges the challenge, novelty, and necessity of her task, writing that "this Genus of composition has never been properly distinguished or ascertained; that it wants to be methodized, to be separated, classed, and regulated."[6] Division, classification, and, importantly, regulation guide her efforts to craft a literary history (and defense) of the Romance, a form of prose fiction distinct from that of the novel and often dealing in reality-defying plots and characters. Twenty-five years later, the poet and critic Anna Laetitia Barbauld (1743–1825) would further develop that history in her introduction to the edited collection *British Novelists*, which brought together a canon of prose fiction prefaced with her explanation and championing of the novel. Reeve and Barbauld were invested in providing a backstory for prose fiction that led to the "modern" novel, and, with it, a guide for readers that covered not only literature but also sociocultural boundaries. The idea of a national – or, more broadly, "Western" – literature looms especially large over both texts. Barbauld's work as an editor, for example, focuses on constructing a specifically British canon; Claudia Johnson notes that *British Novelists* was a "venture explicitly committed to the business of national culture."[7] I would add that hand in hand with the national is a concern with the racial, which the explanatory and didactic work of *Progress* and "Origins" appears to draw upon.

Notions of origin, development, and distinction appear in both women's work outside of their writings on the novel. Their texts aimed at general education actively deploy racial philosophy, including in their pedagogical material training in understanding racial distinction. They build off the idea of monogenism, a belief in a common source for humanity which underlies much of the racial philosophy of the eighteenth century, before clearly stating that not all humans are equal. Reeve's 1792 *Plans of Education* includes in her discussion of how to best educate young ladies a rehearsal of the racial calculations of natural philosophers. In a section describing the ill-effects of racial mixing, she has a character outline racial "gradations from a negro to a white" and claim "he has no doubt to call the negroes an inferior race of men, but still a link of the universal chain."[8] Universality is here cut by hierarchal distinction. Meanwhile, the children's book *Evenings at Home* (1792–96), cowritten by Barbauld and her brother John Aikin, allows, during "a general survey of the different races of men" in the story "A Globe Lecture," that "our human brethren, who, amid all the diversities of character and condition, are yet all *men*."[9] The sentence ends by specifying they are men "filling the station in which their Creator has placed them," with plenty of evidence for the differences in those stations and clear statements about the superiority of some over others throughout the story.[10] Less extreme than a refusal of universal humanity, monogenism might seem to be a progressive alternative to polygenism, which saw racialized beings as different species. However, it could, and did, serve as a precursor to racial division and hierarchy.

Importantly, there were other, less hierarchal models of racial philosophy, espoused by those like their contemporary Thomas Day in his children's book *The History of Sanford and Merton* (1783–89). In this didactic text, Day includes a character simply known as "the Black" who frankly confronts the main character, Tommy, with "how much you white people despise us blacks," shaming him into "blush[ing] a little at the remembrance of the prejudices he had formerly entertained concerning blacks and his own superiority."[11] As Tommy evolves over the course of the story, Day celebrates education as a remedy to racial prejudice: "[Tommy's] heart expanded in the same proportion that his knowledge improved. He reflected, with shame and contempt, upon the ridiculous prejudices he had once entertained; he learned to consider all men as his brethren and equals; and the foolish distinctions which pride had formerly suggested were gradually obliterated from his mind."[12] While elsewhere in the book Day includes echoes of popular rhetoric about savage societies, he also offers resistance to that rhetoric, and to notions of *inherent* racial superiority.

In contrast, neither *Practical Education* nor "A Globe Lecture" seem able to move on from monogenism to racial equality, instead detailing systems of "gradations" and "stations." It is one thing to allow a basic humanity to all people, another to reject a claim to one's "own superiority," and still another to abandon "foolish distinctions." Even a basic capitulation to acknowledging ties to nonwhite "brethren" can serve more than one end. We might read their monogenist rhetoric as sentimental lip-service or as a strategy to lend general credibility to their brand of racialism (again, in contrast to polygenism) but their capitulation to universality also serves a more fundamental role. Laying out how humanity is connected sets up solid ground for subsequent arguments of divergence; their ideas about racial distinction begin with an articulation of common lineage that highlights – indeed, makes possible – the evolution, rise, and *progress* of certain branches of humanity.

Their literary methodologies and judgments mirror, consciously or unconsciously, this racial philosophy. Both *Progress* and "Origins" use the rhetoric and framing of origin and gradation to approach literary development, declaring a monogenic basis for fictional prose. Reeve writes that "Romances or Heroic fables are of very ancient, and I might say universal Origin. We find traces of them in all times, and in all countries: they have always been the favourite entertainment of the most savage, as well as the most civilized people" (13–14). Like Austen's Mr. Darcy, Reeve grants a universal appreciation for prose literature to both the lowest ("the most savage") and the highest ("most civilized") cultures. Barbauld agrees that "[i]f we look for the origin of fictitious tales and adventures, we shall be obliged to go to the earliest accounts of the literature of every age and country."[13] The development of the Romance (and out of it the novel) becomes the lynchpin of their efforts and main subject of their treatises: Reeve proposes "to shew how the modern Novel sprung up out of its [the Romance's] ruins, to examine and compare the merits of both, and to remark upon the effects of them" (7–8). While the content of these works of fiction feature as a topic of interest (and a measure of distinction, in some cases), at the heart of their work is a desire to define forms of writing – specifically, what makes the form of the Romance different from that of the novel.

In another parallel to the construction of racial taxonomies, they name these forms "species"; both texts construct narratives about the "Origins" of the novel reliant on different "species" of writing which are related but distinct. Less clear are the exact boundaries and lines of this genealogy – attempting to delineate what counts as a "Ancient Romance," a "Modern Romance," a "novel," an "Eastern Tale," or an "epic" according to their definitions and breakdowns is difficult, to say the least. For Reeve, while "[n]o writings are more different than the ancient Romance and modern Novel," the modern Romance, a more evolved and European descendant, has more in common with the novel than its ancient predecessor (7). Meanwhile, Barbauld passes between the labels "Romance" and "novel" fluidly until she hits Daniel Defoe in her chronology and begins to use "novel" more consistently. However, in the mess of their attempts to decide what counts as a Romance or novel, some borders stand out, including a consistent connection between older fictional prose forms and non-European (nonwhite) subjects and authors. The earlier (and thus more "primitive") forms, including Romances, tales, and fables, are associated with foreignness, exoticism, and race, from which they seem to try and draw away what they call "the modern novel."

Both deliberately, and perhaps progressively, acknowledge an influential history of non-"Western" literary output. Reeve highlights the existence of Egyptian Romances and cites the belief that Romances made their way to Europe from Africa via the Crusades. Barbauld allows "The East" as a source for prose fiction, one that would go on to inspire the literary production of the "The West," documenting that

> [t]he Eastern nations have always been fond of this species of mental gratification. The East is emphatically the country of invention. The Persians, Arabians, and other nations in that vicinity have been, and still are, in the habit of employing people whose business it is to compose and to relate entertaining stories; and it is surprising how many stories … which have passed current in verse and prose through a variety of forms, may be traced up to this source. (3)

She recognizes the importance of literary production and appreciation in these "Eastern nations," and even suggests that the "East" can be ("surprisingly") credited with not only "invention" of its own stories but also influence on European Romances and epics. However, Barbauld (and Reeve) sees this basic instinct toward recording stories as one that progresses (or does not progress) according to different countries, cultures, and peoples. By the end of their literary histories, the prose of non-European countries is not only associated with but almost defined by an inescapable primitivity, in part due to how this species of writing handles its subject matter.

Uniting early prose pieces is a sense of the unbelievable, of wonder and adventure, connected to exotic, often Orientalist fantasies, unregulated by the boundaries of reason. What Reeve calls Eastern Tales, for example, "are all wild and extravagant to the highest degree; they are indeed so far out of the bounds of Nature and probability, that it is difficult to judge of them by rules drawn from these sources" (57). These works of prose fiction defy reality to the point that they can barely be judged systematically. The supposed improbability of "Eastern" plots and themes informed and was informed by theories about the ignorance and wild imaginations and natures of racialized others, like Kant writing that "we find the Arab to be the noblest human being in the Orient, although with a feeling that very much degenerates into the adventurous ... his tale and history and in general his sentiment always has something marvelous woven into it. His inflamed power of imagination presents things to him in unnatural and distorted images."[14] Like Barbauld, Kant leaves room for a certain appreciation ("noblest human being") but, also like Barbauld, he articulates clear limitations to that appreciation. Kant's racialization of imagination casts literary development as biologically determined; inflammation and subsequent distortion of perspective leads to "marvelous" tales. Here, racial judgment is literary judgment. This species of writing represents – or, rather, channels – something essential about a group of people; both are marked by an inherent flaw that separates them from "civilized" narratives and characters, who might tackle similar themes and subjects but are ruled by reason.

For Kant, and those in agreement, culture – and, thus, cultural and literary development – appears to be tied to the biological. The lesson in "A Globe Lecture" goes on to explain that geographical location impacts neurological development and thus cultural production, whether scientific or artistic:

> The excessive heat, however, of these countries seems of itself to relax the mind, and unfit it for its noblest exertions. And I question if a single instance could be produced of an original inhabitant of the tropics, who had attained to eminence in the higher walks of science. It is their general character to be gay, volatile, and thoughtless, subject to violent passions, but commonly mild and gentle, fond of society and amusements, ingenious in little arts, but incapable of great or long-continued efforts.[15]

The geotemporally induced indolence, the story argues, impacts technological, artistic, and moral development, rehearsing what David Hume puts quite bluntly: "There never was a civilized nation of any other complexion than white, nor even any individual eminent either in action or speculation. No ingenious manufactures among them, no arts, no sciences."[16] The story specifies that it is the "original inhabitant of the tropics" who suffers an inability to produce "noble exertions," thus excluding those from Europe who live in those same countries and placing biological race, rather than geography or citizenship, as the basis for cultural development. The standards by which it judges artistic exertions are telling; nonwhite peoples are allowed "little arts," but not "great or long-continued efforts." Complexity, greatness, and, interestingly, length, become markers of white artistic prowess.

While Barbauld and Reeve, unlike Hume, give credit to non-European cultures for art like Tales and Romances, they also use this acknowledgment as an opportunity to demonstrate European proficiency in these species of literature. As "A Globe Lecture" puts it, while most of Africa, South America, and Asia are "incapable of those advances in knowledge and vigour which raise and dignify the human character," "Europeans render all countries and climates familiar to them; and everywhere they assume a superiority over the less enlightened or less industrious natives."[17] Part of this superiority is the appropriation and "improvement" of native art forms, a cultural parallel (and part) of colonization. In the realm of the development of prose fiction as documented by Reeve and Barbauld, this manifests in two ways. First, European mastery of older species of prose, especially the Romance but others, too. For example, while translations of "Oriental" or Eastern Tales were popular, so, too, were European pastiches. Reeve actually adds *The History of Charoba, Queen of Egypt*, her own (translated and adapted) Tale, to the end of *Progress* as a specimen. Mastery over the "little arts" of others functions as a logical trick in both *Progress* and "Origins" that makes the nonwhite, non-European influence in the genealogy of European literature more palatable. While Tales and Romances are painted as cultural pinnacles of the non-European world, European versions are a mode of writing that can be attempted, conquered, and moved on from to more sophisticated species like the novel.

The second development was the progress of the prose form: the modern (realist) novel, which could only come from a developed country, since "[a]s a country became civilized, their narrations were methodized, and moderated to probability" (14). Realism, or probability, as Reeve calls it, is at once a literary development and a marker of civilization. She anticipates Georges Cuvier, who would go on to write of races whose civilizations "remained stationary."[18] This is not to say, according to Cuvier that there have not been cultural achievements among non-Europeans, but their literary progress is limited in form and content. Among a racial branch in which he includes Arabs, Jews, Abyssinians, and Egyptians, he writes that "the arts and literature have sometimes flourished among its nations, but always enveloped in a strange disguise and figurative style."[19] The upward progression of artistic development is halted amongst certain people; he claims it is by a "great and venerable branch of the Caucasian stock," which of course includes Europeans, "that philosophy, the arts, and the sciences have been carried to the greatest perfection."[20] In the literary taxonomies of *Progress* and "Origins," it appears that the primitive literary art of Romances, Tales, and fables can, in the right hands, develop into a more perfect species, beyond "strange disguises" and "figurative styles." The Eastern Tales and ancient Romances from which the novel emerges, as well as overtly foreign/foreign-influenced material and authors, do have a place within the literary systems Reeve and Barbauld propose, but are best off in what *Progress* calls a separate "class" (25). They remain a separate class in part because they do not (with the implication that they cannot) develop further – they are instead a sort of persistent, exotic relic born of cultures unable to achieve full civilization.

According to Reeve and Barbauld, a departure from this strangeness and arrival at something like realism leads us (eventually) to the modern novel, by way of the modern Romance or early novel, which itself dealt less in the marvelous and more in the historical. As Barbauld puts it, "a closer imitation of nature began to be called for" which would further develop toward reality: "[a] good novel is an epic in prose, with more of character and less (indeed in modern novels nothing) of the supernatural machinery" (17, 3). Reeve declares that the modern novel embraces nature:

> The Novel is a picture of real life and manners, and of the times in which it is written ... The Novel gives a familiar relation of such things, as pass every day before our eyes, such as may happen to our friend, or to ourselves; and the perfection of it, is to represent every scene, in so easy and natural a manner, and to make them appear so probable, as to deceive us into a persuasion (at least while we are reading) that all is real, until we are affected by the joys or distresses, of the persons in the story, as if they were our own. (111)

The novel, unlike the Romance, is "us" – we can see "our" every day and "our" circle of people, and connect with the story until it is "our own." Removal of the "supernatural machinery" is in part the removal of what gets marked as non-European, both in methods of storytelling and subject. According to Reeve, modern novels are identifiable by their attention to *familiar* reality; correspondingly, the novel is a European endeavor. However, even Europe's attempts are divided. Reeve gives the Italians credit for first succeeding in the form, then Cervantes in Spain, but when one of the interlocuters of *Progress* states confidently "I make no doubt that the seed once sown, produced as plentiful a drop there [Spain], as it did in the rest of Europe" (113), Euphrasia, the main lecturer in the dialogue and most commonly aligned with Reeves, disagrees. It is the French and the English, with their numerous novels, that outpace the rest of Europe – Spain, credited for the Romance via the Moors, falls behind in modern novel writing.

While Reeve does not name any non-European novels (Eastern Tales being firmly a separate "class" of the species), Barbauld includes a single example:

> One Chinese novel ... called *The Pleasing History, or the Adventures of Hau Kiou Choan*. It is said to be much esteemed, but can only be interesting to an European, as exhibiting something of the manners of that remote and singular country ... In short, *Shuy Ping Sin* to a Chinese may possibly be as great an object of admiration as *Clarissa*, but her accomplishments are not calculated for the meridian of this country. (34)

Beside associating *The Pleasing History* with the older forms of the novel in the section on "Origins," where she moves between Romance and novel (its first translation was published nearly fifty years earlier, in 1761), Barbauld essentially dismisses its potential for impact: in a work meant to improve the reputation of the novel form, she reduces this one to a novelty. What's more, it seems to suggest that while European writers can master the Romance, non-Europeans have failed to master the novel, an instance of the kind of nonreciprocal authority that Edward Said calls "flexible positional superiority."[21] Indeed, in 1829, it would be retranslated and renamed *The Fortunate Union: a Chinese Romance*. Its value for a European audience exists only in what it can tell readers about a foreign culture – almost a tool for investigation, rather than an object of literary pleasure or evidence of literary capability. By its very nature, it cannot fit a definition of the novel that depends on a familiarity based in part on "meridian."

The value of this promised familiarity is made clear by both; it is in part what allows Reeve and Barbauld to push back against a narrative that considered the novel as dangerous reading, especially for women. They go so far as to suggest that (some) novels are a less risky alternative to the wild exoticism of the Romance. After all, while (or, rather, because) there is value and pleasure in the adventures and wonders of works like Eastern Tales, they are also marked by danger. Reeve writes:

**Euph.**
... It cannot be denied that some of them are amusing, and catch hold of the readers attention.

**Soph.**
They do more than catch the attention, for they retain it. – There is a kind of fascination in them, – when once we begin a volume, we cannot lay it aside, but drive through to the end of it, and yet upon reflexion we despise and reject them.

**Hort.**
> They are certainly dangerous books for youth, – they create and encourage the wildest excursions of imagination, which it is, or ought to be, the care of parents and preceptors to restrain, and to give them a just and true representation of human nature, and of the duties and practice of common life. (58–59)

These Eastern Tales compel their readers in a manner rather like Othello wooing Desdemona and the Venetian court with his stories of adventure and travel, ultimately leading them into regret. The threat lies in their ability to not only command but retain attention, almost against the reader's will. "Imagination" creates pathways away from "the duties and practice of common life," and an excessive, uncontrolled imagination, according to those like Kant, is itself a racializing marker. It is not only Eastern Tales that ring an alarm for Reeve to address – after a discussion of *Oroonoko*, among other early works of prose fiction, the following judgment is handed down by Sophronia: "It must be confessed that these books of the last age, were of worse tendency than any of those of the present" (120). Tales, Romances, and early novels are not only technically distinct from the modern novel but also have specific moral flaws, based in part on their ability to inspire wildness. Reeve is very clear through Euphrasia's response that they are not necessarily universally "bad," that there are bad books in every age, and that in fact those of the last age can be both valuable and entertaining – in many ways, her project is one of redemption and celebration of these forms of prose. At one point, she even allows a comparison of Homer and *The Arabian Nights* as evidence of the (admittedly lesser) value of the latter. However, the message, mediated across the varying opinions of the three friends, appears to be that while not the worst things in the world, they are potentially dangerous for unprepared readers, especially female readers, who might not be able to approach them with restraint.

The key to handling unruly literature (of all kinds) is the recognition and taming of difference. Reeve and Barbauld present literary systems of distinction that allow for *controlled* engagement with literature, including works by or concerned with the exotic, with race, and with racialized characters. Reeve deliberately shies away from commenting on novels of her own moment, though she sets up not only a genealogy for them but a moral basis for the justification of their consumption. Barbauld more clearly advocates for the modern novel, especially the British novel, as a safer (but still pleasurable) choice. One may or may not learn a lesson from them, but, at the very least, corruption will probably be avoided. As she puts it, "in general our novels are not vicious; the food has neither flavour nor nourishment, but at least it is not poisoned. Our national taste and habits are still turned towards domestic life and matrimonial happiness, and the chief harm done by a circulating library is occasioned by the frivolity of its furniture, and the loss of time incurred" (58). If Reeve articulates a concern with the danger of Eastern Tales "retaining" attention, Barbauld offers the reassurance that the modern British novel will not irrevocably alter them or shift them away from "domestic life." Romances and Tales, originating in racialized, backward cultures, are cast as archaic and potentially disruptive precursors to the progressive novel, which exists not only as the product of a civilized and ever-progressing European society, but also as its protector, affirming a "familiar" (white) domestic reality.

## "Productions of the Present Day"

Barbauld's assurance of the propriety of modern British novels comes against a historical and contemporary literary landscape that seems to challenge promises of respectability. Does the "modern" novel, the novel of the Romantic period, fit into the systems Reeve and Barbauld espouse? What role in the modern novel, in "pictures of *real* life," do nonwhite people, foreign countries and cultures, and the concept of race itself play? Even a brief survey of these novels suggests that, at times, the "national taste and habits" turned to subject matter and even forms that might be considered "poisoned." Some of the very themes Reeve and Barbauld labeled as primitive and "Eastern" were controversial hallmarks of the Romantic novel: "The Romantic novelist was drawn to the period's interest in the subjective and irrational, the oneiric and the outre, as represented in such aesthetic fads as the sublime, graveyard imagery, and the supernatural."[22] The Gothic novel is rife with these so-called "fads," as well as both obvious and sublimated references to race. Mary Shelley's *Frankenstein* (1818), to take one frequently discussed example, incorporates not only "the sublime, graveyard imagery, and the supernatural" but also contemporary political debates, imagery, and scientific theory relating to race – the creature, described as a "mummy" with "yellow skin" and living disconnected from a European society that fears him, has been connected to a number of racialized peoples and events.[23]

Somewhat less canonical works like Elizabeth Hamilton's *Translations of the Letters of a Hindoo Rajah* (1796), Sydney Owenson's *The Missionary: An*

*Indian Tale* (1811), and James Morier's *Hajji Baba* novels (1824, 1828) explored the "East's" relationship with the "West," some continuing in the tradition of adventurous and exotic "Eastern Tales" and others more critical and grounded in urgent questions about British imperialism and conquest. Unsurprisingly, slavery and abolition were discussed in numerous contemporary novels, with varying levels of narrative prominence, from John Moore's *Zeluco* (1789) to Austen's *Mansfield Park* (1814), the former finding a home in Barbauld's own *The British Novelists*. A number of racialized characters appear as love interests and seducers, in fantastical plots, as in Charlotte Dacre's *Zofloya, or the Moor* (1806), but sometimes in ordinary domestic narratives, like Maria Edgeworth's *Belinda* (1801), which features a black servant marrying a white country girl. The mixed-race children resulting from interracial unions likewise feature in novels like Amelia Opie's *Adeline Mowbray, or, The Mother and Daughter* (1804), Mary Ann Sullivan's *Owen Castle* (1816), and Austen's *Sanditon* (1817).

Many novels worked with only the briefest allusions to racialized subjects, glancing mentions that hint at an iceberg of sociopolitical complexity. Austen serves as a perfect example; every one of her novels includes at least one fairly unambiguous reference to loaded, racialized topics (slavery in *Mansfield Park* and *Emma* [1815]), people (savages in *Pride and Prejudice* and Miss Lambe in *Sanditon* [1817]), places (East Indies in *Sense and Sensibility* [1811], West Indies in *Persuasion* [1818]), or objects (India muslin in *Northanger Abbey* [1818]). Other works, like the anonymously published *The Woman of Colour* (1808), existed precisely in order to think about race. *The Woman of Colour* tells the story of the mixed-race heiress Olivia Fairfield in letters "collected" by the anonymous editor; it begins by explicitly addressing prejudice and equality and ends with an explicit reminder of the book's purpose, engaging with ideas about race in order to influence the reader's racial perception. As the editor puts it, they hope that the novel will at least "teach one skeptical European to look with a compassionate eye towards the despised native of Africa."[24]

Does the presence of these subjects, themes, and characters in novels of the Romantic period signal a failure of racial distancing? In their respective texts, Reeve and Barbauld create what amounts to a racial theory of the novel, one that aligned the literary species of the modern novel explicitly with Europe and implicitly with whiteness. They do so against a backdrop of contemporary novels that seem to resist their classifications and borders, perhaps inspiring (or at least adding to) their desire for defined boundaries. However, besides leaving an "out" in their systems amounting to "there are good and bad examples of each level of prosaic achievement," what remains the backbone of their argument is an interest in the boundaries of form. The Romance processed the world in a certain way; the novel offered new and powerful frameworks to manage and present that same world. In their systems, a novel is itself a type of mastery over the world; a novelist, they claim, sees, captures, and creates reality. A literary species defined by and created by those gifted with "reason" will then, presumably, deal in racial "reality."

Racialized themes and characters did not need to vanish from the literary landscape – perhaps they simply had to be "reasonable." Olivia Fairfield does not stay in England as a happily married women, Frankenstein's creature does not integrate into society, and glancing mentions of slavery in *Mansfield Park* are carefully met with silence. This stands in direct contrast to many of the works predating the modern novel referenced across *Progress* and "Origins," which dealt in what Barbauld and Reeve probably considered racial fantasy. For example, in *Chariclea*, an Ethiopian queen gives birth to a white child due to maternal impression, while Barbauld stresses the particularly fantastic nature of *The History of Gaudentio di Lucca* (1737), "an account of an imaginary people in the heart of Africa," which "is the play of a fine imagination delighting itself with images of perfection and happiness, which it cannot find in any existing form of things" (36–37). *Gaudentio di Lucca*, she argues, is an exercise in pure fantasy; a utopia (an *African* one, no less) cannot exist, and is, in fact, against the "form of things." Importantly, Barbauld does not unilaterally disapprove of these texts – in fact, she is often complimentary of them as significant works, or at least exciting curiosities. Similarly, Reeve finds great value in Romances and Tales from across the world and time. However, they are clearly stepping stones on the path to the modern, British novel. In Romances and Eastern Tales, racial boundaries and stereotypes are porous, changeable, and impossible, the opposite of the orderly mandate of the modern novel to present "a familiar relation of such things, as pass every day before our eyes."

The novel, then, does not deal in impossibilities, racial or otherwise – in theory. In practice, some novelists arguably crossed the limits of racial reason. In these cases, literary systems like Barbauld's own could sometimes enforce "reality" through exclusion or editing. For example, miscegenation was edited out of Edgeworth's *Belinda* prior to the novel's inclusion in *British Novelists*, drawing out narrative "poison" in service to "domestic" purity. And, of course, what remained could actively bolster the kind of racial imagining Barbauld and Reeve both subscribe to and create. Sir Walter Scott's *Ivanhoe* (1819), for example, "adumbrates the future fusion of the Norman and Saxon races and, partly through this racial harmonization, the emergence of modern Great Britain."[25] Novels dealing in "reasonable" racial engagement were not only permissible but celebrated. If, as Robert Miles writes, "the Romantic Novel" pre-Scott was (and to some extent still is) a "source of embarrassment for its critics," it seems telling that Scott acts as a turning point, away from the embarrassments of the early Romantic novel and toward the realist, modern, *estimable* novel.[26]

Much of the work of establishing the novel form in the Romantic period was in this "turn," in the crafting of the idea of a "natural" trajectory of literary progress. The stakes in remaining a part of that advancement, as a critic and reader, were high. In 1802, Barbauld, languishing in the country without contact with the latest the literary world had to offer, wrote a letter in which she compared herself to a Hottentot:

> I see no new books now ... I live in utter ignorance of all literary matters. I could tell you perhaps how many pearls were showered upon the head of the bride of Almamon, & how much marrow & sugar with how many baskets of eggs & fig's Sultan Solyman eat for breakfast, for I have just been reading it in Gibbon, but for the productions of the present day I know no more of them than a Hottentot.[27]

She refers to Edward Gibbon's *The History of the Decline and Fall of the Roman Empire* (1776–89), which not only addresses and relies on Romances and "the Orient" in its journey into antiquity, but also chronicles, though problematically and dismissively at times, "Eastern" advancements and victories. The chapter she references in the letter appears to be one in which Gibbon describes not only conquests of Europe but also the Romances that kept them living on in memory, imagining a Europe – specifically, an England – that might have existed if those victories had continued. In "Origins," Barbauld takes a cooler tone toward the anxiety of "Eastern" influence than Gibbon, who seems at turns disapproving and forcibly comic. She does not imagine a world in which that influence could radically shift the groundwork of British life – it remains only an important stepping-stone on the path to "Western" literary modernity. However, her letter offers another perspective, one that sees Gibbon himself as representative of an archaic, stifling "Orient." A lack of literary access beyond Gibbon traps Barbauld in what might be called the world of the Romance, of distant and exotic events and people of little importance to her contemporary world. In the absence of "the productions of the present day," she finds herself uncomfortably aligned with "inhabitants of the tropics," who likewise have little access to the literary technologies and trends she sees paving the future. Novelty itself, or at least access to novel works, becomes a marker of superiority, again tied to race; to be left out of "progress" is to be left behind. Less than a decade later she would write "Origins," attempting to master the history of the novel as a preface to its future.

Even while documenting the evolution of a new species called the modern novel, Reeve does not claim that the Romance, or other more primitive forms of fictional prose, will go extinct: "They were the delight of barbarous ages, and they have always kept their ground amongst the multiplied amusements of more refined and cultivated periods … " (xvi). These literary histories clearly (and sometimes radically) appreciate all forms of literature, including non-European prose, and some of the works included in Reeve's recommendations and Barbauld's own series of novels confront and play with race in unexpected ways. But Reeve and Barbauld are clear that, regardless of the worth of Romances and other forms of prose literature, readers should also invest in the modern novel and its progress away from a racialized literary past, to the extent that literary novelty and newness become socioracial markers themselves. Of course, these efforts were in no way definitive – arguments about the definition and provenance of the Romance and the novel persisted in their time (within their own work, even) and continue still to this day. However, in separating the Romance from the modern novel, Reeve and Barbauld draw a line between prose aligned with nonwhite, non-European subjects, authors, and cultures, and evolved, modern, civilized literature. Using systems of organization that echo those of natural philosophers, they attempt to place narrative forms associated with race, the exotic, and foreign others outside the bounds of "reality" in boxes marked "primitive" and, perhaps, "perilous," insisting that "it is necessary to make this distinction." Their work and methodologies demonstrate how contemporary efforts to define race, create boundaries between people, and preserve artificial divisions haunted and informed attempts to categorize, divide, and claim literature.

## Notes

1. Jane Austen, *Pride and Prejudice*, ed. James Kinsley and Fiona Stafford (Oxford: Oxford World Classics, 2004), 18.
2. Fiona Stafford, "Introduction," in Austen, *Pride and Prejudice*, 315.
3. Hugh Blair, *Lectures On Rhetoric and Belles Lettres* (London: W. Strahan, T. Cadell … and W. Creech, 1783), 201.

4. Vicesimus Knox, *Essays, Moral and Literary* (London: Edward and Charles Dilly, 1778), 95.
5. *Oxford English Dictionary*, s.v. "novelty (*n.* and *adj.*)," www.oed.com/dictionary/novelty_n.
6. Clara Reeve, *The Progress of Romance, Through Times, Countries, and Manners: . . . In a Course of Evening Conversations* (Dublin: Price, Exshaw, White, Cash Colbert, Marchbank and Porter, 1785), 7–8. Further references will be given in the text.
7. Claudia L. Johnson, "'Let Me Make the Novels of a Country': Barbauld's *The British Novelists* (1810/1820)," *NOVEL: A Forum on Fiction* 34/2 (2001), 167.
8. Clara Reeve, *Plans of Education; with Remarks on the Systems of Other Writers. In a Series of Letters Between Mrs. Darnford and Her Friends* (London: T. Hookham, and J. Carpenter, 1792), 90–92.
9. John Aikin and Anna Letitia Barbauld, "A Globe Lecture", in *Evenings at Home; or, The Juvenile Budget Opened. Consisting of a Variety of Miscellaneous Pieces*, 5 vols. (London: J. Johnson, 1796), 5:131, 144. For more on the specifics of their coauthorship, see Michelle Levy and Richard de Ritter.
10. Aikin and Barbauld, "Globe Lecture," 131, 144.
11. Thomas Day, *The History of Sandford and Merton* (London: John Stockdale, 1795) 3:222.
12. Day, *History*, 250.
13. Anna Letitia Barbauld, *The British Novelists; With an Essay, and Prefaces, Biographical and Critical by Mrs. Barbauld* (London: F. C. and J. Rivington, 1810), 1:3. Further references will be given in the text.
14. Immanuel Kant, "Observations on the Feeling of the Beautiful and Sublime (1764)," in *Kant: Observations on the Feeling of the Beautiful and Sublime and Other Writings*, ed. Patrick Frierson and Paul Guyer (Cambridge: Cambridge University Press, 2011), 58.
15. Aikin and Barbauld, "Globe Lecture," 134–35.
16. David Hume, *Essays and Treatises on Several Subjects. A New Edition* (London: A. Millar, 1758), 125.
17. Aikin and Barbauld, "Globe Lecture," 134, 141.
18. Georges Cuvier, *The Animal Kingdom Arranged in Conformity with Its Organization* (New York: Carvill, 1831), 52.
19. Cuvier, *The Animal Kingdom*, 52–53.
20. Cuvier, *The Animal Kingdom*, 53.
21. Edward W. Said, *Orientalism* (New York: Vintage Books, 1979), 7.
22. Robert Miles, "What Is a Romantic Novel?" *NOVEL: A Forum on Fiction* 34/2 (2001), 180.
23. Mary Wollstonecraft Shelley, *Frankenstein; Or the Modern Prometheus* (London: Lackington, Hughes, Harding, Mavor & Jones, 1818), 3:101, 98.
24. Anonymous, *The Woman of Colour*, ed. Lyndon J. Dominique (Peterborough: Broadview, 2007), 189.

25. Patrick Brantlinger, "Race and the Victorian Novel," in *The Cambridge Companion to the Victorian Novel*, ed. Deirdre David (Cambridge: Cambridge University Press, 2012), 131.
26. Miles, "What Is a Romantic Novel?" 180.
27. Anna Letitia Barbauld, "ALB to Lydia Rickards 6 Aug 1802," New York Public Library, Carl H. Pforzheimer Collection, Misc 4351.

CHAPTER 12

# Reading Race Along the "Bounding Line"

## Lauren Dembowitz

During the 1790s, intense debates over the transatlantic slave trade breached the official halls of parliament, permeating all forms of popular culture, including plays, poetry, and, especially, images. London printsellers enjoyed a booming market in satirical prints which ridiculed both pro- and antislavery advocates, selling mass-produced images by the thousands.[1] These images were a ubiquitous feature of the urban landscape: they were "hung on walls, stuck onto … furniture, circulated among friends, or viewed in shop windows, alehouses, coffeehouses, [and] workshops."[2] Much as social media has facilitated the proliferation of (mis)information and the polarization of civil discourse around controversial issues like race and racism, developments in affordable print technologies meant that pro- and antislavery images – and the conceptions of racial difference embedded within them – reached a wider audience than ever before.[3] This chapter explores how one popular visual trope of the slavery debates – that of the Black Venus – delineates racial categories in the early Romantic period. I use the term "delineate" because questions of race are also questions of line – how artistic lines translate to conceptual boundary lines. The images I examine here are often understood to have constructed the Black Venus as a pernicious stereotype of hypersexuality which circumscribed Blackness and whiteness as rigidly oppositional categories. However, by layering pro- and antislavery Black Venus images over one another, this chapter reveals that these racial categories and the lines that define them are more porous than the framework of the stereotype allows.

### The Black Venus and the Limits of Stereotype

The Black Venus is most often exemplified by the curvy, two-dimensional silhouette of Sarah Baartman, the so-called Hottentot Venus. In 1810 this Khoisan woman was put on display in London for her – by European standards – unusually large posterior. Baartman was exploited first as an exotic spectacle, then as a comedic caricature, and finally as pseudoscientific evidence of all African women's primitive sexual appetites. By layering the racial qualifier "Hottentot" onto the Roman goddess Venus, Baartman's imposed moniker transformed a celebrated symbol of love and beauty into a mocking oxymoron that marked the failure of African women to live up to white European standards of beauty and virtue. More precisely, the term "Hottentot Venus," like "Black Venus" before it, recast the sexual exploitation of African and African-descended women as their categorical inclination to seduction and promiscuity. Baartman's apparent stereotyping resonates today in the ongoing objectification of Black women's bodies, but the almost unanimous tendency to interpret her along polarized racial lines risks flattening "race [into] an historically timeless concept."[4] In what follows, I suggest that defining the Black Venus as a stereotype is similarly reductive.

If questions of race are also questions of line – of how artistic lines translate to conceptual boundary lines – it bears defining what kind of line a stereotype forms. We are most familiar with the conceptual meaning of a stereotype as an oversimplified and prejudiced characterization of a person or group that is widely held and uncritically repeated."[5] However, a "stereotype" also refers to a mode of printing in which an entire page of print could be cast in a mold for easy and precise reproduction. Is the Black Venus stereotype defined, then, by the mode of its conception – repeatedly imagining Baartman as an abstraction representing all Black women as hypersexualized? Or is it determined by the mode of its production – the actual reproduction of Baartman's silhouette on a page? What other Black Venuses have the fixed contours of the Hottentot Venus occluded? To what extent has the scholarly conception of the Black Venus as a static stereotype flattened the dynamics of racial formation more broadly in the early Romantic period? And how might unsettling the seeming simplicity of the Black Venus outline – both conceptually and materially – reframe the discrete racial binary she is thought to sustain? I begin to answer these questions by way of an anecdote about my own encounter with a different kind of Black Venus outline which the stereotype could not explain.

### Redrawing Racial Lines: The Black Venus Beyond Binaries

John Gabriel Stedman's memoir, *Narrative of a Five Years Expedition Against the Revolted Negroes of Surinam* (1796), includes a disturbing image engraved by William Blake (after Stedman's drawing). Titled "The

Flagellation of a Female Samboe Slave," it illustrates Stedman's encounter with an enslaved woman whose refusal of an overseer's sexual advances is punished with 200 rending lashes. Stedman's efforts to intervene result only in a doubling of the punishment, at which point he runs away from the scene, leaving the brutalized woman hanging by her wrists from a tree. The image has circulated widely as evidence of the pornography of slavery's violence – its central figure an indirect invocation of the Black Venus as a sexualized stereotype – and is commonly reproduced in scholarly articles and monographs. Like all of the *Narrative*'s engravings, Blake's "Flagellation" was printed on a single sheet of thicker paper, separated in texture and space from the text of the *Narrative* itself. In at least one copy (held at the Clark Memorial Library in Los Angeles) this seemingly fixed figure has, in fact, moved and changed over time. The linseed oil or other materials in the ink used to print the image has seeped through the paper to leave a ghostly outline of the woman tied to a tree, her eyes and mouth gaping in silent anguish (see Figure 12.1). Her appearance is arresting. She is not supposed to be here; she should not have been able to bound through walls of paper and leave evidence of her passing, but she has.

As I examined this figure, the outlines of two other Black Venus images I had been studying seemed to rise from the contours of her ghostly afterimage. In 1793, Jamaican planter Bryan Edwards commissioned *Voyage of the Sable Venus* to illustrate the Sable Venus Ode for the second edition of his *History of the West Indies*, an influential text on both sides of the slavery debate (see Figure 12.2). Engraved by William Grainger after Thomas Stothard's painting, the image depicts a critical scene in the ode, where Neptune – "The pow'r that rules old ocean wide" – encounters the Sable Venus on her transoceanic journey from Angola to the West Indies.[6] We are told he "Assum'd the figure of a tar, / The Captain of a man of war," which Stothard conveys by having him hold a Union Jack in place of his traditional trident (100–1). The Sable Venus smiles in response "with kind consenting eyes," after which point Neptune raises a murky cloud to shield (for reasons of decency) their emphatically consensual intimate encounter (103). "Sure silence is consent," the ode's narrator proclaims (16). The various ocean fauna and mythical beings in attendance welcome with joy the ensuing "Blest offspring of the warm embrace! / Gay ruler of the saffron race!" (109–10). The "saffron," or mixed-race child of Neptune and the Sable Venus is described and depicted as Cupid, whose "mingled shafts of black and white / Are wing'd with feathers of delight" (112–13). The account makes no mention whatsoever of the Sable Venus's status as chattel. Nor does it reflect her

Reading Race Along the "Bounding Line" 207

Figure 12.1   Reverse of William Blake, "Flagellation of a Female Samboe Slave" in Stedman, *Narrative of a Five Years Expedition against the Revolted Negroes of Surinam*, (London: Printed for J. Johnson, St. Paul's Church Yard, & J. Edwards, Pall Mall, 1796), 2:328. Courtesy of the William Andrews Clark Memorial Library, University of California, Los Angeles.

Figure 12.2  William Grainger after Thomas Stothard, *Voyage of the Sable Venus from Angola to the West Indies,* from Bryan Edwards, *The History Civil and Commercial, of the British Colonies in the West Indies: In Two Volumes* (London: John Stockdale, 1794). Courtesy of the Library Company of Philadelphia.

child's fate to inherit the status of property from his African mother rather than to inherit property itself from his English father.

This image seems to confirm the Black Venus as a proslavery stereotype through its romanticized portrayal of the Middle Passage and its coy reversal of the violent reality in which white men sexually dominated enslaved Black women. The Sable Venus, an African facsimile of Botticelli's Venus, seems to lord over the two white male figures in the image: the British Neptune (left) who gazes up at her from below, and the twisted Triton (right) whose strained efforts to guide her marine entourage seem somewhat feeble when compared with her serene command of the reins. However, when we approach the Sable Venus image as a circulating material object rather than an abstraction, we can better appreciate its participation in a larger market of Black Venus images circulating throughout the slavery debates. Stothard's *Voyage* reads differently when placed alongside – or rather layered over – the other Black Venus image whose outline emerged from that of the ghostly "Female Samboe Slave."

Two years before the publication of Stothard's *Voyage*, Isaac Cruikshank's *Abolition of the Slave Trade* depicted the scandalous case of Captain John Kimber, whose torture and murder of an enslaved African girl aboard the slave ship *Recovery* provided grist for antislavery appeals in parliament (see Figure 12.3). In an uncanny echo of Stothard's *Voyage*, Cruikshank's image features three triangulated figures. In the center, where the queenly Sable Venus had formerly held the reins of her shell-car, a Black woman hangs by her ankle from a rope on the deck of a slave ship. While she faces away from the viewer, her hands grasp her head in visible agony. On the right, where Triton formerly held fast to the dolphin guiding the Sable Venus's car, is a sailor who holds the hanging woman in place on a pulley. His furrowed brow and disapproving remark – "Dam me if I like it I have a good mind to let go" – convey his reluctant participation in the violent spectacle. On the left of the image, where Stothard's Neptune had gazed adoringly at the Sable Venus, stands Captain Kimber, staring directly at the viewer with a lecherous grin and a scourge in his hand. Perhaps Bryan Edwards commissioned the mythical Sable Venus as a politicized rebuttal to Cruikshank's violated and pitiable subject.

Stothard's inversion of Cruikshank's image seems at first to reinforce a binary opposition between pro- and antislavery discourses. However, their layering together in the ghostly outline of the "Female Samboe Slave" casts in relief the elements – material and conceptual – that they share in common. Both images reduce enslaved Black women to instrumental symbols of English innocence and virtue – not for reasons of ethnographic difference, but rather for reasons of political economy. Cruikshank's image showcased the slave trade's brutal violation of African girls and women

Figure 12.3  Isaac Cruikshank, *Abolition of the Slave Trade, Or the Inhumanity of Dealers in human flesh exemplified in Captn Kimber's treatment of a Young Negro Girl of 15 for her Virjen [sic] Modesty* (1792). Courtesy of the Library of Congress.

precisely as Edwards and other planters were lobbying for a drastic increase in their importation.[7] They understood that controlling enslaved women's reproductive labor would be the only way to keep the plantation economy afloat in the eventuality of the slave trade's abolition. The English dependence on hereditary slavery united rather than divided pro- and antislavery advocates. As Sasha Turner has shown, even leading abolitionists like William Wilberforce deemed it critical to their aims to "end colonial dependence on an immoral and inhuman trade" without "jeopardizing British colonial goals or the fortunes of its investors."[8] Neither Stothard's nor Cruikshank's images fixates on the inherent *hyper*sexuality of Black women, but both betray a preoccupation with the *commercialized* sexuality of *enslaved* Black women and the extent of England's reliance on it as a source of national and imperial wealth. They simply disavow English culpability in this violent dependence in different ways.

For example, Edwards does not use the Sable Venus to make light of Black women's sexual commodification so much as he seeks to reframe it as an economic inevitability whose moral vicissitudes are beyond his control.

Throughout his *History* Edwards does not identify himself with the vicious scourge-wielding Captain Kimber, with whose case he was thoroughly familiar. Nor does he position himself as the stately emblem of British Naval authority, the British-flag-waving Neptune. Rather, Edwards presents himself more like the evasive Triton and the reluctant sailor holding the pulley. All, he suggests, are cogs in the commercial machine of Atlantic slavery. In Edwards's rendering, then, white men are not subject to the seductive powers of the Black Venus per se, but rather to the tyranny of the market for which Black Venus ironically becomes an instrumental figure. Cruikshank's image naturalizes the commodification of Black women by domesticating it. The fact that Cruikshank's image hides the enslaved girl's face or that court documents from Kimber's trial never record the girl's name betrays the way abolitionist discourse abstracts suffering Black women into purchasable vehicles of sentimental English outrage not only to rouse support for the abolition of the trade, but also, ironically, to absolve English men and women of their ongoing economic dependence on hereditary slavery. As Kriz reminds us, tangible evidence of Britain's participation in the slave trade manifested not only in the domestic consumption of sugar but also in the domestic luxuries which the profits of that human commerce made attainable.[9] These luxury goods included graphic prints like Cruikshank's and other abolitionist objects which "offered a supplicating slave toward which any Briton could express [their] virtuous involvement in the Atlantic world."[10]

When we revisit Stedman's account of the "Female Samboe Slave," we see that he too evades accountability for the violence of slavery by abstracting the tortured woman he encounters into an instrument of cathartic sentiment. Stedman models how his London readership might consume the image by focusing less on the feelings of the enslaved victim than on his own virtuous response to the "most affecting spectacle" of her victimization.[11] The horizontal lines transecting her afterimage – ink that had transferred over time from the text of Stedman's *Narrative* on the facing page – materialize her incarceration within the sentimental discourse Stedman invokes to domesticate his complicity in slavery's cruel economies of intimacy (see Figure 12.1). Much as the ghostly outline seemed to blend Stothard's poised goddess and Cruikshank's hanging victim, the illegibility of these horizontal lines effectively collapses what seem to be divergent, even oppositional, rhetorical frames for the slavery debates' violent print spectacles: whether they issue justifications or apologies or laments, the victimized women they describe never escape their commodified instrumentality.

As the layered Black Venus emerging from this afterimage unsettled the boundary between pro- and antislavery discourses, she also troubled the racial binary entrenched by the stereotype. Kriz captures this binary when she argues that, "[j]ust as the beauty of black women could not be confirmed within European discourse on aesthetics ... so the virtue of black women could not be confirmed within the discourse of white femininity, since that discourse was predicated on a notion of domestic English womanhood that black women could only threaten, not hope to emulate."[12] Lisa Lowe, Jennifer Morgan, and Saidiya Hartman help us to see what is lost in this rigid framing, namely that white domestic femininity – so often taken for granted as a stable and normative category – was coming into being through an economic dependence on enslaved Black women and a disavowal of that dependence rather than through relations of biological or aesthetic opposition. Hartman calls us to dissociate the category of "woman" from "the white middle-class female subject who norms the category" by illuminating the violent and uneven process through which that norm was being constructed in the eighteenth century. Attending to this process helps us to "understand the racialized engenderment of the black female captive in terms other than deficiency or lack in relation to normative conditions [of womanhood] and instead understand this production of gender in the context of very different economies of power, property, kinship, race and sexuality."[13]

Lowe highlights the dual logic by which the "ideal of bourgeois intimacy" is constructed as distinct from the public realm of the market even as enslaved and colonized labor "founded the formative wealth of the European bourgeoisie" and "colonized workers produced the material comforts and commodities that furnished the bourgeois home."[14] Morgan unveils an even tighter bind between colonial commerce and metropolitan domesticity in the doctrine of *partus sequitur ventrem*, which dictates that a mother's enslaved status is conferred hereditarily upon her child. For Morgan, this doctrine reveals how thoroughly Atlantic slavery's "transformation of kin into commodity" and its "routinized alienation of black life to the marketplace" were "constitutive of the European, and subsequently Euro-American, private sphere."[15] The Black Venus is a flexible emblem of this racial contingency: she marks the troubling fact that slavery's commodification of Black women's maternity helped finance the formation of a white female domestic sphere precisely as that sphere was being defined by its isolation from the corrosive influence of imperial trade. Black womanhood was not aberrant to white womanhood, then; it was constitutive of it. And the Black Venus records the process through which that whiteness was constructed.

If the stereotype proves overly reductive, what alternative model might we employ to understand the relationship between the Black Venus and racial formation at the turn of the nineteenth century? In what follows, I argue that William Blake's theory of the "bounding line" and its realization in his illuminated poem, *Visions of the Daughters of Albion*, helps us theorize the cumulative character of the Black Venus's shifting uses while also attending to the material (re)production of her images, the markets in which they circulated, and the ways in which they responded to one another.

## William Blake's 'Bounding Line' and Racial Representation

In 1809, just a year before Baartman's London exhibition, William Blake articulated his theory of the "bounding line," a union of artistic praxis and radical politics, of artistic line and conceptual boundary line. According to Blake's account in his *Descriptive Catalogue*, "the more distinct, sharp, and wirey the bounding line, the more perfect the work of art; and the less keen and sharp, the greater is the evidence of weak imitation, plagiarism, and bungling."[16] Blake's preference in the *Catalogue* and *Public Address* for the linearism of Michelangelo and Rafael over the chiaroscuro shading styles used by his popular contemporaries Joseph Reynolds and Thomas Stothard (after Rubens and Correggio) is not strictly an aesthetic one. It reflects his fundamental resistance to the increasing commercialization of art, which, in Blake's eyes, degraded alike both painter and painting. More precisely, Blake associates popular colorist styles with the mechanized and extractive operations of the factory because they demand tremendous manual labor performed by underpaid journeymen in their aims to satisfy "the 'insatiable Maw' of the commercial art market."[17] Blake's reflections on painting echo his critique of reproductive printing and his designation of the mass-reproduced book as a "good for nothing commodity."[18]

As a "reproductive engraver," obliged "to faithfully copy prior images into a new medium where they could be rapidly and accurately reproduced in print," Blake was thoroughly immersed in these modes of production.[19] In fact, Blake spent the early years of his professional career producing engravings for Stothard, who was among the most popular and prolific English book illustrators of the eighteenth century. As we know, he also produced engravings for Stedman's *Narrative*, which saw twenty-five editions and was translated into numerous languages. Its tremendous success and long afterlife of sampling and adaptation mean that Blake's contemporaries were more likely to have seen his engravings for Stedman than any of his other work.[20] In other words, Blake's livelihood depended upon a commercial system he recognized as an extension of the reproductive logic governing industrialization's "dark Satanic mills," but also, I would add, the doctrine of hereditary slavery sustaining English commerce across the Atlantic. Consequently, we can best observe Blake's ideal of the "bounding line" in the counter-praxis of his noncommercial work, a revolutionary method of relief etching through which he remakes the Black Venus in *Visions of the Daughters of Albion*.

Developed in 1788, Blake's illuminated printing – also referred to as "the infernal method" – defied the mass reproducibility of the commercial book as a "good for nothing commodity" in large part through an embrace of porousness and palimpsestic layering that recalls the ghostly afterimage of the Female Samboe Slave. To begin with, Blake's infernal method abjured the industrial logic of original and copy and dispensed with the ordered division of labor required for commercial printing by interweaving image and text on a single copper plate through a painstaking manual process. Blake used pens and brushes to draw both designs and words (in mirror image) directly onto his plates using an impervious liquid medium or stop-out varnish. He then subjected the plate to acid, which would burn away the unvarnished negative space, leaving his words and images raised in relief, or, as he articulates in *The Marriage of Heaven and Hell*, revealing "the infinite which was hid" (39). After inking the raised portions of the plate and running them through a rolling press, Blake hand-colored each print. Every copy's distinctiveness – a result of the ways post-printing embellishments layer onto and even obscure the outlines of the copper plate – shows us that Blake's illuminated books signify in excess of their reproducibility. The material logic animating the infernal method affords us a new way to understand Blake's bounding line.

Indeed, we might rethink the bounding line according to the heuristic process Saree Makdisi ascribes to the illuminated book: it is "a performance to be repeatedly recreated without the intervention of a controlling principle designed to guarantee its outcome or meaning – or at least without *absolute* principles, since what we encounter in Blake's work is not really sheer dissemination but rather a series of repetitions through preexisting channels of reiteration."[21] On the one hand, the bounding line reveals the distinctive line which was "bound" or "hid" in the copper plate. On the other hand, such a line is never fixed but bounds outward through accumulating repetitions and alterations, what Blake calls its "infinite inflexions and movements" (550). For example, in isolation, Blake's illuminated poem "The Little Black Boy" from *Songs of Innocence and of Experience* seems to glorify whiteness and naturalize Black subservience. Proclaiming, "I am black, but O! my soul is white," the poem's child narrator becomes a mouthpiece for binary racial thinking wherein whiteness is a default category imbued with angelic purity and worthiness of God's love (2). Blackness, by contrast, represents a marred or imperfect copy of that original goodness. The bounding line of the illuminated poem's varying iterations unsettles this dynamic, and, by extension, the racial categories it circumscribes. The poetic lines do not change; nor do the outlines delineating Blake's figures. However, the little Black boy's skin tone alters dramatically: in some copies, he appears very dark, almost a featureless shadow behind the little white boy he cherishes. In others, he is as fair as his white counterpart. The bounding line which threads together the layers of these divergent iterations denaturalizes Blackness and whiteness as stable categories, foregrounding the relations of material and figurative contingency through which those categories are forged.

As it does so, it bounds beyond "The Little Black Boy" and into the lines of another poem from *Songs* called "The Chimney Sweeper." We first meet the title character as a "little black thing among the [white] snow" (1). His Blackness, we learn, is not linked to complexion but rather to class. The soot that covers him from head to toe is a literally toxic materialization of his exploited labor, which is, in turn, the condition of possibility for the vaunted whiteness of "God & his Priest & King/ Who make up a heaven of our misery" (11–12). Blake does not reduce enslaved labor in the West Indies to a metaphor for exploited labor in England; he layers them to expose their material contingencies. In other words, Blake's illuminated poems do not retread a single linear narrative over and again; their meanings are never foreclosed or identically reproduced. Instead, they proliferate within and beyond the apparent boundaries of any single print or book. In fact, these channels of reiteration extend beyond Blake's own oeuvre to include those graven into his contemporaries' mass-produced texts. Whereas the bounding line of such reiterations was an accident of time in the ghostly afterimage of the "Female Samboe Slave" – which layered Stothard, Cruikshank, and Stedman's images together – Blake enacts it in *Visions*, through his revised Black Venus, Oothoon.

## Retracing Visions of the Black Venus

Published in 1793, *Visions* follows Oothoon as she pursues her virgin love for Theotormon across the Atlantic, whereupon she is raped and enslaved by Bromion. In the aftermath of her rape, Theotormon spurns the now-pregnant Oothoon for her despoiled virtue and is so consumed with sanctimonious self-pity that he is insensible to her protestations. Although *Visions* constitutes his most explicit reference to transatlantic slavery, Blake's Oothoon is not explicitly Black. In fact, she appears white in all of Blake's illustrations and is described as having "snowy limbs."[22] Moreover, Bromion's careless disposal of Oothoon and her child seems discontinuous with the capitalist logic of hereditary slavery. These incongruities make it tempting to read slavery's primary function in *Visions* as a metaphor for domestic forms of patriarchal oppression generally, and the oppression of the white Daughters of Albion specifically, who, the poem's refrain tells us, hear Oothoon's woes and echo back her sighs. To all appearances, Oothoon indeed seems white. However, if we read along the material and conceptual axes of the bounding line, we can see in her the range of Black Venus figures that permeated British popular culture throughout the eighteenth century, including the ones I have traced here.

The triangulated figures of Blake's frontispiece – Bromion, Oothoon, and Theotormon – layer precisely onto those in Stothard's image – Neptune, the Sable Venus, and Triton respectively (see Figure 12.4).[23] Both Bromion and Neptune appear older than their romantic rivals, Triton/Theotormon; both are bearded and well muscled, and Bromion's hair stands on end like Neptune's spiked crown. Theotormon looks away from Oothoon just as Triton looks away from the Sable Venus. Stothard's *Voyage*, we must remember, is itself a mythologized revision of the living – if abstracted – figures in Cruikshank's *Abolition* (1792). Blake's Bromion contains not only Neptune, but also the vicious naval officer John Kimber. Oothoon embodies not only the empowered Sable Venus but the unnamed young, enslaved woman whose murder at Kimber's hands is overwritten by the Sable Venus's majestic agency. We can even see the triangulated figures of Stedman's account of the "Female Samboe Slave" haunting beneath the surface of Blake's frontispiece. The ruthless overseer claiming the enslaved woman as his sexual property easily evokes Bromion, the "flagellated" woman recalls Oothoon's rending by Theotormon's eagles, and the helpless, hand-wringing Stedman blends uncannily into Theotormon.

Figure 12.4  William Blake, *Visions of the Daughters of Albion*, Copy I, 1793, frontispiece. Courtesy of the Yale Center for British Art, Paul Mellon Collection / Public Domain.

By layering these texts one over the other, Blake's *Visions* casts in relief the discursive patterns of violent abstraction that accumulate through their reiteration. More precisely, Oothoon's contours function as a bounding line that blurs the distinction between Black women who circulate as enslaved captives in the West Indies and those who circulate as instrumental print representations in London; between pro- and antislavery discourses; and between racial slavery and white domesticity. In particular, Blake helps us to see how seemingly sympathetic Black Venus images are embedded in the same markets they protest, and how the commercialized sentiment of antislavery culture may not redeem Black subjects so much as it tries to redeem a whiteness forged through the commodification of their suffering.

Blake's *Visions* upends the supposedly consensual romance that Stothard's *Voyage* and its sister ode illustrate between Neptune and the seductive Black Venus. In visual terms, Blake transforms the subtle bands around the Sable Venus's wrists and ankles – the only visual reference to her enslavement – into substantial chains that bind Oothoon directly to her enslaver, Bromion. And, whereas the empowered Sable Venus gazes up at the reins that signal her apparent control over her journey from Angola to the West Indies and her reign as the goddess of Atlantic commerce, Oothoon's gaze is cast down at the floor of the cave where she remains Theotormon's captive. Blake also embeds within his revision a critique of the London print market in which the Sable Venus circulates as an instrument for naturalizing hereditary slavery. Just after Bromion has "rent [Oothoon] with his thunders," he taunts Theotormon:

. . . behold this harlot here on Bromion's bed,
And let the jealous dolphins sport around the lovely maid!
Thy soft American plains are mine, and mine thy north and south:
Stamp'd with my signet are the swarthy children of the sun;
They are obedient, they resist not, they obey the scourge;
Their daughters worship terrors and obey the violent.
Now thou may'st marry Bromion's harlot, and protect the child
Of Bromion's rage, that Oothoon shall put forth in nine moons' time. (4:18–23–5:1–2)

Bromion's identity is delineated in terms of possession and property, namely in his branding of those he enslaves: "Stamp'd with my signet are the swarthy children of the sun" (4:21). Blake maximizes the potential of branding as a material metaphor for commercial printing, where both signal control over the profitable reproduction of that which is possessed as property and reduced to a "good for nothing commodity," be it human or image.

His boast that those he brands (or stamps) "are obedient, they resist not, they obey the scourge," conjures engraving tools that dig into a copper plate as both a scourge and a brand dig into and mark flesh. The Sable Venus is precisely such a stamped figure; she does not resist because she is an image fabricated and disseminated to a political and economic purpose. The same is true of the Female Samboe Slave. In colored versions of the image, her body is striped with red, indicating the numerous sites of contact with the scourge. In uncolored versions, however, the lines delineating her wounds blend in with the engraved lines that compose her image. Blake invites us to read Bromion's boast in a third way. "Stamp'd with my signet are the swarthy children of the sun" betrays the ease with which those who bear Bromion's image – namely the mixed-race children of enslaved women he rapes – slide into the category of chattel, a proliferation of so many coins or profitable prints.

As Blake blurs the distinction between Black female figures who circulate as enslaved captives and those who circulate as instrumental images, he also exposes the imbrication of antislavery material culture with the violent human commerce it decries. Around the time that Blake published *Visions*, antislavery abstention campaigns were replacing the consumption of actual enslaved Black bodies and the products of their labor (like sugar) with the consumption of enslaved suffering emblazoned on abolitionist swag like cameos, snuff boxes, and sugar bowls. These abolitionist objects would then go on to ornament as outward signals of English virtue the same white leisured domesticity which slavery's circuits of commerce helped to finance. We need look no further than Josiah Wedgwood's famous abolitionist emblem of a kneeling enslaved man beseeching "Am I not a man and a brother?" The emblem protests the commodification of human beings as objects for consumption and profitable reproduction. However, its material form and function as a purchasable and reproducible commodity reinforce its participation in a domestic economy inseparable from slavery. By emphasizing Oothoon's materiality as a palimpsestic figure, Blake short-circuits the commercialized sentiment that her isolation as an individual suffering Black female victim would provoke. In so doing, he also exposes the mechanistic way in which English benevolence transforms enslaved Black womanhood into a resource for asserting white domestic virtue. For Blake, virtue thus secured is pathological, an extension of middle-class subjectivity's mind-forged manacles which prompt Oothoon to declare the moralistic man of feeling, Theotormon, "is a sick man's dream" (9:19).

Blake's damning portrait of Bromion notwithstanding, he reserves his most trenchant critique for Theotormon and the white domesticity he seems to guard and symbolize. When we read *Visions* layered over Stothard's Sable Venus narrative, we realize that Bromion and Theotormon are neither strictly romantic rivals nor adversaries in debates over abolition, as Erdman contends. Rather, they are kin: Neptune was Triton's father, so it follows that Bromion is Theotormon's. He does not, therefore, give away his property in Oothoon and their child for free; Theotormon, whom Erdman identifies as a stand-in for the tortured abolitionist, inherits them. Their child, in turn, inherits Oothoon's enslaved status. In this light, Oothoon's designation as a "harlot" within Bromion's preceding rant about reproductive slavery suggests that it is the commercialization of her maternity within an expansive colonial economy, rather than strictly her loss of virginity, that so torments Theotormon throughout the poem. After all, the circuit of inheritance that brings Oothoon home to Theotormon brings with it the intimate commerce of slavery by which Bromion claimed her as his property. Oothoon's subsequent haunting of Theotormon's cave as an enslaved captive, as an English wife, and as an instrumental Black Venus betrays the intrusion of slavery into the domestic spaces – both England and the English home – believed to be guarded against its moral turpitude. As Theotormon sits on the margin uniting the Atlantic site of Oothoon's rape and enslavement and the domestic space founded in that violence, his efforts to wear "the threshold hard" reflect his desperation to eliminate the porousness between these realms and to block out "the voice of slaves beneath the sun, and children bought with money" (5:8).

Attending to this material layering of slavery and English domestic virtue brings to light an alternative reading of Oothoon's disturbing mutilation. In an eerie parallel of the woman's flagellation in Stedman's *Narrative*, Oothoon calls Theotormon's Eagles to "Rend away this defil'd bosom that I may reflect/ The image of Theotormon on my pure transparent breast" (5:14–16). Superficially, Oothoon seems to endorse both Bromion and Theotormon's conclusions that she is tainted, endeavoring to remove that stain at its source: her defiled body. I propose that Oothoon's rending serves not to clear *her* sin, but rather Theotormon's. After all, if we interpret Oothoon's "defil'd bosom" in the same context as her transformation into a "harlot," we might imagine that what defiles her breast is the brand with which Bromion marks as chattel "the swarthy children of the sun." In this scenario, Oothoon is endeavoring to rend away the material reminder of Theotormon's inherited complicity. Both Bromion and Theotormon seek to benefit from Oothoon's rending – once as rape and again as absolution – and the repetition of the term conjures the phonetically similar (if contradictory) "render." While "rend" means to tear apart, "render" means, variably, to reproduce artistically, to give over (as in money), and to melt away.[24] Like branding, rendering evokes both the business and the mechanisms of reproductive printing. Rend and render form a material link between slavery and printing in the intertext of Stedman's *Narrative*: a Bromion-like villain brutally rends (lacerates by flogging) an enslaved women to mark his absolute claim to her as property, and the Theotormon-like Stedman profitably abstracts (or renders) that brutalization into a vehicle for cleansing pity in his mass-reproduced memoir.

At first, the scene of Oothoon's rending seems to follow the affective logic of its parallel scene in Stedman's *Narrative*. As if bound by the centripetal pull of the Black Venus figure's reiterative use, Oothoon presents Theotormon with an escape hatch. Oothoon's mutilation should, in theory, provoke Theotormon's performance of pity, at which point his image of white purity might be projected back to him on Oothoon's "pure transparent breast." But this is not quite what happens:

> The Eagles at her call descend and rend their bleeding prey:
> Theotormon severely smiles; her soul reflects the smile,
> As the clear spring, muddied with feet of beasts, grows pure and smiles. (5:17–19)

In place of cleansing tears, the rending of Oothoon's breast raises Theotormon's grisly smile, reflecting back a corrupted image erected through intimate violence. Here Blake's opposition to calculated pity takes on a distinctly racialized dimension, recoding whiteness dependent on such performances of sentiment as monstrous. The preying of birds upon human flesh proves an aptly grotesque metaphor for the consumptive impulse of commercialized sentiment. For Blake, "'feast[ing] on the consciousness of our own virtue'" in response to the suffering of others "was both self-centered and self-righteous, making pity an ironic form of consumption in that it sickens and devours not only the receiver but also the giver."[25]

It is in the context of this scene, and its rhetoric of reflection and transparency, that I understand the poem's opening motto: "The eye sees more than the heart knows" emerges as a critique of performative sensibility which shows more than the performer necessarily feels. These opening lines layer provocatively onto Stedman's concluding concession in his *Narrative*: "I must have hurt both the Eye and the heart of the Feeling reader," he admits.[26] While Stedman frames this as an apology, it is precisely his hurting of the reader's eye and heart that enable them to demonstrate that they are, in fact, "feeling reader[s]" set apart from the overseers and planters whose callous disregard for their victims gives Stedman's English readers cathartic suffering to consume. According to Vine, Oothoon's rending reveals to her that Theotormon's love "is inseparable from his self-love, and she herself becomes a mere cipher through which Theotormon accumulates his own value."[27] The same is true, I would argue, for Stedman's paying readers. Ultimately, if Theotormon dominates the poem as a figure of white moral purity to which Oothoon initially aspires, Blake recodes that whiteness in terms of pathological consumption – of literal bodies in slavery and abstracted bodies in abolitionist print culture.

Refusing to visually reproduce victimized Black womanhood, then, Blake reveals instead how their repeated instrumentalization accumulates into Oothoon, a figure whose "snowy limbs" obscure where she ends and where the Daughters of Albion begin. These are, after all, *their* visions. And, as the final words of the poem remind us in their reiteration of Blake's refrain, "The Daughters of Albion hear her woes. & echo back her sighs," we can never rest assured that it is Oothoon's lament we are hearing (11:13). Indeed, we don't hear it. We read it along "preexisting channels of reiteration."[28] Much like the affective short-circuiting of Oothoon's rending, the uncertain origin of her lament, and the indecipherable effect of its filtration through the Daughters of Albion who echo it back, thwart desires for the redemptive closure on which pathological white virtue depends. The syntax and punctuation of the poem's opening lines confuse from the start the source of the lament: "Enslav'd, the Daughters of Albion weep; a trembling lamentation/ Upon their mountains; in their valleys, sighs toward America" (4:1–2). While "weep" and "lamentation" undoubtedly link these utterances of despair, the semicolon after "weep" and the subsequent positioning of "lamentation" as the subject of the following phrase untether that lament from the Daughters of Albion. The fact that this disembodied lament imbricates Oothoon and the Daughters of Albion casts doubt on whether or not Blake's Black Venus continues to operate here as an instrument of whiteness, whether or not the women deemed Black Venuses can escape the matrix of material and symbolic currency that has defined the deep channel of the figure's reiteration.

Through the bounding figure of Oothoon, Blake makes visible what Jacques Derrida calls "white mythology," a "metaphysics which has effaced in itself that fabulous scene which brought it into being, and which yet remains, active and stirring, inscribed in white ink, an invisible drawing covered over in the palimpsest" (11). The ghostly afterimage of the Female Samboe Slave does the same: over the course of 200 years, the black ink that formerly held her captive as a material and symbolic tool of whiteness has come to mar that whiteness, to literally stain what should have been the blank reverse page of Blake's engraving with a brownish red reminiscent of dried blood. And yet, her bounding figure also seems to thread together past and present uses of her image. Staring at the stain of the Female Samboe Slave's ghostly outline, her repeated instrumentalization seems to pile up on the page, layer upon layer. As an enslaved laborer, she augmented the wealth of those who claimed her and any children she may have borne as property. As a spectacular victim, she prompted the cleansing sensibility Stedman models for his metropolitan readers. As a commissioned engraving, she put money in Blake's pocket. As portable evidence of slavery's inhumanity, she served as an adaptable tool of abolitionist rhetoric and, much later, as a scholarly exhibit in histories of slavery. The point here is not to collapse the physical and psychological violence of chattel slavery with the representational violence that so frequently marks its afterlives, but rather to see how these technologies of racial formation persist today in ways that the stereotype as an unchanging repetition obscures.

### Open Lines: What to Do (or Not) with Baartman

How might the bounding line's layered reframing of racial formation inform the way we (re)tell Baartman's story or (re)deploy images of her today? Yvette Abrahams suggests "we lack academic studies that view Sarah Baartman as anything other than a symbol. Her story becomes marginalized, as it is always used to illustrate some other topic."[29] In efforts to rescue Baartman from the stereotype, such studies risk replicating it. Qureshi raises similar concerns, arguing that when scholars and artists identify "with Baartman as an ancestral self and her treatment as representative of the negativity of modern depictions of black sexuality," they unwittingly reify Baartman's objecthood – once curiosity, now cultural icon. Indeed, Qureshi alerts us to the fact that it is "precisely the difficulty in recovering [Baartman's] agency that makes her amenable to employment as a cipher."[30] This is as true of Baartman's instrumental politicization by abolitionists in the early nineteenth century as it is of her potent symbolism for antiracist scholars and artists today. Much as abolitionists overwrote her Indigenous identity as a Khoisan woman with her victimized Blackness, so too have contemporary recoveries – particularly in a US context – rendered Baartman "black through the iterability of her representation as a symbol of black pain."[31] In other words, the bounding line reveals not only how our present bears traces of the past, but also how our "ability to read the past is contingent upon a present that transforms it into an image we can recognize" – or, perhaps more pointedly, an image we can *use*.[32]

Complicity in the ongoing circulation of the Black Venus does not operate uniformly. As Kim Hall reminds us, we should confront rather than scour away the ways in which contemporary manifestations of race (and racial violence), as well as the positionality of scholars within those discursive systems, shape the questions and language through which we explore their historical dimensions.[33] Ultimately, reading the Black Venus along the bounding line thwarts the kinds of redemptive closure that the stereotype seems to demand as a response, instead pushing us to contend with the ways we are "intimately connected" with, "bound up in," and "dependent upon" that figure and the real women she overwrites for understanding how racial capitalism lives on in our present.[34]

## Notes

1. Brooke Newman, "Enslaved Women and British Comic Culture," in *A Dark Inheritance: Blood, Race, and Sex in Colonial Jamaica* (New Haven: Yale University Press, 2018), 181.
2. Catherine Molineux, *Faces of Perfect Ebony: Encountering Atlantic Slavery in Imperial Britain* (Cambridge, MA: Harvard University Press, 2012), 245.
3. Kay Dian Kriz, *Slavery Sugar and the Culture of Refinement: Picturing the British West Indies 1700–1840* (New Haven: Yale University Press, 2008), 1.
4. Sadiah Qureshi, "Displaying Sara Baartman, the 'Hottentot Venus,'" *History of Science* 42/2 (2004), 234. For exceptions to this critical tendency, see Robin Mitchell, *Venus Noire: Black Women and Colonial Fantasies in Nineteenth-Century France* (Athens: University of Georgia Press, 2020), 4; and Zine Magubane, "Which Bodies Matter? Feminism, Poststructuralism, Race, and the Curious Theoretical Odyssey of the 'Hottentot Venus,'" in *Black Venus 2010: They Called Her "Hottentot,"* ed. Deborah Willis (Philadelphia: Temple University Press, 2010), 59.
5. *Merriam-Webster*, s.v. "stereotype (*n.*)," accessed September 10, 2022, www.merriam-webster.com/dictionary/stereotype; *Oxford English Dictionary*, s.v. "stereotype (*n.*3)," accessed September 10, 2022, www.oed.com/view/Entry/189956.
6. Isaac Teale, *The Sable Venus: An Ode. Inscribed to Bryan Edwards, Esq.* (Kingston, Jamaica 1765), 97. Further references will be given in the text.
7. Sasha Turner, *Contested Bodies: Pregnancy, Childrearing, and Slavery in Jamaica* (Philadelphia: University of Pennsylvania Press, 2019), 52, 51.
8. Turner, *Contested Bodies*, 4.
9. Kriz, *Slavery Sugar*, 2.
10. Molineux, *Faces of Perfect Ebony*, 244.
11. John Gabriel Stedman, *Narrative of a Five Years Expedition against the Revolted Negroes of Surinam* (London: Printed for J. Johnson, St. Paul's Church Yard, & J. Edwards, Pall Mall, 1796), vol. I, 326.
12. Kriz, *Slavery Sugar*, 105.

13. Saidiya V. Hartman, *Scenes of Subjection: Terror, Slavery, and Self-Making in Nineteenth-Century America* (New York: Oxford University Press, 1997), 99–100.
14. Lisa Lowe, *The Intimacies of Four Continents* (Durham: Duke University Press, 2015), 29.
15. Jennifer L. Morgan, "Partus sequitur ventrem: Law, Race, and Reproduction in Colonial Slavery," *Small Axe* 22/1 (2018), 13.
16. William Blake, *Descriptive Catalogue*, in *The Complete Poetry and Prose of William Blake*, ed. David V. Erdman and Harold Bloom (Berkeley: University of California Press, 2008), 550. This text is also available on the web through the William Blake Archive: https://erdman.blakearchive.org/. All subsequent references to Blake's works – apart from *Visions* – are to this edition, indicated by page or plate and line numbers.
17. Scott J. Juengel, "William Blake's Enemies," *Studies in English Literature* 58/3 (Summer 2018), 714, 715.
18. Blake, *Public Address*, 576.
19. Saree Makdisi, *William Blake and the Impossible History of the 1790s* (Chicago: University of Chicago Press, 2002), 168.
20. G. E. Bentley Jr., "Blake and Stedman as Costumiers: Curious Copies of Blake's Engravings in 1821," *Blake/An Illustrated Quarterly* 46/4 (Spring 2013), 1.
21. Makdisi, 175.
22. William Blake, *Visions of the Daughters of Albion*, ed. Robert N. Essick (San Marino: Huntington Library and Art Gallery, 2004), 5:12. Further references will be given in the text, as plate and line numbers.
23. Alexander S. Gourlay, "'Art Delivered': Stothard's the Sable Venus and Blake's Visions of the Daughters of Albion," *Journal for Eighteenth-Century Studies* 31/4 (2008), 529–50.
24. *Oxford English Dictionary*, s.v. "rend (v.1.)," accessed February 16, 2022, www.oed.com/view/Entry/162382; "render (v.)," accessed February 16, 2022, www.oed.com/view/Entry/162386.
25. Dennis Welch, "Blake and the Web of Interest and Sensibility," *South Atlantic Review: The Publication of the South Atlantic Modern Language Association*, 71.3 (2006), 48.
26. Stedman, *Narrative of a Five Years Expedition,* 2:168.
27. Steven Vine, "'That Mild Beam': Enlightenment and enslavement in William Blake's Visions of the Daughters of Albion." In *The Discourse of Slavery: Aphra Behn to Toni Morrison*, ed. Carla Plasa and Betty J. Ring (London: Routledge, 1994), 57.
28. Makdisi, *William Blake*, 175.
29. Yvette Abrahams, Colonialism Dysfunction and Dysjuncture: The Historiography of Sarah Bartmann, unpublished PhD dissertation, University of Cape Town (2000), 143.
30. Qureshi, "Displaying Sara Baartman," 250, 249.

31. Kellen Hoxworth, "The Many Racial Effigies of Sara Baartman," *Theatre Survey* 58/3 (2017), 279.
32. Jenny Sharpe, *Allegories of Empire: The Figure of Woman in the Colonial Text* (Minneapolis: University of Minnesota Press, 1993), 14.
33. Kim F. Hall, *Things of Darkness: Economies of Race and Gender in Early Modern England* (Ithaca: Cornell University Press, 1998), 260.
34. *Oxford English Dictionary*, s.v. "bound (*adj*.2.)," accessed September 20, 2022, www.oed.com/view/Entry/22039.

CHAPTER 13

# The Racecraft of Romantic Stagecraft

## Yasser Shams Khan

> Chinese vermillion boiled in milk, and then suffered to dry, and afterwards mixed with about half the quantity of carmine, is decidedly the best colour an actor can use; ... previous to painting it is best to pass a napkin, with a little pomatum upon it, over the part [of the face] intended to receive the colour, then touch the cheek with a little hair-powder, which will set the colour, and then lay on the vermillion and carmine. A rabbit's foot is better than anything else for distributing the paint equally.
>
> –Leman Thomas Rede, *The Road to the Stage*

These make-up instructions are found in Leman Thomas Rede's *The Road to the Stage* (1836), a nineteenth-century guide for those who aspire to act in one of the provincial theaters. With interesting details concerning the hours of labor required by an actor to memorize their lines (somewhere around six hours per day), along with other miscellaneous facts about the inner structure and workings of the theatrical institution in London and the provinces, the manual attempts to lay bare the technicalities of stagecraft during the Romantic period, and is thus one crucial piece of evidence, amongst others, to understand the racecraft underlying the stagecraft of racial performances.

Although Rede notes that "Ladies have generally sufficient knowledge of the arts of decking the face divine," he considers it "a performer's duty," regardless of sex, to master the art of making up the face for the stage.[1] The aforementioned directions are intended for the representation of characters whose racial identity Rede does not remark upon; by inference, we can mark these characters as normatively white. Does it surprise us to consider all the effort white British actors put into embodying whiteness, a cosmetic whiteness that supplemented their natural skin? What of racially black characters?

> To produce the black necessary for the negro face of Hassan, Wouski, Mungo, or Sambo, the performer should cover the face and neck with a thin coat of pomatum, or what is better, though more disagreeable, of lard; then burn a cork to powder, and apply it with a hare's foot, or a cloth, the hands wet with beer which will fix the colouring matter.[2]

Nothing is left to nature, not skin color, nor whiskers on the face. Using burnt cork for moustaches might leave a smudge on the fair lady's already made-up face if such intimacy is staged. For a closer imitation of natural facial hair, Rede recommends the use of camel's hair pencil and Indian ink.[3] To avoid the ink running down the face due to the heat from the gaslights used to illuminate the stage since 1817, Rede suggests wetting the brush in gum water. The same Indian ink can be used to line the wrinkles. Such facial art – turning the face into a living canvas, making it into an emblem, ideal, icon of beauty or horror, of youth or age, of whiteness or blackness – was the convention of stagecraft of the period, rendering anything and everything into an illusion fit for a dramatic spectacle.

In this chapter, I will first present the problem of how to understand "race" as a concept of identity in relation to theatrical practices of acting and spectating during the Romantic period, and then introduce Barbara and Karen Fields's useful concept of "racecraft" to frame the discussion of racial dramas in terms of the performative dimension of race. To further explore the racecraft of stagecraft, I offer a reading of John Fawcett's pantomime *Obi; or Three-Finger'd Jack* (1800) that attends to the affordances of props and stage design. This chapter highlights both senses of the word "craft" in that race is a tricky (crafty) concept to get hold of and its theatrical representations require practical knowledge of stagecraft. The craftiness of racecraft during the Romantic period is particularly important since the concept of race itself was a malleable and somewhat undefined construct, slippery, deceitful, and illusory through and through, which informed the manifold techniques of stagecraft – the artisanal form of labor – involved in constructions of race on stage.

## The Performative Dimension of Race

To define race is not easy since the concept is highly elastic. By using "race," one may explain biological, physiological, and social characteristics, one may classify individuals into racial categories, and one may even chastise entire communities for sharing that common something that designates "race" at a preindividual level that supposedly comes to determine individual and, by simple analogical reasoning, collective behaviors.

Its conceptual capacity to shift between starkly different optical lenses of observation (the microscopic and the macroscopic) is what lends this concept its explanatory efficacy.

What becomes apparent in racist discourse is the twin centrality of actions (of doing things, of gestures, of behaving in a certain manner) and of perceptions (microscopic and macroscopic) that is the centrality of acting and spectating. Race is first and foremost a-doing-and-observing phenomenon. Whether race is used to designate actions, looks, or behaviors, it is its classificatory application that emerges as a racist gesture that fixes the act and interpellates the (char)actor into a racial stereotype. A stereotypical act, in this instance, is just another way of saying that the act observed by the spectator has a history of previous iterations. The observation of this iterative performance reifies what is performed into a racial identity.

Consider the case of *Othello*. Eighteenth-century actors such as James Quin, David Garrick, and Spranger Barry had all enacted Othello in blackface, and no comments were made in contemporary reviews of the performances concerning the character's blackness. In 1787, however, a critic for the *Public Advertiser* inquired of John Philip Kemble's performance whether it is "necessary the Moor should be as *black* as a native of Guiney?"[4] As the abolitionist movement was gathering steam during this period, Othello's black facial paint became linked with the African's racialized blackness, enchaining the beauty and nobility of the Shakespearean Moor with the reality of slavery. There was an increasing reluctance amongst critics to imagine Othello, in his blackness, to be visually associated with images of oppressed enslaved people and with Charles Dibdin's iconic performance of Mungo, the wily black servant in Isaac Bickerstaffe's *The Padlock* (1767). In his performance of Othello in 1814, the actor Edmund Kean adorned a lighter tone to play the character, rather than the conventional burnt-cork black, thus establishing a new standard that became conventional practice for the next two decades.[5] Based on Kean's performance, Rede offers advice in his manual for actors that Othello should be performed in a "tawny tinge," a "Spanish brown," rather than the sable hue of the degraded slave-servant character Mungo, thus making a firm distinction between the color of the noble Moor and the burnt-cork black used for enslaved African characters.[6] Although Desdemona was able to entertain Othello's visage in her mind, it was precisely the noble Moor's onstage palpable blackness, thick in its material burnt-corkness, that proved too much for the mind of some critics, notably Charles Lamb.

Lamb, in his 1811 essay "On the Tragedies of Shakespeare Considered with Reference to Their Fitness for Stage Representation," asks his readers whether they did not find "something extremely revolting in the courtship and wedded caresses of Othello and Desdemona; and whether the actual sight of the thing did not overweigh all that beautiful compromise which we make in reading."[7] Lamb's criticism works upon a simple but revealing dichotomy between imagination and sense. While the former is the ruling faculty of the printed word, the latter governs perceptions of spectacles on stage. Lamb stresses the overbearing power of visual perception in his insistent "appeal to [the reader] that has *seen* Othello played," an appeal to one who has witnessed the "actual sight of the thing" and returning near the end of the passage once again to reiterating what it is that we actually "see on stage." The visceral reaction, presented as a natural reaction to which the commiserating reader is expected to nod his head in agreement, is that of extreme revulsion. Lamb's use of "overweigh," "so much," and "overpower" strategically recur in this short passage to convey to the reader that the visual perception of Othello and Desdemona's "courtship and wedded caresses" is too much to bear for any spectator. The scene is reduced to a "thing" that is preferably left undescribed beyond so many words. Beyond this threshold of revulsion, it is better that the reader as spectator shuts his eyes so that the "actual sight of the thing" does not disgrace the beauty of the words that are better appreciated when read than seen enacted on stage. Shakespeare's words, the means of transporting the imagination into realms of transcendent, transracial sublimity, are here, through the visual spectacle, tainted by their material, bodily enactment. The overbearing visuality and materiality that accompanies the words on stage disrupts the plausibility of the narrative, rendering even the internal motives – "that which is unseen" – implausible. The "unassisted" sense of premature sight overpowers the unseen such that the "first and obvious prejudices" remain.

Central to this discussion of Othello's blackness is the intermedial competition between print and performance culture to claim the legacy of Shakespeare as a national heritage untainted by the history of colonial slavery and imperial administration of colonies which nonetheless lie at the heart of Romanticism's Shakespeare project as its racial unconscious; an understanding of the racecraft of Shakespearean stagecraft during the Romantic period is essential to come to terms with Romantic Bardolatry as a racial project. "What we see upon a stage," Lamb concludes, once again drawing attention to the performative dimension of race, "is the body and bodily action."[8] What signifies race in this case is the staged action at once committed, perceived, and categorized as a racial act.

The spectatorial position from which Lamb argues his case is a subject position within the larger theatrical space beyond the stage which the real, empirical theatergoer occupies while viewing the drama. When discussing the agency of the spectator in determining the significance of what is seen on stage, we need to ask what is the subject position that spectators are invited to assume while watching the performance, which already pre-selects for them their gender, class, and, importantly, race. How does the stage select certain kinds of spectatorial positions and exclude others? Indeed, what happens when spectators disagree with the positions on offer?

Taking up the last question, we know from documented evidence of the period that when spectators collectively refused to assume particular positions during a performance, clashes between the theatrical managers and the audience members ensued. The Jewish opposition to how they were portrayed and perceived in Thomas Dibdin's *Family Quarrels* (1802) is but one case in point, wherein Jewish spectators refused to accept the spectatorial position of white English majoritarianism that looked down upon them. The cause of offence was the performance of a song sung by John Fawcett that expressed antisemitic sentiment directed at Jewish women.[9] Michael Ragussis's *Theatrical Nation: Jews and Other Outlandish Englishmen in Georgian Britain* considers such instances of offense and disruption by ethnic audiences of London stage performances, which he frames in terms of a "Family Quarrel," recalling the disturbance of the performance of Dibdin's drama of the same name. The notion of "family" in Ragussis's argument is necessarily conflated with national identity to underscore the assumed sense of social belonging despite differences, thus foregrounding the centrality of the concept of the "nation."[10] National identity is not considered here as a unitary imposition from above, but a complex negotiation ("quarrels") as to what constitutes it. Ragussis's analysis effectively reveals how a national identity ("Briton") attempts to confer political and cultural national unity on a heterogeneous pluri-ethnic state. We should note, however, that the nation, according to Immanuel Wallerstein, is fundamentally a "socio-political category, linked somehow to the actual or potential boundaries of a state," whereas ethnicity refers to a "cultural category" pertaining to a set of attitudes, behaviors, and practices that are distinguishable from other ethnic identities.[11] "Ethnicity" and "nation" are modal categories that define various social identities of a people, and they are usually part of the discourse concerning the contradictions of the project of nation-building, which aspires to create an identity of national belonging, while simultaneously threatening to eliminate ethnic diversity through assimilation. In other words, ethnicization and nationalization revolve around one of the primary contradictions of historical capitalism: the aspiration for theoretical equality and the maintenance of ethnic hierarchies which promote practical inequality.

What is required is a mediating concept that can overcome this conceptual barrier between nation as a sociopolitical category and ethnicity as a cultural category and, might I add, race as a pseudobiological category. Such a possibility is offered by the concept of "racecraft," coined by Karen E. Fields and Barbara J. Fields, a term that refers to a mental terrain and a pervasive belief that nonetheless originates in collective human action and imagination.[12] The same theatrical context that Ragussis examines to explore the crystallization of national identity, with the participative quarrelling amongst recognized ethnicities within London, also unveils the racecraft underlying racial performances.

The concept of racecraft, as originally formulated by the Fields sisters, foregrounds racism as a reality that produces "race" to rationalize the dispossession of wealth, power, and rights and, I would like to add, to justify the exploitation of colonized subjects, enslaved people, and workers. The most consequential illusion of racecraft is "concealing the affiliation between racism and inequality in general."[13] This camouflaging of inequality as difference effectively hides the social relations and processes that reproduce an unequal social order and foregrounds instead observable markers of difference such as skin color, gestures, beliefs, and proclivities. The Fields sisters are explicit about the fact that the existence of inequalities, socially constituted by class relations, results in the need for racecraft. It is not the racist individual that thinks or structures the world; rather, the individual assumes certain positions that compel him to think and structure the world in a particular way, much like the theatergoer who takes up the subject position offered by the theatrical frame. The thinking and active structuring by individuals is the illusion of the liberal form of identity politics.

In an interview with Daniel Denvir, Barbara Fields uses a performance analogy to explain racecraft, comparing it to "a conjuring trick [in a sideshow] that does not need a conjuror."[14] Racecraft, in other words, is an ideological process without a subject. A point that they reiterate throughout the interview is that an analysis of class positions must take primacy before identity politics. The liberal form of identity politics evacuates class content in order to discuss race and racism in a vacuum.[15] Liberal thinking about identity tends to foreground race and race relations in terms of accommodation and integration, promoting interracial relations. Any attempt to bring "class" into dialogue with "race" is considered a distraction from issues of racism. The consequence of the evacuation of the class question is that race is foregrounded as a central concept rather than economics, which is nothing less than a "devastating, intolerable mistake."[16] This is one of the central mystifications of racecraft: the concealing of class content in discussions on identity, thus effectively neutralizing the political-economic critique of racism.

The association of racecraft with witchcraft is intentional as the explanations that racecraft offers precludes and obfuscates the need to get at the root of the problem of racism or even at the structural prerequisites that make possible, sustain, and generate the concept of racecraft. The struggle against inequality takes a racial form only as a superstructural expression of deeper class relations that produce the inequality. However, liberal thinking about racism gives support to the idea that racism emerges out of racial relations, giving legitimacy to race as an originary and essential identity. In other words, we begin with race as a given form of identity from which we develop an understanding of race relations based on the interactions between the given races, deeming only the harmful, negative interactions as racist. From the counter-perspective presented by the Fields sisters, race relations come after the constitution of racial identities, but the constitution of racial identities follows from the work of racecraft: racecraft itself is the mediating concept that re-presents observable patterns of distinction instituted by class relations as racial constructs, which is, from the performative dimension of race, a racist gesture par excellence.[17] Schematically, the difference between the two ways of thinking about race can be presented as follows:

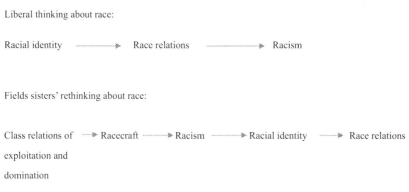

Figure 13.1   Schematic representation of the rethinking of the relations between racial identity and racism.

Racism is the classification of the iterative performance into observable patterns of distinction that makes race look like a real thing. The racial identity is an aftereffect, a consequence of repetition. The act is the performance of a function within the social relation; race is not the relation itself but an expression or imprint of a real social relation. In this context, then, racism – and its categorial byproduct, "race" – can be deconstructed as a very particular performative social act in a socially theatrical event, with its associated actors and spectators.

By using the concept of "racecraft," I hope to overcome the conceptual barrier between nation (a sociopolitical category), ethnicity (a cultural category), and race (a pseudobiological category), thus bridging these groupings of identity in terms of the craft involved in their construction through performance. To elaborate this point, consider the items Rede lists as necessary for any young actor to take up the roles that dominate the theatrical repertoire of the times: a wig to perform Othello; an Indian dress, with head-dress formed of feathers, along with an assortment of bracelets and beads to depict "native" characters like Umba in *Perouse* and Yarico in *Inkle and Yarico*; for more oriental characters ranging from Artaxerxes, Aladdin, Zorayda in *The Mountaineers*, and numerous other Arab, Turkish, Persian, Mughal, and central Asian characters, white satin loose Turkish trousers and of course the iconic slippers turned up at the toes, along with a vest and a turban with birds of paradise plume.[18] These items signify race, ethnicity, nationality, or, more generally, difference itself, which captures the varying shades of all three terms of identification, displaying an iridescence that makes it increasingly difficult to distinguish between them but nonetheless makes evident the ambiguous and somewhat amorphous nature of identity in performance, dependent as it is on material props and signifiers that have no proper referent outside the illusion itself. These items range from costumes, accessories, headwear, and make-up to scenographic elements that generate the illusion of place and identity on a vacant stage. Stagecraft is witchcraft insofar as the spell of the stage creates its own mythical referential world, with its own time and space, in which every element, no matter how minor, is imbued with meaning. The semiotic power of such spellwork collectively conjures for the spectator the illusion itself.

Some of the items that Rede lists function as signifiers of Otherness, capturing in their material bluntness entire civilizations, objects which are powerful in their prosaicness, trapping the exotic in familiar things that can be put on and discarded, owned and disowned at will to stage a dramatic transformation which is an allegory for the march of capitalism on the world stage. The materialization of culture into things makes them liable to appropriation in more ways than one. In George Colman the Younger's opera *Inkle and Yarico* (1787), the low-class comical English character Trudge warns the naïve noble savage Wowski to "Take care of your furs, and your feathers, my girl ... Somebody might steal 'em."[19] The furs and the feathers represent a vulnerability inherent in the exoticization of the Other, for whom these are not items of exchange or supplements to identity but identity itself. The threat and desire of seizure that these items exemplify function in dramas of slavery to stage in a single act both an annexation of property and a stripping of selfhood, an appropriation and an expropriation. The dramatic transformation of such items of personhood into exchangeable commodities is the staging of the history of the encounter of an incipient mercantilist capitalism and a precapitalist social order.

After this encounter, the precapitalist social order forever remains untethered from its own Indigenous history and development, forever arrested for the colonizer into an image of premodernity, as modernity's Other. Modernity is defined by the violent temporal break from this image of a premodern past. But this image of a premodern past exists in the present, beyond the fringes of the empire, and so modernity is also associated with these far-off spaces through a forceful transformative act, the ideologically justified "white man's burden," defined by an aggressive policy of spatial domination or colonialism. The staging of this destructive colonial encounter in terms of objects used to designate racial identities is perhaps best elaborated through a prop-focused reading of John Fawcett's *Obi; or Three-Finger'd Jack* (1800).

### Vectors of Raciality in *Obi; or Three-Finger'd Jack*

John Fawcett's pantomimical drama *Obi; or Three-Finger'd Jack* is about the notorious black outlaw who terrorized Jamaica in the 1780s. "Obi" in the title refers to Caribbean sorcery and is considered a part of Caribbean spiritual practices, much like a charm that protects the possessor of obi. A contemporary account of obi is given by Benjamin Moseley in his *Treatise on Sugar* (1799), where he refers to the practice as an "occult science."[20] Pantomimes were popular forms of entertainment during this period as they permitted managers of minor theaters to circumvent the legal injunction that prohibited the performance of spoken, dialogue-based dramas outside of the patent theaters of Drury Lane and Covent Garden. Despite this limitation, pantomimes evolved into quasi-dramatic forms by reintroducing narrative actions through effective use of song, dance, and mimes to tell stories. The story that Fawcett's play stages is the courtship between a slave planter's daughter, Rosa, and Captain Orford, which is interrupted by Three-Fingered Jack, who imprisons the captain in his hideout in the mountains. In the hope of being granted liberty, two enslaved characters (Quashee and Sam) set out on a mission, accompanied by Rosa (disguised as a boy), to rescue Captain Orford and kill Jack. Rosa gets separated from the group and is caught by Jack, who enslaves her. She eventually manages to rescue her lover and escape from Jack's cave. Jack pursues them, confronting Quashee in a climactic duel that ends in his death.

Staged at the Haymarket Theater for its summer season on July 2, 1800, *Obi; or Three-Finger'd Jack* had a successful run of thirty-nine performances. The play's ideological tensions, its cultural and literary history, and its staging have received much critical attention in recent decades, and various versions of the playtext are also available online.[21] The following reading of the play draws attention to the use of props and scenographic elements, thus shifting the focus from the study of actors (Charles Kemble and Ira Aldridge) performing racial characters (the eponymous Jack) to an object-centric emphasis on racial objects in the service of racecraft. Such a perspective requires viewing objects not just as mere human possessions but as actants with their own "frequencies, energies, and potentials to affect human and nonhuman worlds."[22] Using a variety of sources detailing the performance context of the play, we can recover the various ideological signals emitted by racially charged stage objects as aspects of the racecraft of stagecraft. The sources that are particularly useful for such an analysis include the printed text published in London by Duncombe and Moon (c. 1825), which gives details about stage directions and positioning of scenographic elements; the detailed printed score, which correlates action to music; the published reviews detailing points from the actual performances; and an 1801 watercolor painting of Jack's cave by Sylvester Harrison, engraved by Edward Orme.[23] Although engravings of this sort were a kind of expressive or novelistic interpretation rather than a representation of what the stage set actually looked like, this particular engraving serves as a possible source of evidence for visualizing stage effects since it bears close resemblance to how the Obi Woman's cave is described in the Duncombe and Moon edition. Reading these sources visually requires isolating all the geographical references and prop information given in the scene setting, in dialogues and songs, and in stage directions to create an imaginary map of the landscape and the positioning of the objects in the play, visualizing the ideological world presented onstage.[24] Actors navigate this ideological space and interact with props to embody their characters and enact the drama before an audience. To consider all these elements is to take scenography as a means of making sense of theater from a distinctly visual perspective.

In the first scene, we are introduced to a "View of an extensive plantation in Jamaica" (Act 1.i). There is a large house on the left and sugarhouses at the back of the stage, in front of the scenic painting by Samuel Whitmore drawn "in perspective." It can be assumed from this description that these stage elements collectively represent the flat surface of a plantation that extends far into the horizon. There is a large wheel on the right of the stage. The scene opens with enslaved people and oxen at work tilling the ground at the center of the stage. A group of them carrying sugarcanes are called upon by the Overseer who directs them to the sugarhouses. The playbill of July 1, 1800, claims authenticity in its representation of Jamaica as the painted sceneries are described as "Views taken on the Spot."[25] The enslaved, along with the sugarcanes, sugar houses, the wheel, and the background painting of an extensive plantation, create a horizontal relational nexus across the stage.

The enslaved characters in this opening scene serve only as props necessary to complete the image of a slave plantation. They represent a form of property that has exchange value, procured in slave markets for their use value. In other words, these stage slaves represent slaves figured as commodities and, together with other onstage objects (wheel, sugarcanes) and scenographic elements (view of the plantation, sugar houses), gesture toward the unstaged matrices of physical, socioeconomic, and governmental powers that sustain the institution of slavery and provide the necessary context for the onstage action, thus offering spectators a concrete vision or simplified representation of the actual complex operations of a colonial slave empire. In dramas about slavery, this double aspect of onstage objects (i.e., their material visibility and their invisible relations) is effectively used to create the illusion of a slave plantation.

Of course, the enslaved person is also more than mere property or commodity; they are a person with whom one can develop affective relations of sympathy. The opening thus simultaneously positions the enslaved figures as prop(erty)-objects amidst a theatricalized representation of a slave plantation, and exploits the personhood of the slave-object in terms of the affective value the slave-as-person evokes. In this way, the scene configures both the slave economy and the moral economy through its strategic use of stage objects: the arrangement of these objects signifies the historical circum-Atlantic slave trade that contextualizes the setting of the drama for a contemporary audience; the visible and palpable presence of these objects also conditions the dramatic action, and at times functions to focalize the moral drama between characters. The stage object is ideological insofar as it is present as an onstage material object even as crucial aspects of its objecthood are invisible – namely, its off-stage connotations, which connect the onstage object to its real-world referent and function to instigate a moral drama of affects for the spectator.

As theatrical scholars and practitioners have pointed out, the stage with its material props should be understood relationally. Robin Bernstein considers material objects essential to the performance of identities, raising the key question of how humans perform within racially meaningful, three-dimensional material space.[26] Joseph Roach, Diana Taylor, and Rebecca Schneider have independently focused on this three-dimensional space, uncovering the links between context, meaning, and social practice that form identities through performance.[27] Andrew Sofer's *Stage Life of Props* considers the stage object's "historical, cultural, and ideological baggage," or what constitutes the "symbolic economy of the culture that surrounds it," in order to recover the hidden relations of stage props to their invisible social existence.[28] Stage objects are not autonomous and arbitrary; rather, they are part of the stage design, and collectively as well as relationally impart meaning to the onstage illusion. Actors negotiate with onstage props and navigate set-pieces in order to act out their characters. Importantly, the spatiality of the scene determines actors' movement even before they arrive on stage. The movement of actors, their entries and exits, are conditioned by the stage design. Whether an actor comes in from the left and exits from the right or whether he makes his entry from above and exits through a trapdoor underneath the stage is an ideologically meaningful aspect of stage design that gets overlooked in our studies of dramas as texts rather than as performances. These movements across the stage can be classified in terms of the vectors of horizontality and verticality. Although this aspect of stage design is not particular to *Obi*, I will examine how the representation of slavery in this play makes use of that affordance.

In the opening scene of *Obi*, the actors always make their entry either from the left or the right side of the stage. As pointed out previously, the scene depicts a view of an extensive plantation, so the imaginary topography is flat and horizontal. The sky is above and the sea is at some distance to the left of the visible stage. The movement that such a stage set permits is horizontal, lateral movement. Boundaries and frontiers are nonexistent. This is an ever-expanding territory, defined only by natural barriers which are not really barriers in themselves. The sea might end the stretch of the plantation but the plantation is only one spatial node in the extensive colonial empire; the sea symbolizes the intercontinental expansion of the empire through ships and trade links. The relational nexus between the enslaved, the oxen, the sugarcanes, the sugar houses, the wheel, and the view of the plantation is but part of an extensive network that stretches horizontally and laterally well beyond the confines of the stage scene. In such a scenario, new characters like Captain Orford and his black servant Tuckey can make an entry from one end of the stage precisely because that end symbolically opens the stage to the wider world beyond its confines.

The vector of horizontality in the opening scene can be starkly contrasted to the vector of verticality in scenes that depict spaces that lie outside the plantation economy and beyond the jurisdiction of Britain's slave empire. The central scenes of both acts of the pantomime depict the wild, threatening fringes of colonial power that remain unregulated and unassimilated. These stage sets depict caves, mountains, and subterranean passages, spaces inhabited by the eponymous Jack, the escaped fugitives, and the witch-like character, the Obi Woman.[29] What is clearly distinguishable in the stage design of the Obi Woman's cave (Act 1.iii) as well as Jack's cave (Act 2.iv) is the vector of verticality that spatially structures the stage objects and the scenic apparatus.

In both scenes, the stage design represents an interior cavernous space cut into a large rock with entrances and exits situated at the top of the stage and through trapdoors on the stage floor. This vertical axis determines the movement of characters on stage. In Act 1, scene 3, the black robbers enter the Obi Woman's cave from the top through cavities signalling the entry into a nether world of dark magic. They eventually exit the stage through a trapdoor. In Act 2, scene 2, Jack and Rosa exit the stage through a trapdoor, and make their way through a subterranean passage (Act 2.iii) and in the next scene (Act 2.iv) enter from the top, down a ladder, into Jack's cave, again signalling a retreat from the sun-lit surface into dark, unfathomable depths. At the end of the scene, Rosa rescues Captain Orford and escapes by placing a table "on the sides of the truck over Jack," (Act 2.iv) and then placing a chair on the table, so that they may escape from the top of the stage. Jack pursues them, by placing a ladder before the entrance and climbs up to the surface, only to meet his death in the climactic battle scene with Quashee, Sam, and Tuckey amidst the mountains. The props present in Jack's cave convey not only his perverse domestic arrangement in contrast to the ordered interiors of the Planter's house and the slave huts in previous scenes, but also function as necessary tools of escape within a vertically designed interior space where the coming in and going out of characters is restricted by virtue of its verticality, unlike the lateral relations and expansions permitted by a flat, planar surface with no visible frontier. In these vertical spaces, the walls act like frontiers, physical barriers that squeeze the space in-between like an ever-narrowing vice. The verticality of these interior scenes cuts them from relations of lateral exchange that define the surface of the plantation scenes, with their ever-expanding horizons connecting spaces represented on stage to off-stage extensions into global colonial networks. By contrast, the cave scenes are disconnected from this global colonial network and hence offer a safe space to rebel slaves, robbers, and the Obi Woman from being coerced into relations of domination and exploitation. If horizontality defines the colonial totality, then the verticality of the cave scenes defines the detachment from colonial relations.

This detachment is in fact represented by the props that decorate the walls of the caves and constitute the titular object of fascination: Jack's obi charm. The Obi Woman's cave wall is covered with an assortment of items like feathers, rags, bones, teeth, catskins, broken glass, and parrot's beaks. Similarly, Jack's cave wall, as depicted in the Harrison watercolor/Orme engraving, is covered by skeletons of a turtle and some reptilian creature, and is draped with dead snakes hanging limply on the right (Figure 13.2). From details given in Benjamin Moseley's *Treatise on Sugar* (1799), the original source for Fawcett's pantomime, Jack's obi horn is filled with "a compound of grave dirt, ashes, the blood of a black cat, and human fat; all mixed into a kind of paste."[30] In addition to the goat's horn, Jack's obi bag holds "a black cat's foot, a dried toad, a pig's tail, a slip of parchment of kid's skin, with characters marked in blood on it."[31] A common characteristic of all these items is that they are fragments cut off from whole objects (feathers, teeth, broken glass, beaks etc.) as well as relics of once living creatures (skeletons, skins, ashes, blood, etc.). There is no organic relation between these items except that they are all remnants of things that were previously alive and whole. This collection of dead objects emits quite a clear ideological signal to a contemporary audience: from the evil of witchcraft and black magic to the violence, not to mention the viciousness of the perpetrator, who inflicts such brutality on living things, wrenching parts from bodies and desecrating them further by assembling them into a discontinuous collection of dead matter. The verticality that cuts off the interior space of the caves inhabited by the Obi Women and Jack from the lateral colonial relations

Figure 13.2  The Harrison Watercolor/Orme engraving depicting the scene in Jack's cave (1801), TS 941.5F. Courtesy of the Harvard Theater Collection, Houghton Library.

of the surface also defines the discontinuous and dissociated characteristic of the objects cut off from their origins where they were once still part of a form of living, organic relationality.

If these interior spaces and the objects that they contain work in the service of racecraft to create the stereotypical racial profile of a rebel slave character like Jack, highlighting his villainy, his subversive existence, and his violence against both the natural order and the social order established by coloniality, then they are also the very spaces that are produced by the surface colonial relations as the fringe of colonial order. Although I have presented the axes of horizontality and verticality in terms of contrasting scenes and spaces, it is necessary to note that the lateral colonial relations that spread across the flat surface of the plantation represent a formal equality that masks a relational hierarchy. The Overseer and the enslaved, although present on the same equitable, planar surface, are not equal at all. The master–slave relation is ideologically concealed by the visual horizontality of stage directions. Despite the verticality of the cave scenes that define space in terms of its visible physical hierarchical movements up and down the stage, the scenes themselves enact a more equitable exchange economy. In the Obi Woman's cave, the black robbers exchange their loot for magical obi charms (Act 1.iii). Jack gives the Obi Woman Captain Orford's sash, epaulettes, and gorget as an offering, and, in exchange, she ornaments the sash with obi and fills his obi horn. This pantomimical exchange of gifts between black characters on stage is a stark contrast to the colonial slave economy in which humans themselves become objects of exchange.

Unmasking the politics of verticality in the opening scene that depicts the plantation and the last scene that depicts a flat, open space exposes the ideological obfuscation, engineered by the stagecraft, of the true nature of laterally expanding colonial relations, dependent as they are on structural inequalities. The violence and brutality that is visually associated with Jack and the Obi Woman with their collection of dead items is indicated in the opening verse, sung by two enslaved females (the wives of Quashee and Sam):

> The white man comes, and brings his gold –
> The Slaver meet him on the bay –
> And, oh, poor negro then be sold,
> From home poor negro sails away.
> Oh, it is very, very sad to see
> Poor negro child and father part –
> But if white man kind massa be,
> He heals the wound in negro's heart. (Act 1.i)

The white man cuts the "poor negro" from their origins, takes them away from their traditional, familial relations, transforming a living being into a slave-object plugged into the ever-extensive sugar plantation economy, which consumes the slave's blood, body, and soul to generate its profits. The enslaved, like the dead objects that constitute Jack's obi, are themselves socially dead, a condition detailed in Orlando Patterson's *Slavery and Social Death*.[32]

Indeed, the play may be less about the destruction or extirpation of obeah magic in Jamaica; rather, it stages an assimilation and appropriation of Jack as the British empire's own obi. In the final scene, Jack's body is dismembered, and his head and three-fingered hand is presented as the stage centerpiece:

> As the procession comes down in the centre of the stage, they divide in the front; and march up R. and L. wings, range themselves up the sides in the

order they came on, so as to admit the truck on which Tuckey, Quashee, and Sam are brought on to be placed in the centre of the stage – in front of which is placed Jack's head and hand. (Act 2.viii)

The empire has finally transformed Jack into a fragment of his former self, dissociated from his living body and living relations, much like the components of Jack's obi bag, which contained a parrot's beak, a black cat's foot, and a pig's tail; now it is the empire that possesses a rebel slave's head and a three-fingered hand as a powerful deterrent (charm) against future rebellions. The ritualistic procession that circles around Jack's butchered body parts at the end of the play mimics the witchcraft scene of the Obi Woman, only now witchcraft has been assimilated by the stagecraft of colonial order to display both a patriotic spectacle of triumphant imperialism and its necessary and legitimate form of violence. Elements of racecraft that visually associated witchcraft, violence, brutality, and subversiveness with the illegitimate verticality of the cave scenes are, in the final scene, ideologically assimilated as fundamental aspects of the functioning of the empire's lateral relations.

To conclude, it is the work of the racecraft of stagecraft that legitimizes the empire's necessary violence against the illegitimate transgressions of slave rebellion, that naturalizes the social order of a slave plantation economy visually as an extension of equitable, lateral relations which conceal unequal social hierarchies and obfuscate the inherent brutality of the system, and, finally, that creates, through spatial arrangement of stage design, racialized spaces that sustain the empire's imperial, racial ideology. Highlighting the performative dimension of race allows us to explore race not just as a conscious element of being, nor just as a socially constructed notion, but as a built-in aspect of the performance space as a whole. In the final scene of *Obi*, Jack's decapitated head and three-fingered hand, placed at the center of the stage, coordinate a grand celebratory colonial procession around them – a haunting reminder of the perpetual violence inherent in maintaining any semblance of colonial order. This visual critique of colonial slavery, however, is sonically drowned by the resounding "God save the King" and the final verbal assertion by the Overseer at the end of the play that enforces that spectators perceive the scene only as an imperial fantasy of the legitimacy of British law across the globe: "Here we see villainy brought by law to short duration – / And may all traitors fall by British Proclamation."[33] What remains, just before the curtain closes, is Jack's fragmented body, the brutal cost of empire building.

## Notes

1. Leman Thomas Rede, *The Road to the Stage* (London: Published by J. Onwhyn, 1836), 33, 32.
2. Rede, *The Road to the Stage*, 34. The characters of Hassan, Wowski, Mungo, and Sambo feature in Matthew Lewis's *The Castle Spectre* (1796), George Colman's *Inkle and Yarico* (1787), Isaac Bickerstaffe's *The Padlock* (1768), and Frederick Reynolds's *Laugh When You Can* (1799), respectively.
3. Rede, *The Road to the Stage*, 33.
4. *Public Advertiser*, October 29, 1787.
5. Joyce Green MacDonald, "Acting Black: 'Othello,' 'Othello' Burlesques, and the Performance of Blackness," *Theatre Journal* 46/2 (1994), 231–32.
6. Rede, *The Road to the Stage*, 34.
7. Charles Lamb, *The Works of Charles Lamb* (London: Printed for C. and J. Ollier, 1818), 2:27–28.
8. Lamb, *Works*, 28.
9. Thomas Dibdin, *The Reminiscences of Thomas Dibdin* (London: Henry Colburn, 1837), 1:337–47.
10. Michael Ragussis, *Theatrical Nation: Jews and Other Outlandish Englishmen in Georgian Britain* (Philadelphia: University of Pennsylvania Press, 2010), 13.
11. Etienne Balibar and Immanuel Wallerstein, *Race, Nation, Class: Ambiguous Identities* (London: Verson, 1991), 77.
12. Karen E. Fields and Barbara J. Fields, *Racecraft: The Soul of Inequality in American Life* (London: Verso, 2014), 18–19.
13. Fields and Fields, *Racecraft*, 261.
14. Karen E. Fields and Barbara J. Fields, "Beyond 'Race Relations': Interview with Daniel Denvir," *Jacobin*, January 17, 2018, https://jacobin.com/2018/01/racecraft-racism-barbara-karen-fields (accessed October 10, 2022).
15. Fields and Fields, "Beyond 'Race Relations.'"
16. Fields and Fields, "Beyond 'Race Relations.'"
17. Fields and Fields, "Beyond 'Race Relations.'"
18. Rede, *The Road to the Stage*, 20, 27.
19. George Colman, *Inkle and Yarico*, in *The British Theatre, with Biographical and Critical Remarks by Mrs Inchbald* (London: Printed for Hurst, Robinson, 1824), 20, 33–34.
20. Benjamin Moseley, *Treatise on Sugar* (London: G. G. and J. Robinson, 1799), 170.
21. Charles J. Rzekpa's edited *Obi: A Romantic Circle Praxis Volume* (University of Colorado Boulder, 2002) includes both Fawcett's 1800 pantomimical version and the 1830 melodrama version in which the black actor Ira Aldridge performs the title character, as well as contributions by Jeffrey Cox, Debbie Lee, and Robert Hoskins, https://webarchive.loc.gov/all/20230215190517/https:/romantic-circles.org/praxis/obi/index.html.

22. Marlis Schweitzer and Joanne Zerdy, "Introduction: Object Lessons," *Performing Objects and Theatrical Things*, ed. Marlis Schweitzer and Joanne Zerdy (Basingstoke: Palgrave Macmillan, 2014), 2.
23. The Duncombe and Moon publication is available in digital form in *Obi: A Romantic Circle Praxis Volume*. The printed score is reprinted in Samuel Arnold, "Obi; or, Three-Finger'd Jack," *Series D: Pantomime, Ballet & Social Dance*, vol. 4, ed. John M. Ward, *Music for London Entertainment, 1660–1800* (London: Stainer & Bell, 1996).
24. I take inspiration from Pamela Howard's *What is Scenography?* which offers advice to scenographers on how to interpret the playscript visually to design the sets. See Howard, *What Is Scenography?* (London: Routledge, 2002), 20.
25. Charles Beecher Hogan (ed.), *The London Stage, 1660–1800, Part 5: 1776–1800* (Carbondale: Southern Illinois University Press, 1968), 3, 2290.
26. Robin Bernstein, "Dances with Things: Material Culture and the Performance of Race," *Social Text* 27.4 (2009), 69.
27. See Joseph Roach, *Cities of the Dead: Circum-Atlantic Performance* (NewYork: Columbia University Press, 1996), Diana Taylor's *The Archive and the Repertoire: Performing Cultural Memory in the Americas* (Durham: Duke University Press, 2003), and Rebecca Schneider's *Performing Remains: Art and War in Times of Theatrical Reenactment* (London: Routledge, 2011).
28. Andrew Sofer, *Stage Life of Props* (Ann Arbor: University of Michigan Press, 2003), 17.
29. I have commented on the mapping of the moral-ideological geography onto distinct scenes in this pantomime in "Variant Rebellions: Psychic Compromise in *Obi; or, Three-Finger'd Jack*," *The Eighteenth Century: Theory and Interpretation* 62.3–4 (2023), 259–78.
30. Moseley, *Treatise on Sugar*, 173–74.
31. Moseley, *Treatise on Sugar*, 173–74.
32. Orlando Patterson, *Slavery and Social Death: A Comparative Study* (Cambridge, MA: Harvard University Press, 1982).
33. Jeffrey N. Cox, (ed.), *Slavery, Abolition and Emancipation: Writings in the British Romantic Period*, vol. V: *Drama* (London: Pickering & Chatto, 1999), 219.

# Further Reading

## Chapter 1

Bernasconi, Robert, "Will the Real Kant Please Stand Up," *Radical Philosophy* 117 (2003), 13–22.

Bromwich, David, *A Choice of Inheritance* (Cambridge, MA: Harvard University Press, 1989).

Chandler, James, *Wordsworth's Second Nature* (Chicago: University of Chicago Press, 1984).

Collins, Gregory, "Edmund Burke on Slavery and the Slave Trade," *Slavery & Abolition* 40/3 (2019), 494–551.

Duffy, Michael, *Soldiers, Sugar, and Seapower* (Oxford: Clarendon, 1987).

Hall, Catherine, "The Slavery Business and the Making of 'Race' in Britain and the Caribbean," *Current Anthropology* 61, supplement 22 (2020), S172–82.

Kant, Immanuel, *Anthropology from a Pragmatic Point of View*, trans. and ed. Robert Louden (Cambridge: Cambridge University Press, 2006).

Lee, Yoon Sun, *Nationalism and Irony* (New York: Oxford University Press, 2004).

Mehta, Uday, *Liberalism and Empire* (Chicago: University of Chicago Press, 1999).

O'Neill, Daniel I., *Edmund Burke and the Conservative Logic of Empire* (Oakland: University of California Press, 2016).

Tucker, Irene, *The Moment of Racial Sight* (Chicago: University of Chicago Press, 2012).

Turner, Sasha, *Contested Bodies* (Philadelphia: University of Pennsylvania Press, 2017).

Zammito, John H., *Kant, Herder, and the Birth of Anthropology* (Chicago: University of Chicago Press, 2002).

## Chapter 2

Casimir, Jean, *The Haitians: A Decolonial History*, trans. Laurent Dubois (Chapel Hill: University of North Carolina Press, 2020).

Crawley, Ashon T., *Blackpentecostal Breath* (New York: Fordham University Press, 2016).

Daut, Marlene L., "Beyond Trouillot: Unsettling Genealogies of Historical Thought," *Small Axe* 25/1 (2021): 132–54.
Daut, Marlene L., "'Nothing in Nature is Mute': Reading Revolutionary Romanticism in L'Haïtiade and Hérard Dumesle's Voyage dans le nord d'Hayti (1824)," *New Literary History* 49/4 (2018): 493–520.
Daut, Marlene L., *Tropics of Haiti: Race and the Literary History of the Haitian Revolution in the Atlantic World, 1789–1865* (Liverpool: Liverpool University Press, 2015).
Dubois, Laurent and John D. Garrigus, *Slave Revolution in the Caribbean, 1789–1804: A Brief History with Documents* (New York: Palgrave Macmillan, 2006).
Ferrer, Ada, *Freedom's Mirror: Cuba and Haiti in the Age of Revolution* (Cambridge: Cambridge University Press, 2014).
Ford, Thomas H., *Wordsworth and the Poetics of Air: Atmospheric Romanticism in a Time of Climate Change* (Cambridge: Cambridge University Press, 2018).
Luis, William, *Literary Bondage: Slavery in Cuban Narrative* (Austin: University of Texas Press, 1990).
Scott, David, *Conscripts of Modernity: The Tragedy of Colonial Enlightenment* (Durham: Duke University Press, 2004).
Tremblay, Jean-Thomas, *Breathing Aesthetics* (Durham: Duke University Press, 2022).

## Chapter 3

Anatol, Giselle Liza, *The Things that Fly in the Night: Female Vampires in Literature of the Circum-Caribbean and African Diaspora* (New Brunswick: Rutgers University Press, 2015).
Anyiwo, U. Melissa (ed.), *Race in the Vampire Narrative* (Rotterdam: Brill, 2015).
Aquilina, Conrad, "The Deformed Transformed; or, from Bloodsucker to Byronic Hero – Polidori and the Literary Vampire," in *Open Graves, Open Minds: Representations of Vampires and the Undead from the Enlightenment to the Present*, ed. Sam George and Bill Hughes (Manchester: Manchester University Press, 2013), 24–38.
Berlant, Lauren, and Lee Edelman, *Sex, or the Unbearable* (Durham: Duke University Press, 2013).
Boone, Joseph Allen, *The Homoerotics of Orientalism* (New York: Columbia University Press, 2014).
Bray, Katie, "'A Climate . . . More Prolific . . . in Sorcery': The Black Vampyre and the Hemispheric Gothic," *American Literature* 87/1 (2015): 1–21.
Crompton, Louis, *Byron and Greek Love: Homophobia in Nineteenth-Century England* (Berkeley: University of California Press, 1985).
Donahue, Jennifer, "The Ghost of Annie Palmer: Giving Voice to Jamaica's 'White Witch of Rose Hall,'" *The Journal of Commonwealth Literature* 49/2 (2014): 243–56.
Dyer, Richard, "Children of the Night: Vampirism as Homosexuality and Homosexuality as Vampirism," in *Sweet Dreams: Sexuality, Gender and Popular Fiction*, ed. Susannah Radstone (London: Lawrence & Wishart, 1988), 47–72.

Dyer, Richard, *White: Twentieth Anniversary Edition* (London: Routledge, 2017).
Elfenbein, Andrew, "Byron, Gender, and Sexuality," in *The Cambridge Companion to Byron*, ed. Drummond Bone (Cambridge: Cambridge University Press, 2009), 56–74.
Fincher, Max, *Queering Gothic in the Romantic Age: The Penetrating Eye* (New York: Palgrave Macmillan, 2007).
Gelder, Ken, *Reading the Vampire* (London: Routledge, 1994).
Hartman, Saidiya, *Scenes of Subjection: Terror, Slavery, and Self-Making in Nineteenth-Century America*, Revised and Updated with a New Preface by the Author (New York: W.W. Norton, 2022).
Jenkins, Jerry Rafiki, *The Paradox of Blackness in African American Vampire Fiction* (Columbus: The Ohio State University Press, 2019).
Kent, Sarah, "'The Bloody Transaction': Black Vampires and the Afterlives of Slavery in Blacula and The Gilda Stories," *The Journal of Popular Culture* 53/3 (2020): 739–59.
Koretsky, Deanna P., *Death Rights: Romantic Suicide, Race, and the Bounds of Liberalism* (Albany: State University of New York Press, 2021).
Lansdown, Richard, "The Orient and the Outcast," in *The Cambridge Introduction to Byron*, ed. Richard Lansdown (Cambridge: Cambridge University Press, 2012), 80–96.
McDayter, Ghislaine, *Byromania and the Birth of Celebrity Culture* (Albany: State University of New York Press, 2009).
Moten, Fred, *Black and Blur* (Durham: Duke University Press, 2017).
Moten, Fred, *Stolen Life (Consent Not to Be a Single Being)* (Durham: Duke University Press, 2018).
Moten, Fred, *The Universal Machine* (Durham: Duke University Press, 2018).
Mueller, Monika, "Hybridity Sucks: European Vampirism Encounters Haitian Voodoo in *The White Witch of Rose Hall*," in *Vampires and Zombies: Transcultural Migrations and Transnational Interpretations*, ed. Dorothea Fisher-Hornung and Monika Mueller (Jackson: University Press of Mississippi, 2016), 130–46.
Muñoz, José Esteban, *Cruising Utopia: The Then and There of Queer Futurity*, Tenth Anniversary Edition (New York: New York University Press, 2019).
Parker, Kendra, *Black Female Vampires in African American Women's Novels, 1977–2011* (Lanham: Lexington Books, 2020).
Praz, Mario, *The Romantic Agony* (Oxford: Oxford University Press, 1933).
Rigby, Mair, "'Prey to some cureless disquiet': Polidori's Queer Vampyre at the Margins of Romanticism," *Romanticism on the Net*, no. 36–37 (November 2004). www.erudit.org/en/journals/ron/2004-n36-37-ron947/011135ar/.
Santos, Cristina, *Unbecoming Female Monsters: Vampires, Witches, and Virgins* (Lanham: Lexington Books, 2016).
Sexton, Jared, *Amalgamation Schemes: Antiblackness and the Critique of Multiculturalism* (Minneapolis: University of Minnesota Press, 2008).
Sexton, Jared, "The Social Life of Social Death: On Afro-Pessimism and Black Optimism," *InTensions* 5 (2011): 1–47.

Sharpe, Christina, *In the Wake: On Blackness and Being* (Durham: Duke University Press, 2016).
Twitchell, James, *The Living Dead: A Study of the Vampire in Romantic Literature* (Durham: Duke University Press, 1981).
Vargas, João H. Costa, *The Denial of Antiblackness: Multiracial Redemption and Black Suffering* (Minneapolis: University of Minnesota Press, 2018).
Warren, Calvin, *Ontological Terror: Blackness, Nihilism, and Emancipation* (Durham: Duke University Press, 2018).
Weheliye, Alexander, *Habeas Viscus: Racializing Assemblages, Biopolitics, and Black Feminist Theories of the Human* (Durham: Duke University Press, 2014).
Welter, Barbara, "The Cult of True Womanhood: 1820–1860," *American Quarterly* 18/2 (Summer 1966): 151–74.
Yuan, Yin, "Invasion and Retreat: Gothic Repressions of the Oriental Other in Byron's The Giaour," *Studies in Romanticism* 54 (Spring 2015): 3–31.

## Chapter 4

Baum, Joan, *Mind-Forg'd Manacles: Slavery and the English Romantic Poets* (North Haven: Archon Books, 1994).
De Paolo, Charles S., "Of Tribes and Hordes: Coleridge and the Emancipation of the Slaves, 1808," *Theoria: A Journal of Social and Political Theory* 60 (1983): 27–43.
Dykes, Eva Beatrice, *The Negro in English Romantic Thought, or A Study of Sympathy for the Oppressed* (Washington, DC: Associated Publishers, 1942).
Ebbatson, J.R., "Coleridge's Mariner and the Rights of Man," *Studies in Romanticism* 11/3 (1972): 171–206.
Haeger, J.H., "Coleridge's Speculations on Race," *Studies in Romanticism* 13/4 (1974): 333–57.
Jacobus, Mary, "Southey's Debt to Lyrical Ballads (1798)," *The Review of English Studies* 22/85 (1971): 20–36.
Keane, Patrick J., *Coleridge's Submerged Politics: The Ancient Mariner and Robinson Crusoe* (Columbia: University of Missouri Press, 1994).
Lee, Debbie, "Yellow Fever and the Slave Trade: Coleridge's The Rime of the Ancient Mariner," *ELH* 65/3 (1998): 675–700.
Makonnen, Atesede, "'Our Blackamoor or Negro Othello': Rejecting the Affective Power of Blackness," *European Romantic Review* 29/3 (2018): 347–55.
May, Tim, "Coleridge's Slave Trade Ode and Bowles's 'The African,'" *Notes and Queries* 54/4 (2007): 504–9.

## Chapter 5

Cahillon, Michelle, "Interceptionality, or The Ambiguity of the Albatross," *Sydney Review of Books*, 7 August 2018, sydneyreviewofbooks.com/essay/interceptionality-or-the-ambiguity-of-the-albatross/.

Carretta, Vincent, *Unchained Voices: An Anthology of Black Authors in the English-Speaking World of the Eighteenth Century* (Lexington: University Press of Kentucky, 2003).
Davies, Damien Walford, "Diagnosing 'The Rime of the Ancient Mariner': Shipwreck, Historicism, Traumatology," *Studies in Romanticism* 55/4 (2016): 503–35.
Dykes, Eva Beatrice, *The Negro in English Romantic Thought, or A Study of Sympathy for the Oppressed* (Washington, DC: Associated Publishers, 1942).
Ebbatson, J. R., "Coleridge's Mariner and the Rights of Man," *Studies in Romanticism* 11 (1972): 171–206.
Foucault, Michel, "The Ethic of the Concern of the Self as a Practice of Freedom," in *The Essential Works of Michel Foucault 1954–1984*, ed. Paul Rabinow, trans. Robert Hurley (New York: The New Press, 1994), 281–301.
Fyfe, Christopher, *A History of Sierra Leone* (Oxford: Oxford University Press, 2000).
Gates, Henry Louis, *Figures in Black: Words, Sign, and the "Racial" Self* (Oxford: Oxford University Press, 1987).
Gates, Henry Louis, *The Signifying Monkey: A Theory of Afro-American Literary Criticism* (Oxford: Oxford University Press, 1988).
Hanley, Ryan, *Beyond Slavery and Abolition: Black British Writing, c. 1770–1830* (Cambridge: Cambridge University Press, 2018).
Jager, Colin, "A Poetics of Dissent; or, Pantisocracy in America," *Theory & Event* 10/1 (2007), https://doi.org/10.1353/tae.2007.0042.
Keane, Patrick J., *Coleridge's Submerged Politics: The Ancient Mariner and Robinson Crusoe* (Columbia: University of Missouri Press, 1994).
Kitson, Peter J., "Coleridge's Bristol and West Country radicalism," in *English Romantic Writers and West Country*, ed. Nick Roe (New York: Palgrave Macmillan, 2010), 115–28.
Lee, Debbie, *Slavery and the Romantic Imagination* (Philadelphia: University of Pennsylvania Press, 2002).
Lee, Debbie, "Yellow Fever and the Slave Trade: Coleridge's 'The Rime of the Ancient Mariner,'" *English Literary History* 65/3 (1998): 675–700.
McKusick, James C., "'Wisely forgetful': Coleridge and the Politics of Pantisocracy," in *Romanticism and Colonialism: Writing and Empire, 1780–1830*, ed. Tim Fulford and Peter J. Kitson (Cambridge: Cambridge University Press, 1998), 107–28.
Mix Barrington, Julia, "Phantom Bark: The Chronotope of the Ghost Ship in the Atlantic World," *Gothic Studies* 19/2 (2017), 58–70.
Moss, Sarah, "Class War and the Albatross: The Politics of Ships as Social Space and *The Rime of the Ancient Mariner*," in *Fictions of the Sea: Critical Perspectives on the Ocean in British Literature and Culture*, ed. Bernhard Klein (London: Routledge, 2002), 89–100.
Moten, Fred, *Stolen Life (Consent Not to be a Single Being)* (Durham: Duke University Press, 2018).

Pace, Joel, "Journeys of the Imagination in Wheatley and Coleridge," in *Transatlantic Literary Studies, 1660–1830*, ed. Eve Tavor Bannet and Susan Manning (Cambridge: Cambridge University Press, 2011), 238–53.

Rubinstein, Chris, "A New Identity for the Mariner?: A Further Exploration of 'The Rime of The Ancyent Marinere,'" *The Coleridge Bulletin* no. 3 (Winter 1990), 16–29.

Sandler, Matt, *The Black Romantic Revolution: Abolitionist Poets at the End of Slavery* (London: Verso, 2020).

Schama, Simon, *Rough Crossings: The Slaves, the British, and the American Revolution* (New York: Ecco, 2007).

Shailer, Dan, "Guilt in Coleridge's 'The Rime of the Ancient Mariner,'" *Keats–Shelley Review* 32/1 (2018): 72–76.

Shields, John C., *Phillis Wheatley and the Romantics* (Knoxville: University of Tennessee Press, 2010).

Shuffelton, Frank, "On Her Own Footing: Phyllis Wheatley in Freedom," in *Genuis in Bondage: Literature of the Early Black Atlantic*, ed. Vincent Carretta and Phillip Gould (Lexington: University Press of Kentucky, 2014), 175–89.

Thomas, Helen, *Romanticism and Slave Narratives: Transatlantic Testimonies* (Cambridge: Cambridge University Press, 2000).

Youngquist, Paul, *Race, Romanticism, and the Atlantic* (New York: Taylor & Francis, 2016).

## Chapter 6

Anderson, Glenn B., and Lindsay M. Dunn, "Assessing Black Deaf History: 1980s to the Present," *Sign Language Studies* 17/1 (Fall 2016): 71–77.

Annamma, Subini Ancy, David Connor, and Beth Ferri, "Dis/Ability Critical Race Studies (DisCrit): Theorizing at the Intersections of Race and Dis/Ability," *Race Ethnicity and Education* 16/1 (2013): 1–31.

Barclay, Jenifer L., *The Mark of Slavery: Disability, Race, and Gender in Antebellum America* (Champaign: University of Illinois Press, 2021).

Baynton, Douglas, "Disability and the Justification of Inequality in American History," in *The New Disability History: American Perspectives*, ed. Paul K. Longmore and Lauri Umansky (New York: New York University Press, 2001), 33–57.

Bell, Chris, "Introducing White Disability Studies: A Modest Proposal," *The Disability Studies Reader*, ed. Lennard J. Davis, 2nd ed. (New York: Routledge, 2006), 275–82.

Bell, Chris, "Introduction," *Blackness and Disability: Critical Examinations and Cultural Interventions*, ed. Christopher M. Bell (East Lansing: Michigan State University Press, 2011), 1–7.

Boster, Dea H., *African American Slavery and Disability: Bodies, Property, and Power in the Antebellum South, 1800–1860* (New York: Routledge, 2013).

Challis, Debbie, "'The Ablest Race': The Ancient Greeks in Victorian Racial Theory," in *Classics and Imperialism in the British Empire*, ed. Mark Bradley (Oxford: Oxford University Press, 2010), 94–120.

Cleall, Esme, *Impairment and Otherness Across Britain and its Empire, c.1800–1914* (Cambridge: Cambridge University Press, 2022).

Crenshaw, Kimberlé, "Mapping the Margins: Intersectionality, Identity Politics, and Violence against Women," in *Critical Race Theory: The Key Writings that formed the Movement*, ed. Kimberlé Crenshaw, Neil Gotanda, Gary Pellar, and Kendall Thomas (New York: New Press, 1996), 357–83.

Dolmage, Jay, 'Disabled upon Arrival: The Rhetorical Construction of Disability and Race at Ellis Island', *Cultural Critique*, 77 (2011): 24–69.

Earle, William, *Obi; Or, The History of Three-Fingered Jack*, ed. Srinivas Aravamudan (Peterborough: Broadview, 2005).

Equiano, Olaudah, *The Interesting Narrative and Other Writings*, ed. Vincent Carretta (New York: Penguin, 1995).

Ervelles, Nirmala, and Andrea Minear, "Unspeakable Offenses: Untangling Race and Disability in Discourses of Intersectionality," *Journal of Literary and Cultural Disability Studies* 4/2 (2010): 127–145.

Fausto-Sterling, Anne, "Gender, Race, and Nation: The Comparative Anatomy of 'Hottentot' Women in Europe, 1815–1817," in *Deviant Bodies: Critical Perspectives on Difference in Science and Popular Culture*, ed. Jennifer Terry and Jacqueline Urla (Bloomington: Indiana University Press, 1995), 19–42.

Field, Corrine T., *The Struggle for Equal Adulthood: Gender, Race, Age, and the Fight for Citizenship in Antebellum America* (Chapel Hill: University of North Carolina, 2014).

Finkelstein, Victor, *Attitudes and Disabled People: Issues for Discussion* (New York: World Rehabilitation Fund, 1980).

Garland Thomson, Rosemarie, *Extraordinary Bodies: Figuring Physical Disability in American Culture and Literature* (New York: Columbia University Press, 1997).

Goffman, Erving, *Stigma: Notes on the Management of Spoiled Identity* (New York: Touchstone, 1986) [orig. publ. 1963].

Hairston, Ernest, and Linwood Smith, *Black and Deaf in America: Are We That Different?* (Silver Spring: T. J. Publishers, 1983).

Hevey, David, "The Enfreakment of Photography," in *The Disability Studies Reader*, ed. Lennard Davis, 4th ed. (New York: Routledge, 2013), 432–46.

Hunt-Kennedy, Stephanie, *Between Fitness and Death: Disability and Slavery in the Caribbean* (Urbana: University of Illinois Press, 2020).

James, Jennifer C., and Cynthia Wu, "Race, Ethnicity, Disability: Intersections and Interventions," *MELUS* 31/3 (2006): 3–13.

James, Jennifer C., and Cynthia Wu (eds.), Special Issue: Race, Ethnicity, Disability, and Literature *MELUS* 31/3 (2006).

Jarman, Michelle, "Race and Disability in US Literature," in *The Cambridge Companion to Literature and Disability*, ed. Clare Barker and Stuart Murray (Cambridge: Cambridge University Press, 2018), 155–69.

Jarrett, Simon, *Those They Called Idiots* (London: Reaktion Books, 2020).
Joshua, Essaka, *Physical Disability in British Romantic Literature* (Cambridge: Cambridge University Press, 2020).
Klages, Mary, *Woeful Afflictions: Disability and Sentimentality in Victorian America* (Philadelphia: University of Pennsylvania Press, 1999).
Knadler, Stephen, "Dis-abled Citizenship: Narrating the Extraordinary Body in Racial Uplift," *Arizona Quarterly*, 69/3 (2013): 99–128.
Krentz, Christopher, *Writing Deafness: The Hearing Line in Nineteenth-Century American Literature* (Chapel Hill: University of North Carolina Press, 2007).
Lawrie, Paul, "Race, Work, and Disability in Progressive Era United States" in *The Oxford Handbook of Disability History*, ed Michael Rembis, Catherine Kudlick, and Kim E. Nielsen (Oxford: Oxford University Press, 2018).
Linton, Simi, *Claiming Disability: Knowledge and Identity* (New York: New York University Press, 1998).
Mitchell, David, and Sharon Snyder, "The Eugenic Atlantic: Race, Disability, and the Making of an International Eugenic Science, 1800–1945," *Disability & Society* 18 (December 2003): 843–64.
Nussbaum, Felicity, *The Limits of the Human: Fictions of Anomaly, Race, and Gender in the Long Eighteenth Century* (Cambridge: Cambridge University Press, 2003).
Oliver, Michael, *The Politics of Disablement* (London: Macmillan, 1990).
Oliver, Michael and Colin Barnes, *The New Politics of Disablement* (Houndsmills: Palgrave Macmillan, 2012).
Prince, Mary, *The History of Mary Prince*, ed. Sara Salih (London: Penguin, 2004).
Robey, Kenneth L., Linda Beckley, and Matthew Kirschner, "Implicit Infantilizing Attitudes About Disability," *Journal of Developmental and Physical Disabilities* 18/4 (2006): 441–53.
Samuels, Ellen, *Fantasies of Identification: Disability, Gender, Race* (New York: New York University Press, 2014).
Samuels, Ellen, "Reading Race through Disability: Mark Twain's *Pudd'nhead Wilson* and 'Those Extraordinary Twins'," in *The Oxford Handbook of Nineteenth Century American Literature*, ed. Russ Castronovo (Oxford: Oxford University Press, 2012), 59–80.
Schaffer, Talia, *Communities of Care: The Social Ethics of Victorian Fiction* (Princeton: Princeton University Press, 2020).
Schalk, Sami, *Bodyminds Reimagined: (Dis)ability, Race, and Gender in Black Women's Speculative Fiction* (Durham: Duke University Press, 2018).
Schalk, Sami and Jina B. Kim, "Integrating Race: Transforming Feminist Disability Studies," *Signs: Journal of Women in Culture and Society* 46/1 (2020): 31–55.
Sherry, Mark, "Overlaps and Contradictions between Queer Theory and Disability Studies," *Disability & Society* 19/7 (2004): 769–83.
Stapleton, Lisa, "When Being Deaf Is Centered: d/Deaf Women of Color's Experiences with Racial/Ethnic and d/Deaf Identities in College," *Journal of College Student Development* 56/6 (2015): 570–86.

Stone, Andrea, "The Black Atlantic Revisited, The Body Reconsidered: On Lingering, Liminality, Lies, and Disability," *American Literary History*, 24/4 (2012), 814–26.

Stone, Deborah A., *The Disabled State* (Philadelphia: Temple University Press, 1984).

Tyler, Dennis, Jr., "Jim Crow's Disabilities: Racial Injury, Immobility, and the 'Terrible Handicap' in the Literature of James Weldon Johnson," *African American Review*, 50/2 (2017): 185–201.

Vernon, Ayesha, "The Dialectics of Multiple Identities and the Disabled People's Movement," *Disability & Society* 14/3 (1999): 385–98.

Williams, Cynric R., *Hamel, The Obeah Man*, ed. Tim Watson and Candace Ward (Peterborough: Broadview, 2010).

## Chapter 7

Allard, James Robert, *Romanticism, Medicine, and the Poet's Body* (New York: Routledge, 2007).

Alexander, Simone, *African Diasporic Women's Narratives: Politics of Resistance, Survival, and Citizenship* (Gainesville: University Press of Florida, 2014).

Barcia, M., *The Yellow Demon of Fever: Fighting Disease in the Nineteenth-Century Transatlantic Slave Trade* (New Haven: Yale University Press, 2020).

Bancel, N., David, T., and Thomas, D., eds. *The Invention of Race: Scientific and Popular Representations* (London: Routledge, 2014).

Barclay, Jenifer, "Differently Abled: Africanisms, Disability, and Power in the Age of Transatlantic Slavery." In J. Byrnes and J. L. Muller (eds.), *The Bioarchaeology of Impairment and Disability: Theoretical Ethnohistorical, and Methodological Perspectives* (Cham: Springer International Publishing, 2017), 77–94.

Barclay, Jenifer, *The Mark of Slavery: Disability, Race, and Gender in Antebellum America* (Champaign: University of Illinois Press, 2021).

Bell, Christopher, *Blackness and Disability: Critical Examinations and Cultural Interventions* (East Lansing: Michigan State University Press, 2012).

Bewell, Alan, *Romanticism and Colonial Disease* (Baltimore: Johns Hopkins University Press, 1999).

Bradshaw, Michael (ed.), *Disabling Romanticism: Body, Mind, and Text* (Basingstoke: Palgrave Macmillan, 2016).

Bradshaw, Michael, "'Its Own Concentred Recompense': The Impact of Critical Disability Studies on Romanticism" *Humanities* 8/2 (2019): 103.

Boster, Dea, *African American Slavery and Disability: Bodies, Property and Power in the Antebellum South, 1800–1860* (New York: Routledge, 2013).

Crais, Clifton and Pamela Scully, *Sara Baartman and the Hottentot Venus: A Ghost Story and a Biography* (Princeton: Princeton University Press, 2010).

Curran, Andrew, *The Anatomy of Blackness: Science and Slavery in an Age of Enlightenment* (Baltimore: Johns Hopkins University Press, 2011).

De Almeida, Hermione, *Romantic Medicine and John Keats* (Oxford: Oxford University Press, 1991).
De Barros, Juanita, *Reproducing the British Caribbean: Sex, Gender, and Population Politics after Slavery* (Chapel Hill: University of North Carolina Press, 2014).
Diaby, Bakary, "Feeling Black, Feeling Back: Fragility and Romanticism," *Symbiosis: A Journal of Transatlantic Literary & Cultural Relations* 23/1 (April 2019), 117–38.
Downs, J. T., "The Continuation of Slavery: The Experience of Disabled Slaves during Emancipation." *Disability Studies Quarterly* 28/3 (2008), n.p.
Downs, J. T., *Maladies of Empire: How Colonialism, Slavery, and War Transformed Medicine* (Cambridge: Belknap Press, 2021).
Ernst, Waltraud, and Bernard Harris, *Race, Science and Medicine, 1700–1960* (London: Routledge, 1999).
Garland-Thomson, Rosemarie, *Freakery: Cultural Spectacles of the Extraordinary Body* (New York: New York University Press, 1996).
Garland-Thomson, Rosemarie, "Integrating Disability, Transforming Feminist Theory." *NWSA Journal*. 14/3 (2002), 1–32.
Hobson, Janell, *Venus in the Dark: Blackness and Beauty in Popular Culture*, 2nd ed. (New York: Routledge, 2018).
Hogarth, Rana, *Medicalizing Blackness: Making Racial Difference in the Atlantic World, 1780–1840* (Chapel Hill: The University of North Carolina Press, 2017).
Holmes, Rachel, *The Hottentot Venus: The Life and Death of Saartjie Baartman, Born 1789– Buried 2002* (London: Bloomsbury, 2007).
Hunt-Kennedy, Stefanie, *Between Fitness and Death: Disability and Slavery in the Caribbean* (Urbana: University of Illinois Press, 2020).
Joshua, Essaka, *Physical Disability in British Romantic Literature* (Cambridge: Cambridge University Press, 2020).
Knadler, Stephen, *Vitality Politics: Health, Debility, and the Limits of Black Emancipation* (Ann Arbor: University of Michigan Press, 2019).
Lawrence, Christopher, *Medicine in the Making of Modern Britain, 1700–1920* (New York: Routledge, 1994).
Lettow, Susanne, ed. *Reproduction, Race, and Gender in Philosophy and the Early Life Sciences* (Albany: SUNY Press, 2014).
Mitchell, David and Sharon Snyder, "The Eugenic Atlantic" Race, Disability, and the Making of an International Eugenic Science, 1800–1945." *Disability & Society* 18/7 (2003): 843–64.
Mitchell, Piers, *Anatomical Dissection in Enlightenment England and Beyond: Autopsy, Pathology and Display* (New York: Routledge, 2012).
Mulderink, Carrie Elizabeth, "The Emergence, Importance of #DisabilityTooWhite Hashtag." *Disability Studies Quarterly* 40/2 (Spring 2020), n.p.
Nussbaum, Felicity and Helen Deutsch (eds), *"Defects": Engendering the Modern Body* (Ann Arbor: University of Michigan Press, 2000).
Owens, Deirdre, *Medical Bondage: Race, Gender, and the Origins of American Gynecology* (Athens: University of Georgia Press, 2017).

Pickens, Therí, ed. "Special Issue: Disability and Blackness." *African American Review* 50/2 (Summer 2017): 93–250.

Pinto, Samantha, *Infamous Bodies: Black Women's Celebrity and the Afterlives of Rights* (Durham: Duke University Press, 2020).

Pladek, Ben, *The Poetics of Palliation: Romantic Literary Therapy, 1790–1850.* (Liverpool: Liverpool University Press, 2019).

Qureshi, Sadiah, "Displaying Sara Baartman, the 'Hottentot Venus'." *History of Science* 42/2 (June 2004), 233–57.

Qureshi, Sadiah, *Peoples on Parade: Exhibitions, Empire, and Anthropology in Nineteenth-Century Britain* (Chicago: University of Chicago Press, 2011).

Rusert, Britt, *Fugitive Science: Empiricism and Freedom in Early African American Culture* (New York: New York University Press, 2017).

Sappol, Michael, *A Traffic of Dead Bodies: Anatomy and Embodied Social Identity in Nineteenth-Century America* (Princeton: Princeton University Press, 2004).

Schalk, Sami, *Bodyminds Reimagined: (Dis)ability, Race, and Gender in Black Women's Speculative Fiction* (Durham: Duke University Press, 2018).

Schiebinger, Londa, *Secret Cures of Slaves: People, Plants, and Medicine in the Eighteenth-Century Atlantic World* (Palo Alto: Stanford University Press, 2017).

Senior, Emily, *The Caribbean and the Medical Imagination, 1764–1834: Slavery, Disease, and Colonial Modernity* (Cambridge: Cambridge University Press, 2018).

Seth, Suman, *Difference and Disease: Medicine, Race, and the Eighteenth-Century British Empire* (Cambridge: Cambridge University Press, 2018).

Sheridan, Richard, *Doctors and Slaves: A Medical and Demographic History of Slavery in the British West Indies, 1680–1834* (Cambridge: Cambridge University Press, 1985).

Stanback, Emily, *The Wordsworth–Coleridge Circle and the Aesthetics of Disability.* Basingstoke: Palgrave Macmillan, 2016.

Stepan, Nancy, *The Idea of Race in Science: Great Britain, 1800–1960* (Houndsmills, Basingtoke: Palgrave Macmillan, 1982).

Strings, Sabrina, *Fearing the Black Body: The Racial Origins of Fat Phobia* (New York: New York University Press, 2019).

Sugg, Richard, *Murder after Death: Literature and Anatomy in Early Modern England* (Ithaca: Cornell University Press, 2007).

Turner, David, *Disability in Eighteenth-Century England: Imagining Physical Impairment* (New York: Routledge, 2012).

Turner, Sasha, *Contested Bodies: Pregnancy, Childrearing, and Slavery in Jamaica* (Philadelphia: University of Pennsylvania Press, 2017).

Wallen, Martin, *City of Health, Fields of Disease: Revolutions in the Poetry, Medicine, and Philosophy of Romanticism* (New York: Routledge, 2004).

Wang, Fuson, "The Historicist Turn of Romantic-Era Disability Studies or Frankenstein in the Dark," *Literature Compass* 14/7 (2017): https://doi.org/10.1111/lic3.12400.

Wheeler, Roxann, *The Complexion of Race: Categories of Difference in Eighteenth-Century British Culture* (Philadelphia: University of Pennsylvania Press, 2000).

Willis, Deborah, *Black Venus, 2010: They Called Her "Hottentot."* (Philadelphia: Temple University Press, 2010).

Young, Hershini Bhana, *Illegible Will: Coercive Spectacles of Labor in South Africa and the Diaspora* (Durham: Duke University Press, 2017).
Youngquist, Paul, *Monstrosities: Bodies and British Romanticism* (Minneapolis: University of Minnesota Press, 2003).

## Chapter 8

Ahearn, Stephen (ed.), *Affect and Abolition in the Anglo-Atlantic, 1770–1830* (London: Routledge, 2013).
Ahmed, Sara, *Complaint!* (Durham: Duke University Press, 2021).
Aljoe, Nicole, *Creole Testimonies: Slave Narratives from the British West Indies, 1709–1838* (London: Palgrave MacMillan, 2011).
Brown, Christopher, *Moral Capital: Foundations of British Abolitionism* (Chapel Hill: University of North Carolina Press, 2006).
de Man, Paul, "Anthropomorphism and Trope in the Lyric," in *The Rhetoric of Romanticism* (New York: Columbia University Press, 1984), 239–62.
Hamacher, Werner, "Remarks on Complaint." In *On the Brink: Language, Time, History, and Politics*, ed. Jan Plug (London: Rowman & Littlefield, 2020), 107–126.
Hessell, Nikki, *Sensitive Negotiations: Indigenous Diplomacy and British Romantic Poetry* (Albany: SUNY Press, 2021).
Lee, Debbie, "Black Single Mothers in Romantic History and Literature," in *Race, Romanticism, and the Atlantic*, ed. Paul Youngquist (London: Routledge, 2013), 165–82.
Mackey, Nathaniel, *Discrepant Engagement: Dissonance, Cross-Culturality and Experimental Writing* (Cambridge: Cambridge University Press, 1993).
McKauley, Kirk, "Anti-Slavery Poetry," in *Encyclopedia of Romantic Literature*, ed. Frederick Burwick, Nancy Goslee, and Diane Hoeveler (Oxford: Wiley-Blackwell, 2012), 38–47.
Moten, Fred, "Knowledge of Freedom," *CR: The New Centennial Review* 4/2 (Fall 2004), 269–310.
Ortiz, Ivan, "Lyric Possession in the Abolition Ballad," *Eighteenth-Century Studies* 51/2 (2018): 197–218.
Philip, M. Nourbese, *A Genealogy of Resistance: And Other Essays* (Toronto: Mercury Press, 1997).
Sandler, Matt, *The Black Romantic Revolution: Abolitionist Poets at the End of Slavery* (London: Verso, 2020).

## Chapter 9

Allewaert, Monique, *Ariel's Ecology: Plantations, Personhood, and Colonialism in the American Tropics* (Minneapolis: University of Minnesota Press, 2013).
Bergren, Katherine, *The Global Wordsworth: Romanticism Out of Place* (Newark: Rutgers University Press, 2019).

Bhandar, Brenna, *Colonial Lives of Property: Law, Land, and Racial Regimes of Ownership* (Durham: Duke University Press, 2018).
Brady, Andrea, *Poetry and Bondage: A History and Theory of Lyric Constraint* (Cambridge: Cambridge University Press, 2021).
Chakrabarty, Dipesh, *The Climate of History in a Planetary Age* (Chicago: University of Chicago Press, 2021).
Chander, Manu Samriti, *Brown Romantics: Poetry and Nationalism in the Global Nineteenth Century* (Lewisburg: Bucknell University Press, 2017).
Chen, Mel Y., *Animacies: Biopolitics, Racial Mattering, and Queer Affect* (Durham: Duke University Press, 2012).
Chuh, Kandice, *The Difference Aesthetics Makes: On the Humanities "After Man"* (Durham: Duke University Press, 2019).
Ellis, Cristin, *Antebellum Posthuman: Race and Materiality in the Mid-Nineteenth Century* (New York: Fordham University Press, 2018).
Ferdinand, Malcolm, *Decolonial Ecology: Thinking from the Caribbean World* (Cambridge: Polity Press, 2022).
Garofalo, Devin M., "Lyric Geology: Anthropomorphosis, White Supremacy, and Genres of the Human," *Diacritics* 50/1 (2022): 32–61.
Ghosh, Amitav, *The Nutmeg's Curse: Parables for a Planet in Crisis* (Chicago: University of Chicago Press, 2021).
Grove, Richard H., *Green Imperialism: Colonial Expansion, Tropical Island Edens and the Origins of Environmentalism, 1600–1860* (Cambridge: Cambridge University Press, 1995).
Hartman, Saidiya, *Scenes of Subjection: Terror, Slavery, and Self-Making in Nineteenth-Century America* (Oxford: Oxford University Press, 1997).
Jackson, Virginia, and Yopie Prins (eds.), *The Lyric Theory Reader: A Critical Anthology* (Baltimore: Johns Hopkins University Press, 2014).
Jackson, Zakiyyah Iman, *Becoming Human: Matter and Meaning in an Antiblack World* (New York: New York University Press, 2020).
Kaul, Suvir, *Poems of Nation, Anthems of Empire: English Verse in the Long Eighteenth Century* (Charlottesville: University of Virginia Press, 2000).
Khalip, Jacques, *Last Things: Disastrous Form from Kant to Hujar* (New York: Fordham University Press, 2018).
King, Tiffany Lethabo, *The Black Shoals: Offshore Formations of Black and Native Studies* (Durham: Duke University Press, 2019).
Makdisi, Saree, *Making England Western: Occidentalism, Race, and Imperial Culture* (Chicago: University of Chicago Press, 2014).
Makdisi, Saree, *Romantic Imperialism: Universal Empire and the Culture of Modernity* (Cambridge: Cambridge University Press, 1998).
McKittrick, Katherine (ed.), *Sylvia Wynter: On Being Human as Praxis* (Durham: Duke University Press, 2015).
McLane, Maureen N., *Romanticism and the Human Sciences: Poetry, Population, and the Discourse of the Species* (Cambridge: Cambridge University Press, 2004).
Menely, Tobias, *Climate and the Making of Worlds: Toward a Geohistorical Poetics* (Chicago: University of Chicago Press, 2021).

Neeson, J. M., *Commoners: Common Right, Enclosure and Social Change in England, 1700–1820* (Cambridge: Cambridge University Press, 1993).
Nersessian, Anahid, *The Calamity Form: On Poetry and Social Life* (Chicago: University of Chicago Press, 2020).
Reed, Anthony, "The Erotics of Mourning in Recent Experimental Black Poetry," *The Black Scholar* 47/1 (2017): 23–37.
Sharpe, Christina, *In the Wake: On Blackness and Being* (Durham: Duke University Press, 2016).
Song, Min Hyoung, *Climate Lyricism* (Durham: Duke University Press, 2022).
Viswanathan, Gauri, *Masks of Conquest: Literary Study and British Rule in India* (New York: Columbia University Press, 2015).
Weheliye, Alexander G., *Habeas Viscus: Racializing Assemblages, Biopolitics, and Black Feminist Theories of the Human* (Durham: Duke University Press, 2014).
Wynter, Sylvia, "On How We Mistook the Map for the Territory, and Re-Imprisoned Ourselves in Our Unbearable Wrongness of Being, of Désêtre," in *Not Only the Master's Tools: African-American Studies in Theory and Practice*, ed. Lewis R. Gordon and Jane Anna Gordon (Boulder: Paradigm Press, 2006), 107–69.
Wynter, Sylvia, "Unsettling the Coloniality of Being/Power/Truth/Freedom: Towards the Human, After Man, Its Overrepresentation – An Argument," *CR: The New Centennial Review* 3/3 (2003): 257–337.
Yusoff, Kathryn, *A Billion Black Anthropocenes or None* (Minneapolis: University of Minnesota Press, 2018).

## Chapter 10

Fulford, Tim, and Kevin Hutchings (eds.), *Native Americans and Anglo-American Culture, 1750–1850: The Indian Atlantic* (Cambridge: Cambridge University Press, 2009).
Gannon, Thomas C., *Skylark Meets Meadowlark: Reimagining the Bird in British Romantic and Contemporary Native American Literature* (Lincoln: University of Nebraska Press, 2009).
Hess, Scott, "Aotearoa New Zealand, Traditional Ecological Knowledge, and a Relational Method for the Environmental Humanities," *Studies in Romanticism* 62/1 (2023): 27–35.
Hessell, Nikki, "The Indigenous *Lyrical Ballads*," in *The Cambridge Companion to Lyrical Ballads*, ed. Sally Bushell (Cambridge: Cambridge University Press, 2020), 253–68.
Hessell, Nikki, *Romantic Literature and the Colonised World: Lessons from Indigenous Translations* (Basingstoke: Palgrave, 2018).
Hessell, Nikki, *Sensitive Negotiations: Indigenous Diplomacy and British Romantic Poetry* (Albany: State University of New York Press, 2021).
Hessell, Nikki, and Elizabeth Potter (eds.), "Forum on Re-Indigenizing Romanticism," *Studies in Romanticism* 6/4 (2022).
Hutchings, Kevin, *Transatlantic Upper Canada: Portraits in Literature, Land, and British-Indigenous Relations* (Montreal: McGill-Queen's University Press, 2020).

Richardson, Robbie, *The Savage and Modern Self: North American Indians in Eighteenth-Century British Literature and Culture* (Toronto: University of Toronto Press, 2018).
Rifkin, Mark, *Speaking for the People: Native Writing and the Question of Political Form*, (Durham: Duke University Press, 2021).
Walkiewicz, Kathryn, *Reading Territory: Indigenous and Black Freedom, Removal, and the Nineteenth-Century State* (Chapel Hill: University of North Carolina Press, 2023).
Wisecup, Kelly, *Assembled for Use: Indigenous Compilation and the Archives of Early American Literature* (New Haven: Yale University Press, 2021).

## Chapter 11

Ballaster, Ros, "Narrative Transmigrations: The Oriental Tale and the Novel in Eighteenth-Century Britain," in *A Companion to the Eighteenth-Century English Novel and Culture*, ed. Paula R. Backscheider and Catherine Ingrassia (Malden: Blackwell, 2005), 75–96.
Baugh, Victoria, "Mixed-Race Heiresses in Early-Nineteenth-Century Literature: Sanditon's Miss Lambe in Context," *European Romantic Review* 29/4 (2018): 449–58.
Horejsi, Nicole, "Whose 'Wild and Extravagant Stories'? Clara Reeve's *The Progress of Romance* and *The History of Charoba, Queen of Ægypt*," in *Novel Cleopatras: Romance Historiography and the Dido Tradition in English Fiction, 1688–1785* (Toronto: University of Toronto Press, 2019), 166–98.

## Chapter 12

Ahmed, Sara, "A Phenomenology of Whiteness," *Feminist Theory* 8/2 (2007): 149–68.
Allen, Regulus, "'The Sable Venus' and Desire for the Undesirable," *Studies in English Literature* 51/3 (2011): 667–91.
Bruder, Helen P., *William Blake and the Daughters of Albion* (Basingstoke: Macmillan Press, 1997).
Bush, Barbara, "'Sable Venus,' 'She Devil,' or 'Drudge'? British Slavery and the "Fabulous Fiction' of Black Women's Identities c. 1650–1838," *Women's History Review* 9 (December 2000): 761–89.
Erdman, David, "Blake's Vision of Slavery," *Journal of the Warburg and Courtauld Institutes* 15 (1952): 242–52.
Essick, Robert N., and Joseph Viscomi, "An Inquiry into Blake's Method of Color Printing," *Blake/An Illustrated Quarterly* 35 (Winter 2001/2): 73–102, www.blakequarterly.org.
Gilman, Sander, "Black Bodies, White Bodies: Toward an Iconography of Female Sexuality in Late Nineteenth-Century Art, Medicine, and Literature," *Critical Inquiry* 12/1 (1985): 204–42.
Hartman, Saidiya V., "The Dead Book," in *Lose Your Mother: A Journey Along the Atlantic Slave Route* (New York: Farrar, Straus and Giroux, 2008), 136–53.

Holcomb, Julie, "Blood-Stained Sugar: Gender, Commerce and the British Slave-Trade Debates," *Slavery & Abolition* 35/4 (2014): 611–28.

Ibata, Hélène, "'Blotting and Blurring Demons'? The Paradoxical Place of Colour Printing in Blake's Theory of Art," *XVII–XVIII*, 75 (2018). https://doi.org/10.4000/1718.1144.

Kitson, Peter, "'Candid Reflections': The Idea of Race in the Debate over the Slave Trade and Slavery in the Late Eighteenth and Early Nineteenth Century," in *Discourses of Slavery and Abolition: Britain and Its Colonies, 1760–1838*, ed. Brycchan Carey, Markman Ellis, and Sarah Salih (Houndsmills: Palgrave Macmillan, 2004), 11–25.

Lee, Debbie, "Intimacy as Imitation: Monkeys in Blake's Engraving for Stedman's Narrative." In *Slavery and the Romantic Imagination* (Philadelphia: University of Pennsylvania Press, 2004), 66–119.

Makdisi, Saree, "The Political Aesthetic of Blake's Images," in *The Cambridge Companion to William Blake*, ed. Morris Eaves (Cambridge: Cambridge University Press, 2003), 110–32.

Matthew, Patricia A., "Look before You Leap: Seeing What's Right in Front of Us in Portraits from the Past," *Lapham's Quarterly*, November 4, 2019, www.laphamsquarterly.org/roundtable/look-you-leap.

Matthew, Patricia A., "Race, Blackness, and Romanticism: Dialogues with Professors Simon Gikandi and Lisa Lowe." University of Buffalo. 10 March 2021. *Studies in Romanticism* 61/1 (2022): 137–50. https://doi.org/10.1353/srm.2022.0012.

McCrea, Rosalie S., "Dis-Ordering the World in the Eighteenth Century: The Voyage of the Sable Venus: Connoisseurship and the Trivialising of Slavery." In *Beyond the Blood, the Beach and the Banana: New Perspectives in Caribbean Studies*, ed. Sandra Courtman, 275–97. (Kingston: Randle, 2004).

Mellor, Anne, "Sex, Violence, and Slavery: Blake and Wollstonecraft." *Huntington LibraryQuarterly*, 58/3–4 (1995): 345–70.

Mitchell, Robin, *Venus Noire: Black Women and Colonial Fantasies in Nineteenth-Century France* (Athens: University of Georgia Press, 2020).

Moyer, James F., "'The Daughters Weave their Work in loud cries': Blake, Slavery, and Cotton," *Blake/An Illustrated Quarterly* 48/3 (Winter 2014–15).

Odumosu, Temi, *Africans in English Caricature 1769–1819: Black Jokes White Humour* (London: Harvey Miller, 2017), 30–39.

Otto, Peter, "Politics, Aesthetics, and Blake's 'bounding line,'" *Word & Image* 26/2 (2010): 172–85.

Phillips, Michael, "'Printing in the infernal method': William Blake's Method of 'Illuminated Printing,'" *Interfaces* 39 (2018): 67–89.

Rice, Alan J., "'Food for the Sharks': Constructions and Reconstructions of the Middle-Passage Imaginary in the Transatlantic Economy," in *Radical Narratives of the Black Atlantic* (London: Continuum, 2003), 48–81.

Sharpley-Whiting, T. Denean, *Black Venus: Sexualized Savages, Primal Fears, and Primitive Narratives in French* (Durham: Duke University Press, 1999).

Smith McCrea, Rosalie, "Dis-Ordering the World in the Eighteenth Century: *The Voyage of the Sable Venus*: Connoisseurship and the Trivialising of Slavery," in

*Beyond the Blood, the Beach and the Banana: New Perspectives in Caribbean Studies*, ed. Sandra Courtman, (Kingston: Randle, 2004), 275–97.

Tate, Shirley A., "Looking at the Sable-Saffron Venus: Iconography, Affect and (Post)Colonial Hygiene," in *Black Women's Bodies and the Nation: Race, Gender and Culture* (Basingstoke: Palgrave Macmillan, 2015), 17–46.

Vine, Steven, "'That Mild Beam': Enlightenment and enslavement in William Blake's Visions of the Daughters of Albion." In *The Discourse of Slavery: Aphra Behn to Toni Morrison*, 40–63, ed. Carla Plasa and Betty J. Ring (London: Routledge, 1994).

Viscomi, Joseph, "Illuminated Printing," in *The Cambridge Companion to William Blake*, ed. Morris Eaves (Cambridge: Cambridge University Press, 2003), 37–62.

Wood, Marcus, *Blind Memory: Visual Representations of Slavery in England and America 1780–1865* (London: Routledge, 2000).

## Chapter 13

Botkin, Frances R., *Thieving Three-Fingered Jack: Transatlantic Tales of a Jamaican Outlaw, 1780–2015* (New Brunswick: Rutgers University Press, 2017).

Bratton, J. S., Richard Allen Cave, Breandan Gregory, Heidi J. Holder, and Michael Pickering, *Acts of Supremacy: The British Empire and the Stage, 1790–1930* (Manchester: Manchester University Press, 1991).

Cox, Jeffrey N. (ed.), *Slavery, Abolition and Emancipation: Writings in the British Romantic Period*, vol. V: *Drama* (London: Pickering & Chatto, 1999).

Dellarosa, Franca, *Slavery on Stage: Representations of Slavery in British Theatre 1760s–1830s* (Bari: Edizioni dal Sud, 2009).

Dykes, Eva Beatrice, *The Negro in English Romantic Thought, or A Study of Sympathy for the Oppressed* (Washington, DC: Associated Publishers, 1942).

Gibbs, Jenna M., *Performing the Temple of Liberty: Slavery, Theater, and Popular Culture in London and Philadelphia, 1760–1850* (Baltimore: Johns Hopkins University Press, 2014).

Khan, Yasser Shams, "Theorizing the Performance of Blackness: Relations, Processes, and Possibilities," *Studies in Romanticism* 61/1 (2022): 91–99.

MacDonald, Joyce Green, "Acting Black: 'Othello,' 'Othello' Burlesques, and the Performance of Blackness," *Theatre Journal* 46/2 (1994): 231–49.

Morrison, Toni, *Playing in the Dark: Whiteness and the Literary Imagination* (Cambridge, MA: Harvard University Press, 1992).

Nussbaum, Felicity, "Theatre of Empire: Racial Counterfeit, Racial Realism," in *A New Imperial History: Culture, Identity, and Modernity in Britain and the Empire, 1660–1840*, ed. Kathleen Wilson (Cambridge: Cambridge University Press, 2004).

Oldfield, J. R., "The 'Ties of Soft Humanity': Slavery and Race in British Drama, 1760–1800," *Huntington Library Quarterly* 56/1 (1993): 1–14.

O'Quinn, Daniel, "Theatre and Empire," in *The Cambridge Companion to British Theatre, 1730–1830*, ed. Daniel O'Quinn and Jane Moody (Cambridge: Cambridge University Press, 2007), 233–46.
Orr, Bridget, "Empire, Sentiment, and Theatre," in *The Oxford Handbook of the Georgian Theatre, 1737–1832*, ed. Julia Swindells and David Francis Taylor (Oxford: Oxford University Press, 2014), 621–40.
Ragussis, Michael, *Theatrical Nation: Jews and Other Outlandish Englishmen in Georgian Britain* (Philadelphia: University of Pennsylvania Press, 2010).
Roach, Joseph R., *Cities of the Dead: Circum-Atlantic Performance* (New York: Columbia University Press, 1996).
Valladares, Susan, "Afro-Creole Revelry and Rebellion on the British Stage: Jonkanoo in Obi; or, Three-Fingered Jack (1800)," *The Review of English Studies* 70/294 (2019): 291–311.
Van Kooy, Dana, and Jeffrey N. Cox, "Melodramatic Slaves," *Modern Drama* 55/4 (2012): 459–75.
Vaughan, Virginia Mason, *Performing Blackness on English Stages, 1500–1800* (Cambridge: Cambridge University Press, 2005).
Waters, Hazel, *Racism on the Victorian Stage: Representation of Slavery and the Black Character* (Cambridge: Cambridge University Press, 2007).
Worrall, David, *Harlequin Empire: Race, Ethnicity and the Drama of the Popular Enlightenment* (London: Pickering & Chatto, 2007).

# *Index*

ableism, 101, 104, 106, 118, 124
ableist, 3, 101, 112, 118, 121, 124, 125, 126
abolition, 3, 22, 26, 28, 53, 58, 59, 70, 71, 108, 138, 139, 163, 198, 210, 211, 219
abolitionist, 3, 50, 56, 57, 58, 59, 60, 66, 68, 70, 79, 90, 98, 100, 103, 107, 109, 110, 130, 134, 137, 138, 140, 141, 145, 163, 164, 211, 219, 220, 222, 223, 229
affect, 236
Afropessimism, 2, 37, 53, 55
Alps, 158, 161, 162, 163, 166, 167
anti-Blackness, 112
atmosphere, 13, 22, 23, 24, 25, 29, 30, 31, 34

*Belinda* (1801), 198
Black Loyalists, 3, 78, 79, 80, 81, 82, 83, 84, 85, 86, 87, 88, 89, 90, 91, 92, 93, 95
Blackness as, 121, 122, 124, 126
Boston, 36, 78, 80, 86, 87, 88, 94, 95, 96
Britain, 7, 9, 57, 60, 61, 78, 80, 81, 84, 91, 92, 93, 111, 114, 132, 139, 140, 141, 174, 177, 200, 211, 224, 231, 239

Caribbean, 23, 24, 27, 28, 30, 34, 35, 40, 48, 60, 78, 85, 94, 133, 137, 140, 146, 147, 162, 235
Cherokee, 4, 179, 180, 182
complaint, 4, 57, 130, 131, 132, 133, 134, 135, 136, 137, 138, 139, 140, 141, 142, 143, 145, 146, 147, 148, 170
Cuba, 23, 29, 30, 32, 33, 35, 36

debates, 68, 98, 100, 102, 108, 125, 197, 204, 209, 211, 219
disability, 3, 98, 99, 100, 101, 102, 103, 104, 105, 106, 107, 108, 110, 111, 113, 115, 117, 118, 120, 121, 122, 124, 125, 126
domesticity, 39, 45, 47, 91, 212, 217, 219

empire, 7, 8, 9, 52, 91, 106, 136, 159, 163, 235, 237, 239, 242, 243
England, 6, 16, 17, 26, 35, 45, 66, 78, 79, 85, 88, 89, 90, 92, 94, 107, 114, 122, 134, 135, 156, 167, 184, 199, 200, 210, 215, 220, 226
experiment, 87, 117

French Revolution, 2, 16, 160, 161, 162

geology, 160
Germany, 56, 68, 69, 76
*Guide to the Lakes*, 150, 151, 154, 166

Haitian Revolution, 2, 22, 23, 24, 27, 28, 32, 33, 34, 35, 36, 83, 162, 163
hereditary, 9, 16, 17, 18, 20, 72, 121, 210, 211, 214, 216, 218

imperialism, 70, 106, 126, 169, 173, 174, 178, 198, 243
Indigenous, 4, 118, 152, 155, 168, 169, 170, 171, 172, 173, 174, 175, 176, 177, 178, 179, 180, 181, 182, 183, 223
Indigenous studies, 168, 169
institutional, 38, 101
intersectionality, 104

Jamaica, 27, 28, 36, 47, 54, 83, 107, 122, 128, 137, 224, 235, 237, 242

Lake District, 92, 150, 154, 178, 180, 184
law, 9, 20, 26, 131, 133, 135, 141, 144, 146, 147, 148, 160, 180, 182, 243
lectures on *Othello*, 73
lyric, 4, 130, 131, 132, 134, 136, 139, 140, 143, 144, 145, 146, 147, 148, 151, 160, 164, 165, 166, 179, 180, 181

medical history, 116, 117
medicine, 4, 116, 117, 118, 119, 121, 122, 123, 125
Middle Passage, 26, 30, 64, 66, 87, 92, 208

*Narrative of a Five Years Expedition Against the Revolted Negroes of Surinam* (1796), 205
nature, 3, 4, 9, 11, 12, 13, 18, 20, 28, 40, 49, 63, 68, 73, 89, 108, 127, 132, 135, 136, 150, 151, 154, 155, 159, 160, 163, 173, 179, 180, 181, 194, 195, 196, 199, 228, 234, 242
Nova Scotia, 85, 86, 87, 89, 90, 95

Ojibwe, 4, 174, 179, 180, 182
*Obi*, 107
*Othello*, 56, 73, 74, 75, 196, 229, 230, 234, 244

performance, 85, 171, 187, 214, 221, 229, 230, 231, 232, 234, 235, 236, 238, 243
*Philosophical Enquiry into the Origin of our Ideas of the Sublime and the Beautiful* (1757), 9
play, 87, 104, 105, 126, 130, 172, 178, 197, 199, 201, 229, 236, 238, 242, 243
printing, 205, 213, 214, 218, 220
props, 228, 234, 236, 237, 238, 239, 240
prosopopoeia, 131, 136, 140, 141, 147, 148
pseudo-, 56, 70, 175, 232, 234

racecraft, 5, 227, 228, 230, 232, 233, 234, 236, 241, 243, 244
racial, 3, 4, 5, 7, 9, 12, 17, 20, 46, 50, 56, 66, 67, 68, 70, 71, 72, 73, 75, 76, 81, 89, 98, 105, 107, 108, 109, 112, 118, 119, 121, 124, 131, 134, 135, 138, 139, 145, 146, 155, 163, 186, 187, 188, 189, 190, 192, 193, 198, 199, 201, 204, 205, 212, 213, 215, 217, 223, 224, 227, 228, 229, 230, 232, 233, 234, 235, 236, 241, 243
racism, 3, 5, 6, 13, 38, 39, 52, 54, 56, 70, 74, 75, 77, 85, 88, 101, 104, 112, 118, 122, 124, 160, 187, 204, 232, 233, 234, 244
reproductive futurity, 43, 44

science, 5, 56, 68, 75, 118, 119, 124, 152, 192, 235
scientific, 1, 2, 3, 6, 13, 16, 26, 56, 70, 116, 117, 118, 119, 121, 122, 124, 126, 160, 187, 192, 197
sentiment, 73, 83, 131, 134, 192, 211, 217, 219, 221, 231
settler colonialism, 140, 169, 183
Sierra Leone, 23, 78, 80, 83, 87, 89, 90, 91, 92, 93, 94, 95, 97

slave trade, 7, 22, 26, 28, 29, 30, 33, 60, 61, 62, 63, 64, 65, 66, 67, 68, 71, 75, 78, 93, 125, 204, 209, 211, 238
slavery, 2, 7, 9, 20, 22, 23, 30, 33, 35, 39, 40, 48, 54, 56, 57, 59, 61, 62, 64, 66, 69, 75, 78, 81, 83, 84, 89, 93, 94, 98, 103, 105, 108, 109, 110, 111, 118, 124, 131, 133, 135, 136, 137, 138, 139, 140, 142, 143, 145, 146, 148, 162, 163, 198, 199, 204, 206, 209, 210, 211, 212, 214, 216, 217, 218, 219, 220, 222, 223, 229, 230, 235, 237, 238, 243
South Carolina, 80, 184
sovereignty, 2, 4, 24, 33, 125, 168, 169, 174, 176, 178, 179, 180, 181, 182

theodicy, 133, 145
transatlantic, 26, 40, 57, 61, 62, 64, 68, 75, 78, 84, 92, 118, 204, 216
*Two Treatises of Government* (1689), 154

universalism, 152, 174

ventriloquism, 131, 136
Virginia, 20, 35, 80, 85, 96, 164, 167, 184
visual culture, 5

whiteness, 2, 4, 50, 67, 70, 76, 108, 120, 121, 126, 151, 152, 155, 156, 158, 160, 162, 163, 165, 166, 198, 204, 213, 215, 218, 221, 222, 227, 228
women, 2, 5, 20, 23, 38, 43, 45, 46, 48, 49, 54, 79, 87, 88, 94, 108, 123, 141, 172, 173, 174, 184, 188, 195, 199, 205, 209, 210, 211, 212, 217, 219, 220, 222, 224, 231
women and, 94, 123, 172, 173, 210, 212
Wordsworth, William, 151, 183

*Zong!* (2008), 146

# Cambridge Companions To . . .

## AUTHORS

*Edward Albee* edited by Stephen J. Bottoms

*Margaret Atwood* edited by Coral Ann Howells (second edition)

*W. H. Auden* edited by Stan Smith

*Jane Austen* edited by Edward Copeland and Juliet McMaster (second edition)

*James Baldwin* edited by Michele Elam

*Balzac* edited by Owen Heathcote and Andrew Watts

*Beckett* edited by John Pilling

*Bede* edited by Scott DeGregorio

*Aphra Behn* edited by Derek Hughes and Janet Todd

*Saul Bellow* edited by Victoria Aarons

*Walter Benjamin* edited by David S. Ferris

*William Blake* edited by Morris Eaves

*Boccaccio* edited by Guyda Armstrong, Rhiannon Daniels, and Stephen J. Milner

*Jorge Luis Borges* edited by Edwin Williamson

*Brecht* edited by Peter Thomson and Glendyr Sacks (second edition)

*The Brontës* edited by Heather Glen

*Bunyan* edited by Anne Dunan-Page

*Frances Burney* edited by Peter Sabor

*Byron* edited by Drummond Bone (second edition)

*Albert Camus* edited by Edward J. Hughes

*Willa Cather* edited by Marilee Lindemann

*Catullus* edited by Ian Du Quesnay and Tony Woodman

*Cervantes* edited by Anthony J. Cascardi

*Chaucer* edited by Piero Boitani and Jill Mann (second edition)

*Chekhov* edited by Vera Gottlieb and Paul Allain

*Kate Chopin* edited by Janet Beer

*Caryl Churchill* edited by Elaine Aston and Elin Diamond

*Cicero* edited by Catherine Steel

*John Clare* edited by Sarah Houghton-Walker

*J. M. Coetzee* edited by Jarad Zimbler

*Coleridge* edited by Lucy Newlyn

*Coleridge* edited by Tim Fulford (new edition)

*Wilkie Collins* edited by Jenny Bourne Taylor

*Joseph Conrad* edited by J. H. Stape

*H. D.* edited by Nephie J. Christodoulides and Polina Mackay

*Dante* edited by Rachel Jacoff (second edition)

*Daniel Defoe* edited by John Richetti

*Don DeLillo* edited by John N. Duvall

*Charles Dickens* edited by John O. Jordan

*Emily Dickinson* edited by Wendy Martin

*John Donne* edited by Achsah Guibbory

*Dostoevskii* edited by W. J. Leatherbarrow

*Theodore Dreiser* edited by Leonard Cassuto and Claire Virginia Eby

*John Dryden* edited by Steven N. Zwicker

*W. E. B. Du Bois* edited by Shamoon Zamir

*George Eliot* edited by George Levine and Nancy Henry (second edition)

*T. S. Eliot* edited by A. David Moody

*Ralph Ellison* edited by Ross Posnock

*Ralph Waldo Emerson* edited by Joel Porte and Saundra Morris

*William Faulkner* edited by Philip M. Weinstein

*Henry Fielding* edited by Claude Rawson

*F. Scott Fitzgerald* edited by Ruth Prigozy

*F. Scott Fitzgerald* edited by Michael Nowlin (second edition)

*Flaubert* edited by Timothy Unwin

*E. M. Forster* edited by David Bradshaw

*Benjamin Franklin* edited by Carla Mulford

*Brian Friel* edited by Anthony Roche

*Robert Frost* edited by Robert Faggen

*Gabriel García Márquez* edited by Philip Swanson

*Elizabeth Gaskell* edited by Jill L. Matus

*Edward Gibbon* edited by Karen O'Brien and Brian Young

*Goethe* edited by Lesley Sharpe

*Günter Grass* edited by Stuart Taberner

*Thomas Hardy* edited by Dale Kramer

*David Hare* edited by Richard Boon

*Nathaniel Hawthorne* edited by Richard Millington

*Seamus Heaney* edited by Bernard O'Donoghue
*Ernest Hemingway* edited by Scott Donaldson
*Hildegard of Bingen* edited by Jennifer Bain
*Homer* edited by Robert Fowler
*Horace* edited by Stephen Harrison
*Ted Hughes* edited by Terry Gifford
*Ibsen* edited by James McFarlane
*Kazuo Ishiguro* edited by Andrew Bennett
*Henry James* edited by Jonathan Freedman
*Samuel Johnson* edited by Greg Clingham
*Ben Jonson* edited by Richard Harp and Stanley Stewart
*James Joyce* edited by Derek Attridge (second edition)
*Kafka* edited by Julian Preece
*Keats* edited by Susan J. Wolfson
*Rudyard Kipling* edited by Howard J. Booth
*Lacan* edited by Jean-Michel Rabaté
*D. H. Lawrence* edited by Anne Fernihough
*Primo Levi* edited by Robert Gordon
*Lucretius* edited by Stuart Gillespie and Philip Hardie
*Machiavelli* edited by John M. Najemy
*David Mamet* edited by Christopher Bigsby
*Thomas Mann* edited by Ritchie Robertson
*Christopher Marlowe* edited by Patrick Cheney
*Andrew Marvell* edited by Derek Hirst and Steven N. Zwicker
*Ian McEwan* edited by Dominic Head
*Herman Melville* edited by Robert S. Levine
*Arthur Miller* edited by Christopher Bigsby (second edition)
*Milton* edited by Dennis Danielson (second edition)
*Molière* edited by David Bradby and Andrew Calder
*William Morris* edited by Marcus Waithe
*Toni Morrison* edited by Justine Tally
*Alice Munro* edited by David Staines
*Nabokov* edited by Julian W. Connolly
*Eugene O'Neill* edited by Michael Manheim
*George Orwell* edited by John Rodden
*Ovid* edited by Philip Hardie
*Petrarch* edited by Albert Russell Ascoli and Unn Falkeid

*Harold Pinter* edited by Peter Raby (second edition)
*Sylvia Plath* edited by Jo Gill
*Plutarch* edited by Frances B. Titchener and Alexei Zadorojnyi
*Edgar Allan Poe* edited by Kevin J. Hayes
*Alexander Pope* edited by Pat Rogers
*Ezra Pound* edited by Ira B. Nadel
*Proust* edited by Richard Bales
*Pushkin* edited by Andrew Kahn
*Thomas Pynchon* edited by Inger H. Dalsgaard, Luc Herman and Brian McHale
*Rabelais* edited by John O'Brien
*Rilke* edited by Karen Leeder and Robert Vilain
*Philip Roth* edited by Timothy Parrish
*Salman Rushdie* edited by Abdulrazak Gurnah
*John Ruskin* edited by Francis O'Gorman
*Sappho* edited by P. J. Finglass and Adrian Kelly
*Seneca* edited by Shadi Bartsch and Alessandro Schiesaro
*Shakespeare* edited by Margareta de Grazia and Stanley Wells (second edition)
*George Bernard Shaw* edited by Christopher Innes
*Shelley* edited by Timothy Morton
*Mary Shelley* edited by Esther Schor
*Sam Shepard* edited by Matthew C. Roudané
*Spenser* edited by Andrew Hadfield
*Laurence Sterne* edited by Thomas Keymer
*Wallace Stevens* edited by John N. Serio
*Tom Stoppard* edited by Katherine E. Kelly
*Harriet Beecher Stowe* edited by Cindy Weinstein
*August Strindberg* edited by Michael Robinson
*Jonathan Swift* edited by Christopher Fox
*J. M. Synge* edited by P. J. Mathews
*Tacitus* edited by A. J. Woodman
*Henry David Thoreau* edited by Joel Myerson
*Thucydides* edited by Polly Low
*Tolstoy* edited by Donna Tussing Orwin
*Anthony Trollope* edited by Carolyn Dever and Lisa Niles
*Mark Twain* edited by Forrest G. Robinson
*John Updike* edited by Stacey Olster
*Mario Vargas Llosa* edited by Efrain Kristal and John King

*Virgil* edited by Fiachra Mac Góráin and Charles Martindale (second edition)
*Voltaire* edited by Nicholas Cronk
*David Foster Wallace* edited by Ralph Clare
*Edith Wharton* edited by Millicent Bell
*Walt Whitman* edited by Ezra Greenspan
*Oscar Wilde* edited by Peter Raby
*Tennessee Williams* edited by Matthew C. Roudané
*William Carlos Williams* edited by Christopher MacGowan
*August Wilson* edited by Christopher Bigsby
*Mary Wollstonecraft* edited by Claudia L. Johnson
*Virginia Woolf* edited by Susan Sellers (second edition)
*Wordsworth* edited by Stephen Gill
*Richard Wright* edited by Glenda R. Carpio
*W. B. Yeats* edited by Marjorie Howes and John Kelly
*Xenophon* edited by Michael A. Flower
*Zola* edited by Brian Nelson

# TOPICS

*The Actress* edited by Maggie B. Gale and John Stokes
*The African American Novel* edited by Maryemma Graham
*The African American Slave Narrative* edited by Audrey A. Fisch
*African American Theatre* edited by Harvey Young
*Allegory* edited by Rita Copeland and Peter Struck
*American Crime Fiction* edited by Catherine Ross Nickerson
*American Gothic* edited by Jeffrey Andrew Weinstock
*The American Graphic Novel* edited by Jan Baetens, Hugo Frey and Fabrice Leroy
*American Horror* edited by Stephen Shapiro and Mark Storey
*American Literature and the Body* edited by Travis M. Foster
*American Literature and the Environment* edited by Sarah Ensor and Susan Scott Parrish
*American Literature of the 1930s* edited by William Solomon
*American Modernism* edited by Walter Kalaidjian
*American Poetry since 1945* edited by Jennifer Ashton
*American Realism and Naturalism* edited by Donald Pizer
*American Short Story* edited by Michael J. Collins and Gavin Jones
*American Travel Writing* edited by Alfred Bendixen and Judith Hamera
*American Utopian Literature and Culture since 1945* edited by Sherryl Vint
*American Women Playwrights* edited by Brenda Murphy
*Ancient Rhetoric* edited by Erik Gunderson
*Arthurian Legend* edited by Elizabeth Archibald and Ad Putter
*Australian Literature* edited by Elizabeth Webby
*The Australian Novel* edited by Nicholas Birns and Louis Klee
*The Beats* edited by Stephen Belletto
*The Black Body in American Literature* edited by Cherene Sherrard-Johnson
*Boxing* edited by Gerald Early
*British Black and Asian Literature (1945–2010)* edited by Deirdre Osborne
*British Fiction: 1980–2018* edited by Peter Boxall
*British Fiction since 1945* edited by David James
*British Literature of the 1930s* edited by James Smith
*British Literature of the French Revolution* edited by Pamela Clemit
*British Romantic Poetry* edited by James Chandler and Maureen N McLane
*British Romanticism* edited by Stuart Curran (second edition)
*British Romanticism and Religion* edited by Jeffrey Barbeau
*British Theatre, 1730–1830* edited by Jane Moody and Daniel O'Quinn
*Canadian Literature* edited by Eva-Marie Kröller (second edition)
*The Canterbury Tales* edited by Frank Grady

*Children's Literature* edited by M. O. Grenby and Andrea Immel

*The City in World Literature* edited by Ato Quayson and Jini Kim Watson

*The Classic Russian Novel* edited by Malcolm V. Jones and Robin Feuer Miller

*Comics* edited by Maaheen Ahmed

*Contemporary African American Literature* edited by Yogita Goyal

*Contemporary Irish Poetry* edited by Matthew Campbell

*Creative Writing* edited by David Morley and Philip Neilsen

*Crime Fiction* edited by Martin Priestman

*Dante's 'Commedia'* edited by Zygmunt G. Barański and Simon Gilson

*Dracula* edited by Roger Luckhurst

*Early American Literature* edited by Bryce Traister

*Early Modern Women's Writing* edited by Laura Lunger Knoppers

*The Eighteenth-Century Novel* edited by John Richetti

*Eighteenth-Century Poetry* edited by John Sitter

*Eighteenth-Century Thought* edited by Frans De Bruyn

*Emma* edited by Peter Sabor

*English Dictionaries* edited by Sarah Ogilvie

*English Literature, 1500–1600* edited by Arthur F. Kinney

*English Literature, 1650–1740* edited by Steven N. Zwicker

*English Literature, 1740–1830* edited by Thomas Keymer and Jon Mee

*English Literature, 1830–1914* edited by Joanne Shattock

*English Melodrama* edited by Carolyn Williams

*English Novelists* edited by Adrian Poole

*English Poetry, Donne to Marvell* edited by Thomas N. Corns

*English Poets* edited by Claude Rawson

*English Renaissance Drama* edited by A. R. Braunmuller and Michael Hattaway (second edition)

*English Renaissance Tragedy* edited by Emma Smith and Garrett A. Sullivan Jr.

*English Restoration Theatre* edited by Deborah C. Payne Fisk

*Environmental Humanities* edited by Jeffrey Cohen and Stephanie Foote

*The Epic* edited by Catherine Bates

*Erotic Literature* edited by Bradford Mudge

*The Essay* edited by Kara Wittman and Evan Kindley

*European Modernism* edited by Pericles Lewis

*European Novelists* edited by Michael Bell

*Fairy Tales* edited by Maria Tatar

*Fantasy Literature* edited by Edward James and Farah Mendlesohn

*Feminist Literary Theory* edited by Ellen Rooney

*Fiction in the Romantic Period* edited by Richard Maxwell and Katie Trumpener

*The Fin de Siècle* edited by Gail Marshall

*Frankenstein* edited by Andrew Smith

*The French Enlightenment* edited by Daniel Brewer

*French Literature* edited by John D. Lyons

*The French Novel: from 1800 to the Present* edited by Timothy Unwin

*Gay and Lesbian Writing* edited by Hugh Stevens

*German Romanticism* edited by Nicholas Saul

*Global Literature and Slavery* edited by Laura T. Murphy

*Gothic Fiction* edited by Jerrold E. Hogle

*The Graphic Novel* edited by Stephen Tabachnick

*The Greek and Roman Novel* edited by Tim Whitmarsh

*Greek and Roman Theatre* edited by Marianne McDonald and J. Michael Walton

*Greek Comedy* edited by Martin Revermann

*Greek Lyric* edited by Felix Budelmann

*Greek Mythology* edited by Roger D. Woodard

*Greek Tragedy* edited by P. E. Easterling

*The Harlem Renaissance* edited by George Hutchinson

*The History of the Book* edited by Leslie Howsam

*Human Rights and Literature* edited by Crystal Parikh

*The Irish Novel* edited by John Wilson Foster

*Irish Poets* edited by Gerald Dawe

*The Italian Novel* edited by Peter Bondanella and Andrea Ciccarelli

*The Italian Renaissance* edited by Michael Wyatt

*Jewish American Literature* edited by Hana Wirth-Nesher and Michael P. Kramer

*The Latin American Novel* edited by Efraín Kristal

*Latin American Poetry* edited by Stephen Hart

*Latinalo American Literature* edited by John Morán González

*Latin Love Elegy* edited by Thea S. Thorsen

*Literature and Animals* edited by Derek Ryan

*Literature and the Anthropocene* edited by John Parham

*Literature and Climate* edited by Adeline Johns-Putra and Kelly Sultzbach

*Literature and Disability* edited by Clare Barker and Stuart Murray

*Literature and Food* edited by J. Michelle Coghlan

*Literature and the Posthuman* edited by Bruce Clarke and Manuela Rossini

*Literature and Religion* edited by Susan M. Felch

*Literature and Science* edited by Steven Meyer

*The Literature of the American Civil War and Reconstruction* edited by Kathleen Diffley and Coleman Hutchison

*The Literature of the American Renaissance* edited by Christopher N. Phillips

*The Literature of Berlin* edited by Andrew J. Webber

*The Literature of the Crusades* edited by Anthony Bale

*The Literature of the First World War* edited by Vincent Sherry

*The Literature of London* edited by Lawrence Manley

*The Literature of Los Angeles* edited by Kevin R. McNamara

*The Literature of New York* edited by Cyrus Patell and Bryan Waterman

*The Literature of Paris* edited by Anna-Louise Milne

*The Literature of World War II* edited by Marina MacKay

*Literature on Screen* edited by Deborah Cartmell and Imelda Whelehan

*Lyrical Ballads* edited by Sally Bushell

*Manga and Anime* edited by Jaqueline Berndt

*Medieval British Manuscripts* edited by Orietta Da Rold and Elaine Treharne

*Medieval English Culture* edited by Andrew Galloway

*Medieval English Law and Literature* edited by Candace Barrington and Sebastian Sobecki

*Medieval English Literature* edited by Larry Scanlon

*Medieval English Mysticism* edited by Samuel Fanous and Vincent Gillespie

*Medieval English Theatre* edited by Richard Beadle and Alan J. Fletcher (second edition)

*Medieval French Literature* edited by Simon Gaunt and Sarah Kay

*Medieval Romance* edited by Roberta L. Krueger

*Medieval Romance* edited by Roberta L. Krueger (new edition)

*Medieval Women's Writing* edited by Carolyn Dinshaw and David Wallace

*Modern American Culture* edited by Christopher Bigsby

*Modern British Women Playwrights* edited by Elaine Aston and Janelle Reinelt

*Modern French Culture* edited by Nicholas Hewitt

*Modern German Culture* edited by Eva Kolinsky and Wilfried van der Will

*The Modern German Novel* edited by Graham Bartram

*The Modern Gothic* edited by Jerrold E. Hogle

*Modern Irish Culture* edited by Joe Cleary and Claire Connolly

*Modern Italian Culture* edited by Zygmunt G. Baranski and Rebecca J. West

*Modern Latin American Culture* edited by John King

*Modern Russian Culture* edited by Nicholas Rzhevsky

*Modern Spanish Culture* edited by David T. Gies

*Modernism* edited by Michael Levenson (second edition)

*The Modernist Novel* edited by Morag Shiach

*Modernist Poetry* edited by Alex Davis and Lee M. Jenkins

*Modernist Women Writers* edited by Maren Tova Linett

*Narrative* edited by David Herman

*Narrative Theory* edited by Matthew Garrett

*Native American Literature* edited by Joy Porter and Kenneth M. Roemer

*Nineteen Eighty-Four* edited by Nathan Waddell

*Nineteenth-Century American Literature and Politics* edited by John Kerkering

*Nineteenth-Century American Poetry* edited by Kerry Larson

*Nineteenth-Century American Women's Writing* edited by Dale M. Bauer and Philip Gould

*Nineteenth-Century Thought* edited by Gregory Claeys

*The Novel* edited by Eric Bulson

*Old English Literature* edited by Malcolm Godden and Michael Lapidge (second edition)

*Performance Studies* edited by Tracy C. Davis

*Piers Plowman* edited by Andrew Cole and Andrew Galloway

*The Poetry of the First World War* edited by Santanu Das

*Popular Fiction* edited by David Glover and Scott McCracken

*Postcolonial Literary Studies* edited by Neil Lazarus

*Postcolonial Poetry* edited by Jahan Ramazani

*Postcolonial Travel Writing* edited by Robert Clarke

*Postmodern American Fiction* edited by Paula Geyh

*Postmodernism* edited by Steven Connor

*Prose* edited by Daniel Tyler

*The Pre-Raphaelites* edited by Elizabeth Prettejohn

*Pride and Prejudice* edited by Janet Todd

*Queer Studies* edited by Siobhan B. Somerville

*Renaissance Humanism* edited by Jill Kraye

*Robinson Crusoe* edited by John Richetti

*Roman Comedy* edited by Martin T. Dinter

*The Roman Historians* edited by Andrew Feldherr

*Roman Satire* edited by Kirk Freudenburg

*The Romantic Sublime* edited by Cian Duffy

*Romanticism and Race* edited by Manu Samriti Chander

*Science Fiction* edited by Edward James and Farah Mendlesohn

*Scottish Literature* edited by Gerald Carruthers and Liam McIlvanney

*Sensation Fiction* edited by Andrew Mangham

*Shakespeare and Contemporary Dramatists* edited by Ton Hoenselaars

*Shakespeare and Popular Culture* edited by Robert Shaughnessy

*Shakespeare and Race* edited by Ayanna Thompson

*Shakespeare and Religion* edited by Hannibal Hamlin

*Shakespeare and War* edited by David Loewenstein and Paul Stevens

*Shakespeare on Film* edited by Russell Jackson (second edition)

*Shakespeare on Screen* edited by Russell Jackson

*Shakespeare on Stage* edited by Stanley Wells and Sarah Stanton

*Shakespearean Comedy* edited by Alexander Leggatt

*Shakespearean Tragedy* edited by Claire McEachern (second edition)

*Shakespeare's First Folio* edited by Emma Smith

*Shakespeare's History Plays* edited by Michael Hattaway

*Shakespeare's Language* edited by Lynne Magnusson with David Schalkwyk

*Shakespeare's Last Plays* edited by Catherine M. S. Alexander

*Shakespeare's Poetry* edited by Patrick Cheney

*Sherlock Holmes* edited by Janice M. Allan and Christopher Pittard

*The Sonnet* edited by A. D. Cousins and Peter Howarth

*The Spanish Novel: from 1600 to the Present* edited by Harriet Turner and Adelaida López de Martínez

*Textual Scholarship* edited by Neil Fraistat and Julia Flanders

*Theatre and Science* edited by Kristen E. Shepherd-Barr

*Theatre History* edited by David Wiles and Christine Dymkowski

*Transnational American Literature* edited by Yogita Goyal

*Travel Writing* edited by Peter Hulme and Tim Youngs

*The Twentieth-Century American Novel and Politics* edited by Bryan Santin

*Twentieth-Century American Poetry and Politics* edited by Daniel Morris

*Twentieth-Century British and Irish Women's Poetry* edited by Jane Dowson

*The Twentieth-Century English Novel* edited by Robert L. Caserio

*Twentieth-Century English Poetry* edited by Neil Corcoran

*Twentieth-Century Irish Drama* edited by Shaun Richards

*Twentieth-Century Literature and Politics* edited by Christos Hadjiyiannis and Rachel Potter

*Twentieth-Century Russian Literature* edited by Marina Balina and Evgeny Dobrenko

*Utopian Literature* edited by Gregory Claeys

*Victorian and Edwardian* Theatre edited by Kerry Powell

*The Victorian Novel* edited by Deirdre David (second edition)

*Victorian Poetry* edited by Joseph Bristow

*Victorian Women's Poetry* edited by Linda K. Hughes

*Victorian Women's Writing* edited by Linda H. Peterson

*War Writing* edited by Kate McLoughlin

*Women's Writing in Britain, 1660–1789* edited by Catherine Ingrassia

*Women's Writing in the Romantic Period* edited by Devoney Looser

*World Literature* edited by Ben Etherington and Jarad Zimbler

*World Crime Fiction* edited by Jesper Gulddal, Stewart King and Alistair Rolls

*Writing of the English Revolution* edited by N. H. Keeble

*The Writings of Julius Caesar* edited by Christopher Krebs and Luca Grillo

Printed in the United States
by Baker & Taylor Publisher Services